Global Crises and
Social Movements

About the Book and Editor

Traditionally, scholars have traced the origins and characteristics of social movements to purely local and national determinants. Until recently, the global dimension of such movements has been relatively neglected. This book takes the innovative step of linking social movements to international political and economic crises, identifying the general features of industrial and developing societies that predispose them toward social movements of particular kinds.

The book consists of three parts. Part One views the origins of the European working-class collective movement of 1848 from a variety of perspectives. Part Two reexamines the debate on the moral economy of the peasant in terms of "peasant nonrevolt" and global political economy. Part Three considers the emergence of fascist and populist movements in Western Europe and East Asia in their intersocietal dimensions.

Each of the cases has been selected for its strategic contribution to an understanding of the occurrence of social movements in relation to large-scale societal crises. Collectively, the essays underscore the methodological utility of situating such movements in a global context.

Edmund Burke, III, is professor of history at the University of California, Santa Cruz. He is the author of *Prelude to Protectorate in Morocco, 1860–1912: Patterns of Pre-Colonial Protest and Resistance* (1976) and the coeditor (with I. M. Lapidus) of *Islam, Politics and Social Movements* (forthcoming). He is also the author of numerous articles on collective action in the Middle East and on French orientalism. He is presently chair of the Board of Studies in History at UCSC.

Global Crises and Social Movements

Artisans, Peasants, Populists, and the World Economy

edited by
Edmund Burke, III

Westview Press / Boulder and London

Copyright © 1988 by Westview Press, Inc.

Published in 1988 in the United States of America by Westview Press, Inc.; Frederick A. Praeger, Publisher; 5500 Central Avenue, Boulder, Colorado 80301

Library of Congress Cataloging-in-Publication Data
Global crises and social movements: artisans, peasants, populists,
    and the world economy/edited by Edmund Burke, III.
        p. cm.
    "This book brings together a number of papers that were
originally presented at a National Science Foundation–funded
conference on 'Global crises and social movements,' which was held at
the University of California, Santa Cruz, October 23–24, 1981"—CIP
pref.
    Includes index.
    ISBN 0-8133-0609-4
    1. Social movements—History—19th century—Congresses. 2. Social
movements—History—20th century—Congresses. 3. Business cycles—
History—19th century—Congresses. 4. Business cycles—
History—20th century—Congresses. I. Burke, Edmund, 1940–   .
II. National Science Foundation (U.S.)
HN3.G57   1988
303.4'84—dc19   87-20138
                                                                                CIP

Composition for this book originated with conversion of the editor's word-processor disks. This book was produced without formal editing by the publisher.

Printed and bound in the United States of America

The paper used in this publication meets the requirements of the American National Standard for Permanence of Paper for Printed Library Materials Z39.48-1984.

6   5   4   3   2   1

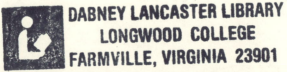

Contents

Tables and Illustrations

Acknowledgments

This book brings together a number of papers that were originally presented at a National Science Foundation–funded conference on "Global Crises and Social Movements," which was held at the University of California, Santa Cruz, October 23–24, 1981. Its purpose was, through a reexamination of international political and economic crises and the social movements that arose from them, to identify features of industrial and developing societies that predispose them toward social movement activities of particular sorts. The conference brought together scholars from anthropology, geography, history, politics, and sociology and was attended by more than 200 students and faculty members from U.C.S.C. and other California colleges and universities. There were nineteen papers and formal comments, including an often very lively discussion among those present. In addition to those whose papers are printed here, thanks are due to Luciano Costa Neto, Michael Hechter, Bernard Magubane, Samuel Popkin, Theda Skocpol, Tony Smith, and Immanuel Wallerstein for their participation and comment.

In putting together this book many have contributed their time and energies. It is appropriate to thank them here. The stimulating intellectual environment of the Comparative and International Studies Organized Research Activity of the University of California, Santa Cruz, led to the generation of the N.S.F. conference proposal. In particular, the intellectual contributions and moral support of Walter Goldfrank, Richard Gordon, Paul Lubeck, and Mark Traugott were crucial all along the way. Without the financial and logistic support of the dean of the Division of Social Sciences of U.C.S.C. and his staff this volume would never have seen the light of day. Wendy Fassett helped with local arrangements for the conference and later with the copy-editing of the volume: In both roles she was indispensable and her ability to function gracefully under pressure sorely tested. Debbie Johnson and Diana Jordan were responsible for preparing the final typescript, in which role they were towers of strength. Susan Szabo also helped with editorial work. Dean Michael Cowan of the Division of Humanities provided much-welcomed support that insured the final publication. Finally, thanks are due to Lea Leadbeater and the editorial staff at Westview Press for their assistance.

Edmund Burke, III
Santa Cruz, California

1

Global Crises and Social Movements: A Comparative Historical Perspective

EDMUND BURKE, III, AND WALTER GOLDFRANK

I

As events have forced social scientists to see the inter-connections of events and processes at the local, national and global levels, historical crises have come to be seen as having an important intersocietal dimension. Thus for example, the concept of a seventeenth century crisis has allowed historians of Western Europe to make sense out of the otherwise chaotic events of the period—wars of religion, large scale peasant insurrections, the emergence of capitalist forces, the development of royal absolutisms, and the decline of the old order (Trevor-Roper, Hobsbawm, Wallerstein 1974, 1980). Similarly, comparative historical studies of the era of the French revolution (Palmer 1959, 1964; Godechot 1965; Rude 1964), the impact of the Bolshevik Revolution outside Russia (Carr 1965, 1967; Carrere d'Encausse and Schram 1965; Ulyanovsky 1979), and the national liberation movements of the 1960s and 1970s (Chirot 1977; Emerson 1960; Huntington 1968; and Schurmann 1974) have accustomed us to understanding political change in a comparative historical context.

Despite the undoubted sophistication and importance of the new scholarship on social movements, however, most works continue to be resolutely local and national in perspective. One of the aims of the present volume is to demonstrate, through an examination of particular cases, the utility of incorporating a global dimension into the study of social movements. For convenience we have selected three areas of research in which recent scholarly debate has significantly altered our prior conceptions, and have invited papers to address the question of intersocietal factors, specifically of global political and economic crises, on the genesis and evolution of particular social movements.

In the present state of the development of the field it seemed strategically important to put together a book that focused upon the occurrence of major social movements during periods of pronounced crisis in the international economy and state system. Accordingly, this volume brings together ten studies of social movements that explore some of the comparative and global dimensions of collective action.

The essays in this volume draw upon recent work in a number of social science fields, especially the recent literature on theories of revolutions (Moore 1966; Skocpol 1979; Tilly 1978; Wolf 1969). Collectively they raise some significant questions about the occurrence of social movements in the context of large scale societal crises. What are the connections between the local, national, and international contexts in situations of severe crisis which are propitious to the emergence of movements of collective action? To what degree are social movements conditioned by economic and political crises at the global level, and to what extent do social movements themselves in turn condition the international political and economic systems? Questions such as these are of undeniable importance to an assessment of the situation which we confront in the 1980s in a context of a severe economic crises in the world economy, the revival of social movements in the developing world (the revolutions in Nicaragua, Iran and the Philippines are notable instances) and generalized tensions in North/South relations.

What is meant by the term "global crises"? The prevailing discourse— indeed, the implicit grammar of our title—suggests that "global crises" refer to periodic disturbances in the world economy; while "social movements" refer to insurgencies in particular national polities, and that the causal relations tend to run from the former to the latter. This is notably the case in the essays included in Section One, where the European revolutions of 1848 are re-examined in a global perspective, and in those of Section Two, where the subject of the moral economy of peasant political action is taken up in the context of the vicissitudes of world market cycles. In the essays in Section Three, "World Market Cycles and Populist Movements in the Twentieth Century" we see the utility of alternative formulations. These place greater emphasis on the *political* dimensions of global structures and crises, on the *international* or even world-wide dimensions of social move- ments, and on the *reverse* causal directionality, i.e., the effects of social movements on the world economy.

Whether one opts for a conception of the world market and the international states system as separate but equally co-determinative, or of the world- system as singular but with multiple dimensions, one can see that world political processes, quite apart from economic fluctuations, entail crises (e.g., of imperial penetration, rivalry and retreat; of war and the threat of war, of hegemonic rise and decline) with profound consequences for social movements and those who would make them. And it is not difficult to point to ways in which social movements help to bring about reorganizations of economic structures (e.g., capital mobility in response to working-class mobilization at the level of the work place and/or the state).

At this point, it seems useful to offer a distinction between crises *in* the world-system, and crises *of* the world-system. Whether economic or political or both, crises *in* the system tend to be cyclical and developmental. They involve "long waves" of expansion and stagnation, and of hegemonic ascent and decline, that have marked the capitalist world-economy over the course of its four centuries' existence. In this volume we focus especially upon crises of this sort, their effects on social groups and state organizations, and the reorganizations of the system that result. By contrast, crises *of* the system refer to epochal disjunctures such as the transition from feudalism to capitalism. Many Marxist intellectuals and organizations discovered too late that the primarily *cyclical* crisis of the inter-war years was not the epochal crisis through which a transition to socialism would issue. This analytic error and its tactical correlates were not without consequences for the grim trajectory of fascist movements and regimes. Currently, while most observers agree that we are once again in a time of cyclical crisis, there exists much debate about whether world capitalism has entered into its epochal crisis as well. (Amin 1975) Whichever the case, and the two are surely not mutually exclusive, none of the papers gathered here contributes to the latter question.

By way of illustrating the above distinctions about causal directionality, and showing too that proletarianization matters even if the industrial working class *per se* can no longer occupy center stage, a few comments about the U.S. civil rights movement in the 1950s and 1960s may be of use. In one of its major aspects, that movement flourished to the degree that it did precisely to forestall global crisis. The United States had emerged from World War II as the unquestioned hegemonic power in the world, trumpeting a liberal democratic ideology as its basic legitimating claim to moral and political leadership. Yet the legally disprivileged position of blacks belied U.S. pretensions on this very basic point. Hence, there was considerable *general* support at high levels in the federal government for the extension of basic civil and political rights to Southern blacks. Simultaneously, the ouster of colonial regimes in sub-Saharan Africa and the success of nationalist movements in other parts of the non-white world put additional pressure on Washington. Concrete instances of the mistreatment of African diplomats in the U.S. capital, or traveling there from United Nations headquarters in New York, together with the U.S. racial situation generally, made competition with the U.S.S.R. for the hearts and minds of the Third World more difficult than it need have been. To exert leadership, then, to avoid global crises, required a more democratic U.S. than existed in the early 1950s; while federal governmental attitudes toward the civil rights movement were ambivalent and contradictory, the primary thrust was one of cautious support, in part by judicial and administrative actions, in part by restraining local government.

At the other end of the movement's trajectory, one can see that its successes were very much part of the mounting pressures on the federal budget that led to the fiscal crisis of the 1970s. The achievement of historic levels of welfare benefits, social services, influence and political consciousness by blacks and other disadvantaged populations increased inflation, made prosecuting and paying for the Vietnam era more difficult, and provided additional incentives for capital flight outside U.S. borders. That the Reagan administration has labored so mightily to reduce social spending suggests that at least at the level of appearances, and probably more substantially, the civil rights movement had economic consequences directly related to the crisis of the 1980s.

Nor need this exemplification of our larger themes stop there. If one looks at the causal dynamics which brought the civil rights movement into being in the first place, one has to acknowledge the massive effects of the world depression of the 1930s and of World War II. Falling prices for agricultural raw materials hit the U.S. South severely, leading to mechanization and reorganization of farming such that large numbers of blacks were forced off the land, into Southern cities and towns and north to the burgeoning ghettos. This movement, followed by wartime recovery, produced a hitherto unknown level of proletarianization among blacks, and the importance of their votes to post-New Deal Democratic Party majorities spurred liberals in the party to challenge the states' rights segregationism of the solid South. As the movement developed beyond its initial civil rights successes in the South, the urban uprisings of the 1960s turned out to be marked by heavy participation by industrial workers. And just as it was for insurgent nationalisms in other parts of the world, the combat and other wartime experiences of black soldiers proved to be critical both for the development of their own political skills and consciousness, and for the ideological lift provided by the struggle to defend democracy against Nazi racism.

II

The chapters in Part One derive from the recent revisionist scholarship on nineteenth century European social movements, the formation of the working class, and the revolutions of 1848 (Noyes 1966; Price 1975; Sewell 1980; Tilly and Lees 1975). Collectively, the scholars working in this field have called into question the Marxian thesis that the proletariat was the leading actor in the successive waves of strikes and collective action which affected Western Europe in the nineteenth century. They have also provided a much more convincing description of the social and cultural life of the artisanal classes, in the process largely undermining both liberal and Marxian accounts of the unfolding of the industrial revolution in Europe. But they have until recently failed to consider the intersocietal aspects of the European labor movement, notably the European economic recession of 1846–7, and the broader political environment of the development of the revolutions of 1848 in Western Europe.

Taking off from this emerging literature, the chapters in Section One consider the concrete mechanisms whereby in the revolutions of 1848 diffuse economic forces were translated into collective action. They also advance explanations for the differing outcomes of the events of 1848 in England, France and Germany.

Mark Traugott's approach emphasizes the role of the great European economic crises of the late 1840s, which he considers as aspects of an interactive system undergoing common economic changes, despite differing productive capacities, access to markets, and capital reserves. Traugott argues that these economic relational factors provide a partial explanation of the differences in the types and levels of social movement activity in Britain and France, but that they cannot explain the striking divergences in the forms they assumed in 1848. His discussion usefully frames the issues pursued in greater detail in the chapters by Bezucha, Calhoun and Stedman Jones.

Robert Bezucha's contribution, "The French Revolution of 1848 and the Social History of Work," through an investigation of the transformation of the construction industry, examines the political forces which brought about the revolution of 1848 in France. Bezucha employs the "cohort hypothesis" of French sociologist Caspard (1974) to argue counter to both Marx and Tilly and Lees (1975) that the difference in behavior between younger and older construction workers in 1848 derived from the differences in their political socialization, as well as to their differential responses to the gradual erosion of their occupational status. He concludes that this, rather than class divisions *per se*, or purely structural forces, was the primary determinant in the revolutionary outcome in France.

A contrasting view is presented by Craig Calhoun. In his "The 'Retardation' of French Economic Development and Social Radicalism During the Second Republic: New Lessons From the Old Comparison with Britain," Calhoun argues that the potential for revolutionary collective action resided in the coalition of skilled workers (and not factory workers, as Marx would have it) whose privileged status within the working class was challenged by the direction of economic change. Contrasting the history of social protest in England in the 1820s and 1830s with the second half of the century, as well as the British and French experiences in 1848, he sees an equation between the more proletarianized conditions of factory work and a reliance upon formal organizations. These he asserts, if they yielded any collective action at all, produced reformist, not revolutionary, politics. France experienced a revolution in 1848 while England did not, he argues, because powerful protest movements were generated by the more artisanal French economy, whose structure enabled workers to mobilize their occupational and neighborhood ties. For Calhoun, changes in the organization of labor are determinative of social relations more broadly, and thus of the likelihood of political mobilization.

Gareth Stedman Jones disputes this view in his paper, "Rethinking Chartism." Stedman Jones disagrees with Calhoun (and implicitly much of the existing literature) over the timing and extent of industrialization as indicated by the concentration of capital, the progress of mechanization, or the degree of proletarianization. He notes the remarkable staying powers of artisans, as well as the fact that workshop production remained predominant in Britain until late in the nineteenth century. But are skilled artisans the revolutionary strata (instead of proletarians), as Calhoun asserts? Here he invokes the German case to argue against explanations which seek to establish in categorical terms the relations between popular politics and class strata, forms of work organization, occupational groups, or elements of popular culture unless they can be demonstrated in specific cases. The differing outcomes of the events of 1848 in Britain, France and Germany can best be explained by the different phases of the development of capitalism in the three countries, involving different structural elements which were shaped decisively by political conditions.

The essays in Part Two take up some of the themes in the recent debate over the moral economy of the peasant. Focused upon rural protest in Vietnam and Southeast Asia, this debate has illuminated the contrasting analytic strategies of social scientists (Paige 1975; Popkin 1979; Scott 1976; Skocpol 1982), and in the process reinvigorated the sociology of peasant movements. The essays of Adas and Watts in this volume broaden the debate by examining cases of non-rebellion in colonial Java, Bihar, and northern Nigeria. A somewhat different critique is developed by Jeffery Paige who seeks to apply to the Guatemalan case the materialist approach (which he calls Marxist) based upon types of export agricultural enterprises which he first employed in his *Agrarian Revolution* (1975).

Michael Adas considers several themes from the moral economy debate in his essay, notably the role of culturally rooted traditions of rural protest, the impact on the old agrarian structures of incorporation into the world market, and the role of the state in the transformation of the countryside. Adas reviews the literature on social protest and agrarian societies in South and Southeast Asia. He stresses the central role it assigns to the development of commercial agriculture as the motor in the transformation of the existing agrarian structures. He suggests that this model is incorrect through an examination of the cases of Java and Bihar. He argues that in these two regions capitalism and colonialism in fact only gradually intruded into the countryside, and did so in such a way as to strengthen (rather than weaken) local and regional elites. The result was that neither Java nor Bihar experienced significant peasant protest movements. In his analysis, Adas argues that the parallel penetration of the capitalist market and colonial bureaucracy to the village level in these societies created a new group of market-oriented tenants, but locked them out of the colonial system. What then were the rural roots of nationalism in these societies? In his conclusion, Adas suggests that nationalism be viewed as the result of a struggle between the market-oriented tenants and the old landlords and the Europeans who supported them.

Michael Watts returns to the subject of the non-occurrence of protest and rebellions among the peasantry in his examination of Northern Nigeria in the period 1900–1945. Despite a series of major famines, a long-term decline in living conditions, and the presence of peasant rebellions elsewhere in Africa, the peasants of the Sokoto Caliphate did not rebel in the period under study. Watts considers the theoretical perspectives of Scott and Popkin (moral economy and political economy) as well as that of British social historian E. P. Thompson (1968) in the light of the Nigerian data, before rejecting all three as inadequate. His conclusion parallels that of Michael Adas: the gradual manner in which Northern Nigeria was incorporated into the world economy and the British empire led to the forging of a class collaboration between local elites and the colonial administration. As a result of the character of elite structural ties to the market and to the British authorities and their institutional solidarity (which limited peasant tactical mobility), agrarian protest was limited to indirect forms. In determining this outcome, Watt suggests, the military power of the colonial state, the role of the Islamic comprador class, and the complex and fluid class relations within the Nigerian state itself also played important roles.

The issues raised in the moral economy debate return again in Jeffery Paige's contribution. In his essay, Paige applies the scholarly theories developed to explain the revolution in Vietnam to the case of Guatemala. He begins by distinguishing three major theoretical orientations in the literature on Vietnam: moral economy, political economy and class conflict. These he connects respectively to the Durkheimian, Millian and Marxian traditions of social science theory. Each, he goes on to suggest, may be associated with a theoretical proposition about the occurrence of peasant revolutions. For Durkheimians, peasant revolutions occur when subsistence minimums, village security systems and patron-client ties are threatened by ecological pressures, the demands of the state and the growth of markets. For Millians, they occur when honest, efficient political entrepreneurs organize the delivery of valuable individual incentives to selected members of an atomized village. Finally for Marxians, peasant revolutions result from the combination of noncultivators dependent upon income from land (e.g., absentee owners) and cultivators dependent upon income from wages (e.g., sharecroppers). In the rest of his essay, Paige seeks to apply each theory to the complex realities of the Guatemalan agrarian system. After a careful review of the facts, he concludes that Marxian class conflict analysis provides the most convincing explanation of agrarian revolution in Guatemala (which as he sees it, is the product of the collision between an agricultural proletariat and capitalist landowning class in a peripheral export economy.)

The essays in Part Three examine twentieth century populism and fascism in a number of world societies from several different perspectives, including Peter Gourevitch's application of a combination of interest group and social forces analysis to the study of Western responses to the Great Depression, Bruce Cumings' emphasis upon the structure of the world economy, product cycles, and regional hegemony in the Northeast Asian political economy, and Walter Goldfrank's use of world systems theory to study the contrasting Japanese and Italian political and economic strategies in the inter-war period.

In contrast to much of the literature on fascism, which focuses upon its social roots, and upon isolating class fractions and strata vulnerable to fascist and populist appeals (Abraham 1981; de Felice 1977; Linz 1976; Mayer 1971; Rogger and Weber 1965), the essays in this book in different ways stress the intersocietal dimension of these movements. They also agree that social movements like fascism and populism can fruitfully be analyzed in terms of elite political and economic strategies within the context of the world market and international system. A final conclusion may be derived from a consideration of the essays included in this section. It calls into question the degree of autonomy that states gain from the adoption of fascist or populist strategies in periods of severe economic crisis. In this connection it seems quite telling that once in power, virtually all the states examined here—including or even especially those which had ridden social movements to power—successfully curtailed the incidence and impact of social movement activity.

Certainly this is the burden of Peter Gourevitch's chapter which considers the contrasting economic and political strategies adopted by Britain, France, Germany, Sweden and the United States in response to the Great Depression. Gourevitch employs the concept of sectors and interest groups differentially linked to the world economy to develop a comparative analysis of economic policy responses to the economic crises of the 1930s: conservative monetarism in Britain, the New Deal in the U.S., social democracy in Sweden, fascism in Germany. Gourevitch's perspective enables him to locate precisely the shifting alliances of farmers, organized workers and distinct sectors of business such that common problems of deflation and unemployment were met in greatly different ways in different states, as differing political combinations had more or less chance of gaining control of the state apparatus.

What fascism looks like when considered from the perspective of world systems theory can be seen in the Walter Goldfrank's chapter "Silk and Steel: Italy and Japan Between the Two World Wars." Goldfrank traces out the efforts of the two powers to move from textile-producing semi-peripheral states to steel-producing core states in the period. He notes the parallel changes in the class structures of Italy and Japan as a result of their efforts to move from the semi-periphery of the world economy to the core. In his comparison, Goldfrank considers each state in turn from the vantage-point of the world system, state structure and internal class cleavages and in the process provides a striking analysis of the reasons for Japanese superiority.

Bruce Cumings presents a synthetic account of the remarkable economic development of the Northeast Asian countries of Japan, Korea and Taiwan from the 1920s to the 1980s. Working back and forth between local and regional investment strategies, military contigencies and opportunities, and world politico-economic constraints, Cumings shows how first the authoritarian Japanese state mobilized for war and industrial growth, and then how Korea and Taiwan, each in slightly different ways, built upon Japanese colonial foundations and U.S. military aid/protection to repeat many aspects of the state-inspired Japanese path. One important conclusion of Cumings' essay is the key role of U.S. and Japanese policy for the region in enabling the emergence of coherent political and economic strategies in post-war Taiwan and Korea.

While the contributors to this volume include a geographer, as well as several historians, political scientists and sociologists and represent a variety of theoretical perspectives, a remarkable confluence of approaches can be observed. The essays in Sections One and Two focus attention on the sequence of changes introduced by the penetration of the world market and state centralization, and their impact upon particular sectors and interest groups. Similarly, those in the section on fascism and populism stresses the utility of a historical examination of each case placed in a global political and economic context. These essays, while differing in their approaches, also employ strategies of identifying particular sectors and economic groups as a way of shedding light on the different outcomes.

In conclusion, as the chapters that follow demonstrate, the interconnections between global crises and social movements are varied and multidirectional. They range from quite general effects of economic fluctuations to specific international influences, like the borrowing of Gandhian strategies of non-violent struggle by Martin Luther King and his followers. Yet all that has been put forward here is but the tip of an iceberg that remains to be explored by submerging ourselves in the chilly currents of modern world history. It is our hope that the explorations continue.

References

Abraham, D. 1981. *The Collapse of the Weimar Republic: Political Economy and Crisis*, Princeton: Princeton University Press.

Amin, A. *et al.* 1982. *Dynamics of Global Crisis*, New York: Monthly Review Press.

Carr, E. H. 1967. *The Impact of the Russian Revolution 1917–1967: The Influence of Bolshevism on the World Outside Russia*, London.

Carrere d'Encausse, H., and S. Schram, eds. 1965. *Le Marxisme et l'Asie 1853–1964*, Paris: A. Colin.

Caspard, P. 1974. "Aspects de la lutte des classes en 1848: le recutement de la Garde nationale mobile," *Revue historique*, No. 511: 81–106.

Chamberlain, W. H. 1965. *The Russian Revolution 1917–1921*, New York.

Chirot, D. 1977. *Social Change in the Twentieth Century*, New York: Harcourt Brace Jovanovich.

de Felice, R. 1977. *Interpretations of Fascism*, Cambridge: Harvard University Press.

Emerson, R. 1960. *From Empire to Nation*, Boston: Beacon Press.

Goldfrank, W. L. 1978. "Fascism and World Economy," in Barbara Hockey Kaplan, ed., *Social Change in the Capitalist World Economy*, pp. 75–117, Beverly Hills and London: Sage.

Godechot, J. 1965. *France and the Atlantic Revolution of the Eighteenth Century*, New York: Free Press.

Hobsbawm, E. J. 1969. "The Crisis of the Seventeenth Century," in Trevor-Aston, ed., *Crisis in Europe, 1560–1660*, London: Routledge and Kegan Paul.

Huntington, S. P. 1968. *Political Order in Changing Societies*, New Haven: Yale University Press.

Linz, J. J. 1976. "Some notes toward a comparative study in sociological historical perspective," in W. Z. Laqueur, ed., *Fascism: A Reader's Guide*, pp. 3–121, Berkeley: University of California Press.

Mayer, A. 1971. *The Dynamics of Counterrevolution in Europe, 1870–1956 An Analytic Framework,* New York: Harper and Row.

Moore, B., Jr. 1966. *Social Origins of Dictatorship and Democracy,* Boston: Beacon Press.

Noyes, P. H. 1966. *Organization and Revolution: Working Class Associations in the German Revolutions of 1848–1849,* Princeton: Princeton University Press.

Paige, J. M. 1978. *Agrarian Revolution,* New York: Free Press.

Palmer, R. R. 1959, 1964. *The Age of the Democratic Revolution,* 2 vols. Princeton: Princeton University Press.

Popkin, S. L. 1979. *The Rational Peasant The Political Economy of Rural Society in Vietnam,* Berkeley: University of California Press.

Price, R., ed. 1975. *Revolution and Reaction: 1848 and the Second French Republic,* London and New York: Croom Helm and Barnes and Noble.

Rogger, H., and E. Weber, eds. 1965. *The European Right,* Berkeley and Los Angeles: University of California Press.

Rude, G. 1964. *Revolutionary Europe 1783–1815,* Cleveland and New York: Meridian.

Schurmann, F. 1974. *The Logic of World Power: An Inquiry into the Origins, Currents, and Contradictions of World Politics,* New York: Pantheon.

Scott, J. C. 1976. *The Moral Economy of the Peasant Rebellion and Subsistence in Southeast Asia,* New Haven: Yale University Press.

Sewell, W. 1980. *Work and Revolution in France: The Language of Labor From the Old Regime to 1848,* Cambridge: Cambridge University Press.

Skocpol, T. 1979. *States and Social Revolutions,* London: Cambridge University Press.

————. 1982. "What Makes Peasants Revolutionary?" in R. P. Weller and S. E. Guggenheim, eds., *Power and Protest in the Countryside: Studies of Rural Unrest in Asia, Europe and Latin America,* pp. 157–179, Durham: Duke University Press.

Thompson, E. P. 1968. *The Making of the English Working Class,* (revised edition) Harmondsworth: Penguin.

Tilly, C., and L. Lees. 1975. "The People of June 1848," in R. Price, ed., *Revolution and Reaction: 1848 and the Second French Republic,* London and New York: Croom Helm and Barnes and Noble.

Tilly, C. 1978. *From Mobilization to Revolution,* Reading: Addison-Wesley.

Trevor-Roper, H. R. 1969. "The General Crisis of the Seventeenth Century," in *The European Witch-Craze of the Sixteenth and Seventeenth Centuries and Other Essays,* New York: Harper and Row.

Wallerstein, I. 1974, 1980. *The Modern World System,* 2 vols. New York: Academic Press.

Wolf, E. R. 1969. *Peasant Wars of the Twentieth Century,* New York: Harper and Row.

————. 1983. *Europe and the People Without History,* Berkeley: University of California Press.

Ulyanovsky, R. A., ed. 1979. *The Comintern and the East,* Moscow: Progress Publishers.

PART ONE

THE MID-CENTURY CRISIS AND THE REVOLUTIONS OF 1848

2

Interdependencies in Global Crisis: France and England in the Mid-Nineteenth Century

MARK TRAUGOTT

My remarks, aimed at providing a descriptive account of the mid-nineteenth century crisis, are essentially introductory. Their purpose is to make the examination of economic crisis in France and England explicitly comparative, thus posing issues in a sharply defined manner and preparing the ground for the next three chapters. First, however, I would like to draw attention to the special appropriateness of a section on the mid-nineteenth century crisis in a volume on *Global Crisis and Social Movements*, since its relevance to the other chapters or to contemporary issues may not be immediately apparent.

The European crisis that culminated in 1848 were perhaps the clearest coincidence of global economic and political instability of which we know. That year witnessed a revolutionary conflagration of continental proportions. In sheer scope it was without precedent; even a century and a half later we have not seen its equal. The three years preceding this outburst had been marked by an economic crisis that though not without precedent, caused acute distress through most of Europe. The nature of significance of the connection between this "global" crisis and these social movements has been the object of considerable speculation. In a passage from "The Class Struggles in France," Marx alluded to the systemic character of the crisis. He attributed the revolutionary eruptions to two "economic world event": the potato blight and crop failures of 1845–1846; and the general and industrial crisis in England. He criticized the French revolutionaries' belief that they could "consummate a proletarian revolution within the national walls of France," for they thus ignored the fact that "French production relations are conditioned by the foreign trade of France, by her position on the world market and the laws thereof." Specifically, Marx asked

This chapter originally appeared as "The Mid Nineteenth Century Crisis" in *Theory and Society* 12/4 (July 1983), pp. 455–468, and is reprinted with permission. Copyright 1983 by *T&S*.

"How was France to break [the web of its relations of production] without a European revolutionary war, which would strike back at the despot of the world market, England?" (Feuer 1959:286–291).

My point in citing the views of Marx is to offer them not as a satisfactory explanation of the events of 1848—we will see that here, as elsewhere, his views are in need of substantial amendment and revision in the light of subsequent empirical research—but as the most apt example of the influence that those events have exerted on our understanding of revolutionary social movements. Through Marx and others the surge of activity that took place in that year ultimately became not just *an* example of the phenomenon we have gathered to discuss, but *the* singular case on which much of the relevant theory, old and new, has been based.

We may, therefore, claim significance for a section devoted to a brief three or four year "incident" of the now distant past on at least these two grounds: that the period neatly encapsulated the dynamic through which global crises and social movement articulate; and that in drawing out the intricacies, some of which have escaped previous analysts for lack of a sufficiently broad unit of analysis, we may hope to correct at their source some of the erroneous conceptions of that dynamic that have survived.

Most serious analyses of the revolutionary movements of 1848 have focused on a single case. The relatively few explicitly comparative treatments have tended to be disappointingly superficial general summaries. Attempts to account for the close parallels among Continental movements—in particular, the way revolution and reaction radiated outward from Paris in rapid succession—have typically pointed to political factors, vaguely conceived. One difficulty has been that in concentrating exclusively on the undeniably striking correspondences in the timing of risings in Paris and Berlin, Brussels and Vienna, Bonn and Rome, too little variation remains, particularly in the dependent variable (social movement activity), to afford much explanatory leverage. In focusing on France and England, the members of this panel take up the potentially illuminating comparison of two nations in which the social movement outcomes differed significantly despite the extensive parallels in short-term economic fluctuations which I now propose briefly to review.

The Old-Style Crisis in France, 1845–1848

One reason for beginning in France is that the general outline of its crisis is readily sketched, since in most respects it conformed to a pattern already well-established under the old regime. The principal distinguishing characteristic of an old-style crisis is that it originated in the agricultural sector. In 1845, the arrival in France of the potato blight reduced the yield in that crop to a level that had not been seen since 1832. While France as a whole was far less dependent on this staple than Ireland, the shortfall caused real distress in the northern provinces. To some extent wheat could be substituted for potatoes in the regions hardest hit, though the 1845 harvest in this crop was also below average. The price of wheat started the year 1845 at a pre-crisis level of about 19 francs per hectoliter. It rose to a plateau of about 22 francs and there it remained through the following summer. By the fall of 1846, however, it had become apparent that the new harvest would be a disaster of major proportions. The price of wheat began an uninterrupted climb that brought it, by mid-1847, to a high of 38 francs, just double its level of two years previous.

France reeled in the face of this agricultural crisis. Among its immediate consequences were food riots, an increased in begging, and an acceleration in the existing pattern of urban in-migration among the poor. It also set off hoarding and speculation among those fortunate enough to possess a disposable surplus of capital, shook the confidence of business circles, and prompted a drastic downward revision of economic expectations in the general population. What began as a severe perturbation of the agricultural sector soon was transformed into a national financial and commercial crisis. What were the mechanisms by which the transformation came about?

The most direct link between agricultural and financial crises derived from the need to import grain in large quantities to feed the population, especially in urban areas. Since nearly all neighboring countries had suffered similarly calamitous harvest, France was not only denied help from habitual suppliers but also entered the market in competition with other European nations. The search for grain drove prices sharply higher. As both the volume and the unit-value of grain imports shot upwards, the French balance of payments quickly turned unfavorable. The bullion reserves of the Bank of France declined precipitously. As the money supply fell, deflation set in, though the drop in the price of non-foodstuffs was never enough to compensate for the loss of earning power on the part of the vast majority of the populations. The urban population was particularly hard hit as an ever increasing share of dwindling family budgets had to be earmarked for the purchase of food. But even among the peasants few benefited, for none but the richest had sufficient surplus to take advantage of the high price of grain.

The process set in motion by the agricultural crisis was at this point greatly exacerbated by its conjuncture with economic circumstances created by the boom that had lasted up to 1845. This preceding period had seen a vast expansion of credit, particularly through speculative investment centered in projects for railway construction. Analysts did agree both as to the utility of these projects in the contemporary state of the French economy and over the question of whether railroad investments had exceeded the limits of the capital resources of the nation and its somewhat antiquated financial system. What is certain is that the lapse in confidence instigated by the agricultural crisis produced a liquidity crunch at just that moment when calls for the unpaid balance on railway shares found French capitalists dangerously over-extended. Most investors had put down 5 percent of the value of their shares, often in the hope of selling them quickly in a rising market to realize a short-term profit. With the market now declining, many were forced to hold on longer than anticipated and were caught short as the balance became due. With credit tightening, the rate at which bills were discounted began to rise when it was possible to discount paper at all. Runs on banks resulted in many failures in the provinces and affected even the Bank of France, which saw its deposits reduced from 320 million francs in June, 1845 to 57 million in January, 1847.

Once the crisis began seriously to impinge on the financial sector, it was inevitable that it should affect industry as well. In rural areas, where grain shortages translated into a reduction in cash income which fell almost heavily upon the great mass of small producers, the result was a decrease in rural purchasing power and demand for urban goods. The market dependence of the growing urban working class left it particularly vulnerable to economic fluctuations. The proportion of the average family's budget that went toward the purchase of bread, which Rudé set at approximately fifty percent at the time of the Great Revolution, had barely declined a half century later. Because demand for bread was relatively in elastic, supply problems implied rising prices and meant that a smaller proportion of family earnings was available to buy other goods. The result was a further reduction in demand for the very goods made by urban workers, a development to which manufacturers responded by cutting back production and laying off employees. A reverse multiplier effect quickly spread throughout the economy, forcing a sharp contraction of industrial production.

By early 1847 French capitalists had to deal with an increasingly depressed domestic market and highly restricted access to credit. This combination overshadowed the few bright spots on the horizon, even the decline in the price of wheat which began in the summer of 1847. France began the year 1848 in serious economic straits, but the worst was yet to come. However, before considering the revolutionary period proper, we should first examine the corresponding events in England.

Economic Crisis in England

Despite minor, if significant, differences, the economic crisis in England initially progressed in a remarkably similar way. Its origins were also agricultural. For a half century Ireland had become increasingly dependent on the potato (Gash 1968). This and climatic considerations contributed to make the effects of the blight of 1846 more devastating in Britain, so that, despite a wheat harvest less disastrous than the French, the net level of distress appears to have been at least equivalent.

In England commercial crisis followed agricultural much as it did in France. The price of wheat in London nearly doubled in the year following June, 1846. But while it began to plummet by the late summer of 1847 in response first to the accumulation of the previous year's heavy imports and then the fall's bountiful harvest, and stayed at or below its pre-crisis level through the whole of 1848, the earlier fluctuations in both price and supply had already induced a financial crisis. Grain purchases abroad, primarily in the United States, threatened to deplete The Bank of England's reserves of gold. The drain began slowly enough, amounting to a mere million pounds in 1846. In the following year, however, the outward flow accelerated, reducing bullion on hand from £13.4 to £9.3 million in the first four months of 1847.

To moderate this crisis, the English used, and to somewhat better effect, the same financial levers exploited by the French. Chief among these were the Bank's manipulation of the discount rate and the imposition in mid-April, 1847 of restrictions on bills acceptable for discounting. On balance, it appears that the liquidity crunch was no less fierce in England than in France through October, 1847; yet, when the government moved to guarantee easier access to credit, the panic-runs instantly ceased, and by late January, 1848 the gold reserves of the Bank of England had returned to the healthy level of £13 million.

The combined effects of the agricultural and financial crises were naturally felt in the industrial sector. Here, however, the parallel with France breaks down to some extent. The relative dimensions of the English industrial crisis were attenuated in certain respects and exacerbated in others, as a consequence of differences in the type and rate of development of the two economies. While the pattern of "old-style" crisis also applied to England, there it was supplemented by a "new-style" crisis in textiles. (The latter must not be confused with the notion of a crisis of overproduction which Marx believed to be the chronic irritant and chief contradiction of capitalist society.) The textile crisis originated in the sub-standard American cotton harvest of 1845. Because the crop was only ten percent smaller than in the previous year, it was possible to draw on stockpiles available in English ports and warehouses and thus maintain production temporarily undiminished. When, however, the crop of the following year was only sixty percent of normal, the cumulative shortage of raw materials produced massive unemployment in Lancashire and Glasgow. In this way, England's greater dependence on foreign markets for industrial raw materials (and the greater market dependence of proletarianized English textile workers that was its concomitant) greatly increased vulnerability to economic upheaval. The industrial slowdown did produce political consequences, notably the passage of the Ten-Hour Bill restricting the length of the working day. But this was possible more because the existence of "short time" undercut the arguments previously made by employers than because of militancy on the part of workers. In general, the unemployed or underemployed textile workers of England were quiescent.

Yet in other respects England's industrial advance mitigated the effects of economic crisis relative to France. This was notably the case in the area if railway construction where both England and France had abandoned themselves to a great surge of speculative investment earlier in the 1840s. Among the dangers of such speculation was that credit, having for a time been too freely extended, would suddenly, in reaction, dry up completely. It was also possible that calls on railway shares would channel too great a proportion of the nation's floating capital into fixed investments and seriously constrain the ability of the economy to meet the capital needs of growing sectors in a flexible manner.

This appeared to have happened in France by 1847. Money was extremely tight, a number of failures occurred among railway companies, and there was widespread stagnation in the industrial sector. In England, these same forces created genuine short-term stringencies, but because the supply of capital proved adequate, these seem to have been more than outweighted by the economic stimulus that railway construction supplied during a period of otherwise reduced demand.

Like the crisis in textiles, the financial problems associated with the railways were largely independent of the agricultural crisis. Already in late 1845, before the effects of massive grain imports had been felt, Parliament had been obliged to take measures to dampen the speculative fever by requiring deposits in bank notes on all railroad projects. The fears expressed by contemporary business opinion that the pool of capital was insufficient to handle the magnitude of investment in railways were not entirely groundless. Nominal investments in English railroads peaked at £132 million in 1846. *The Times* published a calculation that purported to show that the five percent requirement would call for £59 million in bank notes to be placed on deposit at a time when the total value of notes in circulation was only £20 million.

Despite the contribution made by railway investments to the general tightening of credit, the English economy weathered its financial crisis with less upheaval in the industrial sector than the French, in part because railroad construction stimulated iron and steel as well as coal production to an extent that appreciably attenuated the industrial slump of 1845–1847. The best available indices of industrial production show that after fairly rapid advances between 1840 and 1845, total production declined slightly in both 1846 and 1847 before resuming its upward course in 1848 (Mitchell and Deane 1971:271). Moreover, the 4,500 miles of track completed between 1843 and 1850, amounting to an increase of some 200%, constituted infrastructural improvements that continued to provide a return for several decades. These factors seem to justify Ward-Perkins' (1966:273) conclusion that: "the maintenance of the ambitious railway programme, despite the financial uncertainties of 1847 and 1848, was both immediately and ultimately beneficial and had the rare merit of being a countercyclical investment that was in itself productive." Whereas in France the Provisional Government would devise the institution of National Workshops, providing make-work to help alleviate the problems of unemployment, in England: "the continued railway construction was playing, however unconsciously, the part of a public works programme employing in 1848–9, Tooke estimated, upward of 300,000 workmen directly and indirectly, or 10 percent of the industrial labor force" (Ward-Perkins 1966:275).

Thus, between 1845 and 1848 England experienced a multi-staged crisis not unlike that which simultaneously occurred in France. Both experienced

the progression that led from agricultural to financial to industrial disturbances. Yet the course of economic crisis in England appears to have been
somewhat more complex, incorporating old and new-style mechanisms.
Although the shortfall in foodstuffs and the resulting rise in prices were
no less severe than in France, their ramifications in the English industrial
sector were less uniformly negative. The English economy managed to
respond with greater resiliency, so that by early 1848 it had all but recovered
from its slump.

Links Between the Crises in France and England

Thus far we have dealt with our two cases as worlds apart, as if the
patterns displayed were adventitious or merely similar responses to common
external stimuli. It remains to be seen whether the parallels in the patterns
of economic events in France and England in face represented the workings
of systemic forces. Insofar as our two cases permit, we might now ask to
what extent the crisis of the mid-nineteenth century possessed a "global"
character.

The economic history of the period indicates that the French influence
on the crisis in England was rather consistently negative, but not of
overwhelming significance. First, of course, the two countries were rival
bidders for the surplus grain of Russia and the United States, though their
competition was neither direct nor exclusive. Far more important was a
flow of gold from London to Paris, which represented the confluence of
several different sources. One could be traced to the calls of French railway
companies to British shareholders. In 1847 roughly 15 percent of total calls
of some £42 million was foreign, the great bulk of it directed toward the
French lines being constructed, often with English technical as well as
financial cooperation. The monthly value of exports for the United Kingdom
or the magnitude of the gold drain which was causing such concern in
financial circles. Ward-Perkins, however, minimizes the effects of this apparent
outflow of capital on the grounds that much of the money returned via
payments to British engineers, contractors, and workmen involved in overseas
railway construction or via the increase in British exports which these
transfers ultimately stimulated. He concludes that "the net figure cannot
have been serious."

The other main currents of gold directed toward Paris was that intended
to shore up the Bank of France. Despite its own difficulties, the Bank of
England rushed to the aid of its French counterpart since the extensive
involvement of British investors in French projects made the financial crisis
in Paris a major factor in the tightening credit market at home. The Bank
of France was the recipient of a direct loan of £1 million negotiated "through
the Barings—in effect from the Bank of England" even though this tended
to aggravate the latter's reserve position.

In any event, both institutions weathered the crisis. The Bank of France
actually consolidated its position by absorbing several provincial banks and

by acquiring new privileges like the right to issue one hundred-franc notes. For its part, the Bank of England was able to meet its obligations without infringing the provisions of the Bank Charter Act of 1844. The failures after the February Days, of several London houses specializing in trade with France and Belgium were generally surface phenomena and, "despite revolution on the Continent, for Britain 1848 was a year of financial recuperation, although political unrest abroad and at home certainly inhibited a return of long-run confidence."

Looked at from the opposite vantage point, the impact of English industrialism on the French experience of the mid-century crisis was less clearly negative but of far greater moment. The influence of England on the growth of French industry has been described as "all-pervasive and ever-present." This was true not only because England dominated the competition for world markets but also because England was France's prime source of foreign capital and ranked second to the United States among France's own trading partners (Clough 1964:156–157). It was largely because of the sluggishness of the English market that French exports, which had grown steadily in each of the five years since 1842, leveled off in 1846 and declined sharply in 1847. Relative market positions also magnified the effects of the same financial phenomena already noted in England. The use of credit was less extensive in France (Dunham 1955:83). One might think that when the crisis arrived, France would therefore find itself less over-extended. In fact, the limited supply of domestic capital had forced France into an over-reliance on English sources. As the crisis took hold foreign funds were quickly withdrawn from the French market. This tended to ease the situation in England but substantially aggravated conditions in France. A number of French railways, caught in the tightening credit market, were forced to suspend construction. Several failed outright.

The extent of French reliance on English resources was considerable. The same movement of capital from England to France, which amounted to a modest 15 percent of the railroad calls levied on English investors, represented between one-third and one-half of the total investment in French railroads. Tudesq (1956:19) relates that when the *Chemin de fer du Nord* issued a call in mid-1847—one of relatively few that were met quickly and easily—the majority of its shareholders were found to be English. Henderson attributes the halt in the expansion of French railways specifically to the repercussions of the commercial crisis in London (1961:126). While Dunham ends by minimizing the long-term impact of British/French competition for capital, he estimates that half of the total invested in French railways between 1840 and 1848 came from across the channel and notes that its sudden withdrawal between 1845 and 1847 constituted one of the important foreign influences leading to the French industrial crisis (1955:80, 359). Indeed, he concludes that both domestic and foreign influences, independent of one another, were sufficiently important to explain the occurrence of a crisis in France in 1847 (p. 367). Their coincidence in that year simply helps to explain the severity of the one that did occur.

On balance, then, it appears that the interconnections between the crises in France and England were real. They also appear to have been somewhat asymmetric. While those measures that were the result of conscious policy— for instance, bank loans—generally operated to the advantage of the weaker partner, those consequences that were the result of unconscious market forces inevitably favored the stronger. France, with its relatively limited pool of capital and unwieldy system of finance, suffered more from the restriction of European credit. France, with its smaller overall economy and narrower range of trading partners, felt the effects of depressed world trade more quickly. England, though by no means left untouched, was able to exploit its dominant market position and more sophisticated financial institutions to counter the worst effects of the crisis. The gold drain originating in grain imports was compensated to an appreciably extent by the £6 million in continental securities or credits that English investors hurriedly realized during the summer of 1847 (Clapham 1959:494–495).

English investments in France constituted a reserve of capital that in times of easy money, was directed to the Continent to earn a handsome return, often in projects that, like many of the French railway schemes, were actually dominated by English engineering and labor as well as capital. When money grew tight, this surplus was recalled to alleviate the domestic shortage of capital. Conversely, in periods of boom, France might benefit by the use of foreign capital even if this meant that its own nationals sometimes lost in the competition for the choicest investments. In periods of bust, however, capital tended to be withdrawn at precisely that moment when it was needed most. Moreover, this dynamic proved to be self-reinforcing. Once the English began to reclaim their capital, even French investors were inclined to follow suit. They sent their gold to London in search of a security considered to be lacking at home. In all these ways the economic downturn ended by reversing the direction of capital flow and insured that while England would be insulated from the worst effects of the crisis, France would be afflicted to a disproportionate degree.

Global Crisis and Social Movements

Having provided a rough sketch of the economic crisis in France and England, it is now time to step back and see what questions it does and does not help us answer. All analysts concur in the judgment that the French economic crisis of 1846–47 was an important determinant of the revolutionary movement that broke out in Paris in February 1848. They are less unanimous in asserting that economics lay behind the succession of subsequent Continental movements, since "political" factors originating in France offer plausible alternatives. Even more rarely do they venture an explanation of why in England, where economic crisis was also present, no comparable movement caught on. The coincidence of a pan-European depression and an almost equally widespread revolutionary tide will tempt those given to grand-theoretical generalizations. But any general explanation should also account for the relative quiescence in England.

One approach explains the differences in type and level of social movement activity by situating the economies of France and England within the context of nineteenth century capitalist development. In France industrialization had proceeded steadily since the Restoration, but it would be the end of the nineteenth century before the factory would win out over the small workshop. In 1848 the skilled artisan predominated, especially in a center of luxury trades like Paris. This predominance was at first numerical; but the characteristic activism of this privileged stratum of the working class further exaggerated its political presence, giving French movements their radical bias. These conditions can be contrasted with those in England, where factory organization was introduced much earlier. The labor force in textiles, the industrial sector hardest hit by the English crisis of 1846–1847, had already been transformed into a modern industrial proletariat. The extent that differences in the degree of proletarianization can be convincingly associated with differences in the degree and type of political activism to be found within the working class, a potential explanation of the distinctive French and English social movement responses to global crisis begins to emerge.

Alternatively, the difference in social movement response might be thought to derive from the previously mentioned asymmetry in the respective positions of France and England in the world economy. Nations, like individuals, in the view of Burke, may have "equal rights, but not to equal things." Despite evidence that many of the crisis transactions between those countries were intended to work to the advantage of France, it appears likely, in view of what we know of contemporary economics, that conditions of unequal exchange and the privileges conferred on Britain by its dominance of the market were more than adequate compensation. In this view, England—even that miserable English working class that Engels described—was somewhat insulated from the full effects of global crisis and never developed the full-scale social movement symptoms that might otherwise have been expected.

A further possibility also exists. It is suggested by a salient point rarely stressed in comparative context: what ultimately set the industrial crisis in France apart from that in England was the economic impact of the 1848 revolution itself. We have seen that with certain variations in locus and intensity, the crisis pursued much the same course in both countries up to the beginning of 1848. The February Days marked an end to the parallels. Whereas in England 1848 was a year of recovery despite the turmoil on the continent, in France the crisis plumbed new depths, and real signs of recovery would not be seen before 1851. Only the blow to the confidence of business circles delivered by the overthrow of the July Monarchy can explain the dramatic differences in scope and duration that separate the French case from the English. The reaction to the February Days had been immediate. In the fortnight following the declaration of the republic, both three and five percent French bonds lost over a third of their value (Clough 1964:429). By the June Days the price of the 3 percent *rente* had fallen to 32.5 percent of par (Cameron 1961:78).

State bonds fell precipitously and the Bourse closed its doors. Runs on banks began and banks which had large quantities of state bonds in their portfolios were unable to meet their obligations. Several were forced to close and this made it difficult, if not impossible, for commercial houses to discount their bills or notes. Industry was in turn affected and unemployment consequently increased. Paris, with a total male laboring population of about 200,000 at the beginning of 1848 and with 7000 or 9000 unemployed on the eve of the revolution, had, according to an official estimate, 17,000, or according to other sources, 49,000 unemployed on March 1. The increased seriousness of the depression led the provisional government to intervene in economic matters with a vengeance (Clough 1964:165).

The figures of Paris Chamber of Commerce (1851) show that these rates of unemployment would only continue to rise until more than half of the entire industrial labor force was out of work. Intervention by the state, notably in the form of the guarantee of the right to work, produced enrollments of 120,000 workers in the National Workshops and a genuine fiscal crisis. The vacillations of a government torn in its loyalties between "democratic" and "social" republics, between political and social revolution, between bourgeois and working-class objectives, paralyzed the French economy for months. In this case at least, the inescapable conclusion is that the course of political events radically influenced the economic.

Earlier in this paper the unfolding of the economic crisis in France and England was conveniently characterized as a three-step process that progressed from agricultural to financial to industrial sectors. It must now be added that in France, as opposed to England, this progression itself fitted within a larger three-step process in which a depressed economy helped create the preconditions for a revolution that produced in turn a drastic downturn in the French economy. In the attempt to account for both the similarities and divergences, all three of the explanatory alternatives mentioned here are developed in the papers that follow. While compatible in part, they also pose a number of rather stark differences in interpretation which promise to enliven the subsequent discussion. The parallels between the French and English cases may teach us that among the links between global crisis and social movements, the most significant may in fact be counter-intuitive.

References

Cameron, R. E. 1961. *France and the Economic Development of Europe, 1800–1914*, Princeton: Princeton University Press.

Clapham, J. H. 1959. *An Economic History of Modern Britain: The Early Railway Age, 1820–1850*, Cambridge: Cambridge University Press.

Clough, S. B. 1964. *France: A History of National Economics, 1789–1939*, New York: Octagon.

Dunham, A. L. 1955. *The Industrial Revolution in France, 1815–1848*, Hicksville, NY: Exposition Press.

Feuer, L. S., ed. 1959. *Marx and Engels: Basic Writing on Politics and Philosophy*, Garden City, NY: Anchor.

Gash, N. 1968. *The Age of Peel*, New York: St. Martin's Press.

Henderson, W. D. 1961. *The Industrial Revolution in Europe, 1815–1914*, New York: Quadrangle.

Labrousse, C. E. 1956. "Panoramas de la crise," *Etudes de la société d'histoire de la révolution de 1848*, XII:vi.

Mitchell, B. R., and P. Deane. 1971. *Abstract of British Historical Statistics*, Cambridge: Cambridge University Press.

Rude, G. 1973. *The Crowd in the French Revolution*, London: Oxford University Press.

Tudesq, A. J. 1956. "La crise de 1847, vue par les milieux d'affaires parisiens," *Etudes de la société d'histoire de la révolution de 1848*, XII:19.

Ward-Perkins, C. N. 1966. "The Commercial Crisis of 1847," in E. M. Carus-Wilson, ed., *Essays in Economic History*, vol. 3, New York: St. Martin's Press.

3

The French Revolution of 1848 and the Social History of Work

ROBERT BEZUCHA

The remarkable growth of social history during the past two decades has changed substantially what we know and how we think about nineteenth century Europe. In 1963, for example, Peter Amann wrote in the pages of *The American Historical Review* that "For over [a century] the French Revolution of 1848 has proved a source of embarrassment for historians" (Amann 1963:938). He would never say that today. A torrent of books and articles has carried us into the nooks and crannies of life in France around the middle of the past century. We have visited villages in Provence and workshops in Lyon, listened in on Icarian societies and revolutionary clubs, peered over Parisian barricades, tracked down opponents of the *coup d'État*, and even tried to get inside the heads of ordinary workers (Weber 1980). While we now know much more about 1848, one thing was clear when Amann voiced his lament: the Revolution was linked in some way to a general crisis of the French economy. Marx had said as much, of course, but it was not until the publication of a collection of articles edited by Ernest Labrousse in 1956 that historians generally accepted it as true (Labrousse 1956). Because Labrousse was an expert on the economic origins of the Revolution of 1789, it came as a disappointment that, having established its existence, he and his students never got around to probing the precise nature of the relationship between political and economic upheaval in 1848. We haven't made much progress since, either. In their important article "The People of June, 1848," for example, Charles Tilly and Lynn Lees resort to the metaphor of an economic funnel channeling a revolutionary stream of milk (Tilly and Lees 1975:172).

The present volume provides an opportunity to reformulate this long-standing problem and ask about the connection between the development

This chapter originally appeared as "The French Revolution of 1848 and the Social History of Work" in *Theory and Society* 12/4 (July 1983), pp. 469–484, and is reprinted with permission. Copyright 1983 by *T&S*.

of capitalism and the transformation of production, on the one hand, and the revolutionary events of 1848, on the other. This is a large question and I only intend one small answer: a case study of the construction industry of Paris. There is good reason to choose this example, however. Not only were workers in the building trades at the heart of the popular movement from the February Days to the June Days, but their experience also lends support to a statement made by Temma Kaplan about the anarchists of Andalusia and raises it to the level of a general proposition: "Changes in the work process and the politics that developed from them were products of larger social transformations attributable to the growth of capitalism" (Kaplan 1977:37).

The general crisis of the French economy was actually a sequence of three interrelated crises. Its first phase began in 1845, with the loss of the potato crop to the same fungus that was pushing Ireland to the brink of mass starvation. A disastrous harvest the next year drove grain prices to one of the highest levels of the century. By early 1847, they were more than double what they had been two years earlier. An agricultural crisis still meant cascading trouble for the entire economy at this time. Having to pay twice as much for the bread that was the staple of his or her diet, the ordinary person passed up a new shirt; the weaver, whose income was reduced because fewer persons wanted shirts, wore out old shoes; the cobbler postponed buying a stove; the foundry owner laid off workers, and so it went. More than four thousand businesses went bankrupt in 1847 alone.

The *crise de subsistance*, as Labrousse called it, ended with an abundant harvest in 1847. Grain became cheap once again and bread rioting stopped. Contrary to expectations, however, the economy did not recover immediately. Largely as a result of advances made to the panic-stricken government for the purchase of foreign grain, the gold reserves of the Banque de France fell from 201 million francs in June 1846, to 47 million francs in January 1847. The Banque responded by raising its lending rate from 4% to 5%, causing a slowdown in speculation. Some railroad companies were forced to sell their shares in the Banque in order to raise liquid capital. The *Journal des Chemins de Fer* described the credit crunch as "the inevitable consequence of the rapid creation of new instruments of wealth and power." Economic analysts, in other words, were inclined to see it as less the result of the agricultural crisis than of the financial boom that preceded it. In any case, what we recognize as the commercial phase of the general crisis was at the time judged to be over when the Banque lowered its lending rate in December 1847 (Tudesq 1956:4–36).

Labrousse and his colleagues noted that it extended into 1848, but it was the economic historian T.J. Markovitch who later identified the severity of the final phase, which was a crisis of production. All France suffered. Compared to figures from the previous year, coal production fell 77% in 1848. Its impact was most serious in Paris, where the global value of all commerce dropped from nearly a billion and a half francs in 1847, to just over half a billion the following year. Profits in the construction industry were down by 66% and employment dropped 64% (Markovitch 1965). It is impossible to quantify the influence of the collapse of the July Monarchy on the continuing economic disaster, but it is certain that the first months of the Revolution of 1848 were played against a backdrop of serious depression. One consequence of this fact is the notorious "45 centime tax." Frequently called a political blunder because it turned the peasantry against the Provisional Government, this surtax on land was introduced as an emergency measure for the purpose of expanding credit supplies and stimulating industrial production (Gossez 1953).

Let us turn our attention to a second example. Within days of the abdication of the Citizen King, the Provisional Government selected one of its own members, Louis Blanc, to direct a *Commission du Gouvernement pour les Travailleurs*. Concerned with the plight of the worker and fearful of its wrath, the Luxembourg Commission quickly issued its first proclamation. Stated in the rudimentary way that most of us learned it, the length of the working day was reduced to ten hours in Paris and eleven in the provinces (this would be rescinded after the June Days as "harmful to French industry and contrary to worker interests"), and what is often translated as "sweated labor" was abolished (Duveau 1968). Some general histories of the Revolution of 1848 fail to mention the second provision at all (Agulhon 1973). The relevant portion of the text reads as follows:

> Considering . . . that the exploitation of workers by worker subcontractors called *marchandeurs* or *tâcheron* is essentially unjust, vexatious, contrary to the spirit of fraternity. . . . The exploitation of workers by subcontractors, or *marchandage*, is abolished. It is understood that associations of workers whose object is not the exploitation of workers by one another are not considered to be *marchandage* (Levasseur 1904:356).

Since language itself has a history, it would be wrong to assume that *marchandage* and "sweated labor" mean precisely the same thing. Furthermore, the fact that the Provisional Government rushed to abolish *marchandage* and that in doing so it also implied that worker-controlled subcontracting could be fraternal suggests this as an important moment in the social history of work.

Marchandage comes from the word *marchand*, one "whose profession is to buy and sell" (Littré 1878), a *marchandeur* being one who buys and sells the work of others. The synonym *tâcheron* is related to the term for piecework (*ouvrage à la tâche*), but here it refers to the subdivision of labor on a single project (Littré 1878). Something of the contemporary use of the word *marchandage* can be recaptured from Martin Nadaud's *Mémoires de Léonard, ancien garçon maçon*. One of thousands of migrant construction workers who arrived in Paris each spring during the Restoration and the July Monarchy, Nadaud tells of a clever scheme he and his mates had to sell seats on the scaffolding of a building under construction on the Champs Elysees to watch the marriage procession of the Duc d'Orleans in 1837.

"Nous avons beau élever nos prix," he writes, "on ne marchandait pas, on nous prenait au mot" (Nadaud 1976:193). The connotation is clearly one of haggling, or, in this particular case, its absence.

There is a description of how *marchandage* actually operated in the building trades in an account by the *Gazette des Tribunaux* (28 August 1840) of the issues involved in the wave of strikes going on in the capital:

> It has been customary from time immemorial in the professions connected with construction . . . that the contractors [*entrepreneurs*], having won bids on major projects, then subcontract different parts of them with types of foremen [*contremaîtres*] called *tâcherons*: the latter, after having directly recruited workers themselves, execute the work which they have been charged with in a given period of time and at their own risk and peril in consideration for a price fixed in advance. This custom, advantageous to the contractor since it reduces the sum total of his responsibility and oversight, is also advantageous for the *tâcherons*, who, either by paying the workers a wage a little below what they would ordinarily receive or by executing the job with fewer hands or in fewer days than had been foreseen, attain the realization of legitimate profits (Aguet 1954).

Subcontracting in the building trades—among stone cutters, plasterers, masons, roofers, carpenters, joiners, glaziers, locksmiths, and so forth—went back to the Old Regime and, in that sense, had been known "from time immemorial." The system of labor organization known as *marchandage*, however, was the product of three more recent factors: the destruction of self-governing worker *corporations* (guilds) by the Le Chapelier law of 1791; a sharp expansion of the scale of production after 1815; and the development of French capitalism during the first half of the nineteenth century.

The principal reason that contractors found *marchandage* so advantageous around 1840 was that Paris was in the midst of a building boom. Surprising as it may seem, the government spent only 19 million francs for the construction and repair of public buildings under the Empire, whereas state investment rose to over 55 million francs during the Bourbon Restoration (de Sauvigny 1977:51). The figures are even higher for the July Monarchy. In one year alone the public works budget of the Prefect of the Seine grew from 124 million to 140 million francs (Lavedan 1975:366). Private investment was responsible for the construction of 2,671 buildings in the capital between 1817 and 1827 (Bertier de Sauvigny 1977:72). I have no data for the private sector during the July Monarchy, but we know that the lodging-house (*garni*) population—an indirect measure of the number of itinerant workers prevalent in the building trades—rose steadily from 23 thousand in 1831, to 50 thousand in 1846 (Chevalier 1958:275). It is likely, therefore, that the commercial crisis of 1847 struck the construction industry in a position of full extension.

Fortunes were made on speculation in the age of Balzac. "This building mania is attributed to the present scarcity of openings for capital," wrote one author in 1825 (Montigny 1825). "One gambles with construction the way one gambles with bonds," said another. "A building changes hands four or five times a week, another every day" (cited in Bertier de Sauvigny 1977:78). Contractors reaped huge profits by subcontracting for a price fixed in advance. Fortunes could be lost the same way, however. When investors withdrew their capital, as happened during an over-building panic near the end of the Restoration, contractors went bankrupt, *marchandeurs* and *tâcherons* went unpaid, and ordinary workers were left empty-handed. Little wonder that in 1848, construction workers packed the early sessions of the Luxembourg Commission to complain about the "unjust" conditions of their labor (Gossez 1967:26).

The *marchandage* system in the Parisian building trades was only one design in a larger pattern being woven into the western economy at that time. As Christopher S. Johnson has commented: "[The] evolution of industrial capitalism must be understood in terms of *structural* change—from the structure of the world economy at the broadest and most abstract level down to business organization, community structure, and the structure of work in home, shop, and factory" (Johnson 1979:67).

We are only now becoming fully aware of the fact that capitalist expansion around mid-century was due less to technological innovation than to increased exploitation of handwork by means of the division of labor and the simplification of individual tasks. Both, in turn, were made possible by chronic underemployment and a superabundance of labor (Samuel 1977; Gaillard 1977; Johnson 1971). Put into practice it meant that the French tailors who endured the introduction of the piece-work system for producing ready-made clothing, which they called *confection*, would have found a sympathetic ear among the English tailors, who called it "dishonorable labor," and the German tailors, who considered it fit only for a *Pfuscher*, a butcher. As Henry Mayhew wrote in the *Morning Chronicle* of London in 1849: "By this process men gradually become mere machines, and lose all the moral and intellectual characteristics which distinguish the skilled artisan" (Mayhew 1971:340).

The politics that developed from these changes in the work process was highly complex. For this reason historians have chosen to proceed on a case-by-case basis. The remarkable militancy of the Lyonnaise silk weavers rested on a spirit of mutuality among masters and journeymen, a shared sense of vulnerability to the demands of the cloth merchants. In Germany, on the other hand, the split between masters and journeymen lay at the root of their collective failure at the Frankfurt Artisans' Congress in 1848. And London was divided between the "honorable" trades of the West End and the slop shops of the East End (Bezucha 1974, Noyes 1966, Yeo and Thompson 1971). The construction industry of Paris in 1848 offers an even more compelling example, one in which worker fought against worker on the barricades during the June Days. Our task for the remainder of this essay will be to understand how and why this happened.

Let me reiterate a crucial point: with the exception of the substitution of iron for wood in the frames of some public buildings, the scale of the

Parisian building boom was made possible by changes in the organization of the work process rather than by technological innovation (Gaillard 1977:69–70). The *marchandage* system exploited the common laborer and the *marchandeur* alike by encouraging wage-squeezing and discouraging the creation of uniform pay and working conditions in the building trades. It did so, moreover, in the interest of commercial speculation and profit. For over a quarter of a century, as Martin Nadaud told the Legislative Assembly in 1849, contractors had devoted themselves to building housing for the bourgeoisie (Gaillard 1977:23; on London construction, Dyos 1968 and Shepherd 1971:96–105).

Resistance to *marchandage* was an integral part of both great strike waves of the July Monarchy (Shorter and Tilly 1974:107–110, Aguet 1954 and Faure 1974:51–92). We should not conclude, however, either that the industrial militancy of the building workers was uniform in 1833–1834 and in 1840, or that it necessarily had a simple political corollary. The construction industry was riddled by diversity: there was trade rivalry, competition between seasonal laborers and permanent residents, generational conflict, and open disagreement between the craft-conscious members of the *compagnonnages* (the secret journeymen's societies of the Old Regime whose persistence was tolerated by the authorities because they maintained a semblence of order among the so-called "floating population") and unskilled workers simply looking for a job. And the contractors knew how to play on these divisions, moreover. An open letter from the masonry contractors to the stone cutters in 1840 responded to their strike demands by ridiculing the notion that everyone did an equal amount of work in a day, and went on to predict that a fixed daily wage would only bring about closer supervision. When working for a *tâcheron*, they advised, the motto was "The better the man, the better the job":

> You are being deceived over and over again, for all that you want is against your own interest. . . . True workers! Men of stout heart! It is you we address. Our interest in yours, yours is ours—believe us. . . . Present yourselves at your own personal value—your interest, which lies in your work, merits it (Aguet 1954:219).

Such exhortations did not automatically fall on deaf ears. Martin Nadaud was popular enough among his mates to be selected as their representative to the Luxembourg Commission in 1848, yet he was sorely tempted to become a contractor. It is to his credit and our good fortune that he felt ambivalent enough about his ambition to share it in his memoirs (Nadaud 1976:217–218, 229; on the application of psychological categories, Gay 1979:187–204). A mason from the Creuse, Nadaud was present when the cavalry dispersed a mass strike meeting of building workers in 1840, and he imagined the contractors' faces were "radiant, and in their joy they kissed the feet of the ministers." He had seen men shake their fists in frustration when a *marchandeur* told them that a building owner was out of money, and he condemned such "duplicity of which the worker is always the victim." "Voilà!" he wrote, "That is what was called . . . 'freedom to work,' a false doctrine which those who have been my guides in democracy and socialism have counselled me never to accept as true." This was the same person who once secretly agreed to speed-up work on a site for an extra five *sous* a day. "In accepting this proposition," he explained, "we were being selected as *hommes de confiance de la maison*. We weren't betraying our comrades, but were attaching ourselves to the interest of the boss." Nadaud himself acted as a *tâcheron* for three years during the 1840s, all the while wearing a Phrygian bonnet as a symbol of his Republican sentiments.

Call it "false consciousness" if you will, but Martin Nadaud was probably no different from many construction workers who hated the *marchandage* system, and also sat around at night and talked about their illustrious forerunners (he mentions them by name) who began as sons of humble peasants, tramped to Paris as young men, become *ouvriers d'élite*, then contractors, and finally retired to big farms in the Creuse to live out their days surrounded by admiring families. "Success stories" are carrots at the end of the stick of capitalism. Ambition, however, can be a slave-driver setting men against each other. Jules Michelet, who was born among the *menu peuple* and became Professor of History at the *Collège de France*, recognized this when he composed his lyrical essay *Le Peuple* in 1845, the boom year on the eve of the general economic crisis (Michelet 1978:18, 55, 92, 95). "The difficulty is not to rise," he wrote, "but rather, in rising, to remain one's self." Michelet acknowledged that material conditions had improved since the Old Regime and that without the restrictions of workers' *corporations* "the gates are open" to success. Nevertheless, he warned, a "thousand new elements of mental suffering" awaited the artisan seeking to climb "the long ladder of society." A "mental and moral relationship" between workers had been lost, leaving each person prey to a sense of isolation which he called "machinism."

Martin Nadaud neither read Michelet nor understood capitalism, but he learned the meaning of "Egoism," the term workers used for individual competition on the job. Abandoning his position as a *tâcheron* in order to escape "these ruinous speculators," he resolved to find "a good contractor" and serve as a *maître compagnon* training young masons as they worked side-by-side (Nadaud 1976:271). Nadaud's *prise de conscience* serves as a concrete illustration of the emergence of what Bernard Moss has called "the socialism of skilled workers" (Moss 1976). It also parallels the experience of the Parisian master tailors, who began by wholeheartedly supporting "the capitalist condemnation of unruly and unappreciative workers," and by 1848 were attacking *confection* and looking for ways to create a master-worker alliance (Johnson 1975:87–114).

The revival of corporatism, which William H. Sewell, Jr. and Remi Gossez have shown to be at the heart of the popular movement in 1848, was not produced by a desire to restore the Old Regime, as its bourgeois critics charged; rather it was a search for a way around the competition of the *confection* and *marchandage* systems in order to establish a harmonious new world of labor (Gossez 1967, Sewell 1980). Louis Blanc's *Organisation du travail*, written in 1839 and reprinted throughout the 1840s, proposed the use of state capital to create co-operative "social workshops." Once a sympathetic government became "the supreme regulator of production," he reasoned, competition would gradually disappear. Philippe Buchez, by contrast, foresaw that instead of "being emancipated" workers might "emancipate themselves" through the accumulation of "common social capital" (Sewell 1980:203–204, 234–235). In September 1840, the newspaper *L'Atelier* suggested that striking workers adopt self-management:

> You may form small societies of six, eight, and ten members as the case may be. Each society shall choose its most trustworthy member to act as its intermediary with the contractors. He will take the place of the subcontractor, or *marchandeur*, but it will then be to the advantage of all his associates, since the profits will be divided among them according to the amount of work done by each (Aguet 1954:226).

The substitution of democratic, collective *marchandage* for the existing system was frequently discussed by Parisian workers in the years immediately prior to the Revolution of 1848. When the Luxembourg Commission abolished the "exploitation" of the *marchandeur* and left the door open for fraternal labor associations it seemed like more than a political revolution had occurred, therefore (Duveau 1946:263). As if to confirm its intentions, the Commission issued a second proclamation setting fines or a jail term for violations by *marchandeurs*. Numerous mutual aid and other societies based on the principle of collective *marchandage* sprang up in the heady climate of what was called "the Springtime of the People," and, if we accept the word of Ernest Levasseur, a pioneer of French labor history writing eighty years ago, the normal practice of *marchandage* began to disappear (Levasseur 1904:356).

It is rare that workers actually get what they want. Indeed it usually takes a revolution. Why, then, were construction workers fighting each other only a few months later? The answer in its simplest form is that the events of 1848 did not happen in a vacuum. The general economic crisis that helped create a revolutionary situation also stacked the odds against the success of the Second Republic. The Provisional Government ended the February Days by publicly guaranteeing a living wage and the right to work. This was the price it paid for popular support. Frightened businessmen, however, made a run on the Banque de France, whose gold reserves fell 50% within two weeks. Whatever credit had been generated since the Banque lowered its lending rate the previous December now evaporated at the very moment that the winter "dead season" in the building trades was ending. Even if contractors willingly obeyed the authority of the Luxembourg Commission there were few jobs to be found in Paris (Merriman 1978:7, Gossez 1967:101, Duveau 1946:72).

The Provisional Government responded to the massive unemployment with a combination of old and new policies. State-sponsored public works projects were traditional in times of exceptional hardship, but, because the name *ateliers de charitée* sounded objectionable, they were called *ateliers nationaux* in 1848. The National Workshops were unrelated to Louis Blanc's plan for "social workshops," although his presence in the Provisional Government caused some confusion about this at the time. (Here is a classic example of how the growth of social history has refined our understanding of the political history of 1848: it used to be held that the other members of the Provisional Government so feared Blanc's popularity among the working class that they created the National Workshops to undermine his reputation) (Pinkney 1965). In any case, over 100,000 workers had signed up by the time enrollment was closed on 12 May, and the Ministry of Public Works was spending a million francs a week. Although the National Workshops were organized according to a military model into sections, brigades, companies, and units, most men did little more than wield a shovel for a couple of hours in return for one franc, fifty centimes per day. These wages were insufficient for the unskilled day laborers who constituted 13% of the membership and were completely inadequate for trained artisans with families. Research by Tilly and Lees in the dossiers of persons arrested after the June Days suggests that workers continued to look for jobs and considered the National Workshops a last resort (Tilly and Lees 1965:117).

At this point political rivalry did play a role. The moderate faction of the Provisional Government, headed by Lamartine, who had proclaimed the Republic, came to think of the National Workshops as a worker army which could be used to suppress an attempted *coup*. These defenders of the revolutionary *status quo* faced a true dilemma: the expense of supporting the unemployed was costing the regime whatever friends it retained in the business community, while ending the workers' subsidy risked popular retaliation. The bankers won out, and, as is well-known, the announcement that the National Workshops would be closed in Paris and their members enrolled in the army or sent to clear swamps in the provinces was the immediate cause of the June Days. A last-minute promise of an extra payday was to no avail. The success of the June uprising would have meant the victory of the Left and turned the revolution toward the radical program for a "democratic and social Republic." It was put down with such savagery, however, that the Provisional Government itself fell and the republican Right came to power in the person of General Cavaignac (DeLuna 1969). Six months later Louis Napoleon Bonaparte was elected as the first President of the Republic.

Georges Duveau described the National Workshops as "an extra Praetorian guard" to draw attention to the fact that the Provisional Government already had one (Duveau 1946:68). The young regime had also met the unemployment crisis by creating a new institution called the *Garde mobile*. Marx thought of it as nothing more than the *lumpenproletariat* in uniform, but Mark Traugott and others have proved that this special militia was indistinguishable from the National Workshops in occupational terms: a great majority of both was drawn from the artisanal crafts and trades (Traugott 1980a, 1980b,

Caspard 1974; Amann 1975:303 and Gossez, personal communication in Amann). The Mobile Guard was established in the aftermath of the February Days out of a desire to keep the regular army outside the capital, and also doubts about the loyalty of the National Guard and the ability of this militia to maintain order. Members of the Mobile Guard received the same wage as in the National Workshops to train and live in barracks. Although the Mobile Guard stood firm and obeyed orders during the *journées* of 16 April and 15 May, a "Proclamation to All Workers of the Seine Department" on 1 June listed socialist candidates for the National Assembly who were said to have been approved by delegates from the worker societies, the National Workshops, the Mobile Guard, and the political clubs (Amann 1975:259). Fears about its possible radicalization proved unfounded, however, since fourteen thousand of the sixteen thousand men enrolled in the Mobile Guard volunteered to support the Provisional Government in the June Days.

It should be clear by now that the Provisional Government unintentionally facilitated the mobilization of the Paris working class to an extent far beyond what would have been possible through the efforts of the political club movement and the worker societies alone (Tilly and Lees 1975:172–173). The level of popular organization increased, moreover, with the democratic reform of the National Guard. In *Revolution and Mass Democracy*, Peter Amann contends that arming the poor to defend property was "one of the few truly revolutionary . . . social changes initiated by the Second Republic" (Amann 1975:81). Indeed the June uprising did not begin during a protest called by the National Workshops or a speech at the Club of Socialist Republicans, but rather with a demonstration sponsored by the 12th Legion of the National Guard. Units from worker neighborhoods provided the framework for resistance, and the allegience of entire sections of the city during the fighting was largely determined by control of the National Guard infrastructure at the local level (Amann 1975:301, 304–305).

The actual events of June 1848 need not concern us. The important thing for our purposes is the array of forces: around 25,000 troops from the regular army, some *bourgeois* units of the National Guard, plus the Mobile Guard, attacked barricades raised by ten to fifteen thousand insurgents drawn from worker units of the National Guard, the National Workshops, the political clubs, and worker societies, in addition to an unknown number of persons with no organizational affiliation. The size of the uprising alone suggests that a majority of Parisian workers remained passive, if not neutral. Setting aside soldiers in the army, construction workers constituted the largest occupational category on *both* sides of the barricades. They were over-represented, in fact, since members of the building trades made up 19.6% of the adult male population of Paris in 1848, and accounted for 22.4% of the membership of the Mobile Guard and 26.2% of those arrested. According to Mark Traugott's figures the average age of a Mobile Guardsman who took part in the fighting was 22.1 years (i.e. born in 1826), while the average age of an insurgent was 34 years (i.e. born in 1814) (Traugott 1980a:35, 1980b:707). Scholars who have examined the data first-hand agree that age was an important variable, but they become more vague when it comes to explaining why (Amann 1975:303).[1] I hope to convince you that when seen in terms of the social history of work those twelve years probably made the critical difference in how a worker experienced the Revolution of 1848.

Martin Nadaud was born in 1815 (one year later than the average June insurgent) and departed for Paris for the first time in the spring of 1830. He was less than fifteen and a mason's helper when the July Monarchy was born of revolution and full of conciliatory gestures toward the working class. He was nineteen when the government revoked its promises and forebade all unauthorized associations of more than twenty persons. He was twenty-five and had mastered his craft when the 1840 wave of strikes protested the *marchandage* system. He lived through the boom years of the 1840s with the temptation to advance himself individually, and he endured the worsening economic crisis determined to retain his status as a skilled artisan in a future world of fraternal labor.

Martin Nadaud was atypical, of course. His friend Etienne Cabet left to found an Icarian society in America in December 1848, but Nadaud stayed in France and was elected a Deputy by his home department of the Creuse a year after the June Days. He also wrote his memoirs. Nadaud's life as a mason *was* typical of many construction workers his age, however. He had a family at home to help support, a network of friends in Paris, a firm opinion that changes in the work process had undermined craft pride during his lifetime, and a utopian notion that this was wrong and could be corrected. When the revolution came in 1848, his hopes were raised by the abolition of *marchandage*, but when he learned on 30 May that the Provisional Government was going to introduce *tâcheron* in the National Workshops he likely remembered he had seen a government turn on the class that had brought it to power once before (Gossez 1967:101). Nadaud was lucky and found work between February and June, so he never had to enroll in the National Workshops. His exact whereabouts during the June Days have always been a mystery, however (as noted by Agulhon in Nadaud:1976:27–35). My own suspicion is that he fogged over the whole affair in his memoirs because he later felt embarrassed at not having participated. Even in this he was typical of others, although he and they were probably relieved at the time. Thousands of their mates had not been so fortunate.

Nadaud's experience was different from an imaginary counterpart the age of the average Mobile Guardsman, who would have arrived in Paris in 1841, the year after the anti-*marchandage* strikes had been defeated. A mason's helper learning his trade at that time not only was the final link in the chain of production in the construction industry, but also knew nothing about the previous decade of tumultuous labor agitation except what older men told him. When the economy collapsed, moreover, the future seemed more bleak to him than to them because he was the last hired and the first fired. Life in a Mobile Guard barracks must have appeared a better prospect to a bachelor than either seeking work for which others were more qualified, or trying to survive in a *garni* on the dole from the National Workshops.

I concede that this is speculation, but the data so carefully assembled by Traugott, Tilly and Lees, and others make clear that it is not sheer fantasy. Traugott, for example, offers the hypothesis that "economic variables other than strict class affiliation" were operative (Traugott 1980b:710). And Pierre Caspard, who also studied the Mobile Guard, suggests that its members were not "uniformly hostile toward the Parisian proletariat and its aspirations" but had "evolved more and more toward incomprehension and finally antagonism which expressed itself during the course of the June Days" (Caspard 1974:96). The older insurgents, he continues, chose an economic solution to the general crisis by supporting a fundamental transformation of the organization of production, whereas their younger working-class opponents focused on the immediate problem of unemployment. By choosing the relative security of the Mobile Guard they were making what Marx called "a financial decision" (Caspard 1974:106).

I want to make three points in conclusion. First, the seemingly ambiguous political response of the Parisian construction workers at the crossroad of the French Revolution of 1848 is best explained as a combination of differing generational experience with the structural evolution of industrial capitalism, on the one hand, and separate forms of political mobilization after the February Days, on the other. We would expect a similar response from other craft sectors which had undergone "proletarianization without significant mechanization," and the data confirm that clothing workers, the second largest occupational group in the city (14.8% of the adult male population), also made up the second largest categories of Mobile Guardsmen (13.2%) and of persons arrested in June 1848 (14.9%) (Traugott 1980a:35). These facts, in turn, shed interesting light on a long-forgotten incident: during the June Days the warehouse and workshops of a *confectionneur* who supplied ready-made clothing to *La Belle Jardinère* department store were burned to the ground (Johnson 1975:93).

Second, as others have discussed in greater detail elsewhere in this volume, the Irish potato famine and the failure of the wheat crop at home in 1846 and 1847 drew England, too, into a spiral of agricultural, commercial and financial, and industrial crisis. If Henry Mayhew's published 1849 interviews with a variety of London workers are any indication, specialists in English social history should reconsider the proposition that England alone among the Great Powers of Europe failed to catch the French disease of revolution because her economic development was at least a generation ahead of the continent. There is plenty of room for debate here about mid-nineteenth century urban social movements. My own suggestion is that the Cabinet's painstaking preparations to contain the Chartists' demonstration on Kennington Common in April 1848, may turn out to be more important than we have been led to believe. Manchester was a factory city by that time, but the capital of Great Britain more closely resembled Paris in terms of the structure of its local economy and the composition of its working class (on which see Briggs 1960).

This comparison is valid with one major exception, finally. Because London was the financial center of world capitalism, the city's banking and commercial communities were better prepared to deflect or ride out a production crisis than were their Parisian counterparts (Sheppard 1971, esp. chs. 2–3). During the final days of his exile in England, Louis Napoleon Bonaparte volunteered as one of the special constables who protected London from the Chartist throng. After he became Emperor he hired Baron Haussmann to supervise the demolition and reconstruction of central Paris, opening wide boulevards for more efficient crowd control. Napoleon III also reformed the French banking industry by authorizing the establishment of investment and deposit banks such as the *Credit Mobilier* and the *Credit Lyonnais* (Pinkney 1958, Gaillard 1977). At this point, we may say, capitalism and the social history of work in France entered a new stage.

Notes

1. "As to personnel, the only detectable difference between the average February revolutionary and the average June insurgent was one of age: recruitment into the *Garde mobile* drained off the very young workers, who, in June, ended up on the other side of the barricade," Note that Amann does not even hint as to *why* this might have happened.

References

Aguet, F. 1954. *Les grèves sous la Monarchie de Juillet, 1830–1847*, Geneva: E. Droz.
Agulhon, M. 1973. *1848, ou l'apprentissage de la République, 1848–1852*, Paris: Editions du Seuil.
Amann, P. 1963. "The Changing Outlines of 1848," *American Historical Review*, 68:938.
Amann, P. 1975. *Revolution and Mass Democracy: The Paris Club Movement in 1848*, Princeton: Princeton University Press.
Bertier de Sauvigny, G. 1977. *Nouvelle histoire de Paris: La Restauration, 1815–1830*, Paris: Hachette.
Bezucha, R. J. 1974. *The Lyon Uprising of 1834*, Cambridge: Harvard University Press.
Briggs, A. 1960. *The Making of Modern England, 1784–1867: The Age of Improvement*, New York: Harper and Row.
Caspard, P. 1974. "Aspects de la lutte des classes en 1848: le recrutement de la Garde nationale mobile," *Revue historique*, no. 511, 81–106.
Chevalier, L. 1958. *Classes laborieuses et classes dangereuses*, Paris: Plon.
DeLuna, F. A. 1969. *The French Republic Under Cavaignac, 1848*, Princeton: Princeton University Press.
Duveau, G. 1946. *La vie ouvrière en France sous la Second Empire*, Paris: Gallimard.
———. 1968. *1848: The Making of a Revolution*, New York: Vintage Books.
Dyos, H. J. 1968. "The Speculative Builders and Developers of Victorian London," *Victorian Studies*, 9 (Summer Supplement), 641–691.
Faure, A. 1974. "Mouvements populaires et mouvement ouvrier à Paris (1830–1834)," *Le Mouvement Social*, (juillet-septembre), no. 88, pp. 51–92.
Gaillard, J. 1977. *Paris, La Ville, 1852–1870*, Paris: H. Champion.

Gay, P. 1979. "On the Bourgeoisie: A Psychological Interpretation," in P. Merriman, ed., *Consciousness and Class Experience*, New York: Holmes and Meier.

Gossez, R. 1967. *Les Ouvriers de Paris, I: L'Organisation, 1848–1851*, La Roche sur Yonne: Bibliothèque de la Révolution de 1848.

———. 1953. "Les quarante cinq centimes," *Etudes: Recueil publié par la société d'histoire de la révolution de 1848*, 15: 89–132.

Johnson, C. H. 1971. "Communism and the Working Class Before Marx: The Icarian Experience," *American Historical Review*, 76:642–689.

———. 1975. "Economic Change and Artisan Discontent: The Tailors' History, 1800–1848," in R. Price, ed., *Revolution and Reaction: 1848 and the Second French Republic*, London and New York: Croom Helm and Barnes and Noble Books.

———. 1979. "Patterns of Proletarianization: Parisian Tailors and Lodève Woolens Workers," in J. M. Merriman, ed., *Consciousness and Class Experience in Nineteenth Century Europe*, New York and London: Holmes and Meier.

Kaplan, T. 1977. *The Anarchists of Andalusia, 1868–1903*, Princeton: Princeton University Press.

Labrousse, E. 1956. *Aspects de la crise et de la dépression de l'économie française au milieu du XIXe siècle, 1846–1851*, La Roche-sur-Yonne: Bibliothèque de la Révolution de 1848.

Lavedan, P. 1975. *Nouvelle histoire de Paris: Histoire de l'urbanisme à Paris*, Paris: Hachette.

Levasseur, E. 1904. *Histoire des classes ouvrières et de l'industrie en France de 1789 à 1870*, II. 2nd edition. Paris: Rousseau.

Markovitch, T. J. 1965. "La Crise de 1847–1848 dans les industries parisiennes," *Revue del'histoire économique et sociale*, 43:256–260.

Merriman, J. M. 1978. *The Agony of the Republic: The Repression of the Left In Revolutionary France, 1848–1851*, New Haven: Yale University Press.

Michelet, J. (D. McKay, translator). 1978. *The People*, Urbana: University of Illinois Press.

Montigny. 1825. *Provincial à Paris*, cited in L. Chevalier, 1958, *Classes laborieuses et classes dangereuses*, Paris: Plon.

Moss, B. 1976. *The Origins of the French Labor Movement: The Socialism of Skilled Workers, 1830–1914*, Berkeley and Los Angeles: University of California Press.

Nadaud, M. 1976. *Mémoires de Léonard, ancien garçon maçon*, Edition établie et commentée par Maurice Agulhon, Paris: Hachette.

Noyes, P. H. 1966. *Organization and Revolution: Working-Class Associations in the German Revolutions of 1848–1849*, Princeton: Princeton University Press.

Pinkney, D. H. 1965. "Les Ateliers de secours à Paris (1830–1831): précurseurs des ateliers nationaux de 1848," *Revue d'histoire moderne* 12:65–70.

———. 1958. *Napoleon III and the Rebuilding of Paris*, Princeton: Princeton University Press.

Price, R. 1975. *Revolution and Reaction: 1848 and the Second French Republic*, London: Croom Helm.

Samuel, R. 1977. "The Workshop of the World: Steam Power and Hand Technology in Mid-Victorian Britain," *History Workshop*, 3:6–72.

Sewell, W. H. 1980. *Work and Revolution in France: The Language of Labor from the Old Regime to 1848*, New York: Cambridge University Press.

Sheppard, F. H. W. 1971. *London, 1808–1870: The Infernal Wen*, Berkeley: University of California Press.

Shorter, E., and C. Tilly. 1974. *Strikes in France, 1830–1968*, New York: Cambridge University Press.

Tilly, C., and L. Lees. 1975. "The People of June, 1848," in R. Price, ed., *Revolution and Reaction: 1848 and the Second French Republic*, London and New York: Croom Helm and Barnes and Noble Books.

————. 1980a. "Determinants of Political Orientation: Class and Organization in the Parisian Insurrection of June 1848," *American Journal of Sociology*, 86:32–49.

————. 1980b. "The Mobile Guard in the French Revolution of 1848," *Theory and Society*, 9:683–720.

Tudesq, A. J. 1956. "La Crise de 1847 vue par les milieux d'affaires parisiens," in E. Labrousse, ed., *Aspects de la crise et de la dépression de l'économie française au milieu du XIXe siecle, 1846–1851*, La Roche-sur-Yonne: Bibliotheque de la Revolution de 1848.

Weber, E. "The Second Republic, Politics, and the Peasant," *French Historical Studies*, 11,4: 521–550.

Yeo, E., and E. P. Thompson, eds. 1971. *The Unknown Mayhew*, New York: Schocken Books.

4

The "Retardation" of French Economic Development and Social Radicalism During the Second Republic: New Lessons from the Old Comparison with Britain

CRAIG CALHOUN

Nineteenth century France was rocked by repeated revolutions in which workers played a major part, but in which they never succeeded in capturing and holding state power. Until recently, historians have tended to seek reasons for their "failure" in France's "backwardness." This backwardness has been seen sometimes as a retardation of political maturity. Tudesq (1965), for example, seems to suggest that France was not ready for democracy in 1848, that the people were conservative at heart and that many more craved authority and order than craved freedom and self-government. Other times, commentators see the issue as economic. Following Marx (1850, 1852) many suggest that modern capitalist industry was too little developed to have proletarianized a sufficient proportion of the populations, and that the proletarians who were around were too little aware of their true interests. Realizing the confusion in Marx's classification of all workers as proletarians, more recent authors have stressed the predominance of artisans and other pre-industrial workers over factory workers in the revolutionary struggles. Price (1972), for example, disagrees with Marx on a number of points including this, but ends up with a more extreme version of Marx's argument that France was insufficiently advanced for the social revolution to succeed. There is an irony in all these views of French backwardness as explanation for the failure of French revolutions, especially 1848. France is being compared

Portions of this chapter originally appeared in altered form in "Industrialization and Social Radicalism: British and French Workers and the Mid Nineteenth Century Crisis" in *Theory and Society* 12/4 (July 1983), pp. 485–504, and are reprinted with permission. Copyright 1983 by T&S.

to more advanced England, and industrializing England had no revolutions at all. The key nineteenth and early twentieth century examples of revolutions occurred in countries wracked by economic transformation, usually in the direction of capitalist industrialization. Most, if not all, later revolutions have followed this pattern. The advanced capitalist (and socialist) societies have seen struggles, to be sure, but no revolutions. In the present paper I shall argue that many of the comparisons—implicit as well as explicit—of nineteenth century France and Britain have been misleading. I shall criticize arguments as to France's economic retardation and failure to industrialize as well as arguments concerning the source and outcome of radical mobilizations. I shall suggest the radical importance of continuity with preindustrial social organization for the struggle to create a "democratic and social republic" between 1848 and 1851. And I shall suggest that workers' political struggles may have played an important role in steering France onto a course of more gradual and autocentric development than Britain's, a course which was at once more humane and better economic strategy than trying to follow directly in Britain's wake. In the background of my comparison will be a critique of a misunderstanding of the history of British popular radicalism. (This I have developed in more detail elsewhere, though concentrating on an earlier period.) In the foreground will be the social struggles of the Second Republic, though I shall not attempt to develop a very detailed or comprehensive narrative.

Economic Change in France and Britain

From being one of the richest and by far the largest of European economies, nineteenth century France fell behind in growth rate and eventually in overall wealth. "Throughout the first half of the nineteenth century and probably as late as 1860 France was the world's wealthiest nation" (Cameron 1972:429). By the end of the century Britain had overtaken France as Europe's most productive and powerful economy, and Germany was close behind. France's retardation has seemed to need explanation, and the failure to industrialize has been the foremost candidate. The English case has overwhelmed economic and historical imagination; France has been judged constantly by comparison. Even as study of the modern Third World has brought theories of unilineal development into disrepute, such notions have still been applied to French economic history. Recently, however, O'Brien and Keyder have thrown a good deal of doubt on this whole line of reasoning. They argue that one should be "more sceptical about the superiority of Britain's path to the twentieth century and inclined to see a more humane and perhaps a no less efficient transition to industrial society in the experience of France" (1978:197–198). Their argument is based primarily on two observations. First, although the British economy as a whole grew much faster than the French through most of the nineteenth century, the gap in *per capita* commodity output was much narrower (pp. 61–68). France's slow population growth was a crucial condition of her continued prosperity.[1] Secondly, French industrial productivity exceeded that of Britain through most of the century, despite a much slower rate of transition to factory production. It was in agriculture that France lagged farthest behind (see Table 1). Growth in commodity consumption in Britain had at least as much to do with capitalist agriculture, and with British dominance of international trade, as it did with the productivity of domestic industry (though of course the three are interrelated) (O'Brien and Keyder 1978:62–68, 137–139).

Britain was able to add some 12% to the flow of commodities available for domestic consumption by a surplus of imports over exports maintained throughout the century. France, in a peak year, added only 5%. Between 1815 and 1864 France actually showed a net deficit in commodity exchange; the French people had less to consume than they produced (see Table 2). Failure to consider this impact of differing terms of international trade and income from international investment makes industrialization look both easier and better for mid-nineteenth century France than it probably would have been. And to the extent that "industrialization" conjures up some images of highly mechanized factories, we would do well to remember that even in Britain the growth of such industrial production was relatively gradual, while many workers remained in domestic and small workshop production. Productivity was increased through continual division of labor and pressure on the workforce (Samuel 1977). The comparison with France suggests, though, that these measures, however much they helped capital accumulation and net production, did not add dramatically to productivity; it was the *number* of industrial workers employed that gave Britain its industrial strength. It was only at the very end of the century that British industrial productivity overtook French. Throughout the century French industry was more capital intensive than British, though by a diminishing margin (O'Brien and Keyder 1978:91, 148, 150).

In Britain at mid-century industrial labor produced only 84% as much, *per capita*, as agricultural labor. In France at the same time industrial labor produced more than two and a half times as much *per capita* as agricultural labor (O'Brien and Keyder 1978:95). It is, perhaps, easy to understand why contemporary observers and economic historians alike have criticized France for "failing" to move more people into industrial production, and for tolerating the backwardness and inefficiency of smallholder agriculture (Kemp 1971:ch. 1). It is a little harder to understand why some writers would imply that this was a failure of capitalization of French industry (Henderson 1961:91–95). The return on industrial capital was noticeably higher in France than in Great Britain (O'Brien and Keyder 1978:148); if anything, a failure to invest in capitalist agriculture ought to be the charge. Let us consider, however, that capitalist agriculture would have meant dispossessing millions of peasants and moving an enormous landless workforce into industry. There was no guarantee—or even real likelihood—that a large addition could be made to the French industrial labor force without greatly reducing productivity. Maintaining an urban population would have been much more

TABLE 1

Labor Productivity in Agriculture and Industry (pounds sterling)

Periods	Productivity in agriculture Great Britain	Productivity in agriculture France*		Productivity in industry Great Britain	Productivity in industry France*	
		(a)	(b)		(a)	(b)
1781-90	24.7	25.6	25.2	22.3	77.3	53.2
1803-12	52.2	44.8	39.4	38.4	111.2	48.3
1815-24	45.6	32.9	31.3	38.4	56.8	41.2
1825-34	44.3	34.2	32.4	39.2	54.6	42.8
1835-44	50.3	29.9	28.8	44.5	61.6	49.7
1845-54	53.0	29.7	28.9	44.3	64.8	53.5
1855-64	58.4	36.7	36.0	50.7	71.2	60.1
1865-74	67.0	41.9	43.2	62.3	96.5	86.7
1875-84	67.0	33.4	33.8	68.5	85.1	76.4
1885-94	68.8	31.5	31.2	75.0	82.6	74.3
1895-1904	64.6	27.3	26.6	83.7	70.0	73.1
1905-13	64.3	41.6	44.1	90.4	85.2	88.3

* (a) and (b) columns represent conversions from francs to pounds in terms of exchange rate based on French and British output respectively.

Source: O'Brien and Keyder 1978:91.

TABLE 2

Import Surplus as Percentage of Domestic Commodity Output

Periods	Great Britain	France
1781-90	9.8	0.8
1803-12	6.7	0.5
1815-24	3.8	-0.3
1825-34	9.3	-0.6
1835-44	8.1	-0.6
1845-54	9.3	-1.2
1855-64	13.8	-0.7
1965-74	12.4	0.0
1875-84	22.6	5.0
1885-94	18.2	4.7
1895-1904	22.8	2.2
1905-13	16.4	3.5

Source: O'Brien and Keyder 1978:67.

expensive than maintaining a more self-sufficient rural one, especially in the absence of a strong network of internal transportation, which would itself have been expensive to create. The natural endowments of French agricultural areas did not necessarily equal those of Britain. Britain's move to capitalist agriculture was in any case started long before the industrial revolution, and such key steps as the various waves of enclosure were both cruel and contested; they would only have been more so if France had attempted to impose them rapidly in the nineteenth century (as peasant opposition to the confiscation of common lands and forests shows). Britain's early moves in enclosure were linked to an emphasis on animal husbandry which remained key to her greater agricultural productivity in the nineteenth century.[2]

The fundamental differences in British and French growth patterns, then, had been set in the eighteenth century, before either country had begun to industrialize with any considerable use of factories or mechanization. Britain had superior endowments of coal and other important raw materials, and by 1800 had already established much of her historic specialization in heavy industry and mass production. France, on the other hand, was known for the quality of work performed by her artisans, and for highly specialized crafts and distinctive designs which set fashions for all of Europe. France's highest levels of productivity remained in traditional high-skilled crafts. A move to focus capital and labor primarily in factory industry would have played to Britain's strengths and France's weaknesses—hardly a good strategy. France's opportunities to crack Britain's advantage in international trade were precious few, if any. An effort was made in textiles, where France's exports came primarily from the relatively industrialized Alsace. Yet, in 1827–29 the total value of all French cotton cloth exports was only about one-tenth that of Britain, and by 1844–45 it had fallen to about one-fifteenth (Milward and Saul 1973:317–318). If France could not rival Britain in textile industrialization for export, it was hardly likely that it could overcome its lack of key resources as well as Britain's headstart in basic metals or other important branches of large-scale industrial production. What France could successfully export were high quality consumer goods—silks, fine prints, and ribbons were the best textile exports, for example (Dunham 1955:378–381).[3]

In terms of both the markets in which it could best compete, and the industries in which it could be most productive, France was well advised to retain a good deal of artisan and small workshop production. In the 1840s French industrial productivity exceeded British only in food and chemicals, among major, mass-market industries. In mining, metals, leather, and wood it was way behind; in textiles and paper somewhat so (O'Brien and Keyder 1978:157). At the same time, while British productivity in these major industries was above the national average, in France it was not the major industries but the variety of smaller, more specialized branches which had the highest productivity. *Specialization* was important to France's continuing prosperity, not following the British example. Britain's example was a potent political and economic force, however, as was Belgium's to a lesser (but perhaps even more galling) extent. Sherman (1970:198) reports the emphasis public debate put on the obviously modern branches of production, such as textiles and metals, rather than realizing the importance of luxury goods such as wine and silk in which France would have had more comparative advantage. Sherman presumes, however, that a liberal, free trade policy was the progressive stance for France:

> Officials often did not fully appreciate the more subtle points of classical economic liberalism which argued the advantages of trading one kind of manufactured good, produced with comparative efficiency in France, for another, produced more cheaply in another country. They tended to categorize countries as having either manufacturing or nonmanufacturing economies (1970:80).

A glance at the contemporary Third World may suggest the plausibility of such a categorization, and may also suggest that trade was not the only route to development for France. Protectionism, however much it ran afoul of classical economic liberalism, was a plausible strategy in a country which; as we have seen, showed a net loss in the exchange of commodities. French officials who argued that liberal policy was appropriate to England but inappropriate to France (Sherman 1970:86) were not fools. Indeed, the very size of France's domestic market was a plausible argument for protectionism. Autocentric development was, at least in part, a reasonable option.

The period between the decades of the 1820s and 1860s was that in which capitalist industry conquered Britain (see, for the general story, Deane and Cole 1969; Clapham 1926). In one industry after another, new capital was introduced, often accompanied by mechanization or the building of factories. By the 1840s handloom weaving had been virtually eradicated and there had been two major waves of factory-building in the cotton industry (Mitchell and Deane 1962:187; Gayer, Rostow, and Schwartz 1975:198). Steam power was becoming widespread and production units were becoming larger (Musson 1976b). Railroad construction proceeded rapidly; coupled with the preceding era's completion of thousands of miles of canals, it made Britain a much more unified market than France. All this does not mean that local markets or handcrafts had ceased to exist. Rather, a balance had been tipped, and there was no retreat from the spread of modern capitalist production and distribution, at least not for a long time. Samuel (1977) has stressed the gradualness of the eradication of hand production, but it should be borne in mind that by mid-century the leading sectors of the economy had been conquered by machines. Mechanization itself, as Samuel stresses, created new handcrafts, or swelled the ranks of old ones, only to destroy them a short time later when it overcame the last of the bottlenecks in a particular production process. Resistance to such a spread of capitalist industry and destruction of smaller scale and especially hand craft work had been much greater before 1820. From the first rumblings of such industrialization in the 1780s through 1820 there had been a growing populist attack on the new system. This continued through the 1820s and 1830s and was important in the birth of Chartism. The growth of a population for whom factories were the source of livelihood, rather than a threat to a way of life, greatly undermined this resistance. Industrial strikes supplanted machine-breaking and populist attacks on the corruption of elites not because the same people were becoming more modern in their attitudes, but because a new working class was supplanting the members of the older, more heterogenous trades of pre-industrial Britain. By mid-century most Britons were anxious for the prosperity they expected to come with further development of capitalist industry. Several rural crafts, and rather more of the high-skilled urban artisanal trades, survived with some prosperity into the last part of the century. They were, nonetheless, vanishing one by one from the 1820s on. The very gradualness of mechanization may have made resistance harder; unlike a cyclical depression which affected everyone, it was an isolating experience to be replaced by machines. The early years of textile industrialization had threatened more unified craft communities. Handworkers were concentrated together in villages like those of the Pennines where they completely predominated. In the Victorian period artisans and craftsmen occupied an ever-shrinking niche in the larger economy, and in larger population aggregates. When the pressure came, many of the crafts simply petered out, unable to support the children of once-proud master craftsmen.

In France factories came much more slowly, and in the end, much less completely. Part of the reason was the preference of French capitalists for government finance over industrial investments. Landes (1972) has noted the small size of establishments, the preponderance of very cautious family firms, and the delay of corporate financing until the boom of the 1850s and 1860s. Most of the old crafts persisted, many even finding a way to adapt to partial mechanization. When factories did come in France, they tended to be smaller than in Britain (O'Brien and Keyder 1978:170–171). In France, moreover, the industries characterized by small-scale establishments were the ones with the highest productivity, which gave them a greater resilience.[4] New transportation and communication industries were also relatively slow to develop in France. The canal age was virtually bypassed and railways lagged well behind Britain (Dunham 1955:14–84). This was, in fact, one of the reasons for the severity of the 1846–47 agricultural crisis in the northern portion of the country. Most of all, the French people stayed on the land. We saw earlier the enormous difference in the ratios of industrial to agricultural productivity for France and Britain. The other side of this coin is the fact that at mid-century, when 67% of the British labor force was employed in industry (O'Brien and Keyder 1978:94),[5] the same percentage of the French labor force was employed in agriculture. The vast majority, moreover, were owner-occupiers with only a few hectares of land—nearly 40% less land per agricultural worker than in England. And not only was land scarce, but France had much less animal power to use in agriculture, perhaps only half as much and as good as Britain (O'Brien and Keyder 1978:105, 117, 127). France was, indeed, even more rural than the predominance of peasant agriculture suggests, for rural handcrafts were common. These workers were often impoverished, but estimates of their wages have little significance, since they generally retained either small plots of land or close kinship ties to peasants which subsidized their cost of living. Domestic textile crafts were more widely dispersed in the France of 1847 than they had been in the Britain of thirty years before.

No look at the economies of nineteenth century France and Britain is fully intelligible without consideration of the large differences in rates of population growth. During the nineteenth century France's population increased gradually from 18 million to 38 million, while Britain's exploded from 11 million to 36 million despite a higher rate of emigration. The difference is to be accounted for overwhelmingly by Britain's higher birth rate.[6] One of the key reasons French people were able to preserve as much of their traditional crafts and communities as they did was that they refrained from breeding as fast as the British. It may be, of course, that causality runs both ways. In any case, the relative stability of the French population was great, both in terms of numbers and in terms of location and style of life; this is a key difference from Britain, essential to understanding the difference courses of political and economic radicalism in the two countries.

Radicalism and Industrialization

Since the early nineteenth century an enormous volume of literature has linked the progress of industrialization to radical politics. France's revolution of 1848 and the Chartist movement prominent during the 1830s and 1840s in Britain figure prominently in arguments for such a linkage. One might even suggest that they figure in an unfortunately fused manner, since Marx, like some other contemporaries, tended to draw examples of political radicalism and socialism from the French Second Republic, and a model of capitalist industrialization from Britain. Such a fusion is misleading indeed, for it is with good reason that the more industrial country was the less radical. The confusion did not necessarily originate with Marx or other radicals. It is at least as likely to have come first from "men of order" as French Legitimists call themselves, who conceived of popular agitation as both stemming from and producing "disorder."[7] For a long time the propertied classes of both France and Britain had seen the "lower orders" as lacking in self-control, disorderly, and in need of moral discipline. Underestimating the extent of organization which it took to produce a food riot or political protest, they saw these as the results of failures of order and discipline. It was but a short step from this longstanding view to the notion that industrialization brought a breakdown in the moral order, in which people's baser passions were set free to wreak havoc on respectable life. This view is evident in the reports of mid-century doctors and others sent out to investigate the living conditions of the poor in industrial centers (cf. Sewell 1980:223–232 on Villermé; Inglis 1971 on the British equivalents). Sexual license, thievery, and socialism appeared as more or less comparable results of social disorganization.

This popular "breakdown of order" view of the linkage of industrialization to radical political agitation has been widely incorporated into academic thought, where it is sometimes called the mass society view.[8] It posits essentially that people are normally, and ideally, conservative, and that only a breakdown in the socio-psychological relations which maintain moral restraint among them can lead to collective behavior. Collective behavior is, in Smelser's words, based on a "short-circuit" in ordinarily rational thought processes, which introduces "generalized beliefs akin to magical beliefs" (1962:71, 78). It is not industrial life which produces this irrational collective behavior, but rather the disruptive process of industrialization. Smelser thus finds the sources of early nineteenth century English radicalism, including Chartism and the factory agitation, in the weakening of the family-based moral system of early factory workers (Smelser 1959, 1968). If we see riots or political agitation attending the process of industrialization, we are led to posit that early factory workers will be the central figures because of the breakdown of social organization among them.

The same central empirical assertion—that factory workers should be the predominant figures in protest during the process of industrialization— is the result of a Marxian analysis. Marx, however, worked with a different causal argument. Far from a breakdown, he suggested that industrial workers had a variety of relatively new social strengths because they were united in cities and large workplaces, because they more obviously shared the same experiences of transparent exploitation, and because they were in more similar circumstances.[9] The radicalism of the new proletariat, of which factory workers are the core, will thus not be a transient phenomenon, in this view, but will grow as capitalism grows, leading eventually to a working class revolution. In his essays on the French revolution of 1848 and the class struggles of the Second Republic, Marx (1850, 1852) is insistent about the centrality of the proletariat and about the novelty of its task. In the famous opening passage of *The Eighteenth Brumaire of Louis Napoleon,* he rejects the "venerable disguise and borrowed language" in which the proletariat carried out its struggle. As he had written two years before: "The revolution could only come into its own when it had won its *own, original* name and it could only do this when the modern revolutionary class, the industrial proletariat, came to the fore as a dominant force" (Marx 1850:74; original emphasis). Marx makes his contempt for the traditional French peasants, "the great mass of the French nation," manifest as he blames them for the success of Louis Napoleon and the failure of the revolution (1852:238–239). Yet abundant evidence from recent research shows first the centrality of urban artisans to the existence of the socialist struggle under the Second Republic, second, the importance of peasants and rural craftsmen in the insurrection of 1851 and the defense of the Republic more generally, and third, the relative unimportance of factory workers to the whole affair (see, among many, Price 1972; Merriman 1978; Margadant 1979; Sewell 1980). Moreover, neither in France nor in Britain, nor anywhere else, has the growth of a factory-based proletariat provided a sufficient social basis for revolutionary mobilization.

I suggest that we need to see revolutions against capitalism as based not in the new class which capitalism forms, but in the traditional communities and crafts which capitalism threatens. I have called the protagonists of such revolutions "reactionary radicals" (Calhoun 1983). It is their rootedness in a social order challenged by industrial capitalism that at once makes their opposition to it radical and gives them the social strength with which to carry out concerted struggle. To be sure, such reactionary radicals are not always the beneficiaries of revolutions in which they fight, and the success of those revolutions depends on a variety of other factors, from weaknesses in state power to the presence of capable organizations to administer the post-revolutionary state. Nonetheless, I think such groups have been, and remain, crucial to a wide variety of struggles, including those of France between 1848 and 1851. And I think that describing them as members of the working class stretches that term beyond all recognizable connection to Marxian theory (cf. Calhoun 1982).

Tilly (1972) has captured something of this in his discussions of the "modernization" of protest in mid-century France, though it is important to keep cross-section as well as developmental differences in mind. Drawing in part on Marx, he has effectively countered the breakdown theories, showing the extensive organization and mobilization of resources necessary to political agitation (see esp. 1978). Tilly has also stressed the importance of repression, suggesting that discontent is quite widely distributed; it is the means and opportunities to act that are scarce. Following Tilly, Merriman (1978) thus sees a radicalization during the Second Republic. The revolution of February, 1848 removed much of the threat of state repression. Peasants, rural craft workers, and others were then able to pursue longstanding collective goals—such as peasants' desire to regain forest rights. But during the course of the Second Republic more and more explicit political claims began to be expressed, intermixed with traditional grievances. Peasants who had previously only been concerned about immediate economic issues began to worry about the future of a republic they had welcomed only cooly, at best. Where the early mobilization was traditional in orientation, based in the formal bonds of local communities, and provoked directly by the agricultural crisis, the later period showed more formal organization, more complex ideology, and a greater independence of immediate circumstances. The mobilizations of the later period, however, faced an intensifying state repression which limited their efficacy and eventual discontent underground during the Second Empire. (Forstenzer 1981 has criticized some of Tilly's and Merriman's views of the repression.)

Tilly situates this scenario within a transition from defensive to offensive, "reactive" to "proactive" forms of collective action (Tilly et al. 1975:46–55).[10] The transition is marked by an increasing importance of formal organizations, and especially coalitions among different organizations each representing special interests, and the corresponding disappearance of communal groups from politics. Reactive struggles occurred largely during the early nineteenth century in France, Tilly suggests, as the state attempted to expand and improve its centralized control. Proactive struggles replaced reactive ones after the state succeeded in asserting its control and a national market had been established; proactive struggles fought for self-consciously chosen goods, with more complexly worked out strategies, within the arena defined by state power.

This approach comes nearer to grasping what had happened than any other, though I think its emphasis lies so much on long-term developments that Tilly does not fully appreciate the implications of the discontinuity he has suggested, and the importance of the collective action of "reactionary radicals." In the first place, Tilly's focus is on the relationship between state formation and the collective action (especially violence) of "common people." He thus tends to underestimate the importance of the growth of capitalism, and the extent to which it was brought about through proactive collective action. His examples of reaction include "the tax rebellion, the food riot, violent resistance to conscription, machine-breaking, and invasions of enclosed land" (Tilly et al. 1975:50), yet surely the actions of elites which prompted these mobilizations also frequently meet his standard for proaction: "They are 'proactive' rather than 'reactive' because at least one group is making claims for rights, privileges, or resources not previously enjoyed" (p. 51). The transformation is largely in the capacity of common people to be proactive, recalling Hobsbawm's salutary suggestion that we should not underestimate the importance of the formal organizations through which people act in a search for the most obscure details of their lives: "Until the past two centuries, as traditional historiography shows, 'the poor' could be neglected most of the time by their 'betters', and therefore remained largely invisible to them, precisely because their active impact on events was occasional, scattered, and impermanent" (1978:48). The capacity of the rich to be proactive is of much older vintage.

Some of the limits of reactive collective action are apparent; we need to ask, however, whether proactive collective action does not also have important limits. I shall suggest two, very briefly. The first is a limit of vision. The sorts of proactive movements Tilly describes, with their formal organizations, literacy, and rational plans tend to grow up within advanced industrial societies, and their vision of alternatives is thereby diminished. With a characteristic rationalism, Marx from the beginning, and a great many would-be radicals and progressives since, have dismissed the traditions of common people as mere hindrances to their future emancipation (cf. Lasch 1981; Calhoun 1983). Yet it may well be that only those with a strong sense of the past, with an immediately lived notion of what a more human, democratic, or socially responsible society would be like, are likely to conceive of a future radically different from that which capitalism and "actually existing socialism" is already bringing. Craft workers and peasants facing industrialization in Britain in the 1810s or France in the 1840s had such a sense. They had it, it is important for purposes of more general analysis to remember, not because they had read more history books, but because they lived within their crafts and local communities another kind of life from industrial capitalism. If they were "traditional" it was because of the manifold immediate exchanges of information in their everyday lives, not because of mere historical recollections. Community life, family life, may still quite often pose that sort of alternative vision to the public life of industrial society. That vision may become part of a radical challenge to trends in the larger society when it is threatened. *Pace* Smelser 1959, then it was not the destruction of the factory workers' families which produced radical mobilizations in early industrial Lancashire, it was the *threat* of such destruction faced by families and communities of handloom weavers (Calhoun 1982:ch. 7).

The second limit on the collective action of Tilly's characteristic proactive groups is organizational. Traditional communities knit people closely to each other and provide social organization ready made to their members. This means not only that members of such communities do not have to pay high initial costs for the creation of organizations to pursue their interests (a strong disincentive to action), but also that they know more readily whom to trust and whom not to. This helps reactive mobilizations—such as that of the Second Republic—to survive in the face of repression. Tilly recognizes this:

> Communal groups, once committed to a conflict, rarely mobilize large numbers of men, rarely have leaders with the authority to negotiate quick compromise settlements, and rarely can call of the action rapidly and effectively; it may

also be true (as it has often been argued) that communal groups have an exceptional capacity to hold out in the face of adversity. Associational groups, on the other hand, tend to become involved in violence as an outgrowth of brief, coordinated mass actions which are not intrinsically violent (Tilly *et al.* 1975:53).

Proactive struggles, based on associational groups, can be much more precise and flexible in their actions; their actions tend, however, to be "large and brief," in Tilly's words. For related reasons, such as their investment in formal organizations and their awareness of numerous possible courses of action, the members of such groups are, I have suggested, not often likely to be very radical in their actions (Calhoun 1983). This is a central reason for the characteristic reformism of the modern working class.

If communal groups are fighting for their very existence, like British handloom weavers and many French peasants and some artisans were, then they are not very likely to want to "negotiate quick compromise settlements." British and French authorities alike were intransigent and offered few compromises, but it is hard to see what they could have done to alter fundamentally the terms of contest other than to abdicate their positions of power. The French bourgeoisie *did* have to sacrifice *its* republic to secure the repression of the "democratic and social" alternative. In the long-run French artisans and peasants got a much better deal than did British handloom weavers, but in the short-run both groups saw a choice between destruction and complete immiseration, or struggle. The choice was easy to make.

Britain: From Radical Politics to Economic Reform

E. P. Thompson has perhaps understood the political implications of the emergence of associational, proactive politics better than anyone else. In a brilliant essay, he stresses the significance of 1832 as a watershed in the history of English popular struggle (Thompson 1965). In the first place, workers in 1832 did not face a relatively amorphous elite class, but a specific, predatory group—notably the landowners who stood to benefit most from high corn prices—that had control of the state apparatus, and therefore made "governing institutions appear as the direct, emphatic, and unmediated organs of a 'ruling class'" (Thompson 1965:258). The strength of popular struggle, however, threatened bourgeois as well as agrarian interests; the bourgeoisie did not make revolution against Old Corruption because it feared the sort of radicalization—I believe it is in line with Thompson to suggest—which did in fact occur in the France of the Second Republic. As a consequence, struggle within the upper classes was resolved in favor of *laissez faire* and moderate reform of Parliament; because landowners in England were also capitalists this was hardly a victory for some ancient aristocracy. On the contrary: "1832 changed, not one game for another but the rules of the game, restoring the flexibility of 1688 in a greatly altered class context. It provided a framework within which new and old bourgeois could adjust their conflicts of interest without resort to force" (1965:260). Because this settlement was reached, the popular insurgents (I have argued (1981), contrary to Thompson (1968), that these were not "the working class") lost a climactic moment and the nature of struggle changed, perhaps permanently. Chartism was not defeated in 1848, Thompson suggests, but pulled apart from within well before that (1965:280). Thompson has throughout his work stressed the importance of "customs in common" as a source of radical visions and unity; he has argued the radical potential of struggles in defense of a "moral economy" (cf. esp. 1968, 1971). He has also recognized that "once a certain climactic moment is passed, the opportunity for a certain *kind* of revolutionary movement passes irrevocably—not so much because of "exhaustion" but because more limited, reformist pressures, from secure organizational bases, bring evident returns" (1965:281). The moment for this sort of revolutionary movement in Britain had passed by the early 1830s. The phase of industrial mechanization and factory building which began in the 1820s introduced a fundamental, if not necessarily insuperable, split into the ranks of workers. Throughout the Victorian era, the gradual transformation from a population of traditional craftsmen to one of modern industrial (including clerical) employees weakened the organizational base for British popular radicalism. It also gave the ascendant "modern" group the opportunity to compare its circumstances favorably to those of the people it was supplanting. The factory working class was stigmatized at its birth as unruly, immoral, and lacking in discipline. Into its maturity much of its effort went into proving itself respectable, in its own eyes and those of its alleged betters.

During the 1830s this long-term quest for respectable status was already underway. Sunday schools—both religious and secular—taught literacy and propriety (Laqueur 1976). The temperance movement campaigned to restore moral discipline and to save working people from the evils of drink and themselves; it was hardly completely a movement imposed from without, but had rather strong resonance among workers (Harrison 1971). This quest for respectability overlapped with political struggles. Workers differed over the extent to which they should allow their institutions to be engaged in political debate—let alone action. The intervention of middle class reformers, like those behind the Society for the Diffusion of Useful Knowledge, militated to put forward an anti-insurgent definition of respectability (Perkin 1969:chs. 7 and 8; Tholfsen 1976:ch. 7; Harrison 1961). There were also traditions emphasizing the inherent dignity and respectability of labor, traditions which were perhaps more widespread among artisans (See Cobbett's *Political Register* or the *Working Man's Guardian* for examples).

Groups like Owenite socialists split somewhat on this wedge. For many members the movement was focused on consumption and was simply an economic tool for providing cheaper goods; these were the famous "shopkeeper socialists." For others Owenism meant producers' cooperatives; success was only occasional at best, and the cooperatives tended to appeal primarily to artisans suffering from extreme hardship (J.F.C. Harrison 1969; Pollard and Salt 1971). For still others Owenism was a political economic movement. Within it, men like Hodgskin (1822) first formulated theories of class exploitation based on a labor theory of value. Such a theory applied most directly to the "new working class," for it was framed mostly in terms of the direct sale of labor rather than sale of goods and services characteristic of most artisans.

These ideological pulls, in short, overlapped with the profound distinction between those workers threatened by industrialization and those dependent on modern industry for their livelihoods. If the first twenty years of the nineteenth century had been dominated by the resistance of reactionary radicals to proletarianization, the second twenty or so years—up to the Chartist convention of 1839 and perhaps the riots and strikes of 1842— were years of ambivalence. Some unity was forged between factory workers, privileged artisans, and degraded craftworkers; it was this unity which gave birth to Chartism. But Chartism was pulled apart by the differences among these groups—differences among both their strengths and their interests. The early years of the movement were the strongest, because the reactionary radicals were still numerous and somewhat optimistic.[11] The latter years saw the movement rent by struggles over whether or not to use the threat of physical force, and how seriously to take Feargus O'Connor and Bronterre O'Brien (Gammage 1854; Slosson 1916:chs. 3, 5; Rosenblatt 1916:ch. 7; Ward 1973:chs. 5–8). Chartism was thus disintegrating throughout the 1840s and 1850s, even while men like Ernest Jones (see *Notes to the People*) were refining its theoretical foundations, and Marx and Engels were trying to push a Chartist revolution along. By the 1860s factory textiles was an old industry; the cotton famine caused much misery and some protest, but little political activism. When popular politics was again important in Britain, it would be as labor politics, with the characteristic reformism of the working class predominant. This is the result moreover, not of some failure of capitalist penetration or capitalist domination of government, as Thompson's opponents Anderson and Nairn would argue, but of the completeness of capitalist transformation. Workers no longer had "radical roots" in preindustrial social organization to any great degree.

From the 1820s unions began to grow in Britain. Their progress was fitful, and it made uneven use of the cultural heritage left by the reactionary radicals (more in craft unions with old trades, like the builders; cf. Postgate 1923; less among newer factory workers like spinners; cf. Kirby and Musson 1975). One of the distinguishing traits of the unions, however, was the distance they kept from Chartism (Read 1959; Turner 1962; Musson 1976:342). In the first place, groups like the textile spinners led by Doherty were a prosperous elite concerned with maintaining their privileged position with industrial production. More generally, trade unionism simply offered workers within "modern" industries a relatively low-risk, controllable, effective line of action. They did not need to turn to politics the way handloom weavers had, because they were neither desperate nor trying to stop a whole pattern of economic change. Because they controlled important steps in a production process, they could strike effectively, even without the collaboration of their fellow workers. They tended thus to stick to themselves; they may have been extreme among the unions, but they were not entirely atypical. The "new model unions" of the 1850s followed similar paths. Factory workers tended, in any case, to pursue sectional interests such as factory reform (Ward 1962). Capitalist industry and elite politics could more readily grant them some concessions; the cause, even though hard-fought, was thus not fundamentally radical.

The very scale of growth of the factory workforce within the textile industry indicates that the reactionary radicals were losing their battle there. There were still riots in the 1820s, and some undercover organizing, in response to the 50% increase in the number of cotton mills during the middle years of the decade and a trebling of the number of power looms during the decade as a whole (Gayer, Rostow, and Schwartz 1975:198). In the early 1830s, during another wave of factory construction, the number of handloom weavers and factory workers in the cotton industry reached parity (Mitchell and Deane 1962:187). The former were much more important to Chartism, disproportionately active and disproportionately in the leadership. Their numbers declined rapidly after 1831. This is one reason why Thompson sees the 1832 mobilization as such a watershed. As the handicraft workers gradually disappeared, cotton workers, the country's largest industrial labor force, would come to follow a separate set of concerns from those of other industries. The overlapping insurgencies of 1832–34 marked the last major eruption left to the old populist radicalism.

Workers reacted to the Reform Act of 1832, which they had thought would bring substantial democratization to public affairs, but which benefitted only the middle class. They reacted to the oppressive and degrading New Poor Law of 1834, with its attempt to coerce the poor into accepting a more disciplined life on the bottom rung of capitalism's ladder (Edsall 1971). They reacted to the artificially high food prices maintained by the Corn Laws. And, in a last major attempt to save traditional crafts and communities, they reacted to the growth of mechanized industry and the national unification of markets. In the course of all these reactions the radical craft workers gave birth to Chartism, but, as a disappearing breed, they were unable to see it through to fruition. The "Plug Plot Riots" of 1842 were the last English riots of any scale to combine politics with anti-industrial agitation. They were part of a wave of agitation which included an attempted Chartist general strike and some specific trades' actions (Mather 1974; Rose 1957). But the events are as significant for the struggles they reveal within Chartism and the workers' movement as for their intensity. Chartism barely limped along for the next several years. During the crisis of 1846–48 it seemed momentarily to take on new life, but this was an illusion; while millions would sign petitions, very few were interested in risking much in an insurrectionary mobilization. O'Brien put on a brave front, but there was no movement behind.

It should be apparent that the argument just presented, together with my discussion elsewhere of the reactionary radicalism of the early nineteenth century (Calhoun 1982), suggests that a major strain of Marxist analysis has been barking up the wrong tree in trying to explain mid-century quiescence by the development of a "labor aristocracy." It may indeed be true that members of the new model unions of the 1850s developed a sense of internal solidarity "by contrasting the character and style of life of the labor aristocrat with those of the common laborer" (Hearn 1978:177). It may also be true that new forms of labor organization within industry led management to enlist some workers as technical or quasi-managerial elites, acting to control the activities of others (Foster 1974:224–238). It may even be that imperialist "super-profits" gave the British bourgeoisie more capacity to split the best paid workers from the rest (Lenin 1920; Hobsbawm 1964) and thus to "restabilize" British society (Foster 1974:204). What must remain in doubt is whether any of this was necessary to the suppression of some previously extant working class radicalism. I have argued, on the contrary, that there was no such movement of class struggle to be stopped. The radical past from which the new working class diverged was not *its* past. The discontinuity lies, rather, between the new working class and the members of older trades challenged by capitalist industrialization. This discontinuity is better dated from the 1820s and early 1830s than from mid-century. The particular strength of the radical movement in 1832 had largely to do with the reaction to the repressive politics of the political regime. As Thompson (1965) suggested, as that particular moment passed, the very nature of popular struggle in England was transformed.

Foster sums up his version of the labor aristocracy argument as follows:

> What really turns the argument is the movement's quite striking loss of initiative in 1846–7. For the first time it failed to rally mass support during a period of unprecedented industrial depression. Still worse, its own leadership started to disintegrate. A significant number of previously loyal working-class leaders now moved into alliance with certain sections of the bourgeoisie. It was this that really confused and dispirited the movement; and did so precisely because it resulted from a new plausibility in arguments for the existing order, not from outright repression (1974:206).

The unprecedented industrial depression, it should be noted, was a relatively mild one nationally. It was particularly acute in textiles because of contraction in markets (including those of the Continent) for mass-produced clothing. As the first technologically advanced, capital-intensive industry, cotton was out of balance with the rest of the economy.[12] But from the late 1840s this was changing. Beginning perhaps most importantly with metals, capital intensive industry was growing outside of textiles. This not only integrated textiles better into the national economy, it multiplied the number of people for whom there could be "a new plausibility in arguments for the existing order," that is to say, the *emerging* order. As Stedman Jones has observed, the term labor aristocracy "has often been used as if it provided an explanation. But it would be more accurate to say that it pointed towards a vacant area where an explanation should be" (1974:61). I think the confusion is even more basic. Analysts keep expecting there to be an explanation for Victorian quiescence in some special *new* phenomenon of that age (see Musson 1976). In fact, the explanation lies farther back in the end of reactionary radicalism. There was, in short, no reason to expect radicalism and political agitation in the *second* half of the nineteenth century in Britain, because capitalism was already secure. Following in Marx's path, analysts have simply assumed the need to explain the abrupt end to the trend of growing class struggle. But if the earlier struggles were based not on an emergent working class, but on traditional communities, then we should realize that the frequent use of the term labor aristocracy—whether accurate as description or not—points to an area where we were mistaken to find the need for an explanation at all.

With the consolidation of industrial capitalism in Britain there came a consolidation of labor reformism. Stable formal organizations could be constructed to carry on long-term campaigns for incremental but certainly not negligible gains. To pursue these struggles, and to recognize the commonality of the members of the modern working class, might well be called "class consciousness." We need always to remember, though, that this was consciousness of the effectiveness of trade unionism and political reformism, not of a need for radical, transformative struggle or revolution. We are well on the way, now, to an understanding of why "backward" France was the scene of radical revolutionary struggle in the middle of the nineteenth century, while "advanced" Britain was relatively calm.

France: The Struggle for a Social Republic, 1848–51

The economic crisis which toppled the July Monarchy began with potato blight and bad harvests; the politics and economics of the period had deep roots in traditional society. The agricultural crisis led to an industrial crisis and that to a financial crisis. Distress was widespread. At first rural areas were hit hardest, but later the new textile industries of the North suffered more because market constriction cut workers' incomes at precisely the time food prices skyrocketed. When harvests improved, textile workers were still unemployed. At this point only does the story become novel. The crisis had deepened into a full-scale depression because the Parisian bourgeoisie, acting in concert with radical artisans and a few others, had toppled the government of Louis Philippe. The February revolution had been remarkably easy, like blowing on a house of cards; still there was panic on the Bourse, and a capital shortage which intensified the industrial crisis. This continuation of the depression, and the government's early tax measures, helped to alienate potential popular support (Price 1972:123). The revolution took the form of a struggle among different factions of property owners—who could eventually be joined in the fear of attacks on the privilege of property.

The ideology of the revolution was republican; it focused on political liberties and allowed its adherents temporarily to paper over their economic difference (see Agulhon 1981:62–99). Though the artisans of Paris had been a crucial revolutionary force, the bourgeoisie remained in firm control of the Provisional Government. Louis Blanc had only a slight influence, and other radicals generally less. In the eyes of the solidly bourgeois republicans, Ledru-Rollin was a dangerous socialist. Still, unemployed workers manned the barricades in Paris and they remained a threatening presence. The government reponded with universal suffrage and make-work programs. The sense of unity and brotherhood of the early spring did not last long. In the countryside, there was an immediate reaction to the power vacuum where the monarchical administration had previously been. Peasants seized forests which had been taken from them, attacked tax collectors and the worst of nobles, and paid only scant attention at first to the ideology of republicanism (Agulhon 1970). Workers, mostly craftsmen, in provincial towns proclaimed the republic and in many cases seized control of local government. They used the opportunity to advance their interests, often a defense of traditional working conditions, against employers (Merriman 1978:3–25). For both peasants and workers, in the provinces and in Paris, the large part of what the revolution offered was a new chance to pursue some traditional goals. Peasants, of course, sought land and freedom from taxation. Workers sought both a respect for their labor and an opportunity to be their own masters and make a decent living. It was in these struggles, which began in tradition and were waged by whole communities, that the revolution was radicalized, as much as in the abstract rhetoric of republicanism and socialism. Indeed, Amann (1975:164) has shown the "purely political" concerns of most of the radical Parisian clubs, and suggested that the social revolution grew up outside and partially despite them.

By June of 1848 the illusion of solidarity between workers and bourgeoisie had broken down. Even the largely middle class political clubs found themselves estranged from the government (Amann 1975). There was an insurrection in Paris, with one or two provincial echoes; it was crushed. A new ministry was formed and the government sped up its separation from its former allies of February; the gradual march into repression was underway. Repression gathered strength when Louis Napoleon was elected president on December 10 of that year. Only in the spring of 1849 did the left begin to gain strength nationally. Where the conservatives and moderates had predominated easily in the elections of April 1848, in May 1849 Red Republicans, bourgeois socialists, and not a few radical artisans were elected representatives. Peasants who had initially been hostile to the republic because of its taxation program were the object of intensive propaganda from the left. It paid off. Through the repression of 1849–50, peasants became increasingly radicalized in many parts of the country, and extreme measures had to be taken against them. The Bonapartist regime was even more concerned to keep the towns in ideologically dependable hands, and it had to win a number of fights to do so. By virtue of extensive repressive efforts, however, the government succeeded in preparing the way for Louis Napoleon's coup d'état of December 2, 1851. The coup was followed by an insurrection, but only some seventeen departments were able to preserve enough strength to mount much of a radical mobilization (Margadant 1979).

In the rest of this section I propose to examine the social and cultural source of the popular struggle to preserve the democratic republic and make it socially responsible. The first point to be made in this regard is that at no stage of the struggle was a proletariat of the sort Marx would define in *Capital* (1867) prominent. In Paris artisans and employees in small workshops formed the mainstay of popular radicalism—and, to a large extent, of popular conservatism (Price 1972:95–154; Traugott 1980a, 1980b). Elsewhere rural craft workers, peasants, and urban artisans were the groups from which "democ-socs" came led sometimes by their own members and sometimes by bourgeois socialists, especially professionals (Margadant 1979). Merriman (1978:138–163) has shown the weakness of support among the industrial workers of Limoges and the Nord, where repression was fairly complete and where radicalism had only prospered a) under outside leadership, and b) through workers' associations devoted primarily to narrow economistic goals. When Marx spoke of the proletariat in his analysis of the Second Republic (1850, 1852) he lumped together a wide variety of workers.

This image of variety is important, for the radical workers of the Second Republic struggled at once for a variety of particular goals and for a common vision of democratic socialism. Construction workers, for example, sought to maintain the abolition of *marchandage* (sub-contracting, with the effect of sweating labor and sometimes cheating workers of wages) which they had gained from the early provisional government. Their struggle was an old one, and until the Second Republic, had been fought out largely through still older corporations, especially the colorful compagnnonages. In this they were particularly remarkable, but not radically different from many other skilled trade. Sewell (1980) has chronicled the rise of the ideology of respectable labor and socialism through the early nineteenth century. He stresses most of all the continuity of the language of labor which motivated the democ-socs of 1848 with the corporate traditions of the old regime. Artisans had come under increasing pressure over the years, both from the excessive competition with trades and the introduction of more capitalist organization. It had grown hard for a journeyman to ever advance to the status of master and for an artisan to find steady work. Radical artisans drew on a notion that had long been developing—that labor is the source of all wealth—to demand that the republic recognize both the right to labor and the sovereignty of labor (Sewell 1980:250). The former called for the Provisional Government to guarantee work to everyone. The latter held that work was to be organized on the principle of association which united men "for the defense of rights and common interests" (Bezucha 1974:105).

> It was by developing the idea of association—that is, the voluntary aggregation of individuals into a constituted "society" of some sort—that workers eventually made their corporate organizations and their projects of collective regulation consonant with the revolutionary tradition (Sewell 1980:201–202).

This idea had been developing through the July Monarchy and had found expression in various smaller protests. By 1848 it had made workers' ideology "distinctly socialist in character" (Sewell 1980:251; see also Sewell 1981).

If Parisian and many other workers had developed a broader socialist sense of commonality by 1848, it was not in opposition to their particular trades' identities and concerns, but though them. Labor was not an undifferentiated category, but rather came in an infinitude of particular varieties; a worker was always a worker at some particular task, with some particular skill. Thus it was that "from the very beginning of the February Revolution, trade communities had acted as units in revolutionary politics" (Sewell 1980:252). This particularism was carried to a fault in the desire of each corporation to have its own deputy in the Assembly (shades of syndicalism) which meant that virtually none could succeed in getting elected because each trade was too small (Amann 1972:117–118; Sewell 1980:262). But trade communities did provide important intermediate associations, making the workers' vision of a democratic and social republic perhaps a more viable one than the radical individualism/totalitarianism of the Jacobin "One and Indivisible Republic." The Jacobin appropriation of Rousseau's general will was an unstable basis for politics; the federalist notion of 1848 was less so. It was also a more direct outgrowth of traditional community and craft life; as such it could have a stronger basis in the provinces.

Part of the corporations' demand for the sovereignty of labor was a call for self-regulation within craft communities. In the countryside the demand for local autonomy was also strong. Joigneaux, a leading Montagnard propagandist and representative of the Cote d'Or, offered a populist message which stressed "the natural organization of the village unit as an 'association' benefitting all of its members" (Merriman 1978:42). Paris had been organized through corporations and political clubs (Amann 1975). Local *chambrées* and *cafés*, with their old traditions and loyal members, became key vehicles of provincial organization (Agulhon 1970:230–245), along with traditional mutual-aid societies, producers' cooperatives, and consumers' cooperatives (Merriman 1978:57–59). Local carnival traditions were harnessed to radical symbolic purposes; singing, allegory, and street theatre were central to the perpetuation and dissemination of the message of the democratic and social republic (Agulhon 1970:407–417). More explicit messages were also spread through traditional relationships. This was important, for it alone allowed the continuation of the Montagnard campaign in the face of the repression; communities knit their members closely together, making it unlikely that anyone would willingly betray other members. In Albi, six masked men buried the Republic shouting "Down with the reaction" amid pomp and ceremony. Twenty-eight witnesses refused to identify them (Merriman 1978:87). As a result, "the repression failed to break completely the links of the radical apparatus at the communal level, especially among many rural artisans and proletarians" (Merriman 1978:191).

The ability of the Montagnard propagandists to find or make supporters of the democratic and social republic in the countryside was dependent on the fact that "they offered economic incentive not to isolated individuals but to groups of men who already shared a sense of collective solidarity" (Margadant 1979:140). It was their ability to work through already existing relationships which first brought the radicals success, and then allowed them to keep up resistance to the repression and ultimately to launch the insurrection following the coup (see Margadant 1979:ch. 7). So closely did lines of radical social organization follow community membership, that "in the eyes of some young men, Montagnard societies were fraternities that they joined for social purposes; not to belong was tantamount to declaring oneself an anti-social being" (Margadant 1979:161). Community was, in short, both the means by which radicals reached and mobilized peasants and rural craft workers, village and Parisian artisans, *and* a part of the value for which they struggled.

The continuity of community life and traditional occupations was greatest in Paris and in small towns and villages. Only a few of the larger towns had comparable craft organizations. Where they did, as in Rouen, there were militant attacks on the factories which threatened traditional livelihoods (Merriman 1978:14). Margadant has indicated that there was a good deal of movement from agriculture to rural crafts under the July Monarchy (1979:ch. 3), but he still shows strong communities both among peasants (ch. 2) and among rural craft workers (chs. 4 and 7). A key reason for this is that French handicrafts were generally rural, set up in or near the villages in which the peasant parents of present-day craftspeople had lived. Networks of kinship and communal relations could be expected to persist. More broadly, we see here the importance of France's relatively stable population. The very fact of rapid growth contributed both to Britain's larger population aggregates and to her higher level of permanent mobility. French workers were much more likely either to remain in the same place or to maintain close ties when migrating. Both comparisons predispose France to a greater extent of communal solidarity (see Calhoun 1980 on the definition of community). France's more even population distribution is of particular significance (Mitchell 1980:68–70, 81–83). The smaller population aggregates within which most French people lived were more likely—sheerly on an argument based on size—to be densely-knit with social relationships (see Calhoun 1983:175–178, 198–202, following Blau 1978). The French also, as we have noted, worked in smaller workshops than their English counterparts; this to, on the same argument, implies a better social basis for mobilization.[13]

In the struggle for a democratic and social republic, artisans and other less privileged craft workers were the most important participants. They were more prominent in urban areas than unskilled workers (Price 1972:163–166; Tilly and Lees 1975; Traugott 1980a). And they were more prominent in rural areas than were peasants (Margadant 1979:92, 98, 100). Merriman finds that concentrations of underemployed and unemployed rural artisans and proletarians characterized the cantons in which Montagnard secret societies successfully organized, mentioning specifically the high incidence of potters, woodchoppers, wheelwrights, day laborers, rural domestics, masons, stonecutters, and quarrymen, as well as weavers and makers of sabots (1978:202–203). Such craft workers were not the worst off people in France, though they were very poor. Paris' urban artisans were quite prosperous by most contemporary standards. Why then should they have been at the center of struggle? The primary motto of the struggle gives a clue. Merriman (1978:51) reports a Parisian placard from June 23, 1848, which defined the democratic and social republic as "democratic in that all citizens are electors . . . social in that all citizens are permitted to form associations for work." To whom could the second phrase mean more than to artisans and craft workers?

Because of their deep roots in traditional crafts and local communities, artisans and their less-privileged fellows had a vision of a self-regulating, community-based social organization. Each tended to work on a whole labor process and sell the goods he finished, rather than simply selling his labor for use by a capitalist within a highly sub-divided production process. This contributed to the notion of society as a federation of more or less comparable associations, and further suggested the only secondary importance of central government or centralized industrial control. This image could be translated, as we saw Joigneaux doing (above, p. 32), into the peasants' experience of village community, kinship, and common lands. Nothing would have pleased peasants more than to be rid of government intervention, which meant primarily tax collectors; even priests were only marginally tolerated outsiders in many areas (Agulhon 1970:168–187). For the most part, neither craft workers nor peasants proposed to abandon private property; though a number of cooperatives were formed, mostly among craft workers, they were both a minority choice and generally focused on only parts of economic life—marketing, or consumption. Peasants and craft workers did not attack property as such, but a new capitalist use of property, in which large properties destroyed smaller ones. It is accurate to say that these groups were "reactive," but not to imply that they were merely reactionary. Their reactions to the incursions of capitalism, and capitalism's government into their lives were quite radical, and used the experience of life in traditional corporations and communities to offer a distinctive alternative vision of a democratic and social republic.

Like the reactionary radicals of early nineteenth century Britain, the democratic socialists of the Second Republic expected to be able to use peaceful persuasion and the vote to effect their programs. As the former group sought to gain universal manhood suffrage, so the latter group sought to retain it. This was not in itself very radical. The right to political participation had come to seem so incontestable that in both countries legislators from the bourgeoisie and even occasionally the aristocracy found themselves granting it—though with ambivalence and occasional impulses to take it back again. Eventually, the vote would be a major tool of working class and popular reform; some radicals would even feel by the turn of the twentieth century that it gave workers too much incentive to "work within the system." The reason elites could tolerate universal manhood suffrage by the late nineteenth century, or at least the early twentieth was that by then "the people" were more fully a part of capitalist industrial society. This was even more true of Britain than of France, but in both cases, though workers might elect socialist representatives, they did not pose such fundamentally radical threats as the reactionary radicals had.[14] The state, in any case, had built up a much more secure base and apparatus of coercion; it could deal with radical syndicalists and unions in a way the early nineteenth century state could not deal with artisans and peasants. When the artisans and peasants sought to protect the republic, with its guarantee of universal manhood suffrage, they had more than continuous reform in mind. They had in mind ideas like a guaranteed right to productive employment for everyone—a "non-reformist reform" in Gorz's (1968) sense, for it could not readily be granted by the emerging capitalist elites without fundamentally altering the nature of their economic system. It was the growth of capitalism which had rendered certain traditional demands quite radical.

In asking why the attempt to radicalize the revolution of 1848 failed, one probably needs to note, most of all, the repression mounted by the elites organized in Louis Napoleon's government. Price (1975), Merriman (1978), Margadant (1979), Forstenzer (1981) have done so, opening important new historical arguments. But it also needs to be observed that the repression and reaction were not the work entirely of the bourgeoisie. As Traugott (1980a, 1980b) has shown, the people on both sides of the barricades during the June days were drawn from similar occupations. Tilly and Lees (1975) have stressed the extent to which the June Days show protest in France becoming more modern. This may have been true to some extent, but their article also suggests that one of the greatest differences between the artisans and workers who fought for the government, and those who fought against it, was that the latter were likely to have been mobilized through corporations and clubs. As Sewell (1980) and Amann (1975) have shown, however, these corporations and clubs were importantly based on tradition and community. In Tilly's (1978:62–64) language (borrowed from Harrison White), these groupings comprised "CATNETs"; that is, they were at once categories which could clearly distinguish their members from their enemies, and dense networks socially binding their members to each other. They were, I suggest, novel or "modern" in the extent to which they mobilized categories through formal organizations, for proactive goals. But, some of the most important of those organizations were themselves quite old. Even more to the point, the workers of the June insurrection, or for that matter of the 1851 insurrection, were not first and foremost categories of individuals mobilized through formal organizations. They were members of close-knit communities, mobilized on the basis of those communities, to pursue ends congruent with and indeed defensiveness of those communities. Amann (1975:esp. p. 84) documents the great extent to which the clubs were local bodies; craft organizations were equally or even more communal. Their members had a new awareness of who they were, shaped in opposition (as Marx was right to note) to their newly manifest enemies in the bourgeoisie, but they were still reactionary radicals.

The research of Gossez (1967), and especially more recently of Traugott (1980a, 1980b), suggests that the clearest objective distinction which can be made between the groups of artisans and workers on either side of the June barricades is one of age. The reason that this factor was so important points up the centrality—and a central weakness—of the corporate source of the radicalism in behalf of the social republic. Under increasing economic pressure, the trade had been transformed since the days of the old regime (see Sewell 1980). First, masters had become more and more capitalist employers, setting themselves apart from even the most skilled of artisans, for whom independence became a distant, if not real, hope. Then, work itself began to become scarce, especially in the crisis of the late 1840s. The more senior journeymen protected their positions not only by political mobilization, but by exclusion of younger, especially immigrant, workers. The latter were more likely to be unemployed; when they had work, it was not likely to be in the highest quality workshops, but in cut-rate shops, sometimes with a greater division of labor, nearly always making cheaper goods. Protecting the pride of the craft meant little to them, and the corporations were hardly their friends, since it was their seniority rules which kept them from working. Though the radicals' demands for full employment would have benefitted these their poorer cousins, they were unable to make common cause with them. The very defensive of the radical orientation was one reason.

The Fruits of Struggle

We can only speculate as to how the political-economic balance of the Second Republic would have been shifted had France been industrializing faster, or had its birthrate been higher. Perhaps the latter circumstance would have meant all the more youthful workers on the government side of the barricades—or perhaps a sufficient weakening of the old communities that there would have been no barricades. But the struggle was fought, and fought in defense of traditional crafts and communities, and in favor of various goals which, though long developing, would have produced a very new society. The mobilization was strong enough to mount a major insurrection against the coup d'état, even after two years of active government repression and a series of defeats beginning with the June Days. This certainly sets it apart from late Chartism, which petitioned and launched an only marginally successful demonstration, but which brought out a much better display of middle class consciousness and strength. The British government made what seemed stringent preparations to preserve public order during the Chartist demonstration in London in 1848, yet its efforts are thoroughly paltry beside the repression mobilized by the government of Louis Napoleon. There had been little if any preemptive action in Britain; that was the order of the day in France. Of course, British workers had not had the earlier boost of a bourgeois revolution. In any case, the struggle in France was a major one by any standards. In order to repress it, indeed, bourgeois leaders, whom we have no reason to suspect of being on principle anti-republican, were forced to connive in the establishment of the Second Empire. The bourgeoisie had to give up its own republic in order to protect its capital and to have a stronger government, in no small part under pressure from below. It is not clear that this cost the bourgeoisie anything economically, but it may well have led the Empire to be cautious in its promotion of social and economic change. There is no doubt that Napoleon III's government was repressive, but it did attempt to avoid being provocative.

The struggles of the French Second Republic may be taken as representative of an important historical type. They began with an agricultural crisis; in other words, the revolution was set off by an "old style" crisis, not by industrial overproduction or some other more "modern" cause. Struggle was conditioned, however, by new possibilities and new threats, even though it was carried out by largely traditional groupings. The radical struggle for a social and democratic republic was the product of a transitional moment. The social foundations of traditional craft corporations and local communities were strong enough to form the basis for the mobilization; at the same time the growth of capitalism and popular recognition of the threat it posed made such a struggle quite radical. Capitalism itself was not so strong that it was necessarily invincible—any more than in Russia in 1917. And capitalism had not yet recreated the majority of the working population in its more individualistic and bureaucratic image. Struggle like this may have been an important limitation on the extent to which capitalism could ever completely destroy traditional communities.

French workers retained much of their specialized industry, including their superior craft skills, for long after 1851. It is arguable that economic development progressed with more sense and reality of community in France than in Britain. I think it is incontestable that capitalism created less of what Ruskin aptly called "illth" in France. And, on a relatively superficial examination, it seems to me that France may have retained a good deal more capacity for popular politics into the twentieth century. Not only the Commune of 1871 but the radical syndicalist movement of the twenty years before World War I show clear signs of the continuing importance of old political traditions, crafts, and communities in French Politics (this was especially true, before the extreme centralization of the Fifth Republic). Throughout the twentieth century French trade unions have been on the average more politicized than British. And if French peasants have been on occasion a conservative force, surely that should not surprise us, for it has presumably taken a great deal of conservative struggle to preserve as much of their traditions and indeed their very existence as they have done— or did until World War II and the Guallist "modernization" of the 1950s.

France could not match Britain's wage levels or aggregate standard of living during the latter nineteenth century. That did not mean that the French people—or a good many foreign travellers—did not think France was a nicer place to live; they did. Standard of living clearly was and is not the same as quality of life. The increased costs of maintaining an urban industrial society are alone enough to call into question smallish differentials in money incomes. As I have already suggested, it is in any case not quite fair to compare France to Britain, the first industrial country, or even to the United States, which had more opportunity to start anew. Perhaps the fairest comparison would be to look at the political, social, and economic costs Germany paid for rapid industrialization. That is better left to another paper (though note that Clapham 1921, finds no substantial difference in prosperity).

I would like to return in closing to the question of paths of economic development. By the mid-nineteenth century what Wallerstein (1974, 1980) has called the capitalist world system had come to have its core conditions set crucially be industrialization. Countries which failed to industrialize, like Portugal, or which waged civil war against their industrial regions, like Spain, remain "underdeveloped" to the present day. It is arguable whether life is better or worse, perhaps, but it is not arguable either that Spain and Portugal lost their positions in the core of the world system (which were already waning) or that they became relatively poor. We may, I think, assume that the French had no desire to be either relatively poor or relatively weak (indeed, Bonapartism suggest that national pride was still moved by military and economic might). This does not, however, imply that the French ought to have moved faster to imitate their British counterparts, as did the Germans. Because France developed within a world system, rather than in a vacuum, its development was conditioned by that of other national economies. An export-oriented France would have had to compete head on with Britain, Germany, and eventually the United States. All were formidable competitors; specialization in certain areas—including certain foodstuffs and craft products—was perhaps a much better strategy than direct confrontation. The existence of the world system also meant that exchange relations within the core of European and North American countries would tend to flow against a trading France, except in those areas—like high-skilled artisanal production—where it enjoyed very high productivity, and those areas—like wines—where it was more or less a monopoly supplier. During any process of rapid industrialization, France's huge "reserve army" of labor would have kept wages down and forced trade of relatively cheap labor for dear.[15] It is likely that, barring a huge and socially disruptive investment, France's industrial fixed capital would have remained for some time inferior to Britain's, Germany's and the U.S.'s, thus exacerbating this tendency.

Autocentrism was a plausible strategy, and partially conceiving of it explicitly, France followed that path for nearly a century. As Sherman (1970) has shown, government officials during the July Monarchy had already recognized some of its advantages and begun to work with a distinction between industrialized and non-industrialized trading partners that continued to inform French mercantile strategy and even colonial efforts. Some of the same officials, of course, were in power again during the Second Empire.

Where a Marxist—or Rostovian—stage theory argues for the essential centrality of heavy industrialization, the experience of France may shed light. Autocentrism probably allowed more nearly full employment during a more gradual—and perhaps more humane—process of economic growth and development. Were the Soviet Union and People's Republic of China wise to pursue strategies of industrialization at any cost? Perhaps the military rationale was important in the former case, but I think the economics were dubious. Such stage theories tend too much to presume discrete national economies; they also tend to neglect the social costs of development.

In conclusion, let me simply suggest that recurrent political struggle may have been crucial to producing a relatively continuous, gradual transition to a modern economy in France. At the same time, economic backwardness may have been an essential condition of radical French politics—including those of the Second Republic which did so much for the development of modern socialism. Chicken, egg; politics, economics.

Notes

1. Some economists and demographers would argue that a large landless population constitutes a push for innovation, and thus might be expected to see France's low rate of population growth as a reason for her failure to industrialize. See Roumasset and Smith (1981).

2. O'Brien and Keyder (1979:ch. 5) summarize this, but see also Chambers and Mingay (1966); Mingay (1968) and for a longer term comparative view, Slichter van Bath (1963:239–324).

3. See also Dean and Cole 1969:208–209, on the effectiveness of the French challenge in silks.

4. It is worth remembering, though, that even in Britain at this time the huge textile factories showed a productivity below the national average (O'Brien and Keyder 1979:157). Economists notwithstanding, increases in size often have much more to do with power than with efficiency or economies of scale.

5. Dean and Cole (1969:142–143) use a narrower definition if industry, but show a comparable proportionate distribution.

6. It may be noted that this runs counter to conventional notions of demographic transition. Here, too, the standard for modernization is based too much on the British experience. The French birthrate fell during the nineteenth century; among European countries this is as unusual as its slow industrialization.

7. Such views may have contributed to the reluctance of the officials of the July Monarchy to develop a fully supportive government industrialization policy: "most of the aspects of economic modernization seem desirable to French officials only when their economic effects were divorced from their social, ethical and political effects. In varying numbers and in varying degrees, officials made connections between elements of economic modernization and numerous new, disturbing developments, such as the undermining of the social and moral benefits of the agricultural way of life, economic rises, unscrupulous pursuit of profit, miseries of working class life, and political threats posed by the working class. (Sherman 1970:204). My suggestion is not that none of this was accurate, but that the last item does not fit with the rest of the lot very well.

8. This literature is enormous, and I do not propose to review it here. See discussion in Tilly (1978).

9. I have reviewed Marx's argument briefly in Calhoun, "The Radicalism of Tradition: Community Strength or Venerable Disguise and Borrowed Language?" *American Journal of Sociology* (1983).

10. Tilly also notes an earlier competitive form of collective action, which is less political and less important to either his or our discussion. Feuds and rivalries between communities are examples.

11. See D. Thompson 1971; these were the years of Lovett's greater importance.

12. But note, *a propos* our earlier discussion, that Foster is wrong to contrast it or this account with British agriculture (1974:21).

13. In Reims the situation resembled the Lancashire of 15–20 years before. Most of the 3,000 spinners worked in factories, but some 7,500 weavers worked in 3,500 shops. They were the most active, though there was more unity than in England (Merriman 1978:70–71). I would suggest that weavers had both a stronger communal basis and a more pressing economic reason for struggle—though their long-term position was weaker. Studying Paris, Tilly and Lees (1974:193) found that a low number of workers per patron implied a low rate of participation for an industry in the June insurrection. The differences are, however, all among relatively small numbers of workers per establishment, and therefore do not seem a direct refutation of this argument. It may be that among artisan shops in Paris the trades with smaller establishments were those least pressured by economic change (see p. 8 above), while the larger one were transitional—artisan production in the process of degradation—which is the group I would expect to see most readily mobilized. The more prosperous and steady traditional crafts offered workers more hope of becoming masters.

14. It is arguable that the accession of fully socialist governments in twentieth century Europe has posed less of a radical threat to the self-interest of bourgeois elites than did insurrection of reactionary radicals a century before. Managers can still manage under collective ownership of modern industry as under private ownership. It was a socialism with more roots in artisan and peasant traditions and production which threatened to do away with them altogether.

15. So Mandel (1975) Amin (1976) and others have suggested with regard to contemporary Third World development.

References

Agulhon, M. 1970. *La République au village*, Paris: Plon.

Amann, P. 1975. *Revolution and Mass Democracy: The Paris Club Movement in 1848*, Princeton: Princeton University Press.

Amin, S. 1976. *Unequal Development*, New York: Monthly Review Press.

Bezucha, R. J. 1974. *The Lyon Uprising of 1834: Social and Political Conflict in a Nineteenth Century City*, Cambridge: Harvard University Press.

Blau, P. M. 1978. *Inequality and Heterogeneity*, New York: Free Press.

Calhoun, C. J. 1980. "Community: Towards a Variable Conceptualization for Comparative Research." *Social History*, 5:105–129.

―――. 1982. *The Question of Class Struggle: Social Foundations of Popular Radicalism During the Industrial Revolution*, Chicago: University of Chicago Press.

―――. 1983. "The Radicalism of Tradition: Community Strength or Venerable Disguise and Borrowed Language?" *American Journal of Sociology*.

Chambers, J. A. and G. E. Mingay. 1966. *The Agricultural Revolution, 1750–1880*, London: Oxford University Press.

Clapham, J. H. 1921. *The Economic Development of France and Germany, 1815–1914*, Cambridge: Cambridge University Press.

Deane, P., and W. A. Cole. 1969. *British Economic Growth, 1688–1959*, Cambridge: Cambridge University Press.

Dunham, A. L. 1955. *The Industrial Revolution in France, 1815–1848*, New York: Exposition Press.

Forstenzer, T. R. 1981. *The French Provincial Police and the Fall of the Second Republic: Social Fear and Counterrevolution*, Princeton: Princeton University Press.

Foster, J. 1974. *Class Struggle and the Industrial Revolution*, London: Weidenfeld and Nicolson.

Gammage, R. G. 1854. *History of the Chartist Movement*, London: Merlin (this edition 1969).

Gayer, A. D., W. W. Rostow, and A. J. Schwartz. 1975. *The Growth and Fluctuation of the British Economy, 1790–1850*, new edition, Hassocks, Sussex: Harvester.

Gorz, A. 1968. *Strategy for Labor*, Boston: Beacon Press.

Gossez, R. 1967. *Les Ouvriers de Paris, I: L'Organisation, 1848–1851*, La Roche Sur Yonne: Bibliothéque de la Révolution de 1848, vol. 24.

Harrison, B. 1971. *Drink and the Victorians: The Temperance Question in England, 1815–1872*, Pittsburgh: University of Pittsburgh Press.

Harrison, J. F. C. 1961. *Learning and Living*, London: Routledge.

———. 1969. *Quest for the New Moral World: Robert Owen and the Owenites in Britain and America*, New York: Scribner.

Hearn, F. 1978. *Domination, Legitimation, and Resistance: The Incorporation of the Nineteenth-Century English Working Class*, Westport: Greenwood Press.

Henderson, W. O. 1961. *The Industrial Revolution on the Continent: Germany, France, Russia, 1800–1914*, London: Cass.

Hobsbawm, E. J. 1964. "The Labor Aristocracy in Nineteenth Century Britain," in E. J. Hobsbawm, *Laboring Men*, London: Weidenfeld and Nicolson.

———. 1978. "Should the Poor Organize?" *New York Review of Books*, March 23, 1978:44–49.

Hodgskin, T. 1822. *Labour Defended Against the Claims of Capital*, New York: Kelley.

Inglis, B. 1971. *Poverty and the Industrial Revolution*, London: Panther.

Kemp, T. 1971. *Economic Forces in French History*, London: Dennis Dobson.

Kirby, R. G., and A. E. Musson. 1975. *The Voice of the People: John Doherty, 1798–1854*, Manchester: Manchester University Press.

Laqueur, T. 1976. *Religion and Respectability*, New Haven: Yale University Press.

Lasch, C. 1981. "Democracy and the 'Crisis of Confidence'," *Democracy*, 1:25–40.

Lenin, V. I. 1920. *Imperialism, the Highest Stage of Capitalism*, in R. Tucker, ed., *The Lenin Anthology*, New York: Norton, 1975.

Mandel, E. 1975. *Late Capitalism*, London: New Left Books.

Margadant, T. 1979. *French Peasants in Revolt: The Insurrection of 1851*, Princeton: Princeton University Press.

Marx, K. 1852. "The Eighteenth Brumaire of Louis Bonaparte," in D. Fernbach, ed., *Surveys from Exile*, Harmondsworth: Penguin.

Mather, F. C. 1974. "The General Strike of 1842: a Study in Leadership, Organization and the Threat of Revolution during the Plug Plot Disturbances," in J. Stevenson and R. Quinault, eds., *Popular Protest and Public Order*, London: Allen and Unwin.

Merriman, J. M. 1978. *The Agony of the Republic: The Repression of the Left in Revolutionary France, 1848–1851*, New Haven: Yale University Press.

Milward, A. S., and S. B. Saul. 1973. *The Economic Development of Continental Europe, 1780-1870*, London: Allen and Unwin.

Mingay, G. E. 1968. *Enclosure and the Small Farmer in the Age of the Industrial Revolution*, London: Macmillan.

Mitchell, B. R. 1980. *European Historical Statistics, 1750-1975*, New York: Facts on File.

Mitchell, B. R., and P. Deane. 1962. *Abstract of British Historical Statistics*, Cambridge: Cambridge University Press.

Musson, A. E. 1976a. "Class Struggle and the Labour Aristocracy, 1830-60," *Social History*, 3:335-356.

_____. 1976b "Industrial Motive Power in the United Kingdom, 1800-70," *The Economic History Review*, 2nd Series, XXIX:415-439.

O'Brien, P. K., and C. Keyder. 1978. *Economic Growth in Britain and France, 1780-1914: Two Paths to the Twentieth Century*, London: Allen and Unwin.

Perkin, H. 1969. *The Origins of Modern English Society, 1780-1880*, London: Routledge and Kegan Paul.

Pollard, S., and J. Salt. 1971. *Robert Owen: Prophet of the Poor*, London: Macmillan.

Postgate, R. W. 1923. *The Builders' History*, London: National Foundation of Building Operatives.

Price, R. 1972. *The French Second Republic: A Social History*, Ithaca: Cornell University Press.

Price, R., ed. 1975. *Revolution and Reaction: 1848 and the Second French Republic*, London: Croom Helm.

Read, D. 1959. "Chartism in Manchester," in A. Briggs, ed., *Chartist Studies*, London: Macmillan.

Rose, A. G. (1957). "The Plug Plot Riots in 1842 in Lancashire and Cheshire," *Transactions of the Lancashire and Cheshire Antiquarian Society*, LXVII:75-112.

Rosenblatt, F. F. 1916. *The Chartist Movement in its Social and Economic Aspects*, London: Cass (this edition 1967).

Roumasset, J. R., and J. Smith. 1981. "Population, Technological Change, and the Evolution of Labor Markets," *Population and Development Review*, 7:401-420.

Samuel, R. 1977. "Workshop of the World: Steam Power and Hand Technology in Mid-Victorian Britain," *History Workshop Journal*, 3:6-72.

Sewell, W. H., Jr. 1980. *Work and Revolution in France: The Language of Labor from the Old Regime to 1848*, Cambridge: Cambridge University Press.

_____. 1981. "La confraternité des proletaires: conscience de classe sous la monarchie de juillet," *Sociétés Urbaines*, pp. 650-671.

Sherman, D. M. 1970. "Governmental Attitudes toward Economic Modernization in France during the July Monarchy, 1830-1848," Unpublished Ph.D. dissertation, University of Michigan.

Slicher van Bath, B. H. 1963. *The Agrarian History of Western Europe*, London: Edward Arnold.

Slosson, R.W. 1916. *The Decline of the Chartist Movement*, London: Cass (this edition 1967).

Smelser, N. J. 1959. *Social Change in the Industrial Revolution*, London: Routledge and Kegan Paul.

_____. 1962. *Theory of Collective Behavior*, New York: Free Press.

_____. 1968. "Sociological History: The Industrial Revolution and the British Working-Class Family," in N. J. Smelser, *Essays in Sociological Explanation*, Englewood Cliffs: Prentice-Hall.

Stedman Jones, G. 1974. "Class Struggle and the Industrial Revolution," *New Left Review*, 90:35–69.

Tholfsen, T. 1976. *Working Class Radicalism in Mid-Victorian England*, London: Croom Helm.

Thompson, D., ed. 1971. *The Early Chartists*, Columbia: The University of South Carolina Press.

Thompson, E. P. 1979. "The Peculiarities of the English," revised edition in E. P. Thompson, *The Poverty of Theory*, New York: Monthly Review Press.

————. 1968. *The Making of the English Working Class*, revised edition. Harmondsworth: Penguin.

Tilly, C. 1972. "How Protest Modernized in France, 1845–55," in W. O. Aydelotte, A. G. Bogue, and R. W. Fogel, eds., *The Dimensions of Quantitative Research in History*, Princeton: Princeton University Press.

————. 1978. *From Mobilization to Revolution*, Reading: Addison-Wesley.

Tilly, C., and H. Lees. 1975. "The People of June, 1848," in R. Price, ed., *Revolution and Reaction*, London: Croom Helm.

Tilly, C., Tilly, L., and Tilly, R. 1975. *The Rebellious Century*, Cambridge: Harvard University Press.

Traugott, M. 1980a. "Determinants of Political Orientation: Class and Organization in the Parisian Insurrection of June 1848," *American Journal of Sociology*, 86:32–49.

————. 1980b. "The Mobile Guard in the French Revolution of 1848," *Theory and Society*, 9:683–720.

Tudesq, A. J. 1965. *L' Élection Presidentielle de Louis-Napoleon Bonaparte, 10 Décembre 1848*, Paris: Presse Universitaire Française.

Turner, H. A. 1962. *Trade Union Growth, Structure, and Policy*, London: Oxford University Press.

Wallerstein, I. 1974, 1980. *The Modern World System*, 2 vols. New York Academic Press.

Ward, J. T. 1962. *The Factory Movement, 1830–1855*, London: Batsford.

————. 1973. *Chartism*, London: Batsford.

5

The Mid-Century Crisis and the 1848 Revolutions: The Case of England

GARETH STEDMAN JONES

In the last two decades the pan-European economic crisis of 1846–1848 and the revolutionary upheavals of 1848 itself have been a chosen testing-ground for the theoretical approaches of some eminent American sociologists and political scientists. The embroilment of France and central Europe in a revolutionary process, and conversely, the absence of any comparable revolutionary challenge in England, have been viewed in the light of large scale evolutionist theories of modernization and stages of economic development. Older emphases upon the political origins of revolution or its absence have been downplayed in favor of comparative social typologies, and the propensity for a politics of confrontation and direct action has been placed within a framework of developmental sociology. In general, what seems to be involved is an inversion of the classical Marxist model of proletarian revolution. Despite the considerable differences of object and emphasis in the work of Barrington Moore, Charles Tilly, and Eric Wolf, one common theme at least emerges. It is that the bearers of anti-capitalist revolution were not the new factory proletariat, but those groups most threatened by industrialization—"pre-industrial" artisans and peasants. Eric Wolf, in his book on *Peasant Wars of the Twentieth Century*, emphasized the revolutionary role of middle peasants, the most vigorous carriers of peasant traditions and a social stratum both willing and still able to organize collective resistance to the incursions of capitalist agriculture and the world market. Barrington Moore, in his latest work on *Injustice*, treats 1848 in Germany as a revolt of guild-masters and pre-industrial journeymen. The new proletariat, so far as they existed, he considers to have possessed no coherent political perspective and to have remained quiescent. Charles Tilly

This chapter originally appeared as "The Mid Century Crisis and the 1848 Revolutions: A Critical Assessment" in *Theory and Society* 12/4 (July 1983), pp. 505–520, and is reprinted with permission. Copyright 1983 by *T&S*.

(as do the many historians of nineteenth century France inspired by his work), has again stressed the role of tight-knit communities of artisans and peasant and correlates their capacity to organize resistance with the traditionalism of their values and goals. Once again the relative insignificance of the new factory proletariat in the revolutionary process of 1848 is emphasized[1] (Moore 1978:esp. pt. 2; Wolf 1969; Tilly 1972).

What emerges from all these accounts is the conservative character of the revolutionary. Just as Trevor-Roper in his account to the English seventeenth century revolution (Trevor-Roper 1957:179–205) assigned the revolutionary role to the declining gentry, so Craig Calhoun, who broadly shares Tilly's approach, states that "we need to see revolutions against capitalism as based not in the new class which capitalism forms, but in the traditional communities and crafts which capitalism threatens." What is stressed in this more or less shared picture of confrontationist and potentially revolutionary social groups is a "rootedness" in a social order under threat, and this pre-existing social order is generally characterized as traditional, pre-industrial, steeped in custom and ritual, dominated by face-to-face social relations, and affective rather than calculative and rational in its social bondings. Paradoxically, however, much of the intellectual authority, both conceptual and empirical, appealed to in recent times by this approach, also derived from the work of two English historians, who stand in a position of self-confessed allegiance to a Marxist tradition of historiography— Eric Hobsbawm and Edward Thompson. However much their ultimate evaluation of the historical process may diverge from some of the American theorists, Hobsbawm's work on *Primitive Rebels* and Thompson's notion of "moral economy" or "customs in common", are not difficult to reconcile with a picture of societal development in the nineteenth and twentieth centuries which derives more inspiration from Weber than from Marx (Thompson 1971; Hobsbawm 1959). What they have strongly reinforced is a notion of the pre-industrial as a coherent system of values and customs not only distinct from emerging liberal capitalism but also, implicitly at least, distinct from later working class life under industrial capitalism.

Another facet of the approach I am attempting to characterize, more prominent perhaps in the United States than in England is its confident, thought not necessarily optimistic, social evolutionism. Particularly salient in Craig Calhoun's contribution to this volume is the notion that France underwent a revolution in 1848 while England did not, because France was two generations or even half a century behind England in terms of economic and social development. There were far fewer factory workers, a still peasant-based agriculture, slower population growth, smaller cities and towns, and hence the presence of more traditionally rooted geographical or occupational communities of peasants and artisans possessing greater will and capacity to mount organized and even insurrectionary resistance. In England, conversely, a higher stage of the development of industrial capitalism had engendered the virtual elimination of these protesting traditional communities and their replacement by a new industrial working class. This class was more distant from, and increasingly without "radical" pre-industrial roots, culturally permeable to ascendant capitalist values, and prone to "respectability" and reformism. England escaped revolution in 1848 because it stood several stages nearer to the evolutionary terminus implied by this model—that in which, according to Craig Calhoun, capitalism would "recreate the majority of the working population into its (own) more individualistic and bureaucratic image."

Having attempted to characterize—I hope fairly—the salient features of what has become perhaps one predominant approach to nineteenth century social development, and in particular to the interpretation of the relationship between industrialization and social movements culminating in 1848, I want for the remainder of the paper to outline some objections to it. These objections are both conceptual and empirical.

The first thing I would like to question about this picture of nineteenth century revolution as the product of threatened social groups of artisans and peasants rooted in pre-industrial values, customs, and communities is its implicit model of capitalist development. Like the *Communist Manifesto* model of Marxism to which it is juxtaposed, it assumes that the destiny of such groups was to disappear in the face of large scale capitalist agriculture and modern factory industry. If, however, we project that model forward in time to the late nineteenth century, or even further into the twentieth, we can see that such a prediction is very misleading. The English model of capitalist agriculture is the exception rather than the rule and may be ascribed to the highly peculiar political framework devised by a seventeenth and eighteenth century agrarian capitalist class, rather than to a universal logic of capitalist development. In Prussia, for example, where the intention of Stein-Hardenberg reforms of 1807–1821 was precisely to promote a form of peasant emancipation that would benefit an English-style class of substantial agrarian capitalist rather than French-style peasant small-holders, peasants in the first half of the nineteenth century sacrificed one million hectares to landed proprietors. Yet even so, by 1869 the peasantry owned 49% of the land, the junkers 45%. The explanation of this paradox is the tremendous extension of cultivation which succeeded emancipation between 1815 and 1848 (Koselleck 1976). The later attempt by the Prussian state to generate a capitalist agriculture was an even more unequivocal failure (Shanin 1972). In general, peasants have not simply disappeared through the logic of capitalist development. Where they have done so, long sustained state pressure or exceptional political violence, from enclosure to collectivization, have been necessary additions. Certainly, peasants in western and central Europe did not disappear, as can be testified by anyone who has studied the politics of the Common Market today.

If we take the case of artisans, defined as skilled workers operating in small units of production, the case is similar. At a theoretical level, Marxist economists have attempted in vain to establish any *consistent* tendency over the last century and a half towards the rising organic composition of capital. To cite West Germany as the most dynamic European example of post-war capitalism, in 1962 there were over 700,000 craft shops employing some 3.5 million people[2] (Fischer 1972:285–349). This was about 12 times the number of industrial enterprises, and the numbers employed amounted to about one-half those in factory employment. The average size of a craft shop was about 5.1 workers and craft workshop production had increased in importance between 1936 and 1962. In the nineteenth century, according to Prussian statistics, craft production in 1815 accounted for 4% of the population; by 1858 it had reached 6%; by 1895 it had fallen back to 4.5%; it then resumed an upward trend. Very generally over the whole period 1815 to 1962, it is estimated by Wolfram Fischer that the craft labor force and its dependents may have increased from 15% of the total population to about 25%.

If we restrict ourselves to nineteenth century Britain, once again a picture of disappearing artisans would be very misleading. Apart from the textile sector and primary iron and steel manufacture, the great bulk of manufacturing activity took place in small workshops and involved a considerable degree of hand labor of various kinds. Both the old research of J. H. Clapham and the more recent exhaustive inquiry by Raphael Samuel suggests that hand labor and workshop production was a buoyant and expanding sector of the economy at any time up to the 1880s (Clapham 1926–38; Samuel 1977). Britain was accurately described not as the factory, but as the workshop of the world.

If we remove *a priori* assumptions about a teleology of modern industry none of the data is particularly surprising. Hand labor of a skilled, semi-skilled, or unskilled kind was the basic form by which the basic demands of an expanding population for housing, clothing, footware, furniture, and consumer durables was satisfied. Since labor was plentiful and cheap, and demand was fashion-prone in addition to being seasonally and cyclically variable, increasing demand was met by the addition of new units of production rather than by economies of scale, and new technology was capital-saving rather than labor-saving in character. This is exemplified not only by the role of the sewing machine, the bandsaw, and the hand lathe in the clothing, furniture, and metal trades, but also by the striking role of skilled hand labor in a completely new industry, the iron shipbuilding industry which took in the second half of the nineteenth century (Reid 1980).

It is important to note that these industries were as much *new* industries of the nineteenth century as mechanical spinning was a distinctive innovation of the eighteenth. It is quite misleading to harp on their "traditional" features, when their working methods, their products, their markets, and the bulk of their labor force were not more or less rooted in pre-industrial customs or values than were their equivalent cotton mills and iron foundaries of the north.

All this leads to a second point which I want to raise: how significant was it—a feature so emphatically reiterated in the recent historical literature of 1848—that the worker activists in Paris and other cities came from workships rather than factories. The polemic between orthodox Marxists and historical sociologists over this issue seems to me somewhat sterile.[3] In my article on "Rethinking Chartism"—whose arguments are much too long to reproduce here—I have argued on the basis of recent research that it is impossible to interpret Chartism as a movement of artisans *as opposed to* factory workers (Stedman Jones 1983:chap. 3). By 1840, Chartist activity in Ashton under Lyme, a purely factory town, was just as militant and extensive as it was in Trowbridge, a declining community of handloom weavers, or Finsbury and Clerkenwell, a classic center of skilled London artisans. Moreover, the rhetoric of Chartist activists was remarkably uniform across the country. After the split-off of a middle class leadership, it did not differ significantly in Birmingham, London, Manchester, Oldham, Nottingham or Brighton. Between 1839 and 1842 all of these were centers of O'Connerite strength. It is certainly not true, despite Craig Calhoun's suggestion that the 1842 strike was "anti-industrial"—whatever that might mean—or that unions in new industries like that of the cotton spinners distanced themselves from the Chartist upheaval. In fact the contrary was true. It was unions in the textile and engineering industries in the Manchester area—not the pre-existing Chartist leadership, not traditional craft workers—who mounted the general strike of 1842. And they did so for Chartist and not purely industrial or wage-bargaining reasons. Chartism had focused on what it call "class legislation" as the principal reason for the affliction of the working classes. Attempts to increase wages by industrial means were rendered nugatory by what was thought of as the political tyranny of the ruling classes or "idle classes" over the unrepresented producers of "industrious classes." This was the Chartist case, and in strike meetings and conferences of delegates throughout Lancashire and the Midlands it was reiterated as the reason for the struggle in that year (see Sykes and Jones in Epstein and Thompson 1982).

If the decline of Chartism after 1842 was not uniform between regions, this again cannot be correlated in any neat way with a division between factory areas, handloom weaving areas, and skilled workshop areas. In part the geography of Chartism after 1842 is defined by areas in which O'Connor's lands plan possessed a particular appeal (for this was the main activity of Chartist activists between 1843 and 1847), in part it is defined by the resilience of some local leadership or modest electoral gains, and in part by fortunes of particular trades. But all this cuts across any neat schematic division between traditional crafts workers and new industrial workers. In 1848, so far as there was a Chartist revival, it was particularly prominent in London and the West Riding (see Belchem in Epstein and Thompson 1982). London, as a center of workshop finishing trades and very little factory production, could easily be fitted into the picture of Paris drawn, for instance, by Robert Bezucha. You would certainly find the same sorts of complaints about *marchangage*. But the most militant center of the West Riding—a virtually insurrectionary town in 1848—was Bradford, the center of the worsted trade, a predominantly factory industry whose market was heavily hit by the revolutionary turmoil in Europe. In fact, however, the feature uniting London, Bradford, Liverpool, and other trouble spots in 1848 probably had less to do with the proportions of the work force employed as artisans, outworkers, or factory hands, than the relative degree of prominence of the Irish immigrants in each of these districts. It was repeal of the Union rather than the six points of the Charter or the formation of the national convention that provoked most of the violent political confrontations in England in 1848 (See Belchem in Epstein and Thompson 1982).[4]

In Germany analogous evidence could be cited from Berlin to establish the relative unimportance of the factory/workshop division. According to Frederick Marquardt, the evidence contradicts the belief that there was a significant division of outlook between those working in large mechanized factories or large non-mechanized "manufactories" on the one hand and journeymen working in small handcraft workshops on the other (Marquardt 1974). There was in fact a considerable interchange of labor between the two. The picture that Marquardt paints of workers' political activity in 1848 rather resembles that which has been unraveled by Jorwerth Prothero's work on London trades, and which fits much of the French evidence as well (Prothero 1971; 1979). That is to say that the division lies rather between richer and poorer trades: the more affluent being mobilized mainly by issues which affected the political and civil status of workers as a whole; the poorer trades being most associative and the backbone of most social and political militancy; and the poorest, through disorganization and poverty, often unable to sustain any effective forms of organized activity at all.

The primary division in England, at least to the end of the 1880s lay not between factory workers and artisans, but between those who possessed a trade (including such factory workers as cotton spinners, power loom weavers, puddlers, block printers, and so on) and those who did not (casual day laborers, porters, navies, quayside workers), a group, in Mayhew's words "as unpolitical as footmen." Harney and Jones, the Chartist leaders vainly talked about attempting to mobilize these groups in 1847 since it was thought Chartism could do with an influx of support from the physically strong. But all the evidence suggest that apart from the very special case of the Irish, their efforts were a total failure, and that some from these groups, the coal heavers most notably, in fact were actively mobilized as special constables by the other side on April 10, 1848.

So far we have argued that skilled artisans did not disappear from the work force in England, France, or Germany in the second half of the nineteenth century, and it would also be necessary to add that they did not retreat from the salient role they had played in labor movements either. In England around the time of the Second Reform Bill they dominated the trades union movement and continued to do so up until the 1880s. Thus, if we are to explain why the capitalist order appeared much more stable in the second half of the nineteenth century, our explanation would have to include artisans within it.

How, then, does the global crisis of 1845–1847 relate to the revolutions of 1848, and why did England escape them? Rather than comparing countries in terms of comparative stages of social and industrial evolution, as the "Communist Manifesto," Rostovian growth theorists, and historical sociologists have alike been prone to do, we should, I believe, think in terms of phases of capitalist development as a global entity, as a system of combined and uneven development which a) should be looked at structurally and synchronically in any given epoch, and b) will be partly inflected by its political conditions of existence and operation in different states.

In the case of the impact to the economic crises in France and England between 1845 and 1848, its incidence has been admirably described by Mark Traugott elsewhere in this volume, so I won't go over the same ground. What I will briefly attempt to do, is to place it in a more epochal framework. My intention in doing this is to suggest that the reason we have fewer social movements in the second half of the nineteenth century is not purely because other countries were now following in the path successfully pioneered by England, but rather because there was greater stability to the capitalist system as a whole.

If we approach the crises of 1845–1847 with the analytical tools provided by Labrousse, we miss, I think, the full dimensions of the crisis (Labrousse 1956). Labrousse suggests, in the case of France, that it was a combination of what he calls "the last crisis of the old type" and a new trade cycle depression in the capital goods sector (rail, coal, and iron). The two crises are seen as largely independent of each other, except through strains on the balance of payments and hence credit. But the 1840s crisis was not simply a combination of industrial depression and exceptional dearth. It was not only a crisis of agriculture, it was also a crisis of textiles in particular. It was a crisis of a more secular kind and it marked a turning point in the history of the Western European economy.

It inaugurated the de-industrialization of the countryside and the pastoralization of extensive areas which until then had combined agriculture and domestic industry, though it did not, in England or elsewhere, eliminate the importance of the small workshop production in the towns (Kriedte, Medick and Schlumbohn, 1977:esp. ch. 6). It precipitated the first massive wave of migration to America from Ireland, southwest Germany, and to a lesser extent France, succeeded thereafter by a continuous stream of migration into the towns, where industrial activity was henceforth increasingly concentrated. The case of Irish demographic involution after the famine is well-known. But other cases should also be mentioned. It is only from 1851 that the English rural population begins to decline in absolute as well as relative terms. Charles Pouthas, in his history of French population in the first half of the nineteenth century, sees French population growth during this period as a continuation of eighteenth century patterns (Pouthas 1956). The turning point came in 1847–50, a period of demographic crisis. In more than half of France population growth halted or began to decline. The areas particularly affected were relatively densely populated regions combining agriculture and industry—especially the cultivation and weaving of linen—Picardy, Normandy, Brittany, Gascony, and across the Belgian borders in Flanders.

In Prussia the increase of population in country and town proceeded in step until 1849. The period 1847–55 was similarly in Germany a period of demographic stagnation and reaction. In the southwestern areas—Baden and Wurttemberg—the population actually declined between 1845 and 1855.

To explain these features we must attempt to place the crisis of the 1840s in the general context of British and European industrialization in the first half of the nineteenth century.

1. Industrialization during this period remained very narrowly based. It was based on the mechanization of cotton spinning, and to a lesser extent that of wool and linen. Mechanization of the weaving sector was a slower process, not effectively accomplished in cotton in Britain until the later 1830s. Cotton was an imported raw material and had few multiplier effects through the rest of the economy.[5] While it adopted machines and steam power, it possessed little capacity to extend their use in the rest of the economy. The other industrialized sector was iron, based more upon fuel than labor economy (coking instead of charcoal, the puddling process, the hot-blast). Iron had been stimulated by wartime demand, but was cursed by overcapacity until the coming of the railways provided it with a steady and expanding international market, further reinforced by the coming of iron ships.

2. The eighteenth century merchanization of the cotton spinning industry had been precipitated by labor scarcity combined with the dominant position of Britain in the export market for cotton piece goods. Between 1790–1794 and 1800–1804 the volume of exports to Europe doubled after several decades of stagnation, while exports to North America rose by 58%. European competitors were crippled by the blockade and the growing British technological lead reinforced by the supremacy of the British fleet. French and German mechanization of cotton was a necessity if their domestic markets were not wholly to be captured, but the internal necessity to industrialize was weak. The Napoleonic wars had deprived them of former export markets, and the technological gap now meant that there was little chance of recapturing them.[6] The effect of this change was most serious on the linen industry, the largest export industry of 18th century Germany (Kriedte, Medick and Schulmbohn 1977). In cotton, both in France and Germany the mechanized spinning sector was confined to the domestic market. In Germany, because of the low rate of protection, the cotton industry remained precarious until the end of the 1840s, while in heavily protected France, the success of the Alsatian industry was largely at the expense of the more backward Norman industry. Success in the export sector in both countries was largely confined to the finishing sector, where the higher proportion of cheap labor input could offset the advantage of machines. Neither in France nor in Germany could the textile sector generate an industrial take-off. This came with railway building in the 1840s which stimulated coal, iron, and engineering activity (*Histoire* 1967; Motteck 1964; Borchardt 1972; Hardrach 1972). In both France and Germany, the first major cycle in the production of capital goods proceeded independently from the cycle of textiles and consumer goods.

3. Compared with the last half of the eighteenth century, the pace of technical change up to the 1840s was slow (as in the slowness of the introduction of mechanical weaving). This was mainly the result of the abundance of labor supply, itself in part a result of the general rise of population, and in part the degree of under-employment resulting from the decline of linen exports and the mechanization of cotton spinning. Proto-industrialization in the eighteenth century had particularly benefited those on the margins of rural society. Areas of proto-industrialization had been characterized by a higher than average birth rate, lower age of marriage, and much literary evidence suggesting higher rates of illegitimacy (Medick 1976; Levine 1977). Moreover, political changes during the French Revolutionary period increased the labor supply. In France the dividing up of the commons and the imposition of a stricter forest law increased the hardship of those beneath the peasant small-holders, and impelled them into whatever subsidiary industrial employments were available. In Prussia the onerous conditions of peasant emancipation, and the proliferation of a practically landless stratum of cottagers dependent on casual labor had a similar effect.

But while the supply of rural labor increased, the demand contracted. The mechanization of spinning in cotton pushed former spinners into weaving. The contraction of the export market for linen had a similar effect. The domestic market did not greatly expand. The debt burdens on the peasantry, if anything, encouraged a tendency towards subsistence. Moreover, the domestic market was subject to the constant pressure of foreign competition. Cottage industry in textiles had to face British machine competition. Cotton prices fell 72% between 1815 and 1851. The price of linen yarn halved between the 1790s and the 1840s.

But in a situation where labor was abundant and agricultural earnings were low, workers in domestic industry reacted to superior factory competition by increasing output and lowering their rates, thus retarding the speed of mechanization. In England, according to Habakkuk, between 1819 and 1829 the number of handlooms increased by between 25–30% and the prices of their products fell (Habakkuk 1962:147). Thus the mechanization of cotton weaving and linen spinning in the 1830s was resisted by domestic workers by a further attempt to increase their output and lower their prices. In Bielefeld it was estimated that the annual income of a five-member linen spinner family between 1800 and 1853 had fallen from 82 to 49 *reichsthaler* (Kriedte, Medick and Schlumbohn 1977:316). Finally, this growing competition between domestic workers was exacerbated by merchants attempting to depress prices still further in order to compete effectively on the world market. The Silesian cotton weavers who revolted in 1844 had only recently abandoned the linen weaving industry and had been incensed by the advantage taken of them by the merchants of Peterswaldau. According to an article in the *Deutsche Vierteljahrsschrift* for 1844 describing the pauperism of the Obererzgebirge: "the cause of the so unexpectedly increasing immiseration lies not alone in a transitory stoppage of trade, which we have already on occasion lived through, but in the fact that the factories in England have captured our manufacture for themselves. Lace manufacture has received nothing less than a death-blow; and this affects thousands of people here for whom the lace frame, summer and winter, was the milk-giving cow" (*Deutsche Vierteljahrsschrift* 1844:315).

It should be clear that pauperism in Europe cannot be explained in purely Malthusian terms as a pre-industrial or pre-capitalist crisis, as it is often represented (Abel 1974; Conze 1976). The extent of overpopulation has to be measured not simply against the resources of the land, but also against the development of the world market. The potato blight and the bad corn harvest of 1845–47 were not merely a Malthusian positive check on population increase, but rather the last straw in a process of progressive deterioration which had set in since the French wars, particularly in the textile sector. It was not just a crisis *de type ancien*, for its parameters were set not merely by the diversion of consumer spending to food goods, but also the finally victorious onset of cotton machine weaving, mechanized flax spinning, and the beginning of the migration of the textile workers to the coalfields. Neither agriculture nor factory employment offered an alternative. Those who could, emigrated; those unable, formed bands of beggars and took to the roads. The crisis of the 1840s began the mid-century European migration to industrial towns, and the process of the ruralization of the countryside which has gone on ever since.

What all this amounts to saying, is that it is misleading simply to see the crisis in Labrousse's terms as a combination of the traditional and the new. Rather, we should look at their dialectical interrelationship, and at the imbalances imposed on every economy in the period, including the British, by the crisis-ridden development of the textile sector which, I would argue, comes to an end with this crisis. The crisis in France and Germany in the countryside was not just a repeat of what had occurred on the eve of the first French revolution. The weakness of Labrousse's model is its failure to consider international trade in the export sector. Rural industry cannot be viewed as merely traditional. From the eighteenth century onwards it had been intimately tied to competition in the world market. The constriction of the export sector in France and Germany from the time of the Napoleonic wars and the large numbers of workers trapped within it, and the recurrent threat of invasion by English goods, accentuated pressure on the domestic market and thus made the crisis seem more traditional than it actually was. Conversely, the superiority of England in the export sector, particularly in extra-European trade by the 1840s, mitigated the impact of the crisis at home. Even with a considerable rise in the price of corn in 1846–47, the domestic market for manufactures was not hit so heavily as in France because unemployment was far less severe in those sectors of the economy dependent on exports.

If we wish to trace the connection between the crisis and the revolution, however, this difference between England and Europe would not be sufficient. Firstly, as Mark Traugott has shown elsewhere in this volume, the crisis in

England, while not as harsh as in France, was nevertheless severe; and conversely, the worst of the crisis in France was over before February 1848. It is impossible, anyway, to explain any revolution in purely or even primarily economic terms. An analysis of economic relations can pinpoint particular antagonisms between class and social groups, but cannot of itself explain why these tensions should not be resolved through particular forms or alliances that would leave the political structure intact. In this sense, it seems to me that what needs to be explained in France is not primarily the lower class discontent which emerged in the streets in February, but rather the defection of the *petit bourgeoisie* of Paris, whose national guardsmen refused to defend the Guizot ministry, and the growing divisions within the ruling notable class itself, which, to everyone's surprise, turned an apparently manageable political agitation within a few days into the headlong collapse of the monarchy and the regime.

I will not speculate about France, but say a few final words about 1848 in England. Firstly, as in France, there had been a growing lower middle class agitation in 1847—partly stimulated by the tight credit conditions—mainly focused around the stated Whig intention to raise the income tax (in fact on the pretext of an invasion scare from France). O'Connor and the Chartist leadership had placed great hopes in this evidence of shopkeeper discontent. But even before April 10 the London lower middle class had been strongly alienated from the Chartists. A meeting at Trafalgar Square, supposed to be addressed by the leader of the middle class agitation, Charles Cochrane, but in fact taken over by the recent Chartist convert G. M. W. Reynold, was followed by a riot and considerable looting in which it was said criminal elements were present. This brought to an end middle class sympathy for Chartism in that year and helps to explain the successful mobilization of the lower middle class as special constables on April 10. In general, the patterns of confrontation in England in 1848 confirm the picture I gave of Chartism having already been politically defeated from the early 1840s.[7] In the first half of the year there were considerable number of unemployment riots. Most contemporaries commented on the general youthfulness of the participants and Chartist activists were forced in several instances to disown these demonstrations even though Chartist slogans were sometimes shouted out. In general, one is struck by the absence of the large, threatening, but controlled meetings which had so impressed observers of Chartism in the late 1830s.

Secondly—and here perhaps is the main connection with the previous agricultural crisis—the momentum of Chartism such as it was in 1848, particularly after April 10, was mainly the result of the alliance between Chartists and Irish. The insurrectionary tone, the propensity to violent struggle, and most of the conspiratorial activity was centered around the Irish issue. Chartism itself was already a spent force. Even its own activists had become skeptical of its methods: the petition, the Convention, the appeal to the disaffected middle class. Only in the West Riding could it be said the movement was more than a shadow of its former self. The reason for this, as I have argued, has little to do with the disappearance of artisans or even outworkers; mainly, it was because Chartism had already been politically defeated in the years up to the repeal of the corn law. While republicanism and socialism proved growth points, capable in certain regions even of uniting towns and county in France between 1849 and 1851, in England the chances of any popular alliance comparable to the red republicans had been academic since the end of the 1830s. The economic stablization which occurred in the 1840s came after the political defeat and merely confirmed this trend, helping to establish the new framework of popular politics—affecting artisan and factory worker alike—which became predominant after the mid-century.

Notes

1. It is only fair to add that Tilly has since distanced himself from the terminology of modernization theory (See C., L. and R. Tilly, 1975:49–50). However, the ease with which his new classification of rebellion into *Competitive, Reactive and Proactive* may be reappropriated into the framework that I am discussing here, is indicated by the use to which these terms are put in Craig Calhoun's essay.
   My critique of Barrington Moore's position is developed in "Barrington Moore on Injustice," *Historical Journal*, v. 23, 4, 1980.

2. The figures, as cited however, I have taken from John Breuilly's stimulating paper comparing numbers, politics and values of British, French and German artisans in the nineteenth century (Breuilly 1980).

3. See for instances, the importance attached to this issue by Roger Price (1972), or from an orthodox Marxist perspective, Foster (1974).

4. The importance of the Irish issue in the Chartist disturbances of 1848 also comes through strongly in Gammage, 1854.

5. This issue is well discussed in Farnie, 1979; on cost and efficiency factors inhibiting the use of steam in the first half of the nineteenth century, see Von Tunzelmann (1978) and also Musson (1976).

6. For an account of the development of this gap, see Leboyer 1964 and 1968. For the way in which this affected the pattern of French industrial development, see Leboyer (1968). See also O'Brien and Keyder (1978).

7. This point is argued extensively in my "Rethinking Chartism" in (Stedman Jones 1983).

References

Abel, W. 1974. *Massenarmut und Hungerkrisen im Vorindustriellen Europa. Versuch Einer Synopsis*, Hamburg: P. Parey.

Belchem, J. 1982. "Feargus O'Connor and the Collapse of the Mass Platform," in J. Epstein and D. Thompson, eds., *The Chartist Experience*, London: Macmillan.

Borchardt, K. 1972. "The Industrial Revolution in Germany 1700–1914," in C. M. Cipolla, ed., *Fontana Economic History of Europe*, Part 1.

Breuilly, J. 1980. Unpublished mss, p. 6.

Clapham, J. H. 1926–38. *An Economic History of Modern Britain*, 3 vols, Cambridge: Cambridge University Press.

Conze, W. 1976. "Vom Pobel zum Proletariat," in H. U. Wehler, ed., *Moderne Sozialgeschichte*, Koln: Kiepenheur and Witsch.

Farnie, D. A. 1979. *The English Cotton Industry and the World Market 1815–1896*, Oxford: Oxford University Press.

Fischer, W. 1972. *Wirtschaft und Gesellschaft im Zeitalter der Industrialisierung*, Gottingen: Vandenhoeck and Ruprecht.

Foster, H. 1974. *Class Struggle and the Industrial Revolution*, London: Wiedenfeld and Nicolson.

Gammage, R. G. 1854. *History of the Chartist Movement*, London.

Habakkuk, H. J. 1962. *American and British Technology in the Nineteenth Century*, p. 147, Cambridge: Cambridge University Press.

Hardrach, K. W. 1972. "Some Remarks on German Economic Historiography and its Understanding of the Industrial Revolution in Germany," *Journal of European Economic History*.

Histoire quantitative de l'economie francaise. 1967. vol. 7, Cahiers de l'ISEA, Paris: Institut économique de statistique appliqué.

Hobsbawm, E. J. 1959. *Primitive Rebels: Studies in Archaic Forms of Social Movement in the Nineteenth and Twentieth Centuries*, Manchester: Manchester University Press.

Koselleck, R. 1976. "Staat und Gesellschaft in Preussen, 1815–1848," in H. U. Wehler, ed., *Moderne deutsche Sozialgeschichte*, Koln: Kiepenheur and Witsch.

Kriedte, P., H. Medick, and J. Schlumbohn. 1977. *Industrialisierung vor der Industrialisierung*, Gottingen: Vandenhoeck and Ruprecht.

Labrousse, E., ed. 1956. *Aspects de la crise et de la depression de l'economie francaise au milieu du XIX siècle*, La Roche-sur-Yonne.

Levy-Leboyer, M. 1964. *Les Banques europeennes et l'industrialisation internationale dans la première moitié du XIX Siecle*, Paris: Presses universitaire de France.

———. 1968. "Les Processus d'industrialisation: Le cas de l'Angleterre et de la France," *Revue Historique*.

Levine, D. 1977. *Family Formation in an Age of Nascent Capitalism*, New York: Academic Press.

Marquardt, F. D. 1974. "Working Class in Berlin in the 1840s" in the H. U. Wehler, ed., *Sozialgeschichte Heute: Festschrift fur Hans Rosenberg*, Gottingen.

Medick, H. 1976. "The Proto-industrial Family Economy: the Structural Function of Household and Family during the Transition from Peasant Society to Industrial Capitalism," *Social History*.

Moore, B., Jr. 1978. *Injustice, The Social Bases of Obedience and Revolt*, New York: Pantheon.

Motteck, H. 1964. *Wirtschaftsgeschichte Deutschland*, vol. 2, Berlin.

Musson, A. E. 1976. "Industrial Motive Power in the United Kingdom, 1800–1870," *Economic History Review*, 2nd series XXIX.

O'Brien, P., and C. Keyder. 1978. *Economic Growth in Britain and France 1780–1914: Two Paths to the Twentieth Century*, London: Allen and Unwin.

Pouthas, C. 1956. *La Population francaise pendant la première moitié du XIXe siècle*, Paris: Presses universitaire de France.

Price, R. 1972. *The French Second Republic: A Social History*, Ithaca, NY: Cornell University Press.

Prothero, I. J. 1971. "London Chartism and the Trades," *Economic History Review*.

———. 1979. *Artisans and Politics in Early Nineteenth Century London*, Folkestone, England: Dawson.

Reid, A. J. 1980. "The Division of Labour in the British Shipbuilding Industry 1880–1920 with Special Reference to Clydeside," Cambridge University Ph.D. dissertation.

Samuel, R. 1977. "The Workshop of the World: Steam Power and Hand Technology in Mid-Victorian Britain," *History Workshop*, no. 3.

Shanin, T. 1972. *The Awkward Class*, Oxford: Clarendon Press.

Sykes, R. 1982. "Early Chartism and Trade Unionism in S.E. Lancashire," and G. Stedman Jones, "Rethinking Chartism," in J. Epstein and D. Thompson, eds., *The Chartist Experience*, London: MacMillan.

Thompson, D. 1982. "Ireland and the Irish in English Radicalism and Chartism," in J. Epstein and D. Thompson, eds., *The Chartist Experience*, London: MacMillan.

————. "The Geography of Chartism," unpub. mss.

Thompson, E. P. 1971. "The Moral Economy of the English Crowd in the Eighteenth Century," *Past and Present*, 50:76–136.

Tilly, C. 1972. "The Modernization of Political Conflict in France," in E. B. Harvey, ed., *Perspectives on Modernization: Essays in Memory of Ian Weinberg*, Toronto: University of Toronto Press.

Tilly, C., L. Tilly, and R. Tilly. 1975. *The Rebellious Century, 1830–1930*, Cambridge: Harvard University Press.

Trevor-Roper, H. R. 1957. *Historical Essays*, pp. 179–205, London: Macmillan.

Von Tunzelmann, G. H. 1978. *Steam Power and British Industrialisation to 1860*, Oxford: Clarendon Press.

Wolf, E. 1969. "On peasant rebellions," *International Social Science Journal*, vol 21.

PART TWO

PEASANTS AND WORLD MARKET CYCLES: THE MORAL ECONOMY OF AGRARIAN SOCIAL MOVEMENTS

6

Market Demand Versus Imperial Control: Colonial Contradictions and the Origins of Agrarian Protest in South and Southeast Asia

MICHAEL ADAS

In the decades since the end of the Second World War, the study of peasant protest and agrarian revolution in Asia has been transformed from a peripheral sub-field, dominated by a handful of scholars and ex-colonial officials, into one of the central concerns of theoreticians, comparativists, and area specialists in virtually every social science discipline. At the most superficial level, this transformation has resulted from a fascination with the global repercussions of the victorious Communist-led peasant revolutions in China and Vietnam.

Many of the scholars—American, Asian, and European—who are engaged in the current discourse on peasant unrest came of age as intellectuals in the turbulent decades of revolutionary upheaval in post-war China and Vietnam's long struggle against foreign domination and rule by indigenous elites. More fundamentally, however, the growth of interest in peasant societies and movement was spurred by the rapid change and agrarian unrest that was associated with the era of decolonization. The centrality of social conflict in the Marxist ideologies that have exerted such a great influence in the emerging states of Asia, and the implicit assumptions of fundamental change and disruption in the tradition/modernity approach to societal development that has come to be regarded by some as a counter to the Marxist challenge, gave great impetus to the study of the sources of rural and urban unrest, of the conditions that made for revolution, and often of the measures needed to prevent them. The credibility of both approaches was in turn enhanced by their emphasis on change, conflict, and social unrest. A vast literature devoted to the "passing of traditional societies," "transitional" groups and institutions, political "disequilibrium," and "revolutions of rising expectations" provides dramatic testimony to the centrality of these concerns. The growing importance of social history and social anthropology which made long-neglected groups—workers, women, the elderly, peasants—the focus of their inquiry gave added importance to the study of agrarian protest. Though much work has been done on rural social structures and economic systems that is not directly related to peasant protest, a disproportionate share of the literature on the Asian countryside has been devoted to the study of peasant unrest.

The growth of interest in peasant societies and movements has produced much that is positive. It has resulted in a relative abundance of well-researched and detailed case studies in a field where reliable data, much less insightful analysis, was often difficult to locate several decades ago. These studies have made major contributions to our understanding of the organization and dynamics of agrarian systems over much of the Asian world. Our theoretical gains with regard to agrarian societies or peasant protest have on the whole been more modest, but existing theories have been tested or reformulated to take into account our greatly improved knowledge, and a number of important debates have been generated. There has also been a necessary reorientation for our approaches from elite- and Western-centric perspectives and political concerns to peasant views and responses and broader social and economic issues. As several scholars have recently argued both implicitly and explicitly, however, this reorientation may have gone too far (Skocpol 1979; Paige 1975). An exclusive or pre-ponderant emphasis on peasant concerns or a neglect of the critical roles of elite groups, whether they be European or Asian, has made for distortions, inaccuracies, and an incompleteness about much of this work that will have to be corrected by coming generations of scholars. The peasant-centric approach has also rendered much of the work that has been done somewhat tedious, increasingly inbred, and aimed at tiny groups of specialists. These tendencies have restricted the audience and blunted the impact of much of the important, recent work on peasant societies.

Although it has resulted in impressive advances in our understanding of peasant conditions and responses, the growing emphasis in the literature on agrarian societies in Asia and elsewhere on protest and rebellion and the conditions which give rise to these has distorted, I believe, our perception of the experience and reactions of the vast majority of agriculturists in the colonized world. The now commonplace assumption that the colonial age was everywhere a time of rapid change, disruption, and disorientation, which in turn produced frequent and widespread agrarian unrest, has gained acceptance as the result of a tendency, often unconscious, to generalize too readily from the experience of peasant groups in China and Vietnam, or turbulent frontier zones like the Panjab in India, the West Coast of Sumatra, or Lower Burma. Though we may well have overstated the extent of the transformations occurring in these societies and the degree of protest involvement by different peasant groups, we have certainly given dispro-portionate attention to these patterns in our attempts to develop general models to explain the peasant experience or rural resistance and protest in the Afro-Asian world. We have also tried to force the historical experience of societies where change was much more gradual, the persistence of pre-colonial institutions and ideas much more pronounced, and the incidence of overt protest rare into the change/conflict models that have come to dominate the literature on agrarian societies. This trend is perhaps most dramatically illustrated by the growing numbers of books and articles, by specialists working on India in a variety of disciplines, devoted to incidents or movements of rural protest. Though the actual "movements" described often amount to little (Jha 1977; Robb 1977; Kling 1966), the extensive coverage given to rural unrest in recent years provides a striking contrast with Barrington Moore's choice nearly two decades ago of India as a counter case—a society where massive poverty and oppression had produced little in the way of overt protest, much less revolution.

Our growing emphasis on socioeconomic disruption and peasant protest has led to a serious neglect of the "negative cases"—those agrarian situations where political and social transformations were less dramatic than we have come to assume and where the spread of agrarian production for the domestic or export market has generated little in the way of sustained protest on the part of cultivating groups. This neglect is particularly serious because the evidence produced to date indicates that these situations were overwhelmingly in the majority. With relatively rare exceptions, peasants have endured (depending on which theory of protest causation one employs) oppression, exploitation, grinding poverty, relative deprivation, the violation of custom and ethical codes, anomie, and alienation. Despite the prevalence of conditions that the models and theories of a growing cadre of social scientists postulate must have driven them to rebellion, there has been a surprising paucity of peasant protest movements in the Afro-Asian world.

The persistence, despite the coming of colonial rule, of long standing systems of social control and effective peasant defenses and non-confrontational modes of protest, rather than innate docility or habitual submission, can best explain the paucity of agrarian risings in the colonial and post-colonial eras in most of the Afro-Asian world. Despite the vision of relentless change and upheaval that has come to be accepted for the colonial era, in many peasant societies, especially those in densely-populated core areas like Bihar in India and Dutch-ruled Java which are the focus of this essay, the impact of European conquest and rule was far less dramatic and far less extensive, particularly at the village level, than recent approaches to colonized peasant societies would lead us to assume. In fact, colonial administrators in these areas deliberately fashioned political economies that promoted preservation, not innovation, security and stability, not risk-taking and rapid change. They sought to shield the areas they ruled from the social upheavals and disruption that they believed would result from too rapid and extensive an exposure to the forces for the global economy. They advocated colonial policies that were aimed at shoring up pre-colonial political institutions, social hierarchies, and patterns of economic exchange based primarily on personal interaction and patron-client bonds, rather than Western European capitalist principles of competition, contracts, and the cash nexus.

For decades the systems that colonial administrators created by incorporating pre-colonial elites, institutions, and symbols into an overarching bureaucratic grid staffed at the highest levels by Europeans, succeeded in limiting change and reducing rural unrest to a minimum. In the last decades of the nineteenth century, however, internal problems and external pressures—demands for reform emanating from Holland and Britain and global market forces—resulted in changes in Bihar, Java, and other similarly ruled Asian core regions, that undermined the systems of colonial control that had been so carefully fashioned. These forces also brought into being new social groups and competing interests that would ultimately bring about an end to European rule. Ironically, however, despite their struggles to end European domination, these groups were careful to preserve, though with significant modifications, the systems of dependence and control that had made centuries of European rule possible. Thus, though they rose up in protest, nationalist agitators—with the exception of important, but minority, radical elements—strove not to destroy the systems which had made possible their rise to prominence, but to "reform" or alter them in ways that would eliminate foreign and weaken indigenous rivals and provide even greater opportunities for them to enhance their wealth and power.

Although Bihar and different areas on Java passed under colonial rule at different times, the transition to European control had little immediate impact upon and went largely unnoticed by the peasants who made up the vast majority of the populations in these regions. In some cases, recalcitrant princes or regional lords were overthrown by the alien conquerors and there were some shifts in the power exercised by local notables and their dependents as they vied for the favor of indigenous leaders allied to the Europeans and occasionally European officials themselves. Little else changed—in some cases for decades. The European overlords, who assumed the responsibility for the governance of these areas in the late eighteenth or early nineteenth centuries, had neither the strength nor the desire to rule them in depth. The British, confidently citing the ideas of the "classical" economists on the advantages of an improving gentry (Guha 1963; Stokes 1959), conceded local authority and control to a motley collection of Bengali and Bihari ex-officials and local notables who were granted landlord status in the Western sense for the first time. Their titles, which ranged from *zamindar* and *jotedar* to *maharaja* and *taluqdar*, and the complex gradation of regional lords and petty notables that had existed in the pre-colonial period were largely retained, though the specific families and kin groups that controlled these positions changed substantially in some areas (Cohn 1969).

In Java, the Dutch also chose to rule though the pre-colonial aristocracy or *priyayi*. In contrast to Bengal and Bihar, the regents, as the Dutch labelled their *priyayi* subordinates, and lower level members of the indigenous administrative corps, were not granted landlord status as such. During the period of the Cultivation System, (1830–c.1870), some were "paid" in part for their services by grants of control over the surplus from specified areas of land (Deventer 1865–6:vol. 2, 141 ff). Nonetheless, for many decades, and in some areas for well over a century, the regents and their client subordinates dominated rural administration, often with only minimal supervision by Dutch officials (Sutherland 1973:chs. 1, 2; Burger 1948–9:390–398; Furnivall 1939:123–126, 141–142). As in most other densely populated Asian areas were European colonizers worked out similar arrangements with indigenous elite groups), petty officials and local notables, who had shared authority in the pre-colonial era, retained, and often improved upon their positions, in the early decades of colonial rule.

In both Java and Bihar the European colonizers enlisted the aid of indigenous elite groups not only because of personnel and resource shortages, but also because by retaining the long-established Javanese or Indian lords and notables they preserved, virtually intact highly developed and well-tested systems of social control. By incorporating indigenous elites into the colonial administrative grid the Europeans gained the institutional and ideological means to pacify and extract revenue on a regular basis from a large portion of the peasantry at various levels from occupant tenants and smallholders to landless laborers. Patron-client networks in different guises, which had formed the backbone of the pre-colonial political economy and had been essential to the maintenance of wealth and authority at all levels, were now drawn into the colonial bureaucratic structure.

In Bihar, as in other lowland areas of India, patron-client links were embedded in the caste hierarchy that had long formed the central and in many ways the defining element in Indian culture and civilization. By elevating patron or *jajman* caste groups to the status of landowners in the Western legal sense, which they had not been previously, and attaching them as political allies and revenue collectors to the British Raj, the colonizers greatly enhanced these groups already considerable control over *kamin* or client caste groups, including tenants, laborers, and village artisans.[1] Patron-client dependency and reciprocity were critical elements in the colonial formula for social control. By buttressing the ancient *jajman* system and caste organization generally, the British, often quite deliberately, reinforced the vertical orientation and compartmentalization that were key characteristics of pre-colonial patron-client systems. The often asserted notion that colonialism and the spread of capitalism and the market system atomized peasant societies and gave rise to competition, individualism, and the primacy of self-interest in the rural sphere, makes little sense when applied to societies like those found in Java and India. Social and economic exchanges were already compartmentalized and identity constricted by patron-client networks of dependency that promoted family and kinship orientations and cooperation. These webs of dependence also greatly impaired, if not altogether blocked, the emergence of even the feeblest sense of class consciousness or organization. Through calculation or instinct, colonial officials came to view these networks of dominance and exchange as essential props for the maintenance of stability and control in the rural sphere.

In Java, from the early 1700s when the Dutch began to assume control of the agrarian hinterland beyond their port centers on the north coast, they sought whenever possible to incorporate the *kawula-gusti* patron-client chains of the *priyayi* aristocracy and local leaders into the administrative hierarchy of the colonial regime. At the village level, and usually through the patronage powers exercised by their regional Javanese allies, the Dutch mobilized labor and extracted resources in collaboration with the *lurahs* or village headmen and the *sikeps* or prominent, usually land controlling families, within each peasant community. The acquiescence of these groups to Dutch rule was essential to control the great mass of the peasantry. (Deventer 1865–6:vol.2, 201; Kartodirdjo 1972:83–7; Onghokham 1975:161–76).

In both Java and India, the cooperation of regional and local elites meant that those groups that had had the broadest and strongest horizontal links, normally operating through kinship lineages or, in India, caste connections (Fox 1971), were firmly drawn into the colonial establishment, thereby eliminating (or at least greatly reducing) the potential for large-scale and widespread risings against European rule. The fact that these groups had often dominated military affairs in the pre-colonial era and that they often retained their weapons and ability to forcibly back up the demands they made of subordinate cultivators at various levels rendered their alliance with the colonizers all the more essential (Deventer 1865–6:vol.2, 201ff). As the British learned in the Indian "mutiny" of 1857–58 (Raj 1965:19–40; Metcalf 1964, 1979) and the Dutch in the Java War of 1825–30 (Palmer 1960:214ff; Schrieke 1966:219ff) when threatened aristocrats and landed groups led tens of thousands of retainers into open rebellions, indigenous elite groups were potent sources of leadership for resistance against colonial rule (Niel 1969:272–3). The co-option of these groups meant that a possible catalyst for dissidence was transformed into a bulwark of social control in the countryside.

In terms of regular revenue extraction and internal repression on a day-to-day basis, the adherence of indigenous elites was essential to the maintenance of colonial rule. Their private forces of armed retainers, which usually included local toughs or *goondas* in India and *jagos* in Java, meant that landlords and local notables could themselves quell disturbances mounted by disgruntled tenants or laborers through a variety of methods that ranged from crop confiscation and ejection to arson, torture, and murder.[2] European courts and laws based on private property and the sanctity of written contracts further buttressed the power of landlords and local officials (Harcourt 1977:332; Robb 1979:110; Kling 1966:51), but through most of the colonial period threats and violent reprisals proved the most expedient means of dealing with village "trouble makers."

The colonizers' decision to exercise their rule through indigenous elite groups at various levels meant that in Bihar and Java institutions and ideas that had given legitimacy to pre-colonial rulers and officials remained effective means of social control (Low 1973:18–21). This pattern contrasts sharply with the fate of elites and institutions in frontier zones like Lower Burma, where they were swept aside or Cochin China, where they were discredited by defeat and collaboration (Adas 1982; Marr 1971:chs. 2,3). In Java experienced Dutch officials stridently rejected suggestions that the status or powers of the *priyayi* be curbed or their roles reduced. Numerous writers argued that the continuance of Dutch rule was impossible without the cooperation for the regents and village. Dutch authors asserted that these indigenous officials possessed an aura of legitimacy and inspired a depth of peasant loyalty that could never be acquired by the Dutch themselves or even by Javanese administrators whom the Dutch appointed, no matter how well the latter were trained. Dutch officials also came to regard regents and other *priyayi* administrators, and the elaborate symbols and rituals of rule which they wielded, as the most potent antidotes to message of sedition and revolt preached by Muslim teachers and holymen (Boeka 1904; Deventer 1865–6:201–208). In fact, the Dutch were so impressed by the splendor and pageantry of the Javanese "theater state"[3] that they themselves adopted the use of gilded umbrellas and other symbols of Javanese authority (Di Nijs 1961, relevant photos). Though the position and powers of the regent allies of the Dutch varied by region and time period in the nineteenth century, their posts became hereditary and they persisted as the symbolic, if not the actual, locus of political authority in rural Java (Sutherland 1973:ch. 2; Palmier 1960).

If the pageantry was less grand in Bihar and the British somewhat less inclined to wield the physical symbols of Indian power, the role of indigenous allies in legitimizing European colonial rule was no less critical. The British periodically held lavish regional and all-India *durbars* to bolster ritually their ties to indigenous lords. But more than etiquette and elaborate costumes were necessary for the maintenance of an official's or estate owner's legitimacy. Donations to local temples and village shrines, the repair and construction of irrigation works, and dramatic gestures of material generosity were expected of those who exercised local power and claimed a share of the cultivator's harvest or his labor services. In Bihar, as in other areas of India, when these obligations were not fulfilled, cultivators grew resentful to the demands of the landlord class and at times openly challenged their authority.[4] Through much of the nineteenth century, however, the British and Dutch preservation of indigenous social hierarchies insured the persistence of peasant acceptance of stratification and inequities in wealth and power as part of the natural order of things—a view which Louis Dumont (1970) has argued has historically been essential to social cohesion and control in India, and, implicitly, in most pre-industrial societies.

Although patron-client ties and shared cultural values bound the peasant populations of areas like Java and Bihar to indigenous elites in a way they could never have been attached to alien European rulers, the exchanges between landed groups and indigenous bureaucrats and the mass of the cultivators heavily favored the form and were often harshly exploitative. Effective checks on excessive elite demands in the pre-colonial era were largely logistical. If ethical, these buffers were personalized and renegotiated with each encounter, rather than embedded in abstract moral codes, though pious injunctions about the welfare of the peasantry certainly existed. Thus, the fact that indigenous lords retained or increased their authority in the early decades of European rule in itself tells us little about the impact of colonialism on cultivating groups at various levels. Paternalist and patron-client ties could be used in ways that were as oppressive and exploitative as those based on impersonal contracts and cash payments. In social systems where patron-client reciprocity comprised the matrix of economic exchanges and socio-political cohesion, the consciousness of subordinate cultivating groups (as Marx n.d.:18–21 has argued, the cultivating classes as a whole) was highly constricted. Their vertical orientation and social compartmentalization meant that it was rare for tenants or laborers to reorganize effectively for bargaining or resistance to the oppressive exactions of landlords or local officials even within a single village. Geographical and occupational mobility were normally limited, and legal means of cultivator redress of grievances—beyond reliance on precedents established by longstanding custom—were virtually non-existent. Protest, on the rare occasions when it took the form of riot or rebellion, was almost always in support of the cultivators' patron or their patron's lord. Protest against their patrons occurred only in the most desperate circumstances and normally involved flight into the wilderness or (preferably) the transfer of the cultivators' allegiance and services to another patron official, religious leader, or bandit chief (Adas 1982:226–239).

Although ruling through the indigenous elites greatly reduced the costs to the British and Dutch of maintaining internal order, it also greatly limited the amount of control which European or European-trained administrators could exert at the village level. In fact, the level of day-to-day contact between European officials and the peasant population was so minimal under regimes that are conventionally classified as those exhibiting direct rule, that one might well conclude that the standard direct/indirect categorization misleads than informs by concealing critical differences within each type and making too sharp a distinction between them. Because ongoing social control was left to indigenous elites and institutions, British and Dutch intervention in local affairs was sporadic and confined to intermittent tours of inspection and occasions where conflict or peasant unrest threatened serious disturbances. The colonizers routinely responded to the latter situations by stationing extra police or regular military forces in the affected areas (BPP). Thus, the overwhelming edge in military technology, organization, and communications which the Europeans possessed by the mid nineteenth century normally played only a passive role in the maintenance of colonial control. It provided the ultimate guarantee of the authority of the Europeans and their indigenous allies, not the omnipresent force that is central to Frantz Fanon's (1968) Manichaean vision of the colonial world. It could, however, be employed with devastating effect when the Europeans' allies or the colonial regime itself were threatened.

The limits to the control over local affairs that the Europeans were able to exercise were most strikingly revealed by the poor quality of colonial population, revenue, and crop yield statistics. In both Bihar and Java, records keeping and revenue collection were left in the hands of village notables and petty functionaries. Because revenue demands in Bihar (and Bengal and Orissa) were fixed by the terms of the Permanent Settlement of 1782 which the British struck with those rural elite groups who would come to make up the landlord class, British officials had little to do with the gathering and compilation of statistics at the village level. These figures were, of course, the basis for all records keeping relating to rural areas throughout the colonial period. Village crop and population statistics were kept either by high caste, literate *patwaris* or low caste, illiterate *chaukidars* depending on the area in question. For different reasons both groups subordinated the demands of supra-village elite groups to village interests. *Patwaris* were normally related to or closely allied with the dominant, land-controlling caste groups within the village they served. Therefore, the consistent under-reporting of population totals and crop production, and hence the amount of services or produce that had to be yielded up to non-village landlords or officials, enriched both the *patwaris* and the dominant caste families in the village. In villages where low caste *chaukidars* were in charge of crop and revenue records, high caste families found it relatively easy, and perhaps less costly than alliances with *patwaris*, to bribe and browbeat these untrained and impoverished functionaries who were usually treated like menial servants (Dewey 1979:280–286; Robb 1979:102–103, 108–110; BAR 1916; 12, 1917:9).

Because the Permanent Settlement barred increases in the revenue demands made by the British, the periodic settlements and revenue revisions that gave the British a much clearer, though by no means wholly accurate, impression of the productivity and manpower resources of areas ruled in greater depth like Burma, Maharashtra, and the Panjab were non-existent in Bihar. Thus, as British revenue officials freely conceded, agrarian statistics were, on the whole, little more than "absurd guesses" through most of the period of British rule (Dewey 1979:283).

In Java, where village headmen and their kin and client allies monopolized records keeping, revenue collection, and census counts, the Dutch and their Javanese and Chinese allies literally had to "dicker" with village leaders to set the amount of revenue due. In the absence of cadastral surveys (which were not carried out until the last decades of the nineteenth century), assessments were "arbitrary and inexact" and village heads were "unusually successful" in disguising the extent of village cultivation and the productivity of the are cropped (Niel 1964:358). A recent estimate based on a careful study of the reports on the working of the Cultivation System in the middle decades of the nineteenth century reveals that on average only 70–75 percent of the population and land cultivated were actually reported in the 1830s and 1840s (Niel 1972:98, 108–109; also Vitalis 1851:2–3). To avoid increases in crop delivery demands or labor services, village and district heads simply neglected to list population growth that resulted from in-migration or natural increase or new lands that came into cultivation. Because the Dutch, like the British in India, did not have the trained personnel to check local returns in a rigorous manner, most reports went un-challenged even though European officials and the regents were well aware that they were riddled with inaccuracies and deliberate attempts to deceive (Fasseur 1978:16, 21–22, 61–62, 98–99; Onghokham 1975:155–156, 212, 216; J. L. V. 1855:6).

In both Java and Bihar alliances struck with indigenous elite groups and the colonizers' failure to intervene effectively at the village level resulted in large losses of revenue to the European overlords. Due to severe shortages of trained administrators and the obsession with low costs of governance exhibited by the officials and legislators who increasingly shaped colonial policy from the European metropolis, there appeared to be no viable alternatives. To effect change at the local level or extract greater revenues, the colonizers had to put pressure on the indigenous elites that had made their low cost rule possible. As the Dutch were reminded by the Java War and the British by the "mutiny," to press these groups too hard, or even worse to attempt to displace them, endangered the longstanding hierarchies of dependence and control that gave some semblance of legitimacy to European rule (Robb 1979:110).

The loss of revenue that resulted from the inefficiency of ruling largely through indigenous elite groups was, as was intended, offset to a considerable degree by the low level of peasant unrest. Compared to the turbulent frontier zones like Lower Burma and the Mekong Delta region of Vietnam, where the collapse of the indigenous order and far-reaching social and economic changes severely eroded the efficacy of pre-colonial systems of social control, overt peasant resistance was rare in Java and Bihar. This contrast is even more striking if one takes into account the fact that the population of Bihar and Java, both in density and in absolute terms, was far greater than that in Lower Burma or Cochin China, where peasant risings were far more frequent. In part this difference can be attributed to the contrasting fates of the elites and symbols of legitimacy in each region. Equally critical, however, to the lower level of overt resistance to colonial rule in areas like Bihar and Java was the persistence beneath the highest levels of administration of pre-colonial systems of social control and revenue extraction. The survival of indigenous elites and institutions, especially at the village level, meant that most modes of ongoing defense and non-confrontational resistance that cultivating groups had devised in the pre-colonial period to buffer elite demands and check oppression remained viable well into the colonial era, they were usually small-scale and infrequent. Rather, the great majority of the cultivators continued to rely on evasive techniques of defense and protest. Thus, Judith Brown's (1972:464) contention that Indian peasants, before the emergence of Gandhi, had no protest alternatives other than rioting, not only gives undue emphasis to confrontational modes of agrarian resistance, it conveys a distorted image of the nature of the social and political framework in which peasants acted and the economic conditions to which they responded.

As in the pre-colonial period, poor records and the failure of the bureaucracy to penetrate to the village level left ample openings for concealment and evasion which had long been the first line of peasant defense. The complex maze of rights and sub-rights to the land that had evolved over the centuries in Bihar and Java made it possible for local officials and village notables in charge of tax collection or labor recruitment to baffle even the most diligent landlords' agents in Bihar or revenue officials in Java. Even in areas where landlords employed overseers or relatives to check up on local conditions, crop returns were grossly under-reported, newly cultivated fields went unrecorded, and the actual state of land control in the village—which in Bihar was normally dominated by tenants and not landowners—remained largely a mystery to supra-village elites, most especially the Europeans. When villages were assessed on a communal basis, as was the case in Java during the period of the Cultivation System, concealment and collusion worked to the advantage of the village as a whole. In both Java and Bihar, however, these modes of peasant defense best served the interests of the dominant land and records controlling groups in the village just as they had in the precolonial period. In some instances (Deventer 1865–6: vol. 2, 195; Vitalis 1851: xiv, 18) the weak control exerted by the colonial overlords led to extortion and excessive demands by petty officials who were not above resorting to torture and force to have their way. As the ties between groups of high caste tenants in Bihar and *sikep* families in Java and subordinate cultivating groups shifted from paternalist, patron-client links to contractual exchanges, tax and labor service evasion increasingly shielded and enriched locally dominant families and ambitious market producers, often at the expense of the great majority of the village dwellers (Robb 1979:119; Fasseur 1978:21–22, 86; Niel 1972; 98, 105).

Because unclaimed arable land and local shortages of labor persisted into the first decades of the twentieth century, flight and migration remained viable peasant defenses against elite oppression, as they had been in the pre-colonial era. In Java disgruntled cultivators migrated, at times *en masse*, from areas where the burdens of the Cultivation System were too great to those where labor and production demands were lighter. Of the crops introduced by the Dutch, indigo was the most demanding in terms of time and labor. The movement of populations from areas where indigo was grown to coffee or sugar growing areas, or those outside the Cultivation System entirely, is particularly notable (Elson 1978:26; Niel 1972:103; Fasseur 1978:39, 53). In some instances dissident cultivators fled into areas still ruled by Javanese lords, albeit under Dutch tutelage (Vitalis 1851:46). In times of soaring rice prices and famine, which were arguably linked to the substitution of export for subsistence crops (Elson 1978:15–16, 22; Soest 1869:3, 109ff; 165ff; 206–207, Pierson 1868:33–34, 152; Vitalis 1851:21, 35, 42, 55–57), there were large-scale migrations from areas where excessive Dutch quotas had resulted in famine conditions (Fasseur 1978:85, 88; Vitalis 1851:xi, 4).

As the most recent major study of the Cultivation System demonstrates (Fasseur 1978), migration was the Javanese peasants' major form of defense against and resistance to the changes and increased burdens which colonial demands introduced into the countryside. Peasant families—including well-to-do households—migrated to escape arrogant officials, increased labor demands, or excessive tribute quotas. The use of migration both as a defense and an act of protest is the most clearly illustrated by instances where peasants who had fled their home villages returned when official abuses ceased or revenue quotas were lowered. In some cases peasants who had fled migrated yet again when officials in the district to which they had first moved tried to force them to perform labor services similar to those which they had originally resisted (Soest 1869:3, 205). In some instances peasant migrants explicitly stated that the reason for their flight was a protest of government demands. Cultivators who had migrated from the Japara region in northeast Java in the late 1840s informed government officials who inquired into the causes for their flight that in addition to customary services they were required to transport sugar cane and firewood—extra services for which they received no wages. They complained that demands linked to the Cultivation System were so heavy that they had little time to cultivate the fields on which they grew the crops for their own subsistence (Soest 1869:3, 205; Vitalis 1851:xiv, 4). Peasants who fled from areas subject to the Cultivation System in the neighboring districts of Demak and Grobgan in the 1850s voiced similar complaints about government demands for tobacco production. The refugees brazenly declared to inquisitive Dutch officials that they had migrated to protest excessive labor demands and that they would not return to their home districts until forced tobacco cultivation there was ended (Pierson 1868:154–155).

In Bihar, as in Java, flight was a major mode of peasant defense. At times large tracts were left virtually deserted by cultivators fleeing special taxes by Indian landlords or the forced exactions of European planters. In the late nineteenth century, British revenue officials remarked on the stronger bargaining position and consequently the better conditions enjoyed by Bihari tenants who lived in areas where uncultivated arable land, and thus the option of flight, was still available (Robb 1979:105). Until the first decades of the twentieth century the possibility for cultivators who worked estates located in the northernmost areas of the district. Marriage alliances with families living in Nepal and the rather meager material possessions of most Bihari tenants and laborers facilitated this movement which severely undercut the productive capacity of affected estates. As in Java, when conditions improved in the area of departure or overly zealous estate agents were dismissed, large numbers of cultivators would return to their home districts (Henningham 1979:55; O'Malley 1907:38–39).

Labor shortages in some areas (particularly those where new lands were being brought into cultivation for the first time) and the consequent competition of land controlling groups for seasonal and long-term workers meant that some possibilities existed for tenants and laborers to escape exploitation by transferring their services to competing landholders (Sinha 1918:18–19, 26–27; Ray 1973:114, 116–117; Robb 1979:113–114; Kumar 1968:45, 47). Though available evidence indicates that this was a preferred mode of peasant defense in the pre-colonial era (Adas 1981:229–232), the rather infrequent mention of it in the available sources makes it difficult to determine if it remained preferred by cultivators to the high risks preferred by cultivators to the high risks and great labor involved in settling unoccupied areas. Its infrequent mention may be due to the fact that wage and contract labor made the severing of landlord and tenant or laborer ties a good deal easier and much more common than in the pre-colonial period and thus it attracted little in the way of special attention.

Because colonial laws and land tenure systems were loaded heavily in favor of landowning and official groups, and resort to court actions was too expensive for most cultivators, legal avenues of grievance redress were seldom employed until the first decades of the twentieth century. The likelihood that tenants or laborers would turn to the local magistrate with their complaints was also limited because the rural police were almost invariably in collusion with or at least under the control of landholders, headmen, and other local notables. The response of one old man to Gandhi's inquiry in Champaran, Bihar, in 1917 vividly dramatizes the peasants' well-founded mistrust of legal channels of redress. This man who had lost his lands and had had his house pulled down by the local landlord's toughs, reported that when he went to the magistrate to complain of his brutal treatment he was rudely dismissed with a clear threat of bodily harm if he should persist with his complaints. The lesson, he concluded, was clear— "all *topiwallahs* (officials) are the same (Prasad 1949:15). A similar attitude was displayed by peasants in north central Java who were migrating to avoid excessive labor demands. When asked by Dutch officials why they had not taken their complaints to local Javanese officials, they responded incredulously that the option simply was not possible for the "little man" or *wong tjilik* (Pierson 1868:155).

Although tenants and laborers avoided the courts and police, they often resorted to petitions and processions of protest to the residences of government officials; these had been standard modes of peasant dissidence in the pre-colonial era (Kling 1966:68, 168; O'Malley 1938:83–85; Henningham 1979:63, 65–66; Kartodirdjo 1973:25, 28–29; Vitalis 1851:46; Fasseur 1978:47). Work refusals are also recorded and these were sometimes combined with protest processions (Pierson 1868:150). Because this sort of dissidence struck at the very heart of the colonial revenue system, it was usually dealt with harshly by colonial officials. At times, however, protest demonstrations or work refusals prompted investigations of local conditions, some concessions to dissident cultivators, and in a number of instances the dismissal or demotion of offending officials (Vitalis 1851:11–13).

The failure of peasant defensive tactics or non-confrontational modes of protest periodically led to the eruption of overt, at times violent, riots or rebellions. Until the first decades of the twentieth century, however, rural disturbances appear to have been surprisingly infrequent, small-scale, and short-lived in both Bihar and Java. Banditry or dacoity was endemic to many areas of both regions (*BPP*, Criminal Caste Reports: *passim*; Sinha

1918:18–19: Onghokham 1975: 231ff; Siau Giap 1968:111–112; Anon. 1861:289–300), but it is difficult to determine the extent to which it was a symptom of social unrest or merely a continuation of the pattern of professional, often hereditary, criminality that was associated with certain social groups in the pre-colonial era. In fact, in many areas bandit gangs remained in collusion with and often linked by kinship ties to local notables and indigenous officials (Vitalis 1851:6–7)—a pattern that had been widespread in the pre-colonial period. Colonial officials understandably tried to play down the degree to which criminal activities were linked to peasant discontent, but in certain instances in both Java and Bihar, clear connections existed between poor economic conditions, cultivators' distress, and increases in banditry and other criminal activities. Due, however, to the much greater risks involved in banditry in the colonial period, when the police and military were better trained and armed than in the pre-colonial era, it is probable that vandalism, arson, crop destruction and theft, and other forms of sometimes violent, but short-term and clandestine reprisal, became the preferred modes of peasant resistance to excessive demands by landlords and tax collectors. Unfortunately, though some of the more notorious incidents involving these forms of protest were recorded in police records (O'Malley 1938:833, 87, 89; Kling 1966:88, 93; Onghokham 1975:226, 230) most were too minor to come to the attention of colonial officials. As a result, it is impossible to estimate how important arson or vandalism became as modes of peasant response—though as I shall argue below, they became widespread in the turbulent first decades of the twentieth century.

Given the large agrarian populations of both Bihar and Java and the long time span during which these areas were under colonial rule, rioting or more sustained agrarian risings were far rarer than our conflict-oriented models of peasant societies would lead us to assume. Though there were disturbances in some parts of Bihar during the Indian "Mutiny" of 1857–58, the most serious challenges to British rule during the crisis in the district came in highland tribal areas, not in the densely populated lowlands where, as in Bengal, most of the rural elite groups and the cultivators subordinate to them remained loyal to the colonial regime or at least refused to support the rebel cause (Majumdar 1963:140–44; Datta 1957). Despite British charges that the district was one of the main centers of Muslim fundamentalist Wahhabite activity (Sen 1957:245–247), there is little evidence that this resulted in overt or violent challenges to colonial rule.[5] Hindus, who made up a large majority of the district's population, would, of course, have had little sympathy for such efforts. In fact, the available evidence suggests that social tensions were more often released through communal clashes than protest against the colonial overlords or their landlord allies. Paralleling these communal disturbances were innumerable petty squabbles between different villages or tenant holders over field boundaries, stray cattle, water rights, and crop shares (*BPP*, 1911–1931, passim). Other than protest aimed at European indigo planters, which will be discussed in more detail below, there is not evidence of major violent risings against the British until the decades of crisis in the early twentieth century. This absence of overt protest provides eloquent testimony to the effectiveness of the British strategy of ruling as much as possible through indigenous elites and institutions.

In Java peasant risings were more frequent than in Bihar, but, relative to the large population ruled, surprisingly few and generally quite feeble. Ironically, despite the greater concern of the Dutch to preserve and themselves adopt the symbols and rituals that had given political legitimacy to the Javanese *priyayi*, conspiracies and peasant risings focusing on the alien and infidel nature of Dutch rule posed a far more serious challenge in Java than in Bihar. The greatest threat to Dutch rule was posed by the risings that were touched off by the spillover of the widespread rebellion led by Prince Dipanagara between 1825 and 1830 which extended beyond the princely states to the north coast residencies and east-central Java. After the rebellion, which had been led by a mix of threatened *priyayi* officials and Muslim religious figures, the Dutch consciously, and by and large successfully, placated *priyayi* resistance by guaranteeing the position of the princes and restoring much of the power and status that the *bupati* regents had lost in the era of reform under Daendels and Raffles in the first decades of the nineteenth century.[6]

Muslim dissidents, however, could not be mollified or coopted by the infidel and secular-minded Dutch. Muslim teachers (*kyais*) and holymen became, therefore, the main foci of anti-colonial resistance in the years after the Java War. Their determination to overthrow the Dutch was exacerbated by the anti-Muslim policies pursued by the Netherlands Indies regime and by contact between Javanese Muslims and Middle Eastern Muslim fundamentalist and revivalist movements through the *hadj* to Mecca (Anon. 1891:1768–1776). The fact that the great majority of Javanese were at least nominally Muslim, in contrast to Bihar where Muslims were in the minority, gave the threat which Muslim holymen and religious teachers appeared to pose for the Dutch added potency. The fears of Dutch officials and planters, which often bordered on paranoia (Shoemaker 1896) were not entirely without foundation, as was demonstrated by periodic risings in west and central Java led by Muslim religious figures. In some instances these risings, which were usually brief and localized, resulted in the deaths of Dutch planters and their families or *priyayi* officials. Most of these outbursts involved small groups of peasants led by Muslim teachers or holymen who, like Dipanagara, relied on amulets, eschatological prophecies, and their ability to inspire fanatical devotion on the part of their followers to rally (Cary 1979:87–91; Kartodirdjo 1966, 1973; Vitalis 1851:8–9). Fortunately for the Dutch, all of these rebellions were small-scale affairs and thus easily suppressed.[7] Therefore, despite the disproportionate attention given in recent years to overt protest in nineteenth century Java, the study of social control and the persistence of pre-colonial modes of non-confrontational defense and protest is of much greater relevance if we are concerned with the condition and responses of the great majority of the rural Javanese population.

If colonial officials had only to maintain the patchwork combinations of European and indigenous officials and institutions that constituted most colonial regimes, it is reasonable to argue that European imperialist dominance would have been far more enduring than it has proven to be. The Indian Civil Service or the Netherlands Indies Binnenlands Bestuur did not operate in a vacuum, however, but were forced to take into account policy directives predicated on the needs and demands of their respective European metropolises, and the requirements of an ever-expanding global market economy. These external forces generated changes that colonial officials often welcomed initially as beneficial for the colonized peoples, but came eventually to regard as fundamentally disruptive to the systems of social control that had so painstakingly been put together in the early decades of European rule. Attempts to improve and extend bureaucratic control of levy new taxes, the spread of new forms of economic activity, and dramatic shifts in demographic patterns produced new social groups and divisions that threatened the alliances on which the Europeans had based their rule and undermined the centuries-old networks of dependence and modes of defense upon which European global dominance had been based.

Many of the administrative changes that upset the fragile balance between European control and intervention and the continued dominance of indigenous elite groups that had been established in the late eighteenth and early nineteenth centuries, were brought about in response to needs and conditions within the colonies themselves. In all cases, however, ideas and demands emanating from Britain and Holland impinged to a greater and greater extent on the formulation of administrative and revenue policy. Proponents of social reform and the cause of the laboring classes in Europe often extended their campaigns to colonial questions involving the peasantry and urban workers (Fasseur 1978: chs. 4,6; Das 1964). By late nineteenth century liberal, socialist, or even reform conservative standards, the social and political systems produced by the Permanent Settlement in Bihar or the Cultivation System in Java were exotic anachronisms riddled with corruption, inefficiency, and openings for the exploitation of the cultivating classes. Scandals in Java that spread to Holland and debates in the Hague were decisive in the Dutch decision to abandon the Cultivation System and inaugurate the highly touted Liberal Policy. Though British officials in India usually acted more on their own initiative than did the Dutch in Java, the heightened sense of responsibility that was enshrined, however hypocritically, in the *"mission civilisatrice"* gave important impetus to efforts to introduce agrarian reforms in the late nineteenth century.

Bureaucratic reform at the most basic level meant better trained administrative personnel which in the late nineteenth century was synonymous with the rapid expansion of Western-language educational institutions among the colonized peoples. This trend gave rise to the new urban-based elite groups that would eventually wrest power from the European overlords and some of their indigenous allies, but its effects were not really felt in rural Bihar or Java until the first years of the twentieth century. Of more immediate significance were the series of agrarian reform bills that were put into effect in India and Java in the late nineteenth century and the growing involvement of colonial officials in local affairs. Though intended to check only the most serious abuses of landlord groups and indigenous officials, agrarian reform measures often provided the basis for fundamental challenges by subordinate groups to the longstanding dominance of indigenous elites. The ability of estate owners in Bihar or local and regional officials in Java to levy special taxes, turn troublesome tenants off their lands, or manipulate the local judiciary or constabulary was restricted at a time when the financial position and authority of these groups were under assault from other quarters (Robinson 1971:314, 328–329; Robb 1979:11).

Most critically, agrarian bills and judicial reforms could provide effective legal buffers for smallholder, tenant, and laboring classes for the first time. The rise of the vernacular press in both Bihar and Java, and the protracted and often polemical struggles that were necessary to enact these reforms, also served to instill an awareness on the part of cultivating groups of their legal rights. Though landlord interests continued to dominate court actions, increasing evidence from different areas in India indicates that court suits had also become a weapon of tenants and smallholders under certain conditions. In Madras, for example, disgruntled tenants used barrages of court cases to wear down financially strapped landlords to the point where rent demands became too expensive to collect (Baker 1976:27–29). More commonly, tenants, often allying themselves with urban-based lawyers connected to the Congress Party and other nationalist organizations, used the courts to challenge the levying of special taxes or gifts by landlords or to establish their claims to occupancy tenant status which gave them secure tenure and other special privileges as a result of the land reform bills of the late nineteenth century (Sengupta 1971:195).

In addition to agrarian reform, there were major efforts in the late nineteenth century in both Java and Bihar to increase the reach of the colonial bureaucracy and promote its involvement in local affairs in the rural areas. In part these initiatives, as well as the economic innovations discussed below, were the responses of financially troubled regimes. As inflation, the need for additional personnel, and soaring military expenses made it increasingly difficult to balance colonial budgets, European administrators sought new ways to raise revenues and insure that a greater share of what they claimed as their due actually reached the imperial coffers. Though income taxes that were introduced in India as one way of keeping up with expenses affected mainly urban groups, they indirectly fueled rural unrest. These taxes, which were linked to the spread of local self-government, angered mercantile and landholding interests that increasingly sought to rally mass support among rural cultivators for their anti-colonial campaigns (Robinson 1971:324–325; Pandey 1978). In both Java and Bihar village dwellers were more directly affected by sanitation campaigns, drives to inoculate peasant families and livestock against disease, efforts to improve roads and build bridges while the colonizers saw these as essential to improvements in rural welfare, they were often regarded by peasants as bothersome sources of extra demands for labor and resources (Furnivall 1956:430–432).

In some cases the tightening of administrative control clearly worked against the interests of subordinate cultivating groups. In their effort to set aside additional forest reserves and improve surveillance over those already established, for example, colonial administrators deprived the peasant populations which lived in areas near woodlands of free firewood and timber for construction, as well as a wide variety of supplementary foods and medicinal plants. In both Bihar and Java (Benda and Castles 1969:212, 221; Henningham 1979:59, 60, 63) access to forest zones and the right to use tree products in cultivated areas became major sources of friction between government officials or landlords and smallholders, tenants, and landless laborers. More pervasive, however, was peasant anxiety about or overt hostility towards government efforts, through special inquiries and regular census counts to gain more accurate estimates of the population, land resources, and landholding patterns in the areas under colonial control. Peasants rightly perceived that these efforts were a vital threat to many of their most potent means of defense against excessive government and elite demands. As a result, despite some improvements in records collecting, government efforts to upgrade the quality of their data on rural conditions were largely frustrated—again by a shortage of personnel and funds and especially local collusion and concealment (J. L. V. 1855:6–7; Fasseur 1978:62; Dewey 1979:302ff).

As important as administrative reforms and land tenure legislation were in eroding the systems of social control which had upheld colonial rule in Java and Bihar through most of the nineteenth century, their impact was far less extensive and disruptive than the market forces that increasingly penetrated these areas from mid-century onwards. A steadily rising demand in industrializing Europe and later North America for foodstuffs (coffee, tea, sugar, groundnuts, rice) and industrial crops (jute, hemp, palm oil, indigo, cotton) gave impetus to a global communications and transport revolution that began to have significant effects on Java and Bihar in the 1840s and 1850s. In the same period there was a related and rapid spread of the production of export crops in colonized areas under a wide variety of production systems ranging from the plantation zones of Sumatra and Assam to the smallholder economies of Ghana and Minangkabau. In most instances the demand for tropical produce was complemented by a need to find new market outlets for cheap consumer goods and, on a more selective and limited basis, investment capital.[8] Roads, canals, and railway lines were constructed, first in India, and later in Southeast Asia, Africa, and the Middle East, to link crop producing areas to port outlets where improved sailing vessels and, increasingly, steamships could carry them to Europe, North America, and, by the 1890s, Japan for processing, consumption, and sometimes reshipment (Harnetty 1972; Allen and Donnithorne 1957). For most crops[9] the last decades of the nineteenth century were an era of steadily rising demand and, as a result, increasing prices. These conditions drew growing numbers of cultivators throughout the colonial world deeply into production for domestic and overseas markets. Though often viewed as essential concomitant of European imperialist expansion and proudly touted by its defenders as an index of the benefits bestowed by colonial rule, this involvement ultimately did much to break the hold which the European colonizers and their indigenous allies had maintained over rural Asia for most of the nineteenth century.

Some colonial officials voiced concern over the disruptive effects of the rapid spread of market production. In both Java and Bihar this concern appeared to be well-founded, in view of the close association that had already been observed in the early and mid-nineteenth century between agrarian unrest and the presence of European-run estates producing for the export market in each area. In Java the *Particuliere Landerijen* or private estates leased to Europeans or Chinese had been the target of peasant uprisings and labor protest with a frequency that was far out of proportion to the small numbers of Javanese cultivators involved in crop production for these enterprises (Kartodirdjo 1973: ch.2). In Bihar disputes between European indigo planters and the Indian laborers and tenants who worked the lands these entrepreneurs leased from Indian landlords were virtually the only agrarian disturbances in the district in the late nineteenth century (Misra 1967). In neighboring Bengal this connection was even more pronounced and indigo disturbances more frequent and far more serious (Kling 1966).

As export production spread beyond the European and great landlord estates, however, the threats which market involvement posed for systems of colonial control in Java and Bihar multiplied rapidly. A new class of market-oriented, relatively prosperous cultivators emerged in each area. For Bihar, and elsewhere in India, this process has been studied in some detail. In Bihar occupancy tenants, usually from high caste groups, appear to have been the main beneficiaries of increased involvement in market production and to have concentrated their efforts on cultivating foodstuffs for sale both domestically and overseas (Fisher 1979:122–128; Charlesworth 1979; Kumar 1968:45, 54–55; Robinson 1971:319–320).

Much less work has been done on the emergence of market-oriented farmers in Java, in part because of the hold which Clifford Geertz's (1966) brilliantly argued concepts of agricultural involution and shared poverty have exercised over a generation of scholars of Indonesian history. In recent years, however, many of Geertz's ideas have been challenged (Kano 1980). As a result, there is a growing body of evidence which indicates, though by no means conclusively, that the levelling process which Geertz pictured for rural Java as a consequence of the Cultivation System and Liberal Policy was by no means all-inclusive (Elson 1978:7–8, 24–25, 30). In some areas of Java, at least (Tjeribon, Semerant, Bagelen), local notables and land-controlling families not only amassed considerable holdings, but achieved positions of wealth and power through a combination of production for the market and their roles as the intermediaries in negotiations between village communities and Dutch entrepreneurs or revenue collectors. From the first years after the imposition of the Cultivation System, dominant families in the areas where it was introduced reaped great profits from the cuts they were given for tribute produce collected, the control they gained over village lands, and their monopoly of lucrative, local administrative posts (Vitalis 1851:10; Niel 1969:269–270, 274–275; 1972:98, 104–105). Thus, in part at least, the social stratification and divisions between landed and landless classes that characterize rural Java today had their roots in the changes in the island's political economy effected by the Dutch in the middle of the nineteenth century (Elson 1978:20–21, 28–29; Onghokham 1975:201, 206–208). Though the Dutch intended to limit the direct involvement of the Javanese peasantry in the market economy through the introduction of the quasi-tribute Cultivations System, the use of cash payments for produce delivered, and the introduction of export crops on a vast scale frustrated the colonizer's aims and revived and expanded the inland marketing network that had been in decline for decades (Fasseur 1978:36–37; Kartodirdjo 1978:88–89).

However small the numbers of cultivators involved, the growth of a market-oriented class of farmers in Bihar and Java proved increasingly troublesome for colonial regimes that rested on alliances with indigenous elites and the preservation of paternalistic networks of dependency and exchange. In Bihar and other areas of India market-oriented tenants, and in some regions smallholders, vied with European estate managers and Indian landlords for control over land, water rights, and labor. For landless laborers or sharecroppers, the rise of market-oriented tenants, and in some regions smallholders, vied with European estate managers and Indian landlords for control over land, water rights, and labor. For landless laborers or sharecroppers, the rise of market-oriented production meant an increased potential for geographical and occupational mobility within Bihar, which complemented the more limited outlets for work which migration overseas or to the plantations of Assam and towns of Bengal had long provided (Zachariah 1964:200ff; Government of India, *Emigration Proceedings*, [hereafter cited as *EP*] 1875). though it is difficult to know whether the living standard of the laboring classes improved or declined, given population increases and presumably growing competition for jobs and inflation through much of the late nineteenth century, their gains in mobility meant a loss of control on the part of landlord groups.[10] The great increase in cash cropping and the shipping of market produce outside of the areas where it was grown also meant local shortages of food. These were often blamed for famine and price inflation and thus became sources of rural discontent and at times outbursts of protest (Robinson 1971:319). Though these patterns need to be explored in greater depth, they appear to suggest the relevance of some aspects of E.P. Thompson's (1971) formulation of the moral economy in the Indian context.

As the late nineteenth century boom gave way in the 1890s and early 1900s to bad weather, poor harvests, declining world market demands, and tightening credit, the market farmers' resentment of and rivalry with European planters and Indian landlords intensified. Market fluctuation that now affected the great majority of Bihari cultivators produced a no-win situation for the beleaguered colonial administration. Food price increases, which were essential to the continued prosperity and contentment of market farming groups, worked to the detriment of landless, wage earning laborers who thus became a potential source of rural unrest. On the other hand, when food prices declined, to the delight of the laboring classes, market-oriented cultivators faced ruinous debts and sharp drops in their standard of living.

The combination of transport shortages, market disruptions, inflation, and social dislocation that struck India during and right after the First World War (Saini 1978:161–173) drove many market producers to support organized protest in Bihar that came to be focused on Mohandas Gandhi's personal, not mass, *satyagraha*. If recent authors on the subject are correct (Pouchepadass 1974; Henningham 1976:68–69), agrarian agitation in Champaran was not a groundswell struggle of impoverished tenants and sharecroppers as it has traditionally been pictured (Prasad 1949; Datta 1957). Gandhi's main allies in the province and the main beneficiaries of his highly publicized campaign against the European indigo planters were the market-oriented tenants who had seen their gains of the late nineteenth century all but wiped out during the war years. Their struggle with the European planters and Indian landlords over what crops should be grown was intensified by population increases which restricted the amount of land available for market production, drove up the purchase price and rental rates on land already under cultivation, and rendered migration and the clearing of new lands no longer a viable option in most areas of the province. As a result, acts of vandalism, arson, and crop destruction increased sharply in the Champaran period and after—despite Gandhi's message of non-violent protest. Petitions and government inquiries also played a prominent role, but work and rent refusals, land seizures, and violent clashes with police and estate agents became frequent and widespread relative to any period prior to World War I, (Misra 1963:102–103, 116, 132, 140, passim; Prosad 1949:passim). Recent work done on Gandhi's equally famous *satyagrahas* in Gujarat demonstrates that the patterns of market farmer support and shifts to confrontational modes of protest found in Bihar were not isolated or exceptional, but widespread (Hardiman 1977; Charlesworth 1979).

Gandhi's mass appeal in the Indian countryside appears to have resulted from different reasons at different social levels. For illiterate and impoverished laborers and non-occupancy tenants, he was a holyman or *sahdu* and, some authors have argued a messiah. These groups turned out in the tens of thousands to perform *darshan*, ritual and religious obeisance, to the frail figure who lived as simply as they did, preached a message they could understand, and convinced them that he was working to improve the conditions under which they had lived their lives—though it is doubtful that they understood his political goals or his tactics (Pouchepadass 1974:83–84; Hardiman 1977:59ff). For the emerging market farmer classes of Bihar, Gujarat, and other provinces, Gandhi was an ally in their struggles against entrenched landlords and British planters and officials. Gandhi and his Congress Party lieutenants provided a focus and the organizational framework that the competitive and independent-minded minority of tenant and small-holder farmers had sorely lacked in the pre-World War I period. In their view, Gandhi supplied both effective channels of communication with the British and potent tactics for protest should the colonizers resist the farmers' demands. The appeal of Gandhian tactics was all the stronger for peasant groups because some of the principles that underlay passive resistance and civil disobedience had considerable affinity with the modes of defense and protest that had long been employed by Indian cultivators (Spodek 1971; Pandey 1978: 173; Hardiman 1977:62–63).

The appeal of Gandhian techniques and the Congress Party for the emerging farmer class can also be traced to the former's non-revolutionary political aims. Though British planter competition and official restrictions were to be eliminated and Indian landlord rivals weakened, the mixed system of market opportunities and patron-client dependencies in which cash farming groups had achieved prosperity was to be preserved. At the same time, Gandhi and other prominent Congress politicans preached class unity, abhorred violence, and promoted alliances between all Indian groups and classes, including the landlords, who were to become the main targets of more radical movements like the *kisan sabhas* in Bihar and the neighboring United Provinces. The co-option or dissolution of these latter movements, which best represented the interests of poor tenants and landless laborers, became major challenges for Gandhi, Nehru, and other socially-committed Congress leaders from the 1920s onwards. Their success rendered the Indian nationalist "revolution" a process of accommodation and limited adjustments, rather than radical upheavals. Though their wealth and status were somewhat reduced and their power restricted, the landlords and dominant caste groups survived (Low 1973:209–211). With the departure of the British, they came increasingly into cooperation with urban politicians and market-oriented farmers out of their mutual concern to shore up badly battered systems of patronage, dependence, and social control (Pandey 1978; Dhanagare 1975; Huawe 1961).

For Java detailed studies of nationalist agitation in the early decades are not available as they are for India on the rural sources of support for Gandhi and the Congress Party.[11] It is difficult to trace with any certainty the links between the emergence of a market-oriented class of cultivators and the spread of nationalism. Sartono Kartodirdjo, who has written the most detailed account to date on the spread of the Sarekat Islam movement to the rural areas of Java, has surprisingly little to say about which social groups actively supported this first wave of nationalist agitation among the rural masses. For the mass of rural dwellers, Sarekat Islam and especially its quasi-messianic leader, Tjokroaminioto, may have had much the same meaning as Gandhi, the holyman, and the Congress Party (Kartodirdjo 1973:ch. 5; Dahm 1969:32–39). The origins of the Sarekat Islam movement in the Indonesian mercantile classes and its anti-Chinese and heavily economic thrust, may well have meant that it was a rallying point for disgruntled, market-oriented landholders in the years of shipping shortages, inflation, and increased exactions during the decade of the First World War. This connection would appear to be reinforced by recent evidence of involvement by prosperous market farmers in the Tjimareme and Afdeelng B disturbances and other localized protest movements aimed against the *priyayi* and the Dutch regime in this period (Chong 1973:22–25; Kartodirdjo 1973:63, 93, 99).

Several general conclusions emerge from this overview of the nature of colonial control systems and rural protest in Java and Bihar. Most striking is the discovery that there was a paucity of confrontational or violent protest at any social level. It is also notable that the most impoverished groups in both of these societies rarely protested in any form, and when they did it was usually in support of rich and powerful patrons. Their quiescence demonstrates in part the strength of the systems of social control and village defense that the Europeans largely preserved after these areas came under colonial rule. Their lack of overt resistance also reflects, as Eric Wolf (1969:289–290) has argued, their deep dependence on other, especially land-controlling groups and the precarious nature of their existence on the edge of subsistence.[12] The fact that well-to-do, market-oriented peasants were those who supported the most strongly confrontational protest movements in both Java and Bihar—even though these were usually led by religious figures—also lends support to Wolf's contention that "middle" peasants are those who are most able and likely to mount sustained movements of protest. Though the "middle" peasants in Bihar were mainly tenants, they had secure control over the lands they worked and had deeply committed themselves to production for the market. Like their landholder counterparts in Java, and in contrast to the groups studied by Wolf, they sought not revolution but limited changes and reforms that would improve their competitive advantage and counter the adverse effects of market reverses and new bureaucratic demands.

If the sharply contrasting fates of societies where these groups threw in their lot with the forces of revolution is indicative, their decisions in Bihar and Java to ally themselves with parties stressing class cooperation and preservation may well have been decisive for the outcome of the Indian and Indonesian nationalist struggles against European colonial dominance.

Notes

1. There is a surprising paucity of secondary studies on caste in rural Bihar. The best source of information on population composition by caste remains the Indian census reports beginning in 1881. For published accounts that are more accessible, see the various Bihar district gazetteers, especially those compiled by L.S.S. O'Malley. See also Brown 1972:55–58. The best account of caste as a patron-client system based on fieldwork in north Indian remains Lewis 1965: esp. chapter two.

2. The role of force in local control in the colonial period has been studied for many regions in India. For Bihar, see Robb (1979:100–101, 115), Jha (1977:550–551), Henningham (1979:69), BPP, (1914:vol. 9546, 6). For other areas in India see Government of Bihar and Orissa (hereafter *BPP*), *Bihar Police Proceedings* (Sengupta

1971:197–201), Hardiman (1977:53, 59), Washrook (1976:42, 151 et passim), Kling (1966:52–54). For examples from Java see, Onghokham (1975:65–66), Vitalis (1851:4–6).

3. For the most elaborate discussion of this concept which Clifford Geertz introduced nearly two decades ago, see his recent work (Geertz 1980). In contrast to Geertz's argument that the Balinese built power and authority to support the pomp and splendor of the court (esp. p. 13), the Dutch clearly sought to make use of the pomp and splendor of their Javanese princely "allies" to bolster their legitimacy and control.

4. For the best discussion of these patterns in the Indian context, see Baker 1976:22–26. For Bihar, see Henningham (1979:59–65).

5. Though a militant, puritanical Muslim sect repeatedly stirred up dissidence among the peasants of parts of Bengal in the mid-nineteenth century (Kling 1966:61, 68).

6. The fullest account of the Java War in print remains Louw and Klerck (1894–1909, 6 vols.). On the *priyayi* restoration see Palmier (1960) or Schrieke (1966). For post-rebellion disturbances that the Dutch argued were linked to the Java War, see Cary (1979:88–89), Deventer (1865–6:vol. 2, 468–469, 471–474).

7. Deventer (1865:vol. 2, 468–474) discusses a number of minor disturbances or rebellious plots that appear to have been mainly linked to official excesses or new government demands. No religious overtones are discussed in Deventer's account, but his analysis of rebel motives and activities is too brief and sketchy for one to be certain that religious motivations were not important.

8. Although the motives for late nineteenth century expansion have been the subject of one of the most heated (and productive) of all historical debates for some decades, major works by authors like D.C. Platt, Hans-Ulrich Wehler, and William A. Williaams have firmly established the importance of a need for raw materials, markets and to a much lesser extent investment outlets in the mix of reasons for that great burst of empire building.

9. For important exceptions, see Hopkins (1973), especially chapter four.

10. Even though the evidence for these patterns is very scanty, Peter Robb (1979:112) has suggested that laborers preferred contracts to paternalistic arrangements.

11. For well-to-do peasant involvement in risings in the mid and late nineteenth century, see Kartodirdjo (1973:47, 51–53, 63, 93, 99).

12. A different view of the implications for protest of the subsistence peasants' precarious position is developed in Scott (1976).

References

Adas, M. 1981. "From Avoidance to Confrontation: Peasant Protest in Precolonia and Colonial Southeast Asia," *Comparative Studies in Society and History*, 23:217–247.

———. 1982. "Bandits, Monks and Pretender Kings: Patterns of Peasant Protest in Colonial Burma, 1826–1941," in R. Weller and S. Guggenheim, eds., *Power and Protest in the Countryside: Studies of Rural Unrest*, Durham: Duke University Press.

Allen, G. C., and A. Donnithorne. 1957. *Western Enterprise in Indonesia and Malaysia*, London: Allen and Unwin.

Anonymous. 1861. "Binnenlandsche onlusten op Java," *Tijdschrift voor Nederlandsch Indie* 23:289–300.

Anonymous. 1891. "De wording en het verloop van de Tjilegonsche troebelen in Juli 1888," *De Indische Gids*, 13:1137–1206.

Baker, C. 1976. "Tamilnad Estates in the Twentieth Century," *Indian Social and Economic History Review*, 13:1–44.

Benda, H., and L. Castles. 1969. "The Samin Movement," *Bijdragen tot de Taal-, Landen Volkenkunde*, 125:207–240.

Boeka, pseud. 1904. "De Hoofden op Java: een studie," *De Indische Gids*, 26:331–361, 516–544.

Brown, J. 1972. *Gandhi's Rise to Power: Indian Politics 1915–1922*, Cambridge: Cambridge University Press.

Burger, D. H. 1948–9. "Sturctuurveranderingen in de Javaanse samenleving," *Indonesie*, 2:381–398.

Cary, P. 1979. "Rich Peasants and Poor Peasants in Late Nineteenth Century Maharashtra," in C. Dewey and A. G. Hopkins, eds., *The Imperial Impact in Africa and South Asia*, London: Institute of Commonwealth Studies.

Cheong, Y. M. 1973. *Conflicts within the Priyayi: World of the Parahyangan in West Java, 1914–1927*, Singapore: Institute of Southeast Asian Studies.

Cohn, B. 1969. "Structural Change in Indian Rural Society, 1596–1885," in R. E. Frykenberg, ed., *Land Control and Social Structure in Indian History*, Madison: University of Wisconsin Press.

Dahm, B. 1969. *Sukarno and the Struggle for Indonesian Independence*, Ithaca: Cornell University Press.

Das, M. N. 1964. *India under Minto and Morley*, London: Allen and Unwin.

Datta, K. K. 1957a. *Agrarian Unrest against British Rule in Bihar, 1831–1859*, Patna: Government of Bihar.

––––––. 1957b. *History of the Freedom Movement in Bihar*, Patna: Government of Bihar.

Deventer, S. V. 1865–66. *Bijdragen tot de kennis van het landelijk stelsel op Java*, Zalt-Bommel: J. Norman en zoon, 3 vols.

Dewey, C. 1979. "Patwari and Chaukidar: Subordinate Officials and the Reliability of India's Agricultural Statistics," in C. Dewey and A. G. Hopkins, eds., *The Imperial Impact in Africa and South Asia*, London: Institute of Commonwealth Studies.

Dhanagare, D. N. 1975. *Agrarian Movements and Gandhian Politics*, Agra: Agra University Press.

Di Nijs, E. B. 1961. *Tempo doeloe: Fotographische Documenten uit het oude Indie*, Amsterdam: Querido.

Dumont, L. 1970. *Homo Hierarchius: The Caste System and Its Implications*, London: Weiedenfeld and Nicolson.

Elson, R. E. 1978. *The Cultivation System and "Agricultural Involution"*, Clayong, Victoria: Monash University Press.

Fanon, F. 1968. *The Wretched of the Earth*, New York: Grove Press.

Fasseur, C. 1978. *Kultuurstelsel en Koloniale Baten: De Nederlandse Exploitatie van Java 1840–1860*, Leiden: University of Leiden Press.

Fisher, C. 1979. "Planters and Peasants: The Ecological Contest of Agrarian Unrest on the Indigo Plantations of North Bihar, 1820–1920," in C. Dewey and A. G. Hopkins, eds., *The Imperial Impact in Africa and South Asia*, London: Institute of Commonwealth Studies.

Fox, R. 1971. *Kin, Clan, Raja and Rule: State-Hinterland Relations in Pre-Industrial India*, Berkeley: University of California Press.

Furnivall, J. S. 1939. *Netherlands India: A Study of Plural Economy*, Cambridge: Cambridge University Press.

––––––. 1956. *Colonial Policy and Practice*, New York: New York University Press.

Geertz, C. 1966. *Agricultural Involution: The Process of Ecological Change in Indonesia,* Berkeley: University of California Press.

————. 1980. *Negara: The Theatre State in Nineteenth Century Bali,* Princeton: Princeton University Press.

Government of Bihar and Orissa. *Reports on the Administration of Bihar and Orissa, 1915–1920,* London: India Office Records.

————. *Bihar Police Proceedings, 1911/12–1924/5,* London: India Office Records.

Government of India. *Emigration Proceedings,* Vol. 932, 1875, No. 8. London: India Office Records.

Guha, R. 1963. *A Rule of Property for Bengal,* Paris: Moulton.

Harcourt, M. 1977. "Kisan Populism and Revolution in Rural Indian: The 1942 Disturbances in Bihar and East United Provinces," in D. A. Low, ed., *Congress and the Raj,* London: Heinemann.

Hardiman, D. 1977. "The Crisis of the Lesser Patidars: Peasant Agitations in Kheda District, Gujarat, 1917–34," in D. A. Low, ed., *Congress and the Raj,* London: Heinemann.

Harnetty, P. 1972. *Imperialism and Free Trade: Lancashire and India in the Mid-Nineteenth Century,* Vancouver: University of British Columbia Press.

Hauser, W. 1961. "The Bihar Provincial Kisan Sabha, 1929–42: A Study of an Indian Peasant Movement," Ph.D. Dissertation, University of Chicago.

Henningham, S. 1976. "The Social Setting of the Champaran Satyagraha: The Challenge of an Alien Elite," *Indian Economic and Social History Review,* 13:59–73.

————. 1979. "Agrarian Relations in North Bihar," *Indian Social and Economic History Review,* 14:53–75.

Hopkins, A. G. 1973. *An Economic History of West Africa,* New York: Columbia University Press.

Jha, H. 1977. "Lower-Caste Peasants and Upper-Caste Zamindars in Bihar (1921–25): An Analysis of Sanskritization and Contradiction between Two Groups," *Indian Social and Economic History Review,* 14:549–559.

J. L. V. 1855. "Bijdrage tot de kennis der residentie Madioen," *Tijdschrift voor Nederlandsch Indie,* 17:1–17.

Kano, H. 1980. "The Economic History of Javanese Rural Society: A Reinterpretation," *Journal of the Developing Economies,* 17:3–22.

Kartodirdjo, S. 1966. *The Peasants' Revolt of Banten in 1888,* The Hague: Njhoff.

————. 1972. "Agrarian Radicalism in Java," in C. Holt, ed., *Culture and Politics in Indonesia,* Ithaca: Cornell University Press.

————. 1973. *Protest Movements in Rural Java,* Singapore: Oxford University Press.

Kling, B. 1966. *The Blue Mutiny: The Indigo Disturbances in Bengal, 1859–62,* Philadelphia: University of Pennsylvania Press.

Kumar, R. 1968. "The Rise of the Rich Peasants in Western India," in D. A. Low, ed., *Soundings in South Asian History,* Berkeley: University of California Press.

Lewis, O. 1965. *Village Life in Northern India,* New York: Vintage.

Louw, P., and E. S. de Klercke. 1894–1909. *De Java-Oorlog van 1825–1830,* 6 vols. The Hague: Nijhoff.

Low, D. A. 1973. *Lion Rampant,* London: Cass.

Majumbar, R. C. 1963. *The Sepoy Mutiny and Revolt of 1857,* Calcutta: K. L. Mukhopadhyay.

Marr, D. 1972. *Vietnamese Anticolonialism,* Berkeley: University of California Press.

Marx, K. and F. Engels. n.d. *The First Indian War of Independence 1857–1859,* Moscow: Foreign Languages Publishing House.

Metcalf, T. R. 1964. *The Aftermath of Revolt: India, 1857–1870*, Princeton: Princeton University Press.

——. 1979. *Land, Landlords, and the British Raj*, Berkeley: University of California Press.

Misra, B. B. 1963. *Select Documents on Mahatma Gandhi's Movement in Champaran 1917–1918*, Patna: Government of Bihar.

Misra, G. 1967. "Indigo Plantations and the Agrarian Relations in Champaran during the Nineteenth Century," *Indian Social and Economic History Review*, 3:332–357.

Moore, B., Jr. 1966. *Social Origins of Dictatorship and Democracy: Lord and Peasant in the Making of the Modern World*, Boston: Beacon.

Niel, R. V. 1964. "The Function of Land Rent under the Cultivation System in Java," *Journal of Asian Studies*, 23:357–375.

——. 1969. "The Introduction of the Government of Sugar Cultivation in Pasuruan, Java, 1830," *Journal of Oriental Studies*, 7:261–276.

——. 1972. "Measurement of Change under the Cultivation System in Java, 1837–1851," *Indonesia*, 14:89–109.

O'Malley, L. S. S. 1907. *Champaran District Gazetteer*, Patna: Government of Bihar and Orissa.

——. 1938. *Champaran District Gazetteer*, Patna: Government of Bihar and Orissa.

Oonghokam. 1975. "The Residency of Madiun Priyayi and Peasant in the Nineteenth Century," Ph.D dissertation, Yale University.

Paige, J. 1975. *Agrarian Revolution: Social Movements and Export Agriculture in the Underdeveloped World*, New York: The Free Press.

Palmier, L. 1960. "The Javanese Nobility under the Dutch," *Comparative Studies in Society and History*, 2:197–227.

Pandey, G. 1977. "A Rural Base for Congress: The United Provinces, 1920–1940," in D. A. Low, ed., *Congress and the Raj*, London: Heinmann.

——. 1978. *The Ascendancy of the Congress in Uttar Pradesh*, Delhi: Oxford University Press.

Pierson, N. G. 1868. *Het Kultuurstelsel: Zes Voorlezingen*, Amsterdam: Van Kampen.

Pouchepadass, J. 1974. "Local Leaders and the Intelligensia in the Champaran Satyagraha (1917): A Study in Peasant Mobilization," *Contributions to Indian Sociology*, 8:67–87.

Prasad, R. 1949. *Satyagraha in Champaran*, Ahmedabad: Navajivan Publishing House.

Raj, J. 1965. *The Mutiny and the British Land Policy in North India*, New York: Asia Publishing House.

Ray, R and R. Ray. 1973. "Officials and Non-Officials and Leaders in Popular Agitation: Shahabad 1917 and Other Conspiracies," in B. N. Pandey, ed., *Leadership in South Asia*, New Delhi: Oxford University Press.

Robb, P. 1977. "Officials and Non-Officials as Leaders in Popular Agitation: Shahabad 1917 and Other Conspiracies," in B. N. Pandey, ed., *Leadership in South Asia*, New Delhi: Oxford University Press.

——. 1979. "Hierarchy and Resources: Peasant Stratification in Late Nineteenth Century Bihar," *Modern Asian Studies*, 13:97–126.

Robinson, F. C. R. 1971. "Consultation and Control: The United Provinces's Government and Its Allies, 1860–1906," *Modern Asian Studies*, 5:313–336.

Saini, K. G. 1978. "The Economic Aspects of India's Participation in the First World War," in D. C. Ellinwood and S. D. Pradhan, eds., *India and World War I*, Columbia: South Asian Books.

Schrieke, B. 1966. "The Native rulers," in *Indonesian Sociological Studies*, The Hague: Van Hoeve.

Scott, J. C. 1976. *The Moral Economy of the Peasant,* New Haven: Yale University Press.

Sen, S. N. 1957. *Eighteen Fifty-Seven,* New Delhi: Government of India.

Sengupta, K. K. 1971. "Agrarian Disturbances in Nineteenth Century Bengal," *Indian Social and Economic History Review,* 8:192–212.

Shoemaker, W. J. 1896. "Het Mohammedaansche fanatisme," *De Indische Gids,* 20:1517–1537.

The Siau Giap. 1968. "The Samin and Samat Movements in Java: Two Examples of Peasant Resistance," *Revue du sud-est asiatique,* 1:63–77, 107–113; 2:303–310.

Sinha, R. 1918. *The Law of the Landlord and Tenant in Bengal and Bihar,* Calcutta: R. Cambray and Co.

Skocpol, T. 1979. *States and Social Revolutions: A Comparative Analysis of France, Russia and China,* Cambridge: Cambridge University Press.

Spodek, H. 1971. "On the Origins of Gandhi's Political Methodology: The Heritage of Kathiawad and Gujarat," *Journal of Asian Studies,* 30:361–372.

Stokes, E. 1959. *The English Utilitarians and India,* Oxford: Oxford University Press.

Sutherland, H. 1973. "Pargreh Pradja: Java's Indigenous Administrative Corps and Its Role in the Last Decades of Dutch Colonial Rule," Ph.D. dissertation, Yale University.

Thompson, E. P. 1971. "The Moral Economy of the English Crowd in the Eighteenth Century," *Past and Present,* 50:76–136.

van Soest, G. H. 1869. *Geschiedenis van het Kultuurstelsel,* H. Nijgh, 3 Vols.

Vitalis, L. 1851. *De Invoering, werking en gebreken van het stelsel van Kultuurs op Java,* Zalt-Bommel: Norman en zoon.

Washbrook, D. 1976. *The Emergence of Provincial Politics: the Madras Presidency, 1870–1920,* Cambridge: Cambridge University Press.

Wolf, E. 1969. *Peasant Wars of the Twentieth Century,* New York: Harper and Row.

Zachariah, K. C. 1964. *A Historical Study of Internal Migration in the Indian Sub-Continent, 1901–1931,* Bombay: Asia Publishing House.

7

On Peasant Diffidence: Non-Revolt, Resistance, and Hidden Forms of Political Consciousness in Northern Nigeria, 1900–1945

MICHAEL WATTS

Classes do not exist as separate entities, look around, find an enemy class, and then start to struggle. On the contrary, people find themselves in a society structured in determined ways . . . , they experience exploitation . . . , they identify points of antagonistic interests, they commence struggling around these issues, and in the process they find themselves as classes (Thompson 1978:50).

Until relatively recently, one of the few terrains on which Marxist and conventional social science thinking actually met in an amicable symbiosis was that of peasant politics. The Marxian legacy of an individuated peasant livelihood and consciousness—"potatoes in a sack" as Marx himself described the French peasantry—profoundly inseparable from the "barbarian" and "vegetable" conditions of rural idiocy, dovetailed perfectly with the "peasants as generic type" literature so fashionable in the 1950s and 1960s. If the *Eighteenth Brumaire* cast the conservative peasant in "stupefied bondage to the old order," the essentialism of Redfield, Foster, Banfield, and Lewis raised the peasant *mentalité* to a personality type: passive, distrustful, fatalistic, incapable of innovation, shackled with an antediluvian outlook and, in what must have seemed a massive affront to a generation of capitalist development theoreticians, thoroughly unable to defer gratification. It is, of course, true that Marx himself anticipated the most revolutionary of all circumstances when landed classes were in the throes of dispossession as market forces developed, but he could hardly have predicted the astonishing peasant mobilizations in the major revolutionary movements of the twentieth century. The more recent emergence of peasant rebellion and agrarian revolution as a field of central theoretical concern reflected, then, a newfound concern with precisely these victorious social movements in China, Vietnam, and Mexico, coupled with the domestic turbulence surrounding American militarism in Southeast Asia and the obvious rural unrest unleashed during an era of decolonization. Mao and Fanon accordingly became the theoretical and political torchbearers for peasant studies. And so much the better, insofar as even the best materialist analyses frequently reduced the popular classes to social residues of a predatory capitalism from whom urban surpluses were inexorably pumped and whose own history lacked any intrinsic meaning or import. The recognition of popular and peasant protest as a politically significant phenomenon within capitalist development itself restored to peasantries everywhere the dignity of their historic agency which had shaped and forged their own destinies. To the extent that the past fifteen years have witnessed a dramatic profusion of studies on peasant protest, dissent, and mobilization, our grasp of agrarian systems in the periphery has improved enormously. On the theoretical plane, however, the genesis of a healthy number of important debates has revealed that there are marked cleavages with respect to the political economic theorization of peasant society. Some of the purportedly "materialist" analyses seem more informed by Rousseau, Hobbes, and Milton Friedman than by Lenin or Kautsky, while a current of populism runs through a great deal of what has now become a huge corpus of well-researched and often insightful peasant case studies.

Theoretical proliferation may indeed be indicative of a sort of intellectual vitality but, unlike the Narodnik-Bolshevik debates on the agrarian question in pre-revolutionary Russia, the effects of the last decade have placed *rebellion* at the center of the stage. As Michael Adas notes (1980 and in this volume), there has been a tendency to generalize on the basis of the Chinese, Mexican, or Vietnamese experience which has bred a type of myopic and peasant-centered analysis. But as Martin Murray (1981) points out in his recent analysis of colonial Indochina, hybrid and contradictory forms of capital emerged in the colonized territories which articulated noncapitalist forms of production into capitalist forms of commodity circulation; not only did noncapitalist forms of production survive, but limits and blockages constrained the extended reproduction of capital.

Colonial capitalism, then, spawned a variety of roads to social differentiation among peasants and, indeed, it was Lenin himself who observed that "our literature contains too stereotyped an understanding of the theoretical proposition that capitalism requires the free landless worker . . . capitalism penetrates into agriculture particularly slowly and in extremely varied forms" (1972:178). The peasant world is not, and was not, a replica of an admittedly turbulent and protest-ridden Lower Burma or Punjab. But precisely because there has been an obsession with the high visibility areas, the record of peasant diffidence or of hidden forms of peasant consciousness and resistance has been rather neglected. Bruce Cumings (1981) has raised the problem of the relative absence of politics (in contradiction to economics, ideology, and interest) in the peasant protest debates. I would suggest that in many instances and for significant periods of time there was indeed little *explicit* formal politics in the countryside, yet this has to be accounted for theoretically by any informed political economy.

All this is simply to say that peasant rebellion has come to be taken for granted when, in the Afro-Asian realm at least, massive impoverishment and colonial oppression was marked by long periods of relative quiescence. Mikiso Hane (1982), in his recent account of the extraordinary process of Japanese modernization from the Meiji Restoration to World War II—a period of huge social dislocation and peasant impoverishment—argues that there were in fact few rebels and few rebellions. Indeed, a specifically Japanese characteristic of this transformation was "the unusually dense and stable structure of a system of hierarchic social relations" (Hobsbawm 1982:16). In Africa, where peasants stood in a weak competitive position with respect to capital and the colonial state, rural protest—with the notable exception of the Maji-Maji and Bambotha rebellions and a spate of peasant insurgencies in the Transkei—was isolated, "passive," covert, and limited (Isaacman *et al.* 1980). This silence in the historical record may, of course, be somewhat specious because, as Alain Touraine (1977:325) observes:

> It is not easy for history and the sociologist to give back their voices to those who were never allowed to speak, who have left us no carved inscriptions, no tablets, no scrolls, whose heralds died on gibbets, on crosses, or as victims of starvation without any memorialist to record their words. Hence the interest of the descents that can today be made into the history of the colonized, of their refusals, their rebellions, and their dreams.

And yet the negative cases, in a simple statistical sense, remain highly significant. The absence of peasant social movements as a focus for intellectual discussion is not simply a corrective to the somewhat exaggerated concern with rebellion, but sheds considerable illumination on the rather murky area of how disaffected peasants move from moral vision or social interest to political action. But the question of what appears as the *absence* of peasant politics has a more complex two-fold nature, for it asks us not only to account theoretically for the absence of social movements *per se* but, more critically, to provide a political economy of *specific* covert manifestations of resistance and hidden forms of peasant consciousness. In other words, in the face of impoverishment and oppression only rarely are peasants passive; rather they resist in a variety of hidden and culturally informed ways despite the fact that their voices are not readily heard or interpreted. A theory of social movements must, therefore, address not so much absence *per se*, as the forms of "passive" protest which peasants so frequently engage in. The question is not only why there was nothing like a major peasant rebellion in, for example, modernizing Japan—with the arguable exception of the rice rebellion of 1918—but why, as Eric Hobsbawm puts it, the historical peculiarities of their country and culture caused the Japanese to resist in other unique ways. Why, then, did the particular patterns of horizontal class formation, ideological and moral disposition, and material self-interest translate into equally specific—local, covert, individuated, and small-scale—forms of peasant politics.

On Moral, Rational and Material Peasants

In much of the theorizing on peasant rebellion the question of non-revolt is of course implicit; indeed, Scott (1976) explicitly devotes an entire chapter of his book to the subject. And yet much of peasant behavior—and indeed the definition of peasant itself—has an apparently digital quality to it; peasants either rebel or they do not. To use a rather mechanistic metaphor, it is as though the trigger mechanism is in dispute, since it underpins peasant mobilization.

But the identification of the catalysts which initiate and sustain peasant politics not only invokes wildly different theoretical interpretations, but frequently has much to say about what one might call, with some trepidation, views of peasant "nature" or "rationality." Among the three theoretical regularities in the peasant social movement literature—which can be conveniently identified with the work of Scott, Popkin, and Paige—it is somewhat ironic that, while each has in varying measure been Marxist influenced or inspired, the fundamental question of peasant differentiation is rarely confronted. For Marx and Lenin, peasants under capitalism were a highly differentiated and transitory class; any discussion of rebellion, then, demands a very careful specification of who exactly one is talking about. Much of Paige's work is, of course, not about peasants at all, while Scott not only relies on a broadly Chayanovian view of household economy (in some measure drawn from outside Southeast Asia), but is forced to employ evidences which pertain to non-peasant, i.e. fully proletarianized, agrarian groups.

I raise these somewhat prosaic issues not simply because I am dealing with *peasant* rebellion—that is to say, social movements among households that have direct access to the means of production (land) and that differentially produce both their means of subsistence and commodities for exchange which enter the circuits of capitalist reproduction—but also to establish that any discussion of peasant dissent under capitalism must treat the differentiation issue; specifically its unique form and its developmental trajectory or road (de Janvry 1981).

In light of the extraordinarily complex forms of social differentiation among peasants, it is ironic that so much theorization of rural rebellion attempts to universalize both peasant behavior and peasant communities. James Scott's Durkheimian perspective locates peasant behavior in the context of "risk aversion" in essentially "traditional," i.e. Rousseanian, corporate villages. Samuel Popkin's gloss on Mill, conversely, constructs an individual peasant "rationality" within a village terrain not unlike a Hobbesian world of wholesale personal gain and competition. The moral economy and political economy (Popkin variety) approaches, accordingly, derive their theses on peasant insurrection from these fundamental postulates. For Scott, traditional society contained a moral order inextricably bound up with subsistence concerns; technical and social arrangements of peasant livelihood forged an indigenous security system which was normatively enforceable. Colonialism wrought untrammeled exploitation which was transmitted to the peasantry as new forms of social differentiation, agrarian dislocation, the erosion of the moral economy, and a predatory capitalism which frequently threatened peasant survival. Scott looks to peasant morality and outrage as necessary responses to an endangered subsistence minimum; rebellions were essentially conservative and restorative.

For Popkin, conversely, traditional society was not less exploitative than colonialism and the social solidarity of the traditional village was almost nonexistent. Colonialism presented differential opportunities (not least for landlords) to which peasants responded rationally, i.e., "individuals evaluated the possible outcomes associated with their choices in accordance with preferences and values" (1980:431–432). Popkin's peasants respond as gamblers with a careful calculative eye on material gain and benefit, especially new markets. Peasant movements were not restorative but sought to tame capitalism; they transpired as political entrepreneurs proved capable of providing individual incentives to essentially atomized and conservative village communities.

Jeffery Paige's *Agrarian Revolution* (1975), on the other hand, hardly deals with morality, ideology or rationality whatsoever. It is above all an analysis predicated on class interest, on what one might term, with some caution, objective vectors under capitalism. Paige examines what people actually do, a critical element of what I refer to as the labor process; in other words, the organization and structure of work, the ecology of production, production of use versus exchange values, and so on. Paige specifically examines the conditions under which agrarian revolt may occur and the forms which peasant (and other) politics actually assume. His Marxian model predicts that agrarian dissent emerges where: (i) a rigid landed class exists based on landed capital (ii) peasants are denied the possibility of upward mobility (iii) work conditions and the nature of work establish collective solidarity. From the specific forms of agrarian class structure Paige is able to derive three distinctive forms of rural politics: rebellions, reform labor movements, and reform commodity movements.

In assessing these debates on rural social movements one cannot help being struck by two obvious tendencies. The first is the implicit assumption of theoretical incompatibility; ideology or moral vision is somehow not contained within the labor process, and individual calculus represents the antithesis of class interest. Indeed, I find it instructive that both Scott and Popkin, in their discussion of moral economy, give remarkably short shrift to Edward Thompson's seminal contributions on the subject (and from which the term is derived) which precisely attempt to forge a link between objective forces and subjective expression, between politics, economy, ideology, and popular consciousness.[1]

And the second is the striking similarity between the peasant rebellion dialogue and recent debates within English historiography, most particularly the arguments centered on "structure" versus "agency" in historical explanation.[2] In this regard, Perry Anderson and Edward Thompson are at least agreed that history cannot be without a subject, and to that extent the experience of men and women converts their objective [structural] determination into subjective [social] initiatives. By invoking choice, action, consciousness, and human agency in social life, one must also somehow recognize that—to paraphrase Thompson—we "make our own history" and yet "history makes itself." Insofar as the peasant rebellion work is situated within this same problematic, rural politics has been posed either as a necessary appendage of class position, a phenomenological residue of moral outrage, or an expression of an individual calculus based on material and rational self-interest. Very little of the discussion on peasant social movements or non-revolt confronts the necessary unity of structural principles and human agency. There is morality but no economy (Scott), just as there is class without politics (Paige), and real interests without political economy (Popkin). And yet as Cumings (1981:495) correctly observes, "economic interest and moral vision march together in politics."

An explanation of why social movements among peasants do or do not occur presupposed, as Touraine notes (1977:322), two kinds of observations:

> On the one hand those that bear upon social conducts and therefore on the orientations, actions, and claims of the actors; on the other hand, those that bear upon the system of social and economic relations, on the nature of accumulation and economic domination. One cannot establish the existence of a system of historical action and of class relations solely on the basis of social conduct and social movements; nor is it any more possible to conceive that a type of historicity and of class relations will not express itself in a certain class consciousness and, therefore, in social movements.

A social movement must therefore be analyzed within a historic field-of-force which contains social forces that are ultimately of a class nature. Social movements in this sense contain a horizontal movement of class interests and are expressive of contradictions which cause a conflict to explode (Touraine 1977:314). Yet these struggles and class interests are defined by a quite specific historical system which identifies specific forms of class actor, specific stakes, specific conflicts, specific moral visions, and so on.

I have chosen the peasant labor process under capitalism as a critical starting point for an analysis of how structure and agency come together in historically specific circumstances (in northern Nigeria) and which goes some way toward comprehending the absence of collective peasant action in the face of obvious material grievances. I have chosen the labor process as a type of middle horizon concept which on the one hand identifies the structural context of aggregate class-based interests, and on the other situates people in relation to local interests, remedies, and tactical mobility. The labor process is one way in which we can come to terms with the manner in which interests that underly action are, or are not, consciously translated through human and moral endeavors into specific types of peasant politics, of which rebellion is one, perhaps exceptional form.

Resistance and the Peasant Labor Process
Under Capitalism

The first question we must ask is how far is it in fact possible to discern the whole economy of a society from inside it? It is essential to transcend the limitations of particular individuals caught up in their own narrow prejudices. But it is no less vital not to overstep the frontier fixed for them by the economic structure of society and establishing their position in it. Regarded abstractly and formally, then, class consciousness implies a class-conditioned unconsciousness of ones' own socio-historical and economic condition (Lukacs 1971:52).

A mode of production combines both the relations that specify determinate ways of appropriating and distributing labor time and the manner in which nature is actually appropriated. What Marx called the relations of production also correspond to another set of relations into which individuals necessarily enter as they transform raw material into use-values. This unity is the *labor process*[3] which Burawoy (1978:15) sees as constituted by two inseparable components—a relational and a practical aspect. The former refers to the social conditions under which production occurs—the relations in production—and the latter to the activities and the organization of work which transforms nature. Each mode of production and labor process contains particular forms of surplus appropriation which demand specific conditions if social reproduction, i.e. the reproduction of the social relations of production, is to be secured. These specific mechanisms and conditions which ensure social reproduction are political and ideological structures.

Peasant production under capitalism has a unique labor process that is defined by the peasant household as both a unit of direct production and a unit of reproduction (of daily and generational labor powers). Following Deere and de Janvry (1979:602), there are four critical moments in the circuit of the peasant household production process: (i) home production, (ii) wage labor, (iii) circulation and especially terms of trade, and (iv) reproduction/differentiation. At a given moment, family labor is reflected in the prevailing domestic division of labor by sex and age in relation to the means of production. Household labor can be deployed for home production (either as use-values or as commodites for exchange) or for sale as wage labor. Commodity production and wage labor generate a gross cash income which covers the purchase of means of subsistence and work, and raw materials. The terms of trade pertaining to commodity and wage exchange clearly influence the manner and scale with which household reproduction is secured (Bernstein 1979). In sum, then:

Means of consumption and means of work thus derived from both home production and purchase sustain the reproduction of the household as both a consumption and a production unit. Reproduction includes both daily maintenance to restore the capacity to work and generational reproductive activities reflected in the size, age, and sex composition of the household. The scale of this reproduction, in turn, determines the pattern of social differentiation and the consequent changing class position and composition of peasants (Deere and de Janvry 1979:602).

The differential scale of reproduction and the forms of social differentiation which accompany expanded commodity production naturally invokes a variety of forms in which surplus peasant labor is appropriated by a non-producing class. Even under colonial capitalism, a plethora of mechanisms for surplus extraction co-existed within the same social formation operating through *rents* in labor service,[4] in land,[5] or in cash (all of which result from private land appropriation), via the *market* (the wage relation, usury, terms of trade), and by the *state* (head, poll, land, or income taxes). In circumstances such as household production under capitalism in which surplus appropriation is transparent and overt—unlike the appropriation of surplus value under capitalism which is "hidden" at the point of production—the extra-economic conditions which guarantee the reproduction of the prevailing social relations are especially critical. The political and ideological conditions entail, in varying combination, force (that is to say, the exercise of state power for particular class interests) and the manufacture of consent (ideological legitimation). Peasant rebellion can in part be understood as conditions in which, during the process of capitalist development, force or consent are incapable of sustaining rural stability. To summarize, then, the peasant labor process under capitalism contains five critical elements. First, the peasant household has direct access to (and usually customary ownership of) the means of production which provides in some measure the domestic means of subsistence. Second, the peasant farmer sets the instruments of production in motion relatively independently of either the state or merchant capital;[6] simple reproduction,[7] then, is achieved through a high degree of self-management and permits the peasant a measure of autonomy, which Hyden (1980) somewhat exaggeratedly refers to as the "exit option." Third, the demand for monetary income (to cover state demands and purchase of necessary items of consumption) not only necessitates commodity production, but also the sale of wage labor which frequently involves seasonal migration, particularly where ecological conditions (for example, climatic seasonality) permits a high degree of geographical labor mobility and new forms of the social division of labor. Fourth, surplus labor is appropriated through a variety of market or state mechanisms which require sturdy politico-ideological conditions for their existence. And fifth, differing scales of reproduction and differential commoditization among peasant households under capitalism present the possibility of complex patterns of long-term differentiation in which some strata can systematically accumulate through agro-merchant channels while others are squeezed at both ends; as semi-proletarians they receive less than the value of their product while as commodity producers they suffer from deteriorating terms of trade. Ultimately, this "simple reproduction squeeze" (Bernstein 1979) may lead to land sale and full proletarianization.

In the following discussion I shall endeavor to show that an understanding of these elemental properties of the labor process provides critical insights into the absence of sustained rebellion in northern Nigeria between 1900 and 1945. However, since the development of capitalism in agriculture has historically been a complex and multifaceted process, the peasant labor process itself, among what is, after all, a *transitional* class under capitalism, may exhibit significant local variability that is of great consequence for peasant politics. Specifically, in northern Nigeria, under the aegis of the colonial state, merchant capital was instrumental in the incorporation of peasants into the circuits of global capitalism, and "subhume[d] the labor process as it found it" (Marx 1967:Vol.I,1021). Since merchant capital cannot create value, its transformative capability is limited and hence, as Banaji (1977:34) maintains, "the capitalist's control over the labor process retains a partial and sporadic character." I shall argue that it was the low level of [peasant] labor's subordination to capital and the specific form of the existing labor process itself which goes some way toward an explanation of both the absence of peasant insurrection under conditions of material impoverishment and exploitation, and also the manner in which peasants nonetheless actually *resisted* in the face of what E.P. Thompson has called "the sharp jostle of experience" (1978:164).

Merchant Capital and Development
of Colonial Capitalism in Northern Nigeria

Capital's struggle to dominate the enterprise of simple commodity producers—to determine the type, quality, quantity and volume of its commercial output—posits as its basis the limitations imposed on its elasticity by a labour process not determined by itself in which the enterprise of small producers retains its independence, if only as a formal independence. . . . Domination over the labour process becomes impossible on this basis within these limits of quasi-independence without these mechanisms which uproot the patriarchal sufficiency of the small enterprise. The compulsory enforced destruction of the small producer's self-sufficiency figures here as the necessary foundation for the dominance of capital (Banaji 1977:33).

During the nineteenth century, the Sokoto Caliphate occupied much of what is now northern Nigeria and south-central Niger. It was the largest, most populous, and very probably the most complex of sub-Saharan African states. But beginning with the fall of Adamawa in 1901 and terminating with the collapse of the powerful central emirates of Kano and Sokoto in 1903, the Caliphate proved to be a rather brittle opposition in the face of the massively superior British colonial armed forces. The imperial regiments were, in fact, never seriously threatened.

The Caliphal conquest brought to a close almost a century of social, economic, and political development which had opened in 1796 with the *jihadi* overthrow of the so-called *sarauta* system of government. By 1809 the holy war (*jihad*) had successfully welded together some thirty emirates that came to be presided over by a Caliph resident in Sokoto. The nineteenth century witnessed a progressive centralization of the state apparatuses, a huge extension of the agricultural frontier assisted by the importation of captive labor from the Nigerian middle belt, a deliberate policy of settlement and agrarian investment, and an expansion of commodity production which included cotton, indigo, and craft items, not least the famous textile industry. By 1900 the Caliphate was an agrarian bureaucracy of continental significance; it consisted of perhaps 10 million free peasant producers, a significant farm slave population, an urban based office-holding class (*sarauta*), an ideologically significant Muslim theologian strata (*ulema*), and an influential group of merchant capitalists who, though subservient to state officials, had an increasingly important role in craft and petty commodity production.

With the notable exception of the early Muslim resistance to Lugard's colonial forces—which included several notable Mahdist uprisings—the period from 1900 to the end of the Second World War is distinguished by the absence of any systematic, large-scale, overt peasant resistance and certainly nothing which might warrant the denotation "rebellion" or "insurrection." The tradition of peasant diffidence in Hausaland is made more incongruous in light of the detrimental effects of the region's incorporation into a world economy which (i) broke the cycle of household reproduction, (ii) exposed rural producers to the vicissitudes of the world market, (iii) placed peasants in new and deleterious relationships with merchant capital and the colonial state, and (iv) insofar as the forces of production remained unchanged, left rural producers vulnerable to a capricious desert-edge climate (specifically drought). All this is to say that non-revolt, but not passivity, should be seen against the backdrop of transformed conditions of peasant reproduction and the very real threat of crises of simple reproduction. The pharaonic series of famines after 1900—in 1908, 1913, 1927, 1942, and 1949—pays stark testimony to the material deprivation and the deterioration of systems of peasant livelihood.

To grasp the specific form in which capitalism developed in northern Nigeria requires, however, a careful reconstruction of the indigenous social formation itself. By the end of the fifteenth century Hausaland had become "fully integrated into the commercial and ideological nexus which linked the Western Sudan societies together [and into] . . . the wide Islamic world" (Adeleye 1971:492). The three centuries of development leading to the *jihad* in 1796 embodied two integrative processes. First, the network of towns, villages, and hamlets encompassing immigrant communities of heterogeneous origin was welded into a political community under a class of kings (*sarakuna*). And second, expanded commodity production, migration, and long distance trade integrated the kingdoms, in varying degrees, into the *bilad-al-Sudan*. Both tendencies were predicated on considerable descent and occupational diversity and on elaboration of central governmental functions, an important consequence of which was the expanded position which Islam came to occupy in social life.

The Islamization of Hausa society seems to have been coterminous with the rise of the city. It began in the fourteenth century when Islam surfaced in Hausaland initially through the efforts of a community of Malian traders and clerics. By the sixteenth and seventeenth centuries Islam had been adopted by a significant proportion of the popular classes (*talakawa*) through-out the closely settled and ethnically diverse rural areas subject to in-migration. In providing a matrix for social cohesion and a code for personal conduct, Islam was especially relevant to those embedded in an emerging commodity economy since it provided an appropriate juridical framework for the proliferation of exchange, trade, and craft production.

Islam gradually penetrated the *sarauta* system and produced a Muslim intelligentsia capable of providing leadership among rural and urban *talakawa* distinct from the office holders. If there were instances of Muslim *sarakuna*— for example Mohammed Rumfa (1463–1499) who in fact adopted Al-Maghili's treatise on Islamic government—who lent support to both Islam and the clerics (*ulema*), the latter as a class were unequivocally distanced from the loci of political authority. Yet the eighteenth century effloresence of state power and the birth of something like an Islamic theocracy, was ultimately built on a rickety, not to say contradictory, foundation. For while the populace was largely Muslim in terms of values, conduct, and identity, the rulers while nominally Islamicized, sustained their authority from a dynastic context welded to the pre-Islamic spirit pantheon. An increasingly influential Muslim intelligentsia had no institutional function in a government overseen by a cadre of slaves and eunuchs.

By the close of the eighteenth century the contradictions had sharpened considerably. There were those between the ideals of Islamic piety and the reality of dynastic practice and sacerdotal kingship; and between an urban elite and a rural peasantry. The tension between social cohesion and political authority was expressed in the fundamental split between the *cikin gida*, the palace clique, and the *cikin fada*, the influential Islamized commoner class. The eighteenth century had, in any case, seen massive political disruption with the collapse of the Kebbit cities and the leveling of the Zamfara Kingdom. In this ethos of great political insecurity, the escalation of inter-city conflict was critical, for it necessitated increased taxation and the growth of military conscription and doubtless much agro-commercial dislocation. It was amidst this enmity and discord that the preachings of the scholars (*mallamai*), and especially of the reformist intelligentsia centered in Usman Dan Fodio, offered an appropriate avenue for the expression of political protest.

Over a relatively short period beginning in 1796 and, more formally, with the defeat of Sarkin Gobir in 1804, Fodio forged a militant community which posed a direct challenge to the hegemony of the *sarauta* system. The *jihad* movement was governed by several distinct military contingents, led by *jihadist* intelligentsia (*mujahidun*) whose legitimacy was grounded in piety, learning, participation in the holy war, and association with the Shehu. Though many have seen the revolutionary disintegration of the *sarauta* government as principally an ethnic conflict in which the Fulani were pitted against the Hausa ruling class, Usman (1973) has drawn the attention to the limitations of sharply drawn ethnic categories which have little explanatory value in themselves other than as means of social identification. While the revolution was necessarily bathed in a religious illumination, the territorial and occupational units which constituted the political constituency from which the *jama'a* was drawn indicate that the *jihad* was principally concerned with authority. From this perspective the following to whom Fodio appealed was, strictly speaking, trans-ethnic; they were principally downtrodden, disenfranchised commoners, who were for the most part heavily taxed, misguided by the officeholders, and inequitably judged.

The social blueprint held by the Muslim intelligentsia was, of course, quite unlike the model of society envisioned by the former Hausa Kings. Fodio, above all else, aspired to establish a community of believers under the aegis of the Muslim state and nourished by the security of *Shari'a* rule. The *jihad* projected a new social order; the king was to be replaced by an emir, a first among equals, whose legitimacy rested on personal piety toward Allah, in whom all authority was ultimately vested. Political process was relatively unbureaucratic, designed to limit the excesses of palace centered *sarauta* rule and to redress the hypocrisy of a nominally Muslim kingship sustained in some measure by local religious belief. The architecture of the new emirate system was explicitly detailed in Fodio's exegesis on the Kano constitution, the *Diya' al-hukkam*, which was modified, adapted, and reformed by the Shehu's Caliphal successors. As Last (1970) has observed, there was a sense in which the political and intellectual history of the nineteenth century was an extended exercise in the implementation and reform of the original blueprint. The practical political consequence of this grandiose social design was the birth of a huge Muslim community, the Sokoto Caliphate, covering some 150,000 square miles.

The *jihad* of the early 1800s, then, established a Muslim emirate aristocracy which ruled, through Islamic law, a community of free and servile peasants (*talakawa*). The emirs allocated land in the form of fiefs to office holding nobles and slaves who were the agents for tax collection. The office holders and the emirs controlled state power, intervened in the production system, and presided over a relatively wealthy urban merchant class. The state extracted surpluses from the *talakawa* as corvée labor, rents in kind (*zakkat*), and money taxes. Central fiscal policy, certainly in Kano emirate, created incentives for immigration, effected tariff controls, and encouraged commodity production. There is every indication that during the nineteenth century the emirates prospered, the state apparatuses became more centralized, while Islamic learning and jurisprudence flourished. As a prosperous formation, ideologically knitted together through Islamic law and culture, the ruling class hegemony was never seriously threatened.

The material basis of the Caliphal state was fundamentally peasant production, although the "commoditization" of the rural economy was clearly limited. The basic unit of production in the Caliphate was the extended household (*gandu*), embracing sons, clients, and slaves in a diffuse domestic structure. Each household head organized agricultural and craft production, the distribution of the product, and payment of taxes. In spite of the juridical ambiguity of land in Muslim society, it seems safe to assume that customary law provided for considerable security of tenure among Hausa farmers. Such household groups, then, possessed the means of production, provided labor, and disposed of at least part of their collective product. But as a totality the Caliphate was neither integrated into a single division of labor nor was it a peripheral dependency of North Africa. Contact with the Muslim diaspora was diffuse and informal, principally through peripatetic scholars, the *hadj*, and the Islamic brotherhoods. The *jihadi* ideology provided both the basis for internal state building and also a cultural link to a more universalistic Muslim community (Lubeck 1979).

The depression of the 1870s, however, changed all this, since it marked the terminal point in Britain's domination of world production and trade. Prices, profits, and trade fell drastically and unemployment grew markedly as Britain faced effective competition and protectionist legislation from newer and more robust European states. Not unexpectedly, the response of British capital was an aggressive search for untapped markets, in tandem with an enthusiastic drive to procure regular, cheap, and abundant supplies of industrial raw materials. For essentially similar reasons other European powers sought to preserve and extend their own regional commercial hegemonies by carving spheres of geopolitical influence, largely through treaties of protection which proved to be the forerunners of formal colonial rule. Such renewed competition and the threat of reduced merchant profits not only provoked a confrontation between West African and European merchant capitals—and particularly eroded the shaky commercial alliance that had emerged during the nineteenth century—but also reaffirmed the necessity of formal control over peasant production; in other words, of a colonial overrule capable of extending cheap bulk transport and consolidating profitable trading networks.

What concerns me here is the manner in which Chamberlain's drive for a "national estate" was ultimately achieved in the face of a complex indigenous social system; how, in other words, did colonial capitalism develop in northern Nigeria, and more specifically, what was the impact of the subsumption of rural producers into the circuits of international capital upon the peasant labor process? At a simple descriptive level the imperial mission was quite transparent. The Colonial Office promoted a system of Indirect Rule, a peculiar synthesis of nineteenth century emirate administration and direct colonial intervention. In the process, the cowry was replaced by a European specie; emirate taxation was simplified, systematized, and incorporated into an embracing system of revenue and assessment; slavery was tardily abolished; and the colonial state organized both voluntary and forced recruitment of labor, principally for construction and porterage. The colonial courts quickly extended their jurisdiction to include the activities of the firms, and their agents, which facilitated the extension of commerce into the interior proper. European companies were free to combine at will, while the conservative fiscal and currency policy of the banks served the firms whose merchant monopoly mitigated against new investment activities. Surplus money capital was repatriated to Great Britain with the profits of the firms and large portions of government salaries.

The theoretical point which I wish to emphasize, however, is the critical role of European merchant capital which, at the beginning of the colonial period, was relatively autonomous in its operation though formally subsumed by industrial capital. As Hesketh Bell and Charles Temple observed, Britain's interests in northern Nigeria were those of trade which did not require "the exclusion of the natives from the land." The dominance of this historic form of capital and its support through an influential cadre of political officers like Sir Percy Girouard averted the creation either of an indigenous landlord class or of a settler economy. Paradoxically, the architect of Indirect Rule, Lord Lugard, wished to convert the Caliphal aristocracy into a landlord class; his vision was of a bureaucratized Islamic theocracy in which the *sarauta* employed ex-slave wage laborers on their farms. As it turned out, the Northern Nigerian Lands Committee of 1910 established, against all manner of information to the contrary, that private property was alien to the native mind and should be, in the tradition of Henry George, nationalized. In this way, the preservation of a land-holding peasantry and the interests of trade were fulfilled while, as H. R. Palmer observed, the usurer and the land grabber were both contained.

The triumph of merchant capital did not alter the fact that the colonial state had to be self-supporting. Shackled by a small colonial office grant-in-aid and huge debt financing in the period up to 1906, the administrative imperative was obviously the securement of sources of revenue for self-finance. As is well known, this was accomplished principally through direct taxation of rural producers. The colonial concern for extending and systematizing pre-colonial taxes meshed nicely with the concerns of the British Cotton Growing Association and its merchant brethren who sought to supply a flagging British economy with strategic raw materials. The rapid introduction of specie in which taxes had to be paid compelled peasant producers to adopt the cultivation of cotton and especially groundnuts. The early territorial, administrative and fiscal reforms which resulted in the Native Administration (NA) system, staffed by a class of salaried bureaucrats and largely controlled by the traditional aristocracy, were attempts to regularize a revenue system to fulfill the demands of the colonial state and interests of the merchants.

The upshot of the first decade of colonial rule, then, was that the colonial state clearly required the Caliphal elite in order to rule. The Europeans feared a rural rebellion, and the shortage of political officers—only a handful of Europeans ran Kano Province with a population of several millions—further fueled their insecurity. Indirect Rule was a political and economic necessity but the conversion of the *sarauta* into NA officials equally necessitated the devolution of much political power. The dependence of the Colonial State on the Caliphal aristocracy was reflected in the manner in which Lugard effectively ignored the continuation of palace slavery in spite of his rhetorical concern with its immediate abolition. The *sarauta* was also the medium through which the international firms gained access to Hausa merchants who were to fulfill the critical local level buying operations in the groundnut and cotton networks.

In short, within the first decade colonial economic interests were achieved through the preservation of the class prerogatives of the *sarauta*. The hegemonic position of the new compradore aristocracy was further deepened by the growth of Islamic influence which colonial rule affected. As Lubeck's work indicates (1979:199), the Islamic nationalist reaction to conquest by Christian infidels consolidated Muslim hegemony in the emirates. Equally, the cultivation of pre-colonial administration and the further centralization of the state supported Islamic institutions, particularly in the absence of a white settler community and a significant missionary vanguard. Indeed, bureaucratization favored the position of emirs and through them elements of the traditional aristocracy who were presented with new offices to bestow on clients. In the Weberian sense, the rationalization of bureaucracy involved no leveling, for the prerogatives of the Muslim ruling class were preserved intact. The rise of a compradore Islamic elite was, thus, expressive of the removal of traditional constraints on centralized emirate power. The emirs, supported by the military and communications apparatus of the colonial state and mediated by a hegemonic Islamic ideology, could retain and even extend their domination over the *talakawa*. As Abdulahi (1977:79) put it, the colonial epoch in the North was above all a reflection of the seemingly endless capacity of the elite to accommodate and contain the British political officers without loosing its hold on the peasantry.

With the consolidation of the new compradore class and the creation of the Native Authorities, the colonial state could proceed with the business of expanding export commodity production and extending its revenue assessment systems. In a system in which rural producers maintain control of the means of production and for whom household reproduction is the priority in their economic calculus, regulation of what is actually produced tends to be highly problematic. In northern Nigeria, tax proved to be a rather blunt instrument for expanding peasant surpluses, and any system which works best during a global crisis—witness the massive increase in commodity production when prices were at their lowest in the 1930s—is necessarily suspect. Though the size of the collective peasant produce was not easily regulated, the growth of commodities in circulation benefited Nigerian merchants who dominated the lower orders of the buying networks. Using capital fronted by the international firms, local merchants, usually working in tandem with village heads and rural NA bureaucrats, developed an advance and crop-mortgage system which used the credit relation as a means for controlling peasant production. By the 1930s rural indebtedness had proliferated enormously.

Certainly by the end of the First World War, commodity production had become "internalized" in the cycle of household reproduction (Berstein 1979). Since the vast majority of middle peasants were concerned with covering the costs of reproduction of labor, the exchange value of their products could fall without forcing them out of production. This is the basis of what Bernstein calls the "simple reproduction squeeze" in which falling commodity prices or a high tax burden is experienced as a deterioration in the terms of exchange of export commodities relative to those needed for simple reproduction. In the 1930s Hausa peasants confronted this crisis by intensifying commodity production and reducing levels of consumption. This intensification of the labor of the household to increase production also involved some sort of ecological deterioration. It was also the basis of the so-called competitiveness of peasant production. The precariousness of the material and technical basis of peasant production in Hausaland combined with the pressures of price and tax variability to render many households vulnerable to massive subsistence crises.

To summarize, the state embodied the tensions and struggles involved in the articulation of Nigerian peasants with various fractions of local and international capital. This process preserved the *form* of peasant production yet transformed the conditions of reproduction. It opened up avenues for the appropriation of an expanded surplus product by European firms; but to accomplish this, class alliances were sealed which ensured that the *sarauta* elites and indigenous merchants also appropriated part of the product. The state, then, was the distillation of those forces involved in the confrontation of European capitals, indigenous modes of production, and local patterns of resource endowment. Of course, the colonial state above all bore the stamp of European merchant capital, but this had to be secured along with the creation of the conditions of existence of the state itself: first, the military and political pacification of the Caliphate; and second, the establishment of mechanisms of administration, revenue, political structure, and communications. It was in this process of state building that conditions and limits on capitalist penetration occurred and during which contradictions emerged.

In northern Nigeria Lord Lugard wished to transform a powerful slave-holding, tribute collecting aristocracy into a class of landlords; he wished to modify their means of controlling labor without reducing its extent. At the same time, he also wished to rationalize tax collection and administration through the *sarauta* elites. But the desire for a productive ruling class simultaneously cut across the basis of that class's power, and what Lugard got was extortion, plunder, and administrative chaos. Fearing popular rebellion, the British backed off, which terminated their attempt to create a Victorian land-holding aristocracy. In any case, Lugard's scheme was undercut by Girouard and the Lands Committee who used the ideas of Henry George, the colonial experience in Lower Burma, and their obdurate claim that private property was foreign to the Hausa mentality, to push through the state control of land. In short, in spite of evidence to the contrary and much shaky reasoning, the land issue was settled in favor of state power rooted in the control of the means of production. This was certainly a reflection and recognition of the power of the Caliphal elites who were accordingly allied with colonial authority, but it no less guaranteed the hegemony of trade interests, which, as Temple implied, were the primary concerns of the Europeans.

If the peasantry clearly emerged as the bedrock of the colonial state it was less evident how their surplus product was to be appropriated and divided. The enormous expansion in commodity production was achieved by a preservation of household production even though the purpose of production underwent a radical transformation. But the state did not necessarily always back the interests of individual capitalists or always intercede with more onerous tax burdens to increase revenue and stimulate export crop production. As Freund (1981) notes, the government generally promoted conservative policies toward pre-capitalist social forms in the interests of stability. It was scarcely a rarity for the state to receive sharp criticism from firms complaining that direct taxes crippled trade. Moreover, the state occasionally attempted to regulate the advance system of the middlemen and to actively support peasant interests:

> Peasants could receive a fair return based on average socially necessary labor time in exchange of their commodities if the struggle between capital and the peasantry had reached a point where it was advantageous for the state to safeguard peasant commodity production against excessive merchant profits (Bryceson 1980:283).

All this is to say that the state, the firms, the Nigeria middlemen, and the *sarauta* all wrestled over the appropriation of the surplus product. But ultimately the entire edifice rested on the millions of peasants doing what they were supposed to do; namely, produce and consume commodities in a predictable way. But smallholders everywhere have been remarkably ornery and this is why the issue of labor control was so central to state operations. Taxation was the fundamental mechanism for compelling peasants to contribute to the cash economy but it was necessarily blunt (Cooper 1981). Monetary demands might be met through craft production, labor migration, or borrowing, as well as by planting groundnuts. Excessive taxation ran the risk, in the early years at least, of resistance or massive emigration. In this limited sense, the partial incorporation of Hausa small holders gave them breathing space; a farmer who owned 4 acres and produced millet was given room to move. He was, in part, "uncaptured"; he was able to hold the market at arm's length. Markets presented alternatives for some which avoided either wage labor or cash crop production.

Yet, as Fred Cooper also noted, the Great Depression revealed that if the market could be held at arm's length, it could not be avoided. Taxes had to be paid, and some purchased consumer items had become obligatory. As he says, the Depression revealed the great virtue of partial commercialization in agriculture: peasants' cash hunger kept them producing cheap commodities, but their subsistence production would take care of their social security. It was precisely because commodities could not be secured simply through conditions of exchange that merchant capital increasingly employed the credit relation to bind peasants, to assert itself at the level of production itself.

What were the direct implications of this retarded form of capitalist development in northern Nigeria for the labor process itself? First, since merchant capital operated principally in the sphere of exchange, it was incapable of transforming the mode of production. Accordingly, capital's control over the labor process was partial and sporadic. Indeed, the colonial state actively inhibited the development of the forces of production, particularly in agriculture, by using state sanctions to increase the extraction of absolute surplus value. Plantations and European agro-capital, for instance, were subservient to domestic or household systems of production and not given the opportunity to develop at the expense of what Governor Clifford called a "natural," "cheap," and "self-supporting" peasant economy.

Second, as a corollary, the process of capitalist development was markedly uneven; non-capitalist forms of production were differentially preserved, wage labor and "commoditization" of land progressed slowly and unevenly, and the appearance of a fully proletarianized class was forestalled (see Murray 1981).

Third, while merchant capital broke the cycle of household reproduction and commodity production expanded—which further "individuated" peasant economy (Bernstein 1979)—it also left peasants with a measure of autonomy; there was, in other words, a low level of labor's subordination to capital.

Fourth, the resilience of a relatively autonomous peasant labor process was a reflection of: (i) the rate of profit which obtained in agriculture and which explains the penetration of capital into the sphere of production (and conversely of the realm of trade as *the* means for local accumulation); and (ii) the emergence of a new social division of labor through expanded long distance, dry season wage labor migration as a major source of non-farm income to secure household reproduction.

And finally, if colonialism centralized and expanded state power, this was sealed through a class alliance with the indigenous *sarauta* who were able to use state power to expand *their* control over peasants. Yet this expanded political authority and the new forms of class power were both legitimated by Islam itself, and specifically through the critical support of the *ulema*.

In the following section I shall argue that this constellation of economic, political, and ideological tendencies—what I have collectively referred to as the peasant labor process under [Nigerian] colonial capitalism—informs any analysis of peasant revolt and resistance. In sum, I believe that one must locate the absence of large-scale insurrection and the emergence of the other "hidden" forms of peasant resistance and political consciousness in the partial and sporadic control of capital[8] over labor and in the political-ideological conditions under which this labor process obtained. Peasant politics in northern Nigeria resides, I believe, in the peculiar and contradictory pattern of relative autonomy and partial control characteristic of the peasant labor process under Nigerian mercantile capitalism.

Peasant Dissent and Hidden Forms
of Consciousness, 1900–1945

In Tanzazia, [the] partial and sporadic [control of labor by capital] is reflected
. . . by labor [which] continues to 'wrestle' (Marx, *Capital*, I, p. 490) with
capital, successfully showing signs of indiscipline and insubordination. These
signs include subverting production when it appears too marginal to produce
positive returns, diverting inputs to food crops when the returns to labour
are higher than cash crops, becoming 'sick,' frying cotton seeds, planting
cassava cuttings upside down, destroying the roots of tobacco plants and
refusing to harvest tea when profits would be slim to nonexistent, following
deductions for inputs, feigning stupidity to avoid certain quality and quantity
controls in the production process, etc. (Mueller 1981:28–29).

From the very first requests by British trading companies for concessionary
privileges, European penetration of the Caliphate was met with obstruction
and hostility. It is clear from the early exchanges between the Sultan of
Sokoto and the colonial forces that Muslim resistance to illegitimate ex-
pansionism by "Christian dogs" was perceived as obligatory. During the
first five years the colonial presence and the overthrow of many of the
emirs lent the mass resistance a distinctive Mahdist tenor. Lugard felt that
Mahdist movements surfaced almost every year between 1900 and 1906,
culminating in one of the last violent reactions to imperial incorporation
at Satiru.

The insurrection at Satiru village in 1906, occasioned by the proclamation
of a *jihad* against the British and the emergence of the village head (Mallam
Isa) as a Mahdi, reached critical levels following the deaths of the Acting
Resident at Sokoto, two officers, and 25 mounted infantry at the hands of
a motley group of peasants armed with bows and arrows. The rebels,
including a new found Mahdi who succeeded Mallam Isa after his death
in combat, had captured a Maxim gun, rifles, and accrued a good deal of
prestige in the process (Adeleye 1971; Tukur 1979). The slaying of a British
officer elicited a particularly brutal response from the colonial state but only
with the complicity of the *sarakuna*. Satiru, in all its bloodiness, was one
of the few instances of collective peasant response, but it also marked the
first instance of class collaboration between the British and the Hausa-
Fulani elites. After 1906 the history of peasant politics was quite different.

In this early period, then, Islam provided the ideological frame and the
means for collective peasant protest; it was ideologically inspired, in some
sense obligatory, and Mahdist in tone. But by 1908, much of the early
dissent and the threat of rural rebellion had disappeared entirely and never
resurfaced. In part, this was an obvious reflection of state power and the
military supremacy of the colonial forces which had slaughtered several
hundred men, women, and children at Satiru and summarily put down the
first small-scale tax riots. In fact, the state had precisely used this superiority
to disarm the districts in 1907. However, what really marked the watershed

of semi-organized peasant militancy in this period was the successful attempt by Lugard to, in his own words, "preserve and strengthen the ruling class" (1970:221). Satiru was critical in this respect because it provided the first instance of class collaboration between the British and the *sarauta:* "the revolt of Satiru changed relations between the British and the ruling Fulani from superordination based upon force to a near parity based on common interests" (Smith 1960:205). Within several years the *sarauta* were salaried employees of the colonial government and there was finally no ambiguity regarding the nature of their allegiance. From the perspective of the peasant, of course, the *sarauta* now not only had the backing of a strong colonial state, but they were also ideologically legitimate in the sense that they had the support of the Muslim clerics.

The outbreak of the First World War, which the Turkish Caliphate had entered on the side of the Central Powers, threatened this class alliance and prompted new British fears of a pan-Islamic revolt. Paranoia among British administrators in the northern emirates sustained the view that wartime insecurities could transform a malleable *talakawa* into visionary *jihadists.* H.R. Palmer presumed, quite correctly as it turned out, that British survival ultimately depended on their support of the emirs they had attempted to co-opt:

> Native rulers and *ulema* are not an absolute guarantee against fanatical outbreaks but they are the most effective buffer that can be devised . . . the judicial councils of the Emirs, the Cadis and Imams are in receipt of substantial salaries from the Native treasuries (Palmer, cited in Osuntokun 1977:143–144).

There was indeed some popular unrest in 1914–1916; a rebel District Head from Fika emirate actually captured Potiskum town in 1915, and a group of peasants were slaughtered near Dambam. Other disquiet was reported in Bornu, Fika, Yola, and Sokoto, but, in what might have been a difficult period, the emirs and Hausa bureaucrats were steadfast in their loyalty to the British. The Mahdist scare and the slight colonial hysteria over Islamic propaganda and radical *ulema* proved to be unnecessary—and unfounded— for the very same reason.

If Satiru was the highwater mark of collective peasant militancy, a more individualized and strategic rural dissent was nonetheless commonplace. Two years after Satiru, Yola was apparently threatened by "propagandistic mallams" (Tukur 1979:331) while a protracted, small-scale guerrilla resistance continued in the swamps of Hadjia and, more persistently, by pagans in and around the Plateau. Protest was certainly sporadic but also strategic, frequently taking the form of cutting telegraph wires. Significantly, some of the early popular protest was directed against the new *sarauta* class who, insofar as they were British electives replacing the deposed emirs, were seen as geneologically illegitimate. Rural hostility toward the new District Heads (*hakimai*)—who, as NA salaried officials stood arm in arm with the British—was especially marked when district reorganization projected the *hakimai* into their rural domiciles. The physical presence of the District

Heads was not only a burdensome affront, but cross-cut already existing patronage ties which were a legacy of the nineteenth century. Some of the early *hakimai* were treated contemptuously and, at very best, with much indifference.

It proved to be taxation which elicited some of the most directed, if localized, peasant reaction. Perhaps the most quoted case surfaced in Dawakin Tofa District in Kano in 1908 in direct response to a new system of assessment. A spontaneous rejection of the new imposition culminated in the outright condemnation of all taxation and the popular deposition of several village heads who were summarily shunted out of their communities altogether. Resident Cargill over-reacted and dispatched 75 mounted troops and a Maxim to Dumbulum and was met with complete diffidence, although he effected a large number of arrests. And this was not unusual; early tax collection in Katsina was conducted with military support and occasional punitive expeditions; several "ringleaders" from Gwadabawa District in Sokoto were arrested in 1909 for tax evasion and imprisoned for 6 months; and blood was spilled in Adamawa in 1909 and again in 1911 among communities that refused to submit to assessment (Tukur 1979:672). Not all of this popular remonstration was particularly expressive of "popular" dissent. MacBride for example, reported considerable agitation in Dawaki ta Kudu District (Kano) against the adoption of the Revenue Survey Assessment, but it was propagated amongst large landowners by "interested persons residing in Kano" (National Archives NPK SNF 17 30261/1937). The previous lump sum system computed by village headmen almost certainly undertaxed influential Kulaks; the revenue assessment conversely carried a much heavier burden for the rich; hence the protest "by these classes with vested interests in the present system, particularly the village headmen" (NAK SNP17 30261/1937).

But much of what passed as resistance to capitalist penetration was of a wholly different order. It was grounded in a longstanding tradition of "dissent from within," to use Last's (1970:356) adage, in which relations between peasant and state were defensive and evasive. For didactic purposes I refer to these as (i) withdrawal, (ii) individuated resistance, and (iii) disinformation. In the case of the latter I include the plethora of communicative devices by which peasants attempted to wriggle from the clutches of colonial officers. The colonial ledgers, and the District Notebooks in particular, are littered with references to farmers ignoring or "forgetting" local ordinances and Provincial dictates; this was especially pronounced in the attempts to hide children and assets, to disguise granaries, in the process of tacit agreement referred to colloquially as *sai abinda ka ce*, and, of course, through outright deceit (Spittler 1979). It is no accident that Resident Temple devoted a wonderfully endearing chapter in his book on Indirect Rule in Northern Nigeria to "the art of lying," which "has reached a very high state of perfection among the natives of the Northern Provinces" (1918:103). Tax collection, according to Temple, could reduce the unwary political officer to a "condition of bewilderment and bemusement so as to render [him] incapable" (p. 113).

By withdrawal, I refer largely to the process of tax avoidance by migration or flight, evasive tactics on the part of Fulani herders in hiding animals, leasing cattle to kin in French or German territory, or simply increasing their mobility. The decision to flee was very much rooted, as Last (1970) shows, in traditions of nineteenth century dissent, though in the course of the twentieth century, land scarcity and the costs of mobility gradually limited its efficacy.

And finally there was individual resistance, which included smuggling (the illicit groundnut trade to Niger), occasional theft (tin stealing on the Plateau), highway robbery (witness the grain thefts in 1914 and 1927), desertion of forced labor from the mines and public works projects, crop destruction, and acts of sabotage (households consumed government cottonseed or used it as rat poison and as livestock feed). Understandably, a good deal of this individual resistance centered on merchant capital; cotton was dampened to increase its weight or sold illegally on the local market; other farmers attempted to withhold commodities, to take advances from buyers when no cotton had been planted (or to take several advances from different buyers for the same crop), assuming quite correctly that debts were not readily enforced in a society in which public criticisms of usury and interest carried some weight (see Lennihan 1982).

In much of this peasant dissent, quietism and diffidence is to be understood as effective protest. Much "protest," such as it was, centered on parochical issues and illuminated a relatively low degree of political consciousness. but there also developed a tradition which subsumed cultural forms of protest—poetry, praise epithets, verse and so on—which, though barely understood by the colonial officers, constituted a symbolic opposition, as Scott (1977) calls it, representing "the functional equivalent of class consciousness in pre-industrial agrarian societies" (p. 284). In this sense, the popular resistance of the peasantry was part of a long historical record of struggles over the disposition of their product. The colonial period simply ushered in a new social field-of-force in which the surplus was appropriated and fought over in new ways.

Why, then, did peasant resistance overwhelmingly assume the form of dissent from within? I have suggested that the specific form which capitalist development assumed in northern Nigeria was both retarded and uneven. As a consequence, to use Cumings' terms, there was no pronounced horizontal vectoring of class based interests in the sense that colonial hegemony witnessed a rapid dispossession of peasant producers. Commoditization expanded significantly at the household level, peasant households, to differing degrees, lost some of their autonomy, and social differentiation assumed a complex stratification based on the extent to which social reproduction was secured through the sale of wage labor, craft production, or mercantile profits. Yet, fundamentally, peasants were not separated from their means of production; labor was only partially subordinated to capital. Accordingly, the peasant labor process under colonial capitalism provided *individual remedies* for household reproduction and circumvented the threat of pro-

TABLE 1

Elements of the Labor Process	Peasant Response	
Land ownership and self-management	1.	'Exit' option
	2.	Self-exploitation
State/political control	1.	Ignorance, deformation
	2.	Evasion/flight/desertion
	3.	Consumption of government seed/crop destruction/smuggling
	4.	Cultural protest
	5.	Theft/sabotage
Surplus appropriation (through tax, usury, unequal exchange)	1.	Deceit
	2.	Sale resistance/smuggling
	3.	Withdrawal/commodity hold-ups
	4.	Market/merchant resistance
	5.	'Overindebtedness'/false loans
Commoditization, differential reward (scale of reproduction)	1.	Migration
	2.	Theft
	3.	Internal domestic conflict
	4.	Labor control

letarianization that has historically been resisted by rural producer everywhere.

Table 1 rather simplistically lays out the relationships between elements of the labor process and forms of peasant resistance. I do not wish to suggest that there exists some form of Pavlovian causality between peasant dissent and the properties of productive relations. Rather, retarded capitalism left a residue of peasant autonomy which was readily exercised; to use Marx's words, peasants wrestled with capital in a manner in which the hegemony of the colonial state or its class allies was far from inevitable. But the absence of peasant rebellion was not simply a reflection of their victorious "autonomy"—indeed their material deprivation and the sequence of colonial famines obviously suggests otherwise—but also that the labor process itself further individuated the social nature of production, limiting the horizontal vectoring necessary for collective action. The labor process ensured that individual remedies were available, but at the same moment increased commodity production, further individuated peasant social life, and effectively limited, at least in the short-term (viz., until the process of proletarianization had progressed significantly), large-scale collective response.

In short, the labor process did not provide the institutional basis for peasant solidarity, yet provided a tactical space with which they could resist in quite specific ways. The negation of an institutional solidarity is reflected in at least five rather obvious tendencies contained within the commodity economy. First, commoditization moved hand in hand with the decline of extended households, the dissolution of collective work groups, the disappearance of supra-household institutions like the *sarkin noma*,[9] and the gradual transformation of these horizontal social linkages which assisted the reproduction of individual households. In this sense, the demise of a moral economy was replaced by a highly individuated petty commodity system in which households increasingly confronted the market as individuals.

Second, up to the 1940s uncultivated bush permitted rural producers the traditional option of flight (or avoidance) rather than face rural landlessness (a condition which is seen by the Hausa themselves as metaphorically akin to slavery) or oppression.

Third, in spite of the threat of material deprivation, especially during the Depression, off-farm incomes enabled rural cultivators to survive through self-exploitation. In particular, in northern Nigeria, dry season migration (usually for 4–6 months following the upland harvest) provided this critical function, and during one year in the early 1950s for example, 230,000 adult males passed through Sokoto Province alone *en route* to the southern cities. This migratory stream created a social division of labor which further spatially and socially fragmented the conditions of peasant livelihood and political socialization.

Fourth, commoditization also acted to differentiate the peasantry in complex forms. For instance, there emerged a wealthy farmer-trader class whose material position was contradictory with respect to the broad mass of rural producers but which was nonetheless ideologically aligned with the peasantry. This also made for a social heterogeneity at the village level rather than a simple horizontal vectoring.

And finally, the fact that groundnuts became the major export commodity in the north—a crop which can be intercropped with millet (the principal means of subsistence)—did not necessitate a massive displacement of foodstuffs but conversely provided some sort of agronomic stability which did not threaten either *sarauta* privilege or household reproduction.

Of course, the labor process presupposed certain ideological and political conditions of existence and I have implied that both are of some consequence in coming to terms with peasant diffidence. On the one hand, the colonial state, if fiscally fragile, was nonetheless capable of a massive military superiority in the countryside, and it is appropriate to recall in this regard that it is state weakness which breeds a dissenting tradition, for "it is the breakdown of a mode of social control which prompts and allows social revolution" (Skocpol 1976:181). On the other hand, the class alliance which the colonial state forged with the indigenous Muslim elites enabled the *sarauta* to use Islam as a means of legitimation and societal control. In this, following Touraine (1977:326), one can quite legitimately talk of peasant "alienation."

Alienation is the fragmentation of the individual or collective consciousness subjected to the contradictory pulls of dependent participation and class consciousness. The first renders it impossible to view society as a set of social relations and imposes the image of a moral order, to which one must adapt in order to avoid guilt. The second forbids that adaptation and produces rejection in default of actual conflict. With the result that the alienated consciousness is imprisoned in a withdrawal.

The popular consciousness was in some sense dominated by alienation which was one pre-condition of non-revolt.

* * *

In this essay I have attempted to chart the rather troubled waters which lead from rural commercialization in its varied forms to the equally varied expressions of peasant politics, specifically non-revolt. Among Hausa peasants in northern Nigeria, I have sought to locate the "dissent from within" in the labor process under a retarded capitalism and within the political-ideological conditions which attended the class alliances upon which the colonial edifice was constructed. I have documented that from within the ranks of a non-insurrectionary peasantry there was nonetheless a sort of subterranean reservoir of consciousness which was given expression in a variety of individuated, if prosaic, forms of protest. In this sense we can follow Edward Thompson when he says that when individuals find themselves in societies structured in determinate ways, they experience exploitation, identify antagonistic interests, and struggle around these issues. But it was not until long after the Second World War that the sociological basis of peasant resistance was markedly broadened, as capital accumulation in Nigeria, fed by OPEC dollars, entered a new phase and peasants faced what John Berger calls the final act of historic elimination. With new and expanded forms of state intervention, the labor process that I have described has been progressively transformed. On some of the large development projects, rural producers face dispossession, and in some areas there is the emergence of a landless class. In these circumstances rural protest has escalated—witness the killings on the Bakalori irrigation project near So-koto—and politicized peasants have turned to the populist People's Redemption Party. This does not imply that dissent from within disappears—indeed the integrated rural development projects are in many ways bound by it—but that such new material circumstances will generate new and perhaps more collectively oriented forms of rural protest.

Notes

Due to the scope of this paper and the limitations of space, my examination of the process of commoditization among Hausa producers is necessarily brief. For a more detailed discussion of this issue and of the "production squeeze," see Watts (1983), esp. Chapters 4, 5 and 6.

1. Thompson's original expanded formulation of the moral economy was a reflection of the contradictory strengths and weaknesses of state power and patrician-plebian

class relations: "But it is not necessary also to say what this hegemony does not entail. It does not entail any acceptance by the poor of the gentry's paternalism upon the gentry's own terms or in their approved self-image. The poor might be willing to award their deference to the gentry, but only for a price. The price was substantial. And the deference was often without the least illusion: it could be seen from below as being one part necessary self-preservation, one part the calculated extraction of whatever could be extracted. Seen in this way, the poor imposed upon the rich some of the duties and functions of paternalism just as much as deference was in turn imposed upon them. Both parties to the equation were constrained within a common field-to-force." (Thompson 1978:163)

2. For a sprinkling of what has become a volatile debate in English historical circles see Anderson (1980), Samuel (1981), McLennan (1982), Thompson (1978).

3. Marx (1967:Vol.I,78) defined the elementary factors of the labor process as (i) the personal activity of man, i.e. work, (ii) the subject of that work, and (iii) its instruments.

4. Corvée labor by a family on a landlord's estate, for example.

5. Sharecropping systems in which the direct produce renders a predetermined share of the household product to the landowner as a rent for access to the means of production. Both corvée and sharecropping, though semifeudal/servile relations of production, may flourish even though peasants are in some sense directly incorporated into an identifiably global capitalist system.

6. I am assuming, as has historically been the case for much of sub-Saharan Africa, that there is no landlord class capable of exacting specific production regimes.

7. "Therefore, it needs to be explained how and under what conditions an interest in the maximization of profit brought about the penetration of capital into the sphere of production. For this to occur, the profit rate that could be expected from production had to be not only equal to, but greater than, the profit rate common in trade alone." (Schlumbohm 1981:103)

8. This partial control and the ability of the peasant to cling to property does not, of course, imply material well-being. Indeed, as Lenin observed: "It is precisely the peasant's property that is the main cause of his impoverishment and his degradation. The protection of the peasantry is not protection from poverty, but the protection that chains the peasant to his property." (1972:Vol.IV,98–99)

9. An ancient but prestigious redistributive office, granted to the largest farmer and which functioned, among other things, as a famine relief system during poor harvests.

References

Abdullah, M. 1977. "The Modernization of Elites in North Western State, Nigeria," Ph.D. dissertation, University of Chicago.

Adas, M. 1980. "Moral Economy or Contest State?" *Journal of Social History*, 15:525–546.

Adeleye, R. 1971. *Power and Diplomacy in Northern Nigeria 1804–1906*, London: Longmans.

Anderson, P. 1980. *Arguments within English Marxism*, London: New Left Books.

Banaji, J. 1977. "Modes of Production in a Materialist Conception of History," *Capital and Class*, 3:1–44.

Bernstein, H. 1979. "African Peasantries: A Theoretical Framework," *Journal of Peasant Studies*, 6:420–443.

Bryceson, D. F. 1980. "Changes in Peasant Food Production and Food Supply in Relation to the Historical Development of Commodity Production in Tanganyika," *Journal of Peasant Studies*, 7:281–311.

Burawoy, M. 1978. *The Manufacture of Consent*, Chicago: University of Chicago Press.

Cooper, F. 1981. "Africa and the World Economy," Paper presented at the Annual African Studies Association Conference, Bloomington, Indiana.

Cumings, B. 1981. "Interest and Ideology in the Study of Agrarian Politics," *Politics and Society*, I:467–495.

Deere, C., and A. de Janvry. 1979. "A Conceptual Framework for the Empirical Analysis of Peasants," *American Journal of Agricultural Economics*, 6:601–611.

de Janvry, A. 1981. *The Agrarian Question and Reformism in Latin America*, Baltimore: Johns Hopkins Press.

Freund, W. 1981. *Labor and Capital in Nigerian Tin Mines*, London: Longmans.

Hane, M. 1982. *Peasants, Rebels and Outcasts: The Underside of Modern Japan*, New York: Pantheon.

Hobsbawm, E. 1982. "The Lowest Depths," *New York Review of Books*, April 15, pp. 15–16.

Hyden, G. 1980. *Beyond Ujamaa*, Berkeley: University of California Press.

Isaacman, A. *et al.* 1980. "'Cotton is the Mother of Poverty': Peasant Resistance to Forced Cotton Production in Mozambique 1938–1961," *International Journal of African Historical Studies*, 13:581–615.

Last, M. 1970. "Aspects of Administration and Dissent in Hausaland, 1800–1968," *Africa*, XL:345–357.

Lenin, V. I. 1974. *The Development of Capitalism in Russia*, Moscow: Progress Publishers.

———. 1972. *Collected Works*, Vols. I-IV. Moscow: Progress Publishers.

Lennihan, L. 1982. "Agency and Structure and the Growth of Wage Labor in Northern Nigeria," Paper presented to a Workshop on State and Agriculture in Nigeria. University of California, Berkeley, (May 7–9).

Lubeck, P. 1979. "Islam and Resistance in Northern Nigeria," in W. Goldfrank, ed., *The World-System of Capitalism*, London: Sage.

Lugard, L. 1970. *Political Memoranda*, London: Cass.

Lukacs, G. 1971. *History and Class Consciousness*, Cambridge: M. I. T. Press.

Marx, K. 1967. *Capital*, Vols. I-III, New York: International Publishers.

McLennan, G. 1982. *Marxism and Methodologies of History*, London: New Left Books.

Mueller, S. 1981. "Barriers to the Further Development of Capitalism in Tanzania," *Capital and Class*, 15:23–54.

Murray, M. 1981. *The Development of Capitalism in Colonial Indochina 1870–1940*, Berkeley: University of California Press.

Osuntokun, A. 1977. *Nigeria and the First World War*, Ibadan: Longmans.

Paige, J. 1975. *Agrarian Revolution*, New York: Free Press.

Popkin, S. 1978. *The Rational Peasant*, Berkeley: University of California Press.

———. 1980. "The Rational Peasant," *Theory and Society*, 9:411–471.

Samuel, R., ed. 1981. *People's History and Socialist Theory*, London: Routledge and Kegan Paul.

Schlumbohm, J. 1981. "Relations of Production," in H. Medick, P. Kriedte, and J. Schlumbohm, eds., *Industrialization Before Industrialization*, Cambridge: Cambridge University Press.

Scott, J. 1976. *The Moral Economy of the Peasantry*, New Haven: Yale University Press.

———. 1977. "Hegemony and Peasantry," *Politics and Society*, 7:267–296.

Skocpol, T. 1976. "France, Russia and China: Structural Analysis of Social Revolutions," *Comparative Studies in Society and History*, 18:175–210.

144   *Michael Watts*

Smith, M. 1960. *Government in Zazzau*, London: Oxford University Press.
Spittler, G. 1979. "Peasants and the State in Niger," *Peasant Studies*, 8:30.
Tahir, I. 1975. "Scholars, Sufis, Saints and Capitalists," Ph.D. dissertation, Cambridge University.
Temple, C. 1968. *Native Races and Their Rulers*, London: Cass.
Thompson, E. P. 1978. *The Poverty of Theory*, New York: Monthly Review.
Touraine, A. 1977. *The Self-Reproduction of Society*, Chicago: University of Chicago Press.
Tukur, M. 1979. "The Imposition of British Colonial Domination on the Sokoto Caliphate," Ph.D. dissertation, Ahmadu Bello University.
Usman, Y. B. 1973. "The Transformation of Katsina," Ph.D. dissertation, Ahmadu Bello University, Nigeria.
Watts, M. 1983. *Silent Violence: Food, Famine and Peasantry in Northern Nigeria*, Berkeley: University of California Press.

8

One, Two, or Many Vietnams?
Social Theory and Peasant Revolution
in Vietnam and Guatemala

JEFFERY PAIGE

When the first American marines arrived in Vietnam in March 1965 they were, according to Philip Caputo, who was one of them, guided to the beaches of Danang (Tourane in Colonial Vietnam) by maps drawn by French cartographers. Similarly, American policy makers would have found, had they chosen to look, their best guide to the sociology of the quagmire in the works of such French scholars as Yves Henry and Pierre Gourou. Gourou's classic *The Peasants of the Tonkin Delta* remains the starting point for all later writing about peasant revolution in Vietnam, but the long American involvement produced what James Scott has called a "boomlet" in the study of peasant revolution in Vietnam and elsewhere (Caputo 1977:44, Henry 1932, Gourou 1955, Scott 1977:21). As the United States increases its military involvement in Central America it seems appropriate to inquire whether any of the scholarly theories developed in the earlier experience in Vietnam might generalize to fit still another peasant revolution half a world a way. Neither sound foreign policy nor good social theory can be based on "explanations" which in fact apply only to one time and place. Consideration of the Central American revolution and the case of Guatemala in particular should provide information about both. The goal of this article, however, is principally theoretical; to test theories developed to explain one case, Vietnam, in a second and largely independent case, Guatemala.

Scholarly analysis of the problem of peasant revolution in Vietnam has led to three different sets of theories, all of which make somewhat different predictions about the causes of peasant revolution in Vietnam and elsewhere and are, furthermore, at least in large part, mutually exclusive. The three theoretical perspectives might be called moral economy, political economy,

This chapter originally appeared in *Theory and Society* 12/4 (July 1983) and is reprinted with permission. Copyright 1983 by Jeffery Paige.

and class conflict. The first two terms were used by Samuel Popkin in his book *The Rational Peasant* to distinguish his own perspective on Vietnam, which he calls "political economy," from the perspective he calls "moral economy," after the title of James Scott's study of depression-era rebellions in Burma and Vietnam, *The Moral Economy of the Peasant.* "Moral economists" include not only Scott but also Eric Wolf, Joel Migdal and, to a lesser extent, Paul Mus and his students John McAlister and Frances Fitzgerald (Popkin 1979, Scott 1976, Wolf 1968, Migdal 1974, McAlister and Mus 1970, Fitzgerald 1972). Since political economy sometime implies the Marxist variety associated, for example, with the Union of Radical Political Economists, it is important to note that Popkin's political economy has a distinctly conservative cast and draws not on Marx but on the work of such American political theorists as Frohlich, Oppenheimer and Young, Mancur Olson, Brian Barry, and even Edward Banfield (Frohlich, Oppenheimer and Young 1971, Olson 1965, Barry 1970, Banfield, 1968). This leaves, obviously, a third interpretation which, to distinguish it from conservative political economy and avoid interminable debate over what is and is not Marxist, might be called "class conflict." This position in the interpretation of the Vietnamese revolution I claim for myself although it is very likely that of the revolutionaries themselves (Paige, 1975, Giap and Chinh 1974).

The three perspectives—moral economy, political economy, and class conflict—are not products of idiosyncracies of the Vietnamese case but rather of regularities in the structure of social movement theory. They are in fact representative of three general traditions in the study of social movements which Charles Tilly has called, respectively, Durkheimian, Millian and, with more courage than I can muster here, Marxist. Popkin and his fellow "political economists" can be unequivocally assigned to Tilly's Millian category by direct attribution. Millians, whom Tilly traces to the Utilitarian tradition of John Stuart Mill, can be identified by their affection for rational individuals guided by explicit decision rules and by their corresponding lack of interest in or, as Tilly would have it, fear of, class-based political action (Tilly 1978:24).[1] Popkin and associates are Millians not only because the subject of his book is "national" peasants but also because he explicitly acknowledges his intellectual debt to theorists such as Mancur Olson and Frohlich, Oppenheimer and Young who are named by Tilly as part of the Millian school (Popkin 1979:xiii, Tilly 1978:27–28). Characteristically, Popkin begins his book by evoking an image of Millian calculation in this quotation from Pierre Gourou: "We cannot help being astonished by the subtlety, the intrigue, of what a simple peasant is capable, when his wretched appearance might make one believe that he doesn't see beyond the muzzle of his buffalo" (Popkin 1979:frontispiece quoting Gourou 1955:311).

The rational peasant, as described by Popkin or by Gourou as well, is constantly plotting his individual advancement; and usually, although not invariably, at the expense of other less fortunate members of the peasant class. Social solidarity insofar as it exists at all in peasant society depends on political stalemate or stable dominant coalitions, not on any particular attachment, either social or emotional, to "folk society" or the "little tradition" or the "closed corporate village."

James Scott, Popkin's exemplary moral economist, begins his book on depression-era rebellions with a quote from Tawney about the position of the rural Chinese population being like " . . . that of a man standing permanently up to his neck in water, so that even a ripple might drown him" (Scott 1976:1).[2] The imagery of isolated individuals clinging to a precarious subsistence in the face of social and economic forces which threaten inundation is a central theme in Scott's book although the problem is not so much that drowning is inconvenient but rather that it is immoral. Such concerns are characteristic of theorists whom Tilly terms "Durkheimian." They share a common fear of the disruptive effects of industrialism and capitalism and view social movement responses to the breakdown of social solidarity during rapid change. It would simplify matters considerably if Tilly classified Scott's intellectual associates as Durkheimian just as he classified Popkin's as Millian. Unfortunately, Eric Wolf, whose *Peasant Wars of the Twentieth Century*, like Popkin's and Scott's books, was written because of and about Vietnam, is directly mentioned by Tilly as an example not of a Durkheimian but, of all things, a Marxist. It is true that Wolf shows a critical concern for the ravages of what he calls "North Atlantic Capitalism," but then Durkheim was equally concerned with the disruptive effects of capitalism on the French side of the North Atlantic and Wolf's comments on the consequences of capitalist expansion have a decidedly Durkheimian ring. Capitalist markets have ". . . torn men up by their roots and shaken them loose from their social relationships," (Wolf 1968:295) and for Wolf the "tactically mobile middle peasantry" is the main carrier of revolution because it is both most vulnerable to the changes wrought by capitalism and most dependent on the solidarity of kin and village which these changes disrupt. It is of course difficult to accept the taxonomy while rejecting the taxonomists's judgements, but Wolf's role in theorizing about Vietnam is too important to be ignored, Tilly's taxonomy, too useful to be dropped, and Wolf, too clearly part of the Durkheimian tradition to be reclassified.

The third classification is the least problematic since Tilly kindly uses *Agrarian Revolution* as an illustration and correctly emphasizes that the work is concerned with the relationship between interest and action, which is the hallmark of his Marxist theoretical type (Tilly 1978:10). Taxonomy is of course a prerequisite, not a substitute, for theory, but the neat parallelism between the directions of explanation of Vietnam and the three traditions in social movement theory indicates that the problems raised by the Vietnamese case are general ones. Their extension to a second case, Guatemala, will answer theoretical as well as substantive questions. To do so requires first that the principle propositions from each theory be extracted from a reexamination of the Vietnamese case.

Durkheim, Mill, and Marx in Vietnam

Durkheim: Moral Economy

Traditional Vietnamese society was, according to the Durkheimian moral economists, held together by three elements, which Popkin calls "safety first," the village and patron/client bonds (Popkin 1979:5–15). Safety first, or the subsistence ethic, is a moral principle which reflects a widely shared view that a peasant deserves just recompense for his labors in the form of a guaranteed if meager subsistence and that it is the responsibility of his superiors to see that their customary rapacity does not extend to the peasant's mite. The peasant may provide, as Eric Wolf notes, "three bags full—one for my master, one for my dame and one for the little boy who lives down the lane," but he must also provide for himself (Wolf 1968:12). It is immoral for the master to steal not the first three bags but only the last, the one that the peasant needs to live. To do so risks not only deprivation but a violation of the implicit social contract and revolt. But such an implicit contract can be and is violated in peasant society by natural disaster or famine beyond even the landlord's control, and, more directly, by the extractions of a strong state or by the inequities of a commercial market in crops or land. The peasant can be drowned by a natural disaster including, literally, a flood, or be submerged by the combined demands of landlords, the market, and the state.

The village, according to Popkin's description of moral economy, functions to ease the subsistence crisis by providing communal resources such as community land, reciprocal labor exchange, ceremonial funds, communal granaries, mutual aid based on kinship or vicinage, or institutionalized social pressures to redistribute wealth to gain status in the village civil-religious hierarchy. Village social structure, then, functions as a form of social insurance to protect peasants from violation of the subsistence minimum.

If village social insurance fails and the subsistence minimum is endangered, the lord may still extend a helping hand in the form of patron-client ties which, whatever their overtones of paternalism and subordination, allow the person one more source of money, political influence, and social prestige when he needs them most. Rents may be forgiven, loans reduced or interest not collected, medical expense paid, burial plots donated, tax collectors suborned, and the sheriff dissuaded by a landlord who values social prestige and political support more than money.

It is, however, at just those times when the subsistence minimum is most endangered that the village's insurance system and the patron's generosity are likely to vanish. Natural disasters impoverish villages and landlords as well as peasants, the market replaces communal ties with calculation and turns patrons into rent collectors, and the state, if strong enough, cannot be denied by village notables or powerful patrons. The failure of all these mechanisms means that the moral economy of the village will be destroyed, that exploitation will become not only unbearable but intolerable, and in such circumstances revolt is inevitable.

Such is the tale of moral economy as told by Popkin. As he admits himself many of the nuances are left out and individual theories blurred to produce a single theme. Still, the main elements—subsistence ethic, village insurance and patrons—are clear. For purposes of this analysis another step is necessary—the formulation of an explicit theoretical statement which, based on Popkin's analysis, might read as follows: *Peasant revolution occurs when the subsistence minimum is endangered and village security systems and patron-client ties destroyed by* (a) *ecological pressures* (b) *the demands of the state or* (c) *the growth of markets.* The worst case for this model would be a situation in which a peasant found himself in a perilous natural environment confronted by a powerful state in the midst of an economic depression without patron or village to protect him. Indeed, this is precisely the situation Scott finds in the Vietnamese provinces of Nghe An and Ha Tinh during the Communist rebellions of 1930–31. Burdened with the worst conditions for agriculture in all of Vietnam in the best of times, the peasants of Nghe An and Ha Tinh, confronted with the worst times in the world depression of 1930 and finding that French colonial policy had brought the traditional village down around them, struck against the state by attacking tax collectors; against the landlord by burning land records, against the market by attacking granaries, and against the moral order by murdering mandarinal officials. They also organized the first People's Soviets in Vietnam and set in motion a revolutionary wave which, building slowly at first, swelled to engulf all of Vietnam in 1975. But this is another story. For Scott and other moral economists the peasant revolutionaries are looking back toward the solidarity of the traditional village not forward toward a new socialist order. If they bring about the latter in pursuit of the former this is simply one of many examples of the unintended consequences of human actions.

Mill: Political Economy

Political economy as developed by Popkin is based on two fundamental assumptions: (1) the social solidarity of the traditional village could not have been disrupted by the state, the market or nature because there was little social solidarity to begin with; and (2) the individualistic actors of the peasant village can only be united by individual incentives delivered by efficient political organizers. It may be the case, Popkin argues, that the peasant village was a corporate communal entity, but within its boundaries (typically a bamboo hedge in Vietnam) the appearance of solidarity often cloaked individual calculation and greed. True, all citizens participated in village affairs, but far from all villagers were citizens; taxes were levied on the village as a whole, but were rigged by village notables so that they fell regressively on the poor and the weak; insurance funds did work, but at a cost paid by the poorer villagers to the rich; communal land existed, but it was often arid or under water and good land was raffled off to the politically influential; ceremonial expenditures were heavy, but they solidified the control of a dominant political machine; village decisions were reached by consensus, but this reflected a fear of the dominant faction, not democracy;

the rich loaned money to the poor but they expected a profit; patrons took as clients only the most servile and only when it increased their own influence. The colonial state and the market made all of these things worse; instead of destroying the village they tightened the control of the wealthy and politically influential, and increased the rewards of graft and the power of the ruthless. But before and after the coming of the colonial economy the village ran on self-interest, a divided collection of potatoes in a sack.

In such an atomized world collective appeals, revolutionary as well as conservative, find little response. Accordingly, the political leader must offer individual incentives such as lower rents, equitable taxation, fair land distribution, insurance that works, irrigation water, or the elimination (often physical) of the landlord; and, if he is to avoid the problem of the "free rider," must extend benefits only to those who support his program. It is helpful if the political organizer is efficient and honest; otherwise he will be seen as just one in a long line of corrupt village tyrants. In Popkin's analysis ideology is unimportant. Catholic priests, Cao Dai warlords, mad Hoa Hao bonzes, and Communist cadre all succeeded because they were honest, efficient, organized purveyors of individual incentives. Popkin's argument reduced to a single hypothesis might read as follows: *Peasant revolution occurs when honest, efficient political entrepreneurs organize the delivery of valuable individual incentives to selected members of an atomized village.* If political entrepreneurs more often succeed in non-traditional than traditional villages it is because both organizational effectiveness and opportunities for the delivery of individual incentives are greater in the former. Popkin notes that a susbsistence crisis preceded the Nghe An-Ha Tinh soviets in 1930–31, but adds that an even worse crisis occurred at the turn of the century with no revolt. The difference? "By 1930 there were more than three hundred Communists . . . actively working among the industrial workers of the area and urban labor organization was already making an impact" (Popkin 1979:248, 249–50). Popkin also notes another fact inconvenient for the moral economy theorists: most protests in the twentieth century in Vietnam occurred in the Mekong Delta of colonial Cochinchina where income and living standards were highest, and none in Tonkin, by far the poorest of the three colonial regions and the closest to the subsistence margin. The colonial region of Annam, almost as poor as Tonkin, was, except for Nghe An-Ha Tinh, generally quiet. Scott's strongest empirical case turns out to have been the exception rather than the rule in Vietnam. The Communists (and the Cao Dai and Hoa Hao before them) succeeded in the Delta because they had more resources to distribute in the form of selective incentives. There was nothing to redistribute in Annam and Tonkin except poverty.

Marx: Class Conflict

Popkin is correct in arguing that the Mekong Delta of colonial Cochinchina was the most rebellious area of Vietnam under the French and that the narrow coastal strip, most of which was included in the colonial administrative division of Annam, and the northern coast and Tonkin Delta (Colonial Tonkin) were generally quiet. Indeed, my own analysis of Vietnam began with a reconsideration of a 1967 RAND corporation report by Edward Mitchell which suggested that in the southern part of a divided Vietnam, the government of the Republic of Vietnam (South Vietnam) found its greatest support in regions of extensive tenancy, large estates, and export agriculture, all of which typify the Delta and that, by contrast, the Communists were strongest in areas of traditional village structure and minute owner-operated holdings in the Coastal Lowlands (Mitchell 1968). Mitchell's analysis was used by Eric Wolf to support his contention that independent small holders, not sharecroppers, were the main carriers of revolution in Vietnam. The contrast between the Mekong Delta on the one hand and the Coastal Lowlands and Tonkin Delta on the other, or, to use the colonial nomenclature, between Cochinchina and Annam and Tonkin, distinguishes the moral economy predictions from those of both political economy and class conflict. On this specific empirical point Mitchell, Wolf, and Scott are almost certainly wrong, as both Popkin and I have argued, although Wolf disputes the clear-cut nature of the comparison and did extend his argument to include the Delta protests of the 1930s (he did not include analysis of other movements in Vietnam) (Popkin 1979, Paige 1975 and Wolf 1977). The Delta was more rebellious not only in the French colonial period but, as Bernard Fall had demonstrated, in the early post-independence period as well (Fall 1958). This does not, however, necessarily imply that Popkin's political economy theory is correct. Considering much the same data on Vietnam but also substantial additional data from world wide patterns of agrarian social movements I concluded that the key element of the Delta economy was its class structure, not its potential for selective incentives. In particular, I proposed that the well documented radicalism of the Delta was a result of class conflict between backward capitalists whose only capital was land and a rural semi-proletariat whose only remaining claim was to a share of the crop as a wage. The landlords, whom I called "noncultivators," relied on political influence to secure land and labor, lacked the resources to share their surplus with their workers, and refused any political compromise. The workers, whom I called "cultivators," severed from the conservative effect of the ownership of even small amounts of land, limited to improvement in the living standards only through group action, and dependent on the worker community for much of what the moral economists called social insurance, demanded radical change. The result was revolution. Indeed, this pattern appeared to be quite general, particularly in agricultural export sectors organized in systems of decentralized sharecropping such as those in the Delta or in colonial estate agriculture employing extensive amount of migratory wage labor. This analysis leads then to the third and final proposition about the causes of revolution in Vietnam, this one of my own: *"A combination of noncultivators dependent on income from land and cultivators dependent on income from wages leads to revolution. Such a combination of income sources is typical of sharecropping and migratory labor estate systems"* (Paige 1975:71). The empirical prediction about the area of greatest revolutionary activity (the Delta) made by this theory is, of course, the same as that made by Popkin. Therefore, although the evidence from Vietnam seems to provide more support for the political economy or class conflict perspectives than it does for moral economy, this evidence alone does not distinguish between the two "economic" theories. The regional distribution of revolutionary activity in Guatemala, the second case of peasant revolution, does permit such a distinction. The predictions of the three theories about the location of revolutionary events in Guatemala are distinct and in general support the class-conflict perspective more than either of the other two.

Guatemala: Peasant Unions, Military Men, and Guerrilleros

In October of 1944, Jorge Ubico (1931–1944), the last in a long line of military dictators, was overthrown and the Guatemalan revolution began. It has not yet ended. The fall of Ubico and the election of Juan José Arévalo began a brief era of democratic reform and popular mobilization. But this was abruptly halted by the flight of Arévalo's successor, Jacobo Arbenz Gúzman, and the collapse of his government in response to an invasion by Guatemalan exiles from neighboring Honduras. The exiles were organized by the United States Central Intelligence Agency but led by a Guatemalan General, Carlos Castillo Armas. Castillo Armas, who was assassinated shortly after assuming power, and a new line of military and civilian dictators have tried, through a combination of medieval barbarity and modern technology, to contain the popular mobilization begun by Arévalo and Arbenz. Despite the slaughter of perhaps 50,000 of their opponents in the years since 1954 (Camposeco 1981) they are at this writing as far from their goal as ever. The Guatemalan revolutionaries, like the Vietnamese, show an amazing persistence, although thus far they have not acquired the military potency of the North Vietnamese infantry.

Although the "terrorists" who have run the Guatemalan government since the fall of Arbenz have not lacked urban opponents, Guatemala, like Vietnam, is an agricultural country and it is rural revolutionaries and their leaders who continue to constitute the greatest threat to the generals' counter-revolution. Rural mobilization has taken place in three distinct episodes: the peasant union movement, 1952–1954; the guerrilla movement, 1962–1967: and the guerrilla movement at present. The Agrarian Reform Laws of 1952 issued in a brief period of intense union activity among the peasantry and led to the formation of some 1,700 peasant unions by 1954 and their integration in the National Peasant Federation of Guatemala (CNCG). The Federation, with a block of perhaps 150,000 votes, formed a decisive political force in democratic elections (Pearson 1969:323–73, Murphy 1970:438–78). The CIA-sponsored invasion ended both the unions and the lives of many of their organizers. The CIA involvement in Guatemala was, however, a decidedly mixed blessing even for the military officers themselves, and the use of a coffee *finca* at Helvetia de Retalhuleu as a training base for exiles for another CIA invasion, this time at the Bay of Pigs, split the military and led to an abortive coup attempt on November 13, 1960. The coup failed but a small number of officers led by Luis Augusto Turcios Lima and Marco Antonio Yon Sosa retreated to the wilds of eastern Guatemala and organized a guerrilla war. Beginning in 1962 it gained considerable momentum, but it was crushed in a massive counterthrust in 1967 by still another military officer, Colonel Carlos Arana Osorio. He earned the nickname the "butcher of Zacapa" for slaughtering 15,000 peasants to eliminate perhaps three hundred guerrillas (NACLA 1974:185, Melville and Melville 1971:1, Gott 1972:99–100). In 1967, their leaders dead or in hiding, their eastern base liquidated, the guerrillas seemed defeated. But by 1980 a reorganized guerrilla movement fielding four separate but loosely coordinated commands was posing the most serious threat the generals had faced since the fall of Arbenz. In 1966 Yon Sosa told Adolfo Gilly that in *two and a half years* of war his guerrilla front had inflicted 142 deaths on the military and police (Gilly May 1965:30). On May 16, 1981 the Organization of the People in Arms (ORPA) claimed that in a single action, a *"claymorazo"* or ambush with Claymore mines, it had annihilated a military convoy killing fifty-nine soldiers and wounding six, and this was not an isolated incident. (*Noticias de Guatemala,* 4 May 1981:19). Regis Debray had said that the Guatemalan guerrillas of the sixties had achieved the greatest mass support of any movement in Latin America, with the possible exception of Colombia (NACLA, 1983). The strength of the current Guatemalan guerrilla movement seems an order of magnitude greater.

The Ecology of Rural Protest

As was the case in Vietnam, rural protest in Guatemala follows clear-cut patterns of geographical concentration, although, unlike Vietnam, the focus of conflict shifts over time. Each of the three movements since the Arbenz period had a different regional and ecological base. The areas of concentration reflect both the nature of the movements and the regional specialization of Guatemalan agriculture. The major ecological regions of Guatemala as they are generally described are shown in Map 1 (Whetten 1961:8–16, CIDA 1965:2–3, West and Augelli 1976:408). The North and the Caribbean Lowlands, frequently discussed together, are regions of forbidding jungle, lowland terrain, sparse population and casual swidden cultivation. They have been largely empty since the fall of Maya civilization in the ninth century A.D., although recently the North has attracted considerable attention as a possible site of a large petroleum deposit. The heart of the current Indian population, however, is in the Central Highlands, shown as the West in Map 1, a rugged, mountainous area with cultivated valleys and barren high plateaus. This is a region of microscopic subsistence holdings, minute parcel subdivision, intensive cultivation, primitive agricultural technology, and acute overpopulation. It is also a region of grinding poverty, backbreaking toil, starvation, and death. It is not uncommon to see a man laden with a burden of fifty pounds or more walking beside a horse lightly

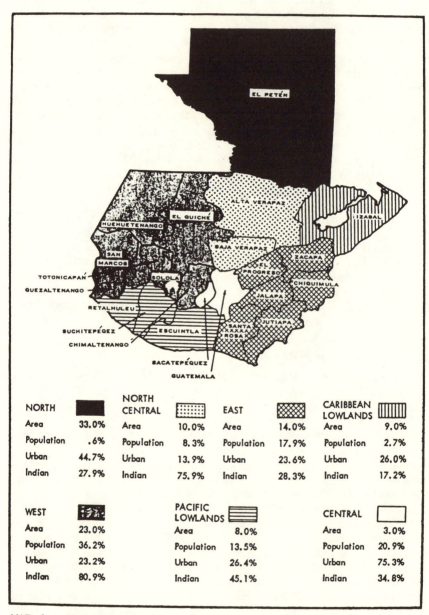

MAP 1   Major Ecological Regions of Guatemala

laden or carrying nothing at all. The horse is valuable; the man, expendable. Every available inch is cultivated, in corn at lower altitudes and wheat at higher ones, and it is not uncommon to see the roots of corn plants protruding through eroded overhangs beside roads, or corn growing on slopes that appear accessible only with the aid of mountaineering equipment. In Vietnam, only in Tonkin and the poorest areas of Annam did one find this desperate overcultivation and degrading substitution of human for animal labor.

Agriculture in the Central Highlands cannot support the population. In some areas virtually all adult males depart to work in the Pacific Coastal Lowlands for six months of the year. The Lowlands departments of Retalhuleu, Suchitepéquez, and Escuintla are major destinations for highland migrants and it is here that most of Guatemala's export crops are produced, and these crops *are* the Guatemalan economy. The nature of coastal agriculture, as West and Augelli have pointed out, depends on altitude (1976:408). The lowest altitudes, tropical in climate, were formerly almost exclusively pasture and as late as 1960 were underdeveloped because of problems of transportation, irrigation, and disease. But since that time pesticides, highways, and bank loans have made possible a massive expansion of cotton production and the lower coast is now the most dynamic agricultural region in Guatemala. (Adams 1970:353–379). In 1973–74, for example, the department of Escuintla alone accounted for 68.5 percent of total Guatemalan cotton production (Guatemala 1976:Quadro 4). At slightly higher altitudes sugar cane, bananas, cardamom and other crops are grown. Still higher, at altitudes from 500 to 1500 meters, is Guatemala's coffee piedmont which stretches through the southern coastal provinces and into the coastal extensions of the highland departments of Quezaltenango and San Marcos. This is the oldest region of export agriculture in Guatemala. Coffee cultivation began on a large scale as early as 1880 (Dessaint 1962) and was, until the sixties, the only major producer of export earnings and the only major consumer of migratory labor from the highlands. The principal producing departments in the coastal coffee piedmont, ranked by production in 1974, were San Marcos, Retalhuleu, Quezaltenango, Santa Rosa, Guatemala, and Chimaltenango (Guatemala 1976:Cuadro 3, 70). It should be noted that in all southern and some western departments, geography and political divisions do not coincide. Many of these departments such as Suchitepéquez, have zones in the Central Highlands as well as in the Coast and Coffee Piedmont. Coffee is also produced in a second distinct zone of relatively poorer soil but abundant and virtually cost-free labor in the north-central province of Alta Verapaz. In both areas coffee is produced almost entirely on large estates by a labor force divided between resident tenants and harvest migrants. The estates are owned by the *ladino* (the Guatemalan term for fictive Hispanic descent) oligarchy and worked by Indian labor.

Since the Central Region is largely urban, the remaining agricultural zone is found in the Eastern Highlands (the East in Map 1). As the data in Map 1 indicate, in comparison to the Central Highlands and the Verapaz, the

TABLE 1

Demographic Findings of Quiché Highlands

Date	Population
1524	50,000 (estimate)
1893	55,000 (first census)
1926	63,000
1940	78,000
1950	81,000
1974	100,000

Source: R. M. Carmack, 1981.

population is predominantly *ladino* rather than Indian and living standards are somewhat higher. Overpopulation is not as serious as in the Highlands, there are considerably more middle-sized holdings, and agriculture is productive enough to eliminate the need to migrate to work in the export sector. In the Eastern Highlands animals rather than people carry the burdens. Although most agriculture is subsistence, the acute agrarian crisis of the Highlands is largely absent in the East.

As the data in Table 1 indicate, the three major agrarian social movements which make up the rural phase of the Guatemalan revolution were each concentrated in a different ecological region. Column 4 in Table 2 shows the number of peasant unions in each province in 1954 as reported by Pearson 1969:323–73). The distribution of coffee production was roughly the same in 1954 and 1974, with the notable exception of Retalhuleu which was not a major producer in the fifties. With a few exceptions unions follow the coffee harvest. San Marcos, the largest producer, has the most unions. Quezaltenango, Chimaltenango, Santa Roasa, and Guatemala in the southern Coffee Piedmont and Alta Verapaz in the North Central producing area all have large numbers of unions. Only Huehuetenango and Escuintla have unions and little coffee and only the former is an exception. The Escuintla unions were on sugar and banana plantations. As Pearson notes, ". . . it is probably not unreasonable to assume there are at least 1,500 active unions in the CNCG based principally on the 1,408 large plantations with over 100 inhabitants on them or the 1,736 plantations producing over 200 bags of coffee per year" (Pearson 1969:350). The Central Highlands, except for Huehuetenango, were quiet during the period of peasant mobilization under Arbenz. The plantation proletariat of Escuintla, particularly the banana workers, and the tenants of traditional coffee estates, were the principal supporters of the CNCG.

The rebels of the sixties did not, however, build on this peasant base in the Coffee Piedmont but rather chose the remote Sierra de las Minas range in the east largely, it appears, for military reasons. The military rebellion of November 13, 1960 involved two garrisons: Matamoros outside Guatemala city and Zacapa in the military district of the same name. The rebels also

took control of the banana port of Puerto Barrios in Izabal until they were dislodged by troops and air strikes flown by Cuban exiles from the training base at Retalhuleu. It was "a typical nationalist revolt" (Gott 1972:32) and the rebel officers, who had no plans to arm the peasantry, seem to have been convinced to continue their struggle by their outlaw status and, according to Gilly, an outright request from eight hundred Zacapa peasants for arms and leadership (Gilly May 1965:14). When, after temporary exile, the rebel officers returned to Guatemala to take up the struggle, it was natural that they would return to Zacapa and Izabal, departments where they could count on peasant support and, at least initially, unenthusiastic military opposition. The mountains and jungles of the east also provided favorable terrain for guerrillas, but there is no scarcity of such terrain in Guatemala. As Gilly reports: "In February 1962 under the name of *Movimiento Guerrillero Alejandro de León 13 de Noviembre*, Yon Sosa's forces began the struggle in the Mountains of Izabal, in the Sierra de las Minas" (Gilly May 1965:17). The Sierra de las Minas are located in the area surrounding the intersection of the departments of Zacapa, Izabal and the southern extension of Alta Verapaz; guerrilla units operated in all three areas (Gilly May 1965:18–19, Gott 1972:52, NACLA 1974:184). As Table 2 indicates, however, there were two principal guerrilla fronts: the first, the original Alejandro León front, led by Yon Sosa named after one of the military rebels killed before the beginning of the guerrilla war. Yon Sosa's organization, called MR-13 after the date of the military rebellion, first allied and then split with a broader protest organization called the Rebel Armed Forces (FAR) initially dominated by the Guatemalan Communist Party (PGT). FAR established a second major guerrilla *foco*, the Edgar Ibarra front, named after a student leader killed in Guatemala City, and led by Tucios Lima, and Zacapa. Despite their differences, including a Trotskyist preference for mass insurrection in MR-13, both organizations, although originally led by nationalist military officers, were both revolutionary and socialist. Yon Sosa makes clear the ideology of his organization in an interview with Gilly in 1964:
How did you all become socialists?

While we were dodging bullets. It's impossible to fight for very long, side by side with peasants, and not become socialist. An armed revolution must become a socialist revolution. Which countries, similar to ours, have been able to have been able to emerge from backwardness? Cuba, China, *North Vietnam*, North Korea—they have all taken the socialist path. A backward country cannot advance the capitalist path, and there is not a third alternative. All you have to do is look around and see what's happening in the world. How could we not be for socialism (Gilly May 1965:32).

The reference to Vietnam (italics mine) was not incidental since Vietnam had been the topic of extended discussion among Gilly, Ysosa, and other guerrillas the night before. Yon Sosa went on to say that both Guatemala and Vietnam were engaged in a common struggle to overthrow imperialism ("a bunch of bastards") and were part of a world-wide military offensive

TABLE 2

Agrarian Social Movements in Guatemala. Peasant Unions 1954,
Guerrilla Fronts 1962-1967, and Guerrilla Fronts and Actions 1980-81, by Department

Department	Guerrilla Actions[a]				Guerrilla Fronts[b]	Guerrilla Front[c]	Peasant Union[d]
	1980-81				1980	1962-67	1954
	EGP	ORPA	N.A.	Total	EGP, FAR	FAR, MR-13	CNCG
Central							
Guatemala	0	4	0	4	Otto Rene Castillo (EGP) Sergio Anibal Ramirez (FAR)		84
Sacatepequez	1	1	1	3			53
West							
Chimaltenango	10	6	2	18			88
El Quiche	21		5	26	Ho Chi Minh* (EGP)		57
Huehuetenango	11	1	7	19	Ernesto Guevera (EGP)		123
Quezaltenango		21	5	26			63
San Marcos		16	1	17			212
Sololá	1	7		8			23
Totonicapan		1		1			24
South							
Retalhuleu		4	1	5			25
Suchitepéquez	6	11	10	27	Luis Turcios Lima (EGP)		48
Ecuintla	2	1	3	6	Oscar Bayesteros (FAR)		170

East					
El Progreso	1	1		Edgar Ibarra	22
Zacapa				(Turcios FAR)	32
Jalapa					54
Chiquimula					28
Santa Rosa	1				<u>86</u>
Jutiapa			1		35
North Central					
Baja Verapaz	<u>8</u>				45
Alta Verapaz	1	3	<u>12</u>		<u>195</u>
North					
Izabal	1			Alejandro León	42
El Petén	3	3		(Yon Sosa MR-13)	4
				Feliciano Argueta Rojas (FAR)	

* also called Frente Guerrillero Edgar Ibarra (FGEI) in EGP documents.

a. Source: Noticias de Guatemala, 55-71, (November 1980 - August 1981). Collection of Ellisa Miller. Lacking 59, 61, 62, 70.

b. Source: EGP, Ejercito Guerrillero de los Pobres, Companero, No. 4 (n.d., probably January 1981), 24; FAR, Fuerzas Armadas Rebeldes, Parte de Guerra, No. 6 (n.d., probably 1981). Collection of Ellisa Miller.

c. Source: North American Congress on Latin America (NACLA) Guatemala (Berkeley 1974) based on Gabriel Aguilera Peralta, Guerrilla y Anti-Guerrilla en Guatemala, (Thesis, Guatemala 1970); Adolfo Gilly, "The Guerrilla Movement in Guatemala," Monthly Review 17, Part I (May 1965): 9-40, Part 2 (June 1965): 7-41; Richard Gott, Guerrilla Movements in Latin America, (Garden City, N.Y.: Anchor, 1972); Eduardo Galeano, Guatemala: Occupied Country, (New York: Modern Reader, 1967).

d. Source: Neal J. Pearson, "Guatemala: The Peasant Union Movement," in Latin American Peasant Movements, ed., Henry Landsberger (Ithaca: Cornell University Press, 1969), 351.

uniting all socialist states. According to NACLA, "By mid-1966 the FAR had influence over a wide area in Izabal, Zacapa and Alata Verapaz, and is some villages virtually coexisted with the local authorities," and MR-13 had a similar influence in the area around Izabal (NACLA 1974:185, 187). The nationalist military officers had attained this following, as Gilly makes clear by adapting their ideology to the desires of the peasants and rural laborers (Gilly May 1965:16–17). Otto Rene Castillo, one of Guatemala's greatest poets, who joined FAR under the command of Turcios Lima in that same year, 1966, puts it best:

> Por ello pido que caminemos juntos. Siempre con los campesinos agrarios y los obreros indicales, con el que tenga un corazcon los campesinos agrarios y los obreros indicales, con el que tenga un corazón para querete.
>
> Vámonos patria a caminar, yo te acompaño.
>
> For this I say let us walk together, always with the agrarian peasants and the union workers with he who has a heart to love you.
>
> Let's go, my country, I will go with you (Castillo 1971).

But 1966 was the guerrillas' high water mark. Turcios Lima was killed in an automobile accident in Guatemala City on October 2, 1966. Colonel Arana's counter-insurgency campaign in the East destroyed the Edgar Ibarra front in 1967 and Turcio's successor, Camino Sanchez, was captured and executed in Guatemala City in 1968. The army also crushed the Alejandro León front of MR-13, driving Yon Sosa, hunted and alone, to seek refuge in Guatemala City. In March 1967 Otto Rene Castillo was captured, tortured for four days, and burned alive. The guerrilla movement of the sixties was over.

Neither Turcios's FAR or Yon Sosa's MR-13 ever successfully extended their operation outside their Sierra de las Minas base in Zacapa and Izabal. MR-13 planned to organize coffee workers (Gilly June 1965:25) but apparently this strategy was never carried out. FAR also organized resistance zones in the Western Highlands near the coast in the departments of Quezaltenango and San Marcos, and these fronts, although never as active as the East, survived the "Butcher of Zacapa" and were still active in the early seventies (NACLA 1974:183, 191). Attempts to extend the guerrilla war to the Central Highlands were, however, a disaster. Turcios Lima describes an attempt in November 1962 to organize a guerrilla front in Huehuetenango:

> It (Huehuetenango) is a very mountainous yet densely populated area. The leaders of the movement had very mountainous yet densely populated area. The leaders of the movement had made no political preparations; they barely knew the terrain and they had no support from peasant organizations. They went round and round in circles, vainly trying to explain in lightning meetings what they were fighting for. A setback. They were all captured and shot . . . [3]

Only in the East did the guerrillas gain any significant support. In the other major ecological regions of Guatemala—the Central Highlands, the South Coast, and the Coffee Piedmont—they were, with the exception of minor FAR activity in Quezaltenango and San Marcos, completely unsuccessful.

In 1975 guerrilla war came to the central Highlands. in the spring of 1975 guerrillas from the Poor People's Guerrilla Army (EGP), a new organization founded in 1973, shot Luis Arenas, the "tiger of Ixcan," an unpopular landowner, as he watched his administrator give his workers their meager pay. The following day the guerrillas returned and occupied Ixcan and other towns in Huehuetenango (Anon. 1980). Many such incidents followed and by 1980–81, as the data in Table 2 indicate, guerrilla actions had engulfed the entire Central Highland region and had extended to the South Coast and Coffee Piedmont as well. But the old areas of FAR and MR-13 strength in Zacapa and Izabal were almost entirely quiet.

The data in the first column of Table 2 were computed by the author from the "Sintesis de Noticias" section of *Noticias de Guatemala*, a publication of the Democratic Front Against Repression which is a broad-based opposition group not limited to the guerrilla organization. The location of the guerrilla fronts as listed in column 2 was derived from press releases and other publications of the guerrilla organizations themselves. In 1974 there were four major guerrilla organizations; they agreed in 1982 to coordinate their formerly separate commands. Two of these organizations, the Poor People's Guerrilla Army (EGP) and the Organization of the People in Arms (OPRA), were new organizations although, in the case of ORPA in particular, they seem to have built on the organizational work of FAR. FAR itself reorganized and shifted its activities to the South Coast and the jungles of the North. The Guatemalan Communist Party (PGT) also launched a guerrilla compaign although their activities were concentrated in urban areas.

Table 2 shows the activities of all four organizations reported in *Noticias* from November 1980 to August 1981, although all but two of the actions carried out by groups whose identity was given were by the EGP and ORPA. This should not, however, be taken as an indication of relative activity since *Noticias* includes both actions culled from the Guatemalan press, in which the identity of the guerrillas, often described as bands of heavily armed men, is not given, and press reports of the guerrilla organizations themselves. Almost all the latter communications are from EGP and ORPA; actions reported in *Parte de Guerra*, the war report of FAR, do not appear in *Noticias*. Communications, needless to say, among these clandestine groups are difficult and the government does its best to disrupt them, so it is not surprising that some groups appear to have better communications channels than others. *Noticias* does report completely and accurately press releases which I have in my possession from both ORPA and EGP. For example, the EGP press release, *Parte de Guerra* of July 24, 1981, lists 24 separate actions commemorating the second anniversary of the Nicaraguan Revolution of July 19, 1979. Every one of these actions is correctly reported and accurately summarized in *Noticias*. Similarly, an ORPA press release of April 13, 1981 *Comunicado a la Prensa, Radio y Televisión* reports a series of actions which also are accurately summarized in *Noticias*. Since the Guatemalan press is heavily if selectively censored and the Army secretive, these may be the best sources available on the location of the contemporary guerrilla.

Table 2 reports only those actions which involve groups, whether or not they are explicitly identififed as guerrillas, who engage in armed action against either military or police forces. This includes attacks on police substations and barracks as well as on mobile units; attacks on economic targets such as plantations and warehouses; and on elements of the infra-structure such as bridges, rail lines, buses, trucks, and oil rigs. It also includes armed actions in which violence does not occur if it involves groups of people initiating and receiving the action. The most frequent action of this type is the armed occupation of a town or farm for purposes of holding a political meeting. It excludes assassinations, which are very numerous (they are called "*ajusticiamientos*," "executions," in *Noticias*) unless they are part of an attack on a group of government, police, or military officials, and bombings, unless part of a general attack by a group. In the latter two cases the responsibility for the action is often difficult to assess and such actions may also be carried out by lone individuals far from the guerrillas' base of operations. It should be noted that only *major actions* are included in Table 2; if assassinations and bombings were included the number would have been considerably larger. Table 2 is limited to actions occurring outside of Guatemala City and its immediate suburbs, such as Amatitlan, but includes any action occurring outside of the Central Region even if it occurs in what passes for a city in rural Guatemala. Actions reported together but occurring in different departments have been counted separately. Most of the actions fall into two general types: (a) ambushes of police and military units (*emboscadas*) and attacks on police stations and military barracks (*ataques*); (b) military occupation of towns and farms and the holding of mass meetings, distribution of propaganda leaflets, and recruitment of supporters (called "*toma de lugares*," "seizure of places," in *Noticias*), and destruction of agricultural machinery, buildings, vehicles, and other elements of the eco-nomic infrastructure, often in conjunction with an armed occupation (*sabotaje*). Below are translated descriptions of actions of each type as they appeared in *Noticias* and the original guerrilla press release.

Guerrilla Actions: A Comparison of Sources

A: Ambushes and Attacks

At 9:45 hours at kilometer 162, jurisdiction of Cuyotenango we carried out a harrassing ambush against a military convoy composed of one truck with 40 soldiers and one jeep. In the operation we detonated 2 claymore mines causing 9 enemy deaths and an indeterminate number of wounded.

(EGP: *Parte de Guerra* press release, July 24, 1981)

Type of Action: Harrassing Ambush against a military convoy. Claymore.

Place: Km. 162 jurisdiction of Cuyotenango Suchitepéquez.

Result: EGP action. Nine soldiers dead and an indeterminate number wounded.

(*Noticias*, August 20, 1981)

B: Occupations and Sabotage

Tuesday April 7. ORPA fighters, in the municipality of Colomba, Quezaltenango, carried out a substantial operation of military occupations which lasted from 5:00 A.M. to 15:00 P.M.

At 5:15 A.M. they occupied the Mujuliá estate and at 6:00 A.M. the estate of Culpan, where they communicated to the workers the message of the revolution and the accomplishments of the popular revolutionary war.

At 7:00 A.M. they captured through military action, the municipal capital of Colomba where the day before the government had forced a demonstration of support for the army and regime by threatening the inhabitants.

The agents of the substation of the national police were forced to withdraw and all the arms of the garrison were recovered and, according to the policy of ORPA, the lives and finances of the police were respects.

Through the local facilities of TGAC and ORPA fighter transmitted a revolutionary message for ten minutes and a meeting with the population was held in the central park.

In the remainder of the action our forces occupied the Transito-Bolivar and Providencia Fernandez estates withdrawing without difficulty at 15:00 hours.

(ORPA: *Comunicado a la Prensa*, April 13, 1981)

Type of Action: Seizure of places and meetings, 4/7/81.

Place: Municipal Capital of Colomba, Quezaltenango, Radio TGAC local facilities Estates of Mujulía Culpán, Tránsito Bolivar and Providencia Fernández.

Result: ORPA action. Distribution of a great quantity of propaganda. Transmission of revolutionary-messages. Recovery of all arms of the garrison.

(*Noticias*, May 4, 1981, p. 19)

The first of these two actions is a typical *"claymorazo"* or ambush with claymore mines, although the guerrillas distinguish two types; harrassing ambushes like this one, and ambushes of annihilation in which the intent is to completely eliminate the opposing force. The ORPA occupation of a muncipal capital and several nearby estates is an example of what has come to be called "armed propaganda" and was one of the most common guerrilla actions both now and in the sixties. The actions reported in *Noticias* are somewhat more likely to be ambushes or attacks on police or military installation than occupations and sabotage, although many occupations may not be reported in the press where *Noticias* gets at least some of its information. The two best-covered guerrilla organizations also differ somewhat in the ratio of the two types of actions, with EGP relying more on military actions (forty ambushes and attacks versus twenty occupations and sabotage actions), and ORPA slightly more on armed propaganda (forty-three ambushes and attacks versus thirty-three occupations and sabotage actions), but clearly the tactics of both are very similar.

The regional distribution of actions by ORPA and EGP differ more markedly. The largest number of EGP actions (twenty-one) occurred in El Quiché which according to guerrilla sources, is the location of the oldest EGP guerrilla organization, the Ho Chi Minh front (also called the Edgar Ibarra front in some EGP press releases). The next most active is the adjacent department of Huehuetenango, the location of the EGP's Ernesto Guevara front. Chimaltenango, at the southern extension of the Ho Chi Minh front, is also the site of many EGP actions. It is clear that the core of EGP strength is the Maya Quiché region of the Central Highlands. The EGP also opened its newest front (Luis Tucios Lima) in the South Coast department of Escuintla and also has been active in the adjacent department of Suchitepéquez.

ORPA, which had organizational links to the old FAR *focos* Quezaltenango and San Marcos, has greatly expanded activity in these two departments and in adjacent Sololá around Lake Atitlán; it has also operated in the southern portions of Chimaltenango while the EGP controls the north. Like the EGP, ORPA is also active on the south coast, particularly in Suchitepéquez, and examination of the municipal location of ORPA actions indicates that its activities cross all three of the department's ecological zones, although tending to concentrate in the Central Highlands' municpalities close to Lake Atitlán.

Actions by groups identified in *Noticias* follow approximately the same general distribution as those of ORPA and EGP, so it is reasonable to assume that many of these actions have been excluded from Table 2 because of the restriction of the population to rural events. The new FAR has, according to its publication *Parte de Guerra*, been active in two distinctly different regions, the remote Peten and the south coast department of Escuintla. Its tactics are much the same as those of the two better described guerrilla organizations.

The most striking difference between this pattern of action and the earlier efforts of FAR, MR-13, and the CNCG is the mobilization of the central Highlands. Huehuetenango, where the original military rebels failed so miserably, is now a center of rebellion. So is adjacent El Quiché which is engaged, as an American embassy spokesmen told the author in August 1980, in "a small scale civil war." That portion of the Highlands not oganized by EGP is controlled by ORPA which has attained success here never reached by the early FAR attempt in the same region. Only FAR remains in the jungle, but even this organization has abandoned its original eastern base and shifted its operations to the even more inaccessible Petén. Both ORPA and EGP have operated in the Coffee Piedmont but this does not seem to be their central focus as it clearly was for the CNCG. Both ORPA and EGP are attempting to extend their operations to the south coast, particularly in Suchitepéquez. But the Central Highlands are clearly their base of operations. In summary, each movement has a distinct regional base; the CNCG in the Coffee Piedmont, the FAR and MR-13 in the Eastern Highlands, and EGP and ORPA in the Central Highlands.

The change in the regional base of the guerrillas does not seem to reflect simple changes in guerrilla strategy but rather far-reaching changes in the structure of Guatemalan agrarian political economy and social sturcture. These changes were particularly dramatic in the Central Highlands and created the conditions for the guerrilla successes of the last year. The starting point for these changes was, as was the case in Vietnam, the traditional peasant subsistence village. Indeed, if one reads the traditional ethnographic literature on peasant communities written before 1970 the village social organization sounds much like the traditional Vietnamese village (Wagley 1949, Tax 1953, Bunzel 1952, Tumin 1952).

At that time (1937) the Indians of Santiago Chimaltenango seldom acknowledged, and most did not even know that they formed a segment of the nation. . . . They considered themselves as Chimaltecos, not Guatemaltecos. They respected their own civil religious officials selected by the elders (*Los Principales*). They considered themselves *"muy buen católicos"* (very good Catholics)—by that term they meant a firm belief in the Saints as local deities, the guardian spirits of the mountains, and the ancestors as supernaturals. They evoked these supernaturals through the power of their own rituals which involved prayers led by their native shaman priests and offerings of incense soaked in turkey blood. Such communities were "localocentric," that is, united against outsiders, non-Indian and other Indians alike, to the extent of refusing to sell land within their territorial boundaries to outsiders. They were endogamous and closed communities and through their localocentrism they had maintained their identity despite exploitation and domination by Spanish colonial and Republican rule for four centuries.[4]

The civil religious hierarchy, the consensual rule of the elders, the cult of the guardian spirit, the integrating power of ritual, the corporate identity, the communal land ownership, the strict closed endogamy, the collective resistence to exploitation will all be familiar to students of Vietnamese peasant communities or indeed to students of any peasant communities. There is something in the traditional literature for political economists too; it was in Panajachel, Sololá that Sol Tax found that rational calculation toward small gain that caused him to refer to its citizens as "penny capitalists" (Tax 1953).

Things have changed in Huehuetenango, where Wagley's village was located, and indeed, his intent in the passage quoted above is to underscore just how much they have changed. On July 19 of this year a detachment of soldiers entered another Huehuetenango village, San Miguel Acatán, not far from Wagley's Santiago Chimaltenango. According to a statement by FP-31, an opposition political group:

The people organized to defend themselves with sticks, stones and machetes. A fierce and unequal battle took place from early morning until mid-afternoon, with the military using a helicopter and a plane to strafe and bomb the population. An estimated 150–300 persons were killed, including children, men, women and aging villagers. "The distance which separated the two forces was only a few meters," stated the FP-31. "The soldiers yelled 'Long live Lucas!' The people cried 'Long live the people and the revolution!'" (*The Guardian*, September 16, 1981:13)

The EGP had held an armed propaganda meeting in San Miguel Acatán in early April 1981 and, judging from the villagers' reactions to the troops, must have received a warm welcome (*Noticias de Guatemala*, May 4, 1981:4). Presumably the soldiers were aware of this when they went to San Miguel. From "*buen católicos*" to desperate revolutionaries in a generation.

There is considerable evidence that these changes are very recent, dating from the late sixties or early seventies, and that the Central Highlands would not have supported the guerrillas earlier no matter how effective or well-informed about local conditions they had been. In 1962 Turcios Lima's guerrillas found no response when they tried the same tactic, armed propaganda, that the EGP has been practicing successfully all over Huehuetenango since 1975. The FAR guerrillas found no peasant organizations because no peasant organization existed. Tragically, they had arrived a scant decade too soon. In 1966–67, for example, Colby and van den Berghe studied the Ixil region of El Quiché, the source of many of the peasants who died in the sit-in at the Spanish embassy in January 1980, and one of the areas where the EGP has been most active, particularly in the towns of Nebaj, Chajul, and Cotzal where Colby and van den Berghe were doing their interviewing (Colby and van den Berghe 1969). The government has been sufficiently concerned about the guerrillas' support in this area that it has carried out massacres of unarmed peasants in both Nebaj, in March 1980, and at Cotzal, in July 1981 (*New York Times*, May 9, 1981:4). Yet Colby and van den Berghe could write, and there is no reason to doubt them, that in 1966–67 ". . . the Ixil community itself exhibits considerable group solidarity. This is clearly illustrated in the recent revival of traditional religion, resentment of the catechists, and recapture of political offices by the traditionalists" (Colby and van den Berghe 1969:178). The "*buen católicos*" of the civil-religious hierarchy with their turkey blood and mountain spirits were holding off catechists who were trying to convert the peasants to catholicism. Where Catholic priests failed, Marxist guerrillas preaching Trotskyist world revolution could hardly be expected to succeed.

But in Aguacatán, less than ten miles from Nebaj, Douglas Brintnall found that by 1975 the village had reached ". . . some kind of critical point at which a major social transformation occurs" (Brintnall 1979:33). The traditionalists had been routed, the civil religious hierarchy of Aguacatán had collapsed, and ancestor worship was as dead as the kinsmen it celebrated. In 1970, for the first time, an Indian was elected mayor and responded by throwing the *ladinos* out of local offices, precipitating a confrontation with the local military commander and a minor skirmish with the army. Although the FAR guerrillas found no peasant organization in 1962, had they returned in 1975 they would have found that a hugely successful one had just been established. On March 2, 1981 an Army convoy moving through Aguacatán was caught in a "*claymorazo*" sprung by the EPG. The army unit was wiped out with thirty dead and twenty wounded (*Noticias de Guatemala*, 23 March, 1981). Revolutionary change in Aguacatán had been terrifyingly compressed into less than a decade.

Similar changes were apparently taking place elsewhere in the Highlands in the same decade. Robert E. Hinshaw surveyed selected villages on Lake Atitlán in 1965 and again in 1974 as part of his restudy of Tax's Panajachel. In Santa Maria Visitación the *cofradías*, religious festivals led by the traditionalists, were disbanded in 1963 and by 1968 the politicized villagers were lobbying the government in Guatemala City for a hydroelectric project. In Panajachel itself Hinshaw found that in 1974 "the *cofradías* were still staffed but with increasing difficulty," and that "Panajachelños participated more actively in the election campaigning that they had the previous decade" (Hinshaw 1975). In San Andreas Semetabaj, also on the lake, Kay Warren found that by 1971 the previously politically passive Indians of what was an unusually wealthy community by Highland standards had staged a strike by refusing to enroll their children in school unless a dispute with the *ladinos* over payment for school lunches was settled (Warren 1978). Here too the civil-religious hierarchy was losing ground to a reform-oriented missionary group.

The guerrillas' success in the Central Highlands reflects deep-seated changes in the social structure of rural Guatemala which created the possibility for an Indian political mobilization. The guerrillas' operations had shifted because the political environment in the Highlands had changed. The location of the three movements as well as the successes of the EGP and ORPA in an area where FAR had failed, raise fundamental question for theories developed in Vietnam. What accounts for the shift in location and the radical transformation of the Highlands? There are of course three distinct answers.

Guatemala: Moral Economy and Political Economy

Moral Economy

The concentration of the contemporary guerrilla movement in the Central Highlands, the Tonkin or perhaps even the Nghe An-Ha Tinh of Guatemala, would seem at first examination to provide considerable support for moral economy. Just as in Vietnam, the region of most intense rebellion is one where the subsistence minimum is threatened by primitive agriculture, acute overpopulation, and unfavorable agricultural ecology. The demands of the state and the pressures of the world market in agricultural commodities are also present in the Highlands although they take a very different form than they did in Vietnam. The failure of the sixties movement in the East also tends to support moral economy theory since the Eastern *ladinos* were considerably further above the subsistence threshold than were the Indians of the Central Highlands. The peasant union movement is, however, a puzzle for the moral economists since it occurred not in the Highlands, but in the Coffee Piedmont among resident estate laborers at at time when world coffee prices were high and there was therefore to immediate threat to subsistence. An even greater problem, however, is the fact that most of the elements of the subsistence crisis have been present in the Highlands since at least the end of World War II, if not earlier, yet, as the analysis of social change in the Highlands indicates, the receptivity of Highland peasants to guerrilla organization is of extremely recent origin.

There is no doubt that the subsistence margin is and has been in danger in the Central Highlands. Statistics on malnutrition and infant mortality make this tragically clear. By one estimate 81 percent of Guatemalan children under six years of age suffer from malnutrition and 42 percent are born below normal weight due to inadequate maternal nutrition (Quan 1981:17). The CIDA examined the Civil Register of San Juan Ostuncalco in Quezaltenango and found that children under the age of six constitute 55 percent of all reported deaths in the municipality, and that in Totonicapán 10 percent of all deaths were from malnutrition (CIDA 1965:109–110). Although export agriculture has sparked a long economic boom, per capita production of food crops did not increase at all between the early fifties and mid-sixties (Adams 1970:152). Between the 1964 and 1973 censuses the population of the northwest zone of the Central Highlands increased at an annual rate of 2.34 percent, but maize production increased at almost precisely the same rate, 2.39 percent (Guatemala, Direccion General de Estadistica 1980). The subsistence crisis did not ease but, significantly, neither did it worsen. However, in the seventies the situation improved. Maize production increased at a rate of 5.9 percent between 1973–74 and 1977–78, more than double the historic population growth rate.

The village studies of Brintnall, Hinshaw and Warren confirm that at least in some areas of the Highlands changes such as the introduction of cash crops, fertilizers, irrigation, and the organization of cooperatives began to dramatically improve Indian agriculture. By 1973 in Aguacatán, for example, despite immense technical difficulties, half of all lands were irrigated. Around Lake Atitlán, Sante Maria Visitación had largely liberated itself from seasonal labor by increased commerce in fruit and vegetables, Panajachel Indians had taken up coffee production and in San Andreas Semetabaj the local wheat growers, whose wealth was based on chemical fertilizers, had expanded their cooperative to include 1,200 members in Sololá, Quiché and Guatemala.[5] All of these changes, however, benefit only the land-owning members of the communities and there are still plenty of poor landless peasants to supply labor for the coastal plantations. The subsistence crisis seems to have eased in the critical decade of the late sixties and early seventies when, according to moral economy theory, it should have deepened.

Pressures on subsistence reached the crisis stage, however, long before this last decade as careful demographic research by Carmack on the central

Quiché Highlands indicates. He estimated that the carrying capacity of maize agriculture under primitive conditions, which were the conditions in most of the Highlands, would support a population of some 50,000 in central Quiché. As the Table 1 indicates, that figure was exceeded as early as the 1920s (Carmack 1981:104–105).

The subsistence crisis was beginning to be serious by the twenties and was acute by 1940. This is also evident in the mass recruitment of Highland workers for the lowland coffee estates described by Dessaint in a review of the earlier ethnographic literature on the Highlands. During the thirties and forties entire villages and even sizable towns were depopulated of adult males for much of the year as the men sought employment on the coffee estates. Around Lake Atitlán men from all the villages except the successful capitalists of Panajachel emigrated; Wagley's Chimaltenango was practically empty during October and November of each year, when as few as fifty able-bodied men (village population 1500) were left; in San Martín Huehuetenango all of the men seen by Tax seemed to go to the coast for half the year; in Chichicastenango church bells tolled regularly to mourn the death of a migrant on a coastal estate, since as many as 15,000 men from the small city worked there (Dessaint 1962:338–339). Escape from the subsistence crisis was not found in local insurance systems but rather by massive employment in wage labor, much as the peasants of Nghe An worked in the nearby industries of the city of Vinh (Scott 1976:136–137).

The moral economists, of course, did not say that the subsistence crisis alone created the potential for rebellion. This occurred only if the crisis were combined with human intervention which politicized discontent. Still, if it were the subsistence crisis which triggered the revolt it should have occurred in 1940, not 1980. Furthemore, the extractions by the state and peasant involvement in the market are also of long standing. In Vietnam the state and the market demanded rice or money; in Guatemala both demanded labor. In Vietnam the French colonial state and its local Vietnamese agents collected taxes while the forces of the market determined the price of rice and the share rents were set by direct negotiations with local landlords. In Guatemala the state and the landlords were virtually indistinguishable and their demands were the same—labor in the coastal estates. There is no doubt that the state threatened the subsistence margin directly by taking time away from subsistence cultivation. The result was the same as in Vietnam, but on a much smaller scale. Colby and van den Berghe report that in Nebaj in 1936 Indians assaulted the local army garrison to protest forced labor and debt servitude in an action reminiscent of the depression era rebellions in Vietnam. It appears that unrest was a chronic problem in Indian communities through much of this century and earlier but before the late seventies it had not, since the early colonial period, led to a general insurrection (Colby and van den Berghe 1969:155).[6] But the state role in labor recruitment was pronounced earlier in the century and, if anything, declined after 1944. Before that time labor was recruited through state enforced debt peonage (1894–1934) or through vagrancy laws (1934–

1944) which required 100–150 days labor a year of Indians (but not *ladinos*) (Whetten 1961:120–121, Dessaint 1962:331). The state role in labor recruitment diminished after 1944 when the revolution abolished the vagrancy code, but by that time the subsistence crisis was sufficiently advanced to compel migrant labor by economic pressure alone. Thus, the demands of the state, the labor market, and subsistence pressures had all reached a crisis stage by 1940, but no revolt occurred until almost forty years later. By then, the subsistence crisis had eased, and although the demand for labor persisted, the state's involvement in labor recruitment had declined. When all three variables specified by the theory were present the general insurrection predicted by the moral economy theory did not occur. Agrarian revolution occurred in the right place but at the wrong time.

Political Economy

For political economy theory agrarian revolution occurred in both the wrong time and the wrong place. Theoretically, the guerrillas should have succeeded in the East in the sixties, but of course they did not. Although it is difficult to assess the effectiveness of a clandestine guerrilla organization independent of how powerful an insurrection it organizes, there is considerable evidence that guerrilla organization and tactics in the sixties were not significantly inferior to those of the seventies, and indeed, the two guerrilla movements showed striking similarities. The actions of FAR and MR-13, like those of EGP and ORPA, were about equally divided between military occupations ("armed propaganda") and small scale ambushes on military units. Indeed, the following description of a FAR armed propaganda action could have been taken from an ORPA press release:

> . . . after Panzo's was occupied by the guerrilla squad of commander Turcios, a public meeting was held in the square at which the entire village was present. The guerrilla squad had confiscated all arms and supplies belonging to the military post; it had bought provisions in local shops, paying prevailing prices. It had then drawn up an agreement which the mayor was obliged to sign in the presence of the villagers (Gilly June 1965:18–19).[7]

The structure of the two organizations as well as their largely middle class and student leadership was also similar; in the case of both ORPA and new FAR there are direct structural links between the old and new guerrillas. Indeed, the division of the guerrilla movement into two phases is somewhat arbitrary since the struggle continued at a reduced level during the intervening years. Even the names of the EGP fronts—Turcios Lima, Edgar Ibarra, Otto Rene Castill—reflect the ideological connections between the two sets of organizations. The development of the ORPA front in Quezaltenango and San Marcos depended on the earlier organizational work of FAR in the late sixties.[8]

The sixties guerrillas also followed Popkin's advice concerning the importance of selective incentives delivered by honest effective political entrepreneurs. Both FAR and MR-13 built their peasant following over a period of years by carefully soliciting and responding to the interests of individual peasants and peasant communities. The principal selective incentive was, of course, land; the Eastern peasantry faced expropriation by expanding cattle ranches that often claimed lands that had been cultivated by peasant communities for years. MR-13 pressured landowners and their administrators and often managed to leave peasants in possession of rent-free land. They instituted a radical tax-cutting program by eliminating the feudal levies of Eastern estate owners. They also established village assemblies for the effective disposition of local disputes outside the rancher dominated local courts and even became involved in the settlement of domestic quarrels. These committees also cared for the families of peasants killed by the army. There were never any charges of dishonesty or major scandals involving the guerrillas and they seem to have attained an almost mythical status among the peasantry (Gilly May 1965:11, June 1965:15–16, Galeano 1967:31–32). There was also no absence of military training or experience among the military men in the first guerrilla wave: Turcios Lima, for example, had received ranger training at Fort Benning, Georgia (Gott 1972:49). All the guerrilla leaders became sophisticated ideologues well versed in the tactics and theory of guerrilla movements in Latin America and around the world. They also had Guatemala's greatest poet and, lest cynics suggest that poets do not revolutionaries make, consider the poems of Agustinho Neto and Ernesto Cardenal. Their organizational cadre was in no way inferior to that of later guerrillas, their tactics the same; yet they failed.

Their failure was a result of the limited potential for mobilization of the eastern peasantry, not the absence of honest, effective political entrepreneurs delivering selective incentives. From the point of view of political economy the East is more promising than the Central Highlands since there are more free resources to distribute and communication is facilitated by a higher level of Spanish literacy. The dirt poor Central Highlands, like Tonkin and Annam, have few incentives, selective or otherwise, to offer anyone. But this analysis ignores the class structure of the Eastern region and this, in the end, appears to have been decisive: ". . . the majority of their peasant base (were) small *ladino* property owners who were particularly susceptible to the government's repressive tactics and some of whom even joined the right wing para-military groups" (NACLA 1974:186). Unlike the Central Highlands, here there were many property owners with medium-sized holdings who were threatened by the encroaching ranches but were united to them by property ownership and *ladino* ethnic background. FAR and MR-13 never managed to reach the Indian population on any significant scale, but the change process in the Highlands was not sufficiently advanced in this period to make such an approach promising. In 1967, while the "butcher of Zacapa" was doing his evil work in Guatemala, another revolutionary *foco* led by a talented guerrilla leader with an impressive track record was eliminated in Bolivia. Che Guevera, like FAR and MR-13, had selected a region where property holdings were small; the owners' conservative instincts ended his revolutionary career (Gott 1972:481). Popkin is right that effective organizational entrepreneurs are indispensable for revolution. But they cannot succeed if the underlying class structure blocks popular support.

Guatemala: Class Conflict
'No necesitan a los indios'

Neither the subsistence crisis nor the guerrilla organization changed much in the decade preceding the rebellion of the late seventies. The organization of production of Guatemala's agricultural export economy, however, changed fundamentally from the traditional Latin American *hacienda* system which had dominated coffee production since the 1890s to a new form of agribusiness based on a migratory rural proletariat working in the new export crops of cardamom, sugar, and, above all, cotton. The change produced a conflict between two classes new to Guatemala: cost-conscious capitalists whose principal form of capital was still land, and migratory rural proletarians who still lived in Highland peasant communities. The results of such a collision between capitalists dependent on land, and a rural semi-proletariat was apparent in the Mekong Delta of Vietnam throughout the twentieth century. In Guatemala the conflict is largely a result of changes in agricultural organization in the last twenty, and especially the last ten, years.

Changes in agricultural organization are in large part a result of the introduction of new export crops, although the structure of the traditional coffee hacienda has been undergoing fundamental change as well. As the data in Table 2 make clear, while production in Guatemala's traditional export crops, coffee and bananas, continues to expand, the most dramatic growth has occurred in new crops, the most important of which is cotton. Although between 1960 and 1978 production of coffee and bananas both increased by almost 40 percent production of cotton more than quintupled in the same period and sugar production, starting from a small base, increased to over 150,000 tons by 1978, nearly tripling in the last decade. Cardamom exports experienced a dramatic increase a decade earlier and, although the quantity by weight is small, this is an extremely valuable spice much prized in the Middle East. All of these new export crops as well as the traditional banana crop are produced in the lower agricultural zones of the South Coast; and this region has also experienced a dramatic expansion of commercial cattle production for export. The long economic boom that Guatemala has experienced in the last to decades is directly attributable to the dramatic expansion of the South Coast agricultural zone.

These new export crops were produced in new forms of agricultural organization rather than in the traditional hacienda which was ill-suited to the highland values and intensive, rationalized production of the South Coast. The hacienda, however, served as the principal vehicle for Guatemalan export production from 1890 until recently and, although modified in form, continues to be important in coffee production. The traditional landowner, concerned about securing a captive labor supply, lured peasant laborers to his estate by giving them small plots of land on which to cultivate subsistence crops in exchange for labor on his estate when it was needed (Hoyt 1955:33–

46, Dessaint 1962, CIDA 1965, Riklin 1980). The workers, called *colonos* or *mozos*, were essentially sub-subsistence farmers (*minifundistas*) who happened to live on an estate and shared many of the social and political characteristics of mini-subsistence farmers of the Highlands or, for that matter, of Tonkin and Annam. Hoyt, describing the situation in 1946–47, notes that the hacienda left Indian culture unchanged and that workers seem unconcerned with changing conditions (Hoyt 1955:41–46). About the latter she was almost certainly wrong since, as we have seen, these workers were active in the peasant union movement less than a decade later. Still, the atmosphere of the hacienda was paternalistic and tightly controlled by the estate owner who held judicial as well as economic power over his workers.

Elsewhere in Latin America, notably in Mexico and Peru, hacienda tenants have resisted peasant revolutionry movements begun by independent communties, and the combination of stable access to a subsistence plot and tight landlord control does not seem to be conducive to mobilization.[9] Both Riklin and Hoyt call the hacienda "feudal" by which they mean manorial, but there is little doubt that as Riklin observes of two farms in the San Pablo region of Quiché ". . . they are a twentieth century incarnation of medieval European feudal estates" (Riklin 1980:10). The landlord's control of his tenant was complete. A landowner in San Pablo forbade his tenants to congregate in groups greater than five and threatened to shoot any priest who set foot on his property (Riklin 1980:10); in 1946–47 it was still common for landowners to keep a jail on their property where they placed offenders against hacienda rules (Hoyt 1955:34). And landowners were so suspicious of outsiders in the early sixties that they refused to allow agricultural extension agents on their property (CIDA 1965:81). On one of Hoyt's estates there had been a radio at one time but the owner took it away because it gave so much time (he claimed) to labor propaganda (Hoyt 1965:37). The owner provided inadequate housing and sometimes took care of older residents after their working lives were over, but he could easily withdraw these privileges at will. Under these circumstances it is surprising not that there was so little labor organization, but rather, so much. During times of national crisis, like the Arbenz period when landlord control was dramatically weakened, such peasants could and did organize on a massive scale. But such times are the exception.

Many of the estate workers, were, of course nonresident migrants from the Central Highlands, but they lived in temporary barracks-like quarters and were clearly subordinate to and largely controlled by both the residential community of permanent tenants and the hacienda administration. The traditional proportion of resident labor was approximately 45 percent; Hoyt reports 12,000 permanent and 16,000 temporary workers on the fifty estates she surveyed; the CIDA found a total of 651 resident and 900 temporary workers in the six Coffee Piedmont estates it surveyed and Schmid found a total of 80,385 resident and 99,000 migrant workers in coffee production in 1950 (CIDA 1965:85, Schmid 1967). With such a large proportion of year-round permanent residents it would be difficult for much independent political organization to develop among the migrants. Furthermore, the migrants were tightly controlled by *ladino* labor contractors, the *enganchadores* *(v.t. enganchar*, to hook), who completely monopolized access to estate labor (Brintnall 1979:108). To work as a migrant meant first subordinating oneself to a *ladino* contractor, then to the estate residential community, and finally to the landlord's law. Contractor, community, and landlord all reinforced traditional patterns of Indian subordination and *ladino* domination. Perhaps this is why San Miguel Acatn, where in 1981 peasants died shouting "long live the revolution," was known in the thirties as "A good village for plantation labor because Indians generally had no serious objections to this type of work" (Dessaint 1962:341). Those with serious objections, of course, could find no *ladinos* to supply them with work.

Stockpiling resident estate labor may have had some utility before the subsistence crisis forced Highlanders into the migratory labor stream, but after 1940 the organization of the hacienda with its inefficient use of land and labor and backward technology could not long survive the rationalizing forces of the international commodity market. As Quan observes, "with the increased possibilities of mechanization, a more than adequate labor supply, and the increasing value of land, this system is no longer the most advantageous for the landowner, and the *colono* is fast disappearing" (Quan 1981:14). The resident Indian estate laborer in export agriculture has become expendable. The current attitude toward Indian resident labor is well-expressed by the chilling phrase heard increasingly in Central America: "*No necesitan a los indios*" (We don't need the Indian anymore).[10] What is needed is labor reduced to commodity status, not Indian residential communities that eat up land and resources. The *colono* system never made any headway on the South Coast which was, from the beginning, organized along rational capitalist lines. In the early sixties the CIDA found that such attitudes were the most striking difference between estate owners in the Coffee Piedmont and the South Coast. South Coast planters were enthusiasts for new ideas and the latest technology; they invested heavily in estate improvements and were not afraid to take risks. According to the CIDA the owners of the most modern coastal estates also wanted to get rid of their permanent laborers to avoid problems of under-employment, evade labor legislation, and rationalize manual work (CIDA 1965:81–82). To a large extent they have succeeded. Thus it is not surprising to find that the ratio of temporary to permanent laborers is higher in the Coast than in the Coffee Piedmont. Adams estimates that there were 4,700 permanent employees and laborers on cotton farms in 1965–66, while there were between 118,000 and 150,000 migrant laborers (Adams 1970:369). Although the South Coast planters have dispensed with resident Indian communities, they have not dispensed with the need for Indian labor. Their economic success ultimately rests on acute deprivation in the Central Highlands.

Even in the Coffee Piedmont the hacienda system is beginning to break down. While in 1950 their proportion was down to about a third. With this change to migratory rather than resident labor in coffee, and the continued expansion of the South Coast migratory labor system, came a fundamental change in the pattern of class relations. The only connection between the South Coast agribusinessman and his worker is money during the harvest season. The rest of the year the worker fends for himself beyond the reach of estate administrative coercion. Since there are no longer extensive residential communities of *colonos*, the inhibiting effect of this conservative strata is removed. Finally, labor recruiting in cotton seems to have slipped out of *ladino* hands and is now controlled by a new class of Indian entrepreneurs (Brintnall 1979:154). Since the Indian migrants now obtain half or more of their subsistence from the South Coast economy their dependence on the good will of local landowners in the Highlands is also greatly reduced. To many Indians it must appear that it is the *ladinos* who are expendable. The fundamental changes which have come to the Indian villages of the Highlands, then, are a result of the fact that many of these villages are not peasant at all but rather temporary homes for agricultural wage laborers. Typical of the effect of such changes is Brintnall's description of how peasant leagues came to Aguacatán. They came in the person of a coastal labor organizer brought to the village by a native returning from seasonal labor. Focusing on labor issues, not on traditional peasant and disputes, the organizer had great success, but only among the poor members of the village, who were still largely dependent on coastal labor, and had not benefitted from the improvements in agriculture in the Highlands. By 1975 there were two noncompetitive leagues with over two hundred members. Poor *ladinos* as well as Indians were admitted, an unheard of breach of local racial etiquette (Brintnall 1979:163). Here was the peasant organization that Turcios's men had sought in vain in the sixties. Aguacatán, as was indicated earlier, is, of course, in the center of current EGP operations including a recent *claymorazo*.

The collapse of the hacienda system and the increasing independence of Indians in agro-export wage labor is also evident in Riklin's account of the origins of a protest march on the Guatemalan congress by twenty-seven Indians from the remote Quiché villages of San Pablo and Chimel (Riklin 1980:10). The problems started when the owner of El Soch, a nearby coffee estate, ordered the peasants, under penalty of death, to make a one and a half hour detour around his estate to go to market. In the past the Indians would have grudgingly obeyed. But, of course, times have changed. The EGP retaliated by killing the owner of El Soch on August 12, 1980 and on August 19 army reprisals, in the form of kidnappings, began. The villages of the Highlands had been long accustomed to losing men to kidnappers both for the army and for forced labor. But this time instead of acquiescing they went to the capital, an act of unheard-of audacity.

The farmers of Chimel and San Pablo are dependent on Coastal wage labor for half or more of their subsistence. They spend that money at the market, which could now be reached only by a forced detour around El Soch. El Soch itself and the adjoining farm of El Rosario are both in economic difficulties since they are traditional haciendas worked by resident *colonos* and their low productivity and poor management have made them increasingly uncompetitive in a coffee economy dominated by agribusiness. It was not the residents of the traditional commercial haciendas who went to Guatemala City but rather the migratory wage laborers who still lived in the independent villages of San Pablo and Chimel. From hacienda to migratory labor estate and from Indian to proletarian; the changes in San Pablo are a microcosm of the shifts in the Guatemalan agricultural economy as a whole. It is these changes, not the subsistence crisis or the EGP's superior organization, which have created the conditions for revolution in the Central Highlands of Guatemala. There is one more piece of evidence supporting the class-conflict interpretation, although it is not beyond dispute: the theories of the guerrillas themselves. As was the case in Vietnam, successful political entrepreneurs seem to view their struggle in class-conflict terms. Here is the EGP's position from its magazine *Compañero*.

> . . . poor peasants . . . *minifundistas* (owners of sub-sistence plots) have no other choice than to migrate periodically to the coast, if they are to survive. This reality constitutes one aspect of the inextricable relationship between the latifundio and the minifundio; the other aspect is the landowners' reliance on this migrant labor force. . . . Within this process of capitalist transformation, the Indian peasants have become wage workers part of the year or *semi-proletarians* (Italics mine.) (*Compañero* n.d. probably 1981:7).

According to the EGP the Indians' only choice is to join the Popular Revolutionary War and it is clear that it is these "semi-proletarians" that it expects will join.

The transformation from hacienda to agribusiness has had one other major effect on the Highland peasantry. Increasing land values and prospects for agro-export development have precipitated large-scale land grabs throughout the Highands, particularly in the so-called Northern Transversal Strip which includes the northern third of Huehuetenango, El Quiché, and Alta Verapaz (Riklin 1980, IWGIA 1978). General Romeo Lucas Garcia himself, Guatemala's most recently deposed presidential general, is rumored to personally own a substantial tract in the area, variously estimated from 18,000, to 130,000 acres.[11] Other large tracts are owned by many other officers as well as by a "Who's Who of Guatemalan society" (Riklin 1980:8). The area is also becoming important as a possible southern extension of the great Mexican petroleum fields (*New York Times* May 8, 1981:29). All of this wealth sits under land occupied by Indian communities and traditional haciendas. *No necesitan a los indios.* The generals' current slaughter of entire Indian villages at Chajul, Cotzal, Nebaj, San Miguel Acatán, San Martin Jilotepeque, and Panzos in this region combines a grim economic as well as political logic. Eliminating the population will eliminate the guerrillas and also free the land for development. The parasitic relationship between the hacienda and the Indian village is being destroyed by military agri-businessmen whose viciousness apparently knows no limits. If they survive the generals' onslaught, the peasants' last connection to the land will be severed and they will be completely dependent on the agro-export wage labor.

In their long involvement in Vietnam, Americans never listened to the revolutionaries' own account of the origins of their conflict. Had they, they would have heard the same message as in the passage from the EGP quoted above: class conflict generated by the collision between an agricultural proletariat and capitalist landowners in a peripheral export economy has the power to generate revolutionary conflict of explosive power. In Vietnam the conflict was between landowners and share tenants, in Guatemala it is between military agribusinessmen and migratory proletarians, but the results have been remarkably similar. Neither moral economy nor political economy has the power to explain the origins of the conflict in both nations or to reflect the views of the revolutionaries themselves. Perhaps it would not surprise Marx to learn that careful analysis of the organization of production would provide the key to an understanding of revolutionary change, but it seems to be something of a surprise to recent theorists of peasant revolution. It is a lesson they could well take to heart.

Notes

This is a revised version of a paper presented at the Conference on Global Crises and Social Movements (Santa Cruz, California, 24 October 1982), and circulated as Working Paper 275, Center for Research on Social Organization, University of Michigan. The data on which the analysis is based extend to August 1981 and so do not reflect more recent developments, especially the rapidly changing situation after the counter-revolutionary offensive launched by Efrain Rios Montt in July 1982. I am grateful to Ellisa Miller for allowing me access to her collection of contemporary Guatemalen oppositon publications and to members of the Guatemalan church in exile, who must remain anonymous, for much helpful information.

1. Tilly's typology includes a fourth tradition, the Weberian, which has no clear representative among scholarly theories about Vietnam.

2. Quote from R.H. Tawney, 1966, pp. 77.

3. *Le Monde*, February 7, 1966, quoted in Gott 1972:56.

4. Charles Wagley, "Forward," in Brintnall, 1979.

5. For Aguacatán see Brintnall 1979:113, for Santa Maria Visitación and Panjachel see Hinshaw 1975:164, 172, for Semetabaj see Warren 1978:157.

6. For unrest in Indian communities, see Herbert, 1970.

7. See also Gilly, May 1965:20–22 and NACLA 1974:182–184.

8. Julio Quan personal communication.

9. In Mexico, Womack 1968:43–50, in Peru, Paige 1975:204.

10. I am indebted to Gilma Tinoco for this observation.

11. Riklin estimates 18,000 (1980:8); IWGIA quoting *Newsweek*, 78,000 (1980:Document 11); and Camposeco, 100,000 (1981:8).

References

Adams, R. N. 1970. *Crucifixion by Power*, Austin: University of Texas Press.

Anon. 1980. "Guatemala! The Terrible Repression and its Roots in the U.S. National Security State," *Green Revolution*, Winter.

Banfield, E. 1968. *The Moral Basis of a Backward Society*, New York: The Free Press.

Barry, B. 1970. *Sociologists, Economists and Democracy*, London: Macmillan.

Brintnall, D. 1979. *Revolt Against the Dead*, New York: Gordon and Breach.

Bunzel, R. 1952. *Chichicastenango*, American Ethnological Society, Publication 22.

Camposeco, J. 1981. "A Testimony on Guatemala," paper presented at the Conference on Land Tenure in Central America, Johns Hopkins University, Washington, DC: Washington Office on Latin America.

Caputo, P. 1977. *A Rumor of War*, New York: Holt, Rinehart and Winston.

Carmack, R. M. 1981. *The Quiche Mayas of Utatlan*, Norman: University of Oklahoma Press.

Castillo, O. R. 1971. *Let's Go! Selections from Vamanos Patria a Caminar*, Margaret Randall, trans., London: Cape Goliard Press.

Colby B. N., and P. L. van den Berghe. 1969. *Ixil Country*, Berkeley: University of California Press.

Comite Interamericano de Desarrollo Agricola (CIDA). 1965. *Tenencia de la Tierra y Desarrollo Socio-Economico del Sector Agricola: Guatemala*, Washington, DC: Panamerican Union.

Companero n.d. probably 1981.

Dessaint, A. X. 1962. "Effects of the Hacienda and Plantation Systems on Guatemala's Indians," *American Indigena*, 22:332.

Fall, B. 1958. "South Vietnam's Internal Problems," *Pacific Affairs*, 31:241 60.

Fitzgerald, F. 1972. *Fire in the Lake: The Vietnamese and the Americans in Vietnam*, New York: Random House.

Frohlich, N., J. A. Oppenheimer, and O. R. Young. 1971. *Political Leadership and Collective Goods*, Princeton: Princeton University Press.

Galeano, E. 1967. *Guatemala: Occupied Country*, New York: Modern Reader.

Giap, V. N., and T. Chinh. 1974. *The Peasant Question (1937–38)*, C. P. White (trans.), *Southeast Asia Program Data Paper #94*, Ithaca: Cornell University Press.

Gilly, A. May 1965. "The Guerrilla Movement in Guatemala, Part One," *Monthly Review*, 17:19–40.

———. June 1965. "The Guerrilla Movement in Guatemala, Part Two," *Monthly Review*, 17:17–41.

Gott, R. 1972. *Guerrilla Movements in Latin America*, Garden City, NJ: Anchor.

Gourou, P. 1955. *The Peasants of the Tonkin Delta*, New Haven: Human Relations Area Files. Originally published as *Les Paysans du Delta Tonkinois*, Paris: Editions d'Art et d'Histoire, 1936.

Guatemala, Direccion General de Estadistica. 1974. *Anuario Estadistico*, Cuadro 4, Guatemala City.

———. 1976. *Anuario Estadistico 1974*, Cuadro 3. Guatemala City.

———. 1980. *Guatemala en Cifras 1964*, Guatemala City.

Henry, Y. 1932. *Economie agricole de l'Indochine*, Hanoi: Governement General de l'Indochine.

Herbert, J. L. 1970. "Expresiones Ideologicas de la Lucha de Clases y de la Discriminacion Racial Institucional a su Mixificacion: El Indigenismo," in C. G. Blocker and J. Herbert, eds., *Guatemala: Una Interpretacion Historico-Social*, Mexico: Siglo XXI Editores.

Hinshaw, R. 1975. *Panajachel: A Guatemalan Town in Thirty Year Perspective*, Pittsburgh: University of Pittsburgh Press.

Hoyt, E. 1955. The Indian Laborer on Guatemalan Coffee Fincas," *Inter-American Economic Affairs*, 9:33–46.

International Work Group for Indigenous Affairs (IWGIA). 1978. *Guatemala 1978: The Massacre at Panzos*, Document 33, Copenhagen.
McAlister, J. T., Jr., and P. Mus. 1970. *The Vietnamese and Their Revolution*, New York: Harper and Row.
Melville T., and M. M. Melville. 1971. *Guatemala: The Politics of Land Ownership*, New York: The Free Press.
Migdal, J. 1974. *Peasants, Politics and Revolution*, Princeton: Princeton University Press.
Mitchell, E. J. 1968. "Land Tenure and Rebellion: A Statistical Analysis of Factors Affecting Government Control in South Vietnam," Rand Memorandum 5181-ARPA, Santa Monica, California. Also published as "Inequality and Insurgency: A Statistical Study of Vietnam," *World Politics*, 20:421–38.
Murphy, B. 1970. "The Stunted Growth of Campesino Organizations," in R. N. Adams, *Crucifixion by Power*, Austin: University of Texas Press.
North American Congress on Latin America. 1974. *Guatemala*, Berkeley: NACLA.
Olson, M. 1965. *The Logic of Collective Action*, Cambridge: Harvard University Press.
Paige, J. M. 1975. *Agrarian Revolution*, New York: The Free Press.
Popkin, S. L. 1979. *The Rational Peasant*, Berkeley: University of California Press.
Pearson, N. J. 1969. "Guatemala: The Peasant Union Movement," in H. Landsberger, ed., *Latin American Peasant Movements*, Ithaca: Cornell University Press.
Quan, J. 1981. "Guatemalan Agriculture in 1981," paper presented at the Conference on Land Tenure in Central America, Johns Hopkins University, Washington Office on Latin America, Washington, DC.
Riklin, S. 1980. "Guatemala: The Revolution Approaches," mimeographed. Rye, NY: n. p.
Schmid, L. 1967. "The Role of Migratory Labor in the Economic Development of Guatemala," Ph.D. Dissertation, University of Wisconsin, quoted in Adams 1970:392.
Scott, J. C. 1976. *The Moral Economy of the Peasant*, New Haven: Yale University Press.
———. 1977. "Peasant Revolution: A Dismal Science," *Comparative Politics*, 9:21.
Tawney, R. H. 1966. *Land and Labor in China*, Boston: Beacon Press.
Tax, S. 1953. *Penny Capitalism: A Guatemalan Indian Economy*, Smithstonian Institution, Institute of Social Anthropology, no. 16, Washington, DC.
Tilly, C. 1978. *From Mobilization to Revolution*,
Tumin, M. M. 1952. *Caste in a Peasant Society*, Princeton: Princeton University Press.
Wagley, C. 1949. *The Social and Religious Life of a Guatemalan Village*, American Anthropological Association, Memoir 71.
Warren, K. B. 1978. *The Symbolism of Subordination*, Austin: University of Texas Press.
West R. C., and J. P. Augelli. 1976. *Middle America: Its Lands and Peoples*, 2nd ed. Englewood Cliffs: Prentice Hall.
Whetten, N. L. 1961. *Guatemala: The Land the People*, New Haven: Yale University Press.
Wolf, E. 1968. *Peasant Wars of the Twentieth Century*, New York: Harper and Row.
———. 1977. "Review Essay: Why Cultivators Rebel," *American Journal of Sociology*, 83:742–50.
———. 1966. *Peasants*, Englewood Cliffs: Prentice Hall.
Womack, J. 1968. *Zapata and the Mexican Revolution*, New York: Random House.

PART THREE

WORLD MARKET CYCLES AND FASCIST AND POPULIST MOVEMENTS IN THE TWENTIETH CENTURY

9

Fascism and Economic Policy Controversies: National Responses to the Global Crisis of the Division of Labor

PETER GOUREVITCH

Two forms of global crisis appear to affect the intensity of domestic social movements most profoundly: war and economic depression. The fascism of the interwar years derived from both: the shocks of wartime continued to ripple through the societies of Europe long after the fighting stopped, and the economic shocks of the war and then the depression of skillful fascist organization.

The economic crises were international ones. The war sped up economic change considerably, inducing considerable investment in agriculture and industry in both old industrial countries and newly industrializing ones. The initial postwar crisis involved the difficulty of readjusting to peacetime, of bringing greatly increased productive capacity back into line with non-military supported demand, and of having national producers absorb the implication of new and modernized production around the world. Agriculture felt the pressures early on and never fully recovered. Industry experienced something of boom in the waning years of the decade, but then the double economic crisis hit: a business cycle downturn combined with unresolved tensions in shifting advantages in the international division of labor brought about by the diffusion of old technologies to new countries and the development of new products and new technologies for older products.

International economic crises wreak their effect on domestic politics by their effects on domestic actors: social forces and interest group organization seek to gratify the policy demands of their members; politicians seek by levels of wealth. As the international economy changes, so does the en-

Reprinted from *International Organization* 38/1 (winter 1984), Peter Gourevitch, "Breaking with Orthodoxy: The Politics of Economic Policy Responses to the Depression of the 1930's," by permission of The MIT Press, Cambridge, MA. Copyright 1984 by the President and Fellows of Harvard College and at the Massachusetts Institute of Technology.

vironment of these domestic actors. One way to highlight these connections is to examine policy debates: the quarrels over how to handle the tremendous shock of international contraction—who will pay the costs, who will reap the benefits of different solutions, through what instruments and modalities, through which political formulae?

The interpretations of fascism are legion. In this essay, I wish to stress the importance of substantive policy issues in affecting the struggle over power and the constitution. The international economy presents specific policy issues. Power is sought for various purposes, but policy goals are certainly a major one. Much can be understood about fascism by exploring the policy battles which express the specific linkage inside between the external pressure of the global crisis in the economy and the domestic social movements in each country.

When the Great Depression rippled around the world in 1929, most countries responded with the same economic policy, deflation. This was the "orthodox" response prescribed by orthodox analyses, but it did not work. After some two to four years of failure, most countries broke with orthodoxy to try "neo-orthodoxy"—devaluation of the currency, tariffs, and some corporatistic regulation of domestic markets. Some countries broke more drastically, either immediately or after a few years of neo-orthodoxy, to try more unusual departures from standard views—demand stimulus through deficit spending, known after the war as Keynesianism, or more drastic forms of state-dominant corporatistic regulation of the domestic economy.

How can this policy sequence be understood; in particular, how can we explain the divergence of countries after the initial similarity in their policy motives? Why did some countries remain with "conventional" breaks from orthodoxy while other experimented more radically? The answers to these questions may shed light on the politics of economic policy. They may also have implications for other outcomes, for the timing of great shifts in policy and great shifts in politics is too close for coincidence. To understand the connections between breaking with economic orthodoxy and the destruction of constitutional government by fascism (Germany), the critical realignment elections (Sweden and the United States), the Popular Front and its demise, the disruptions of the Labour Party and the ascendancy of the Conservatives might be to understand the connection between *economic experimentation* and *political experimentation*.

The answers given to these questions address current controversies over the 1970s and 1980s. Both periods raise conceptual questions concerning the relationship among international economic crisis, the evolution of the international division of labor in different sectors or branches ("the product cycle"), the development of political coalitions among different producer groups within particular countries, the content of government policy, and the character of political forms.

The policy debate around the current crisis challenges a set of political and policy arrangements whose historical origins lie in the earlier crisis— which was, in turn, a challenge to arrangements that had been derived from the economic dislocation of the last quarter of the nineteenth century. In very general terms, the 1930s disrupted a particular set of producer group relationships. The nineteenth century's enmity between agriculture and labor over tariffs and other quarrels turned into farmer-labor alliances albeit of kinds that differed from place to place. The relationship of labor and agriculture to different types of business (some sharply antagonistic, others more cooperative) underwent acute shifts as well (Arndt 1944; Landes 1969; Lewis 1960).

In several countries where constitutional government survived, particularly Sweden and the United States, the outlines of a pattern were emerging by the late 1930s, one that would spread over most of Western Europe in the postwar period. Involving mutual accommodation among elements of labor, business, and agriculture, this pattern is commonly labeled "social-democratic," after the European parties that played a key role in it, or "Scandinavian," after the region that embodies it most clearly. It is built around a set of economic policies that combine Keynesian demand management, an open international economy, trade union autonomy in labor markets, private control of capital in both investment and management, and subsidies for agriculture (Shonfield 1969; on the role of labor unions Ross, Lange et al. 1983; and on the origins of postwar corporatism Katzenstein 1985). It is this social-democratic compromise which is now under sharp challenge: the victories of Reagan and Thatcher represent the unraveling of political relationships built around economic policies dating back to the 1930s, and the many shifts in political majority of recent European elections (Mitterand, Papandreous, Kohl, Gonzalez, Palme) show the political ramifications of current economic disruptions. Unraveling the older pattern is thus instructive both for testing types of explanation for a particular period and for specifying which relationships are now under stress.

Social science is, of course, full of possible explanations for the economic policy outcomes of the 1930s. My focus will be on the "political sociology of political economy"—on the pattern of alliances among social actors whose interactions shape patterns of policy. Certain features of some such alliances are well-known. For example, the iron and rye coalition of late nineteenth century Germany linked industrialists producing "heavy" goods (iron and steel) with grain growers. Together they supported high tariffs in opposition to finished consumer goods manufacturers using advanced technology, meat and dairy farmers, and consumer-oriented labor, all of whom opposed tariffs (Gerschenkron 1966; Lambi 1963). At about the same period, after many years of free trade, Britain experienced a resurgence of sympathy for protectionism, particularly among the metal producers of Birmingham and grain farmers. They opposed the continued economic liberalism of the great finance-shipping-insurance grouping symbolized by the City and allied with labor concerned with cheap food (Brown 1943; Aldcroft and Richardson 1969). American history notes "Gold Democrats," free-trade-oriented merchants and bankers pushed toward the Democratic Party in opposition to their protectionist brethren in the Republican Party. In the post 1945 era, the differences in sectoral preference toward commercial policy have become increasingly obvious: free-trade automobile makers turned protectionist when that industry went into crisis, joining the makers of televisions, shoes, steel, and other products. In America, the internationalism of free trade has historically had some association with Eastern financial circles, while isolationism and economic nationalism have been associated with the manufacturing mid-West (Schattschneider 1963; Williams 1969; for an emphasis on economics, see Taussig 1967; Bauer, et al. 1967). These "sectoral" proclivities are known, and some political scientists have found them worthy of interpretation (Kurth 1979).

In this essay I assume that something can be learned about the 1930s by exploring further the relationship implied by these well-known cases. But I also assume that in analyzing the political and policy relationships among capital, labor, and agriculture, these terms must be disaggregated into sectors, or branches, that have identifiable characteristics. What the industries produce and how, who buys their products, their capital requirements, their labor component, organizational characteristics, international competitiveness, and so on—these elements of a sector shape its *situation*. Situation influences a sector's policy preferences, which in turn affect its political behavior, which ends by affecting politics and policy outcomes.

This is not a new theory. It is a familiar mixture of the interest-group approach, social forces analysis, structural Marxism, rational choice, and old-fashioned liberalism derived from Bentham, Smith, and Mill. The distinctive features of its use here are fourfold. First, I stress sectors, rather than firms or specific organizations. Second, I emphasize the international situation in shaping group behavior; sector policy goals are influenced by location in an international division of labor. Third, I am concerned with the substantive content of sectoral "alliances," which is to say the terms of trade of alliances with other actors. Finally, I focus attention on the importance of politics not as formal institutions but as the forging of coalitions out of social components.

The interest-group and social forces approaches have had many valid criticisms leveled against them. The journey from the first step (group situation) to the last (policy or other outcomes) can be quite long, and there are certainly intervening variables (ideology, institutions, leadership, and security issues, to name but a few) that affect the interplay of situation, preference, and political outcomes.

Knowing "interests," whether of an individual, a group, or a class, poses its own problems. To say that a group takes a particular position because "it is objectively in its interest to do so" is a form of proposition requiring its own sort of justification. In this article, however, I mean to explore a sociological proposition, not a philosophical one. From knowing a group's situation, we may generate an expectation about various behaviors (policy preferences and political alignments) and thereby gain leverage to explain policy outcomes. I assume that groups frequently pursue policies that are not optimal, that reality is sufficiently ambiguous as to provide a multitude of calculi from which a variety of behaviors could be drawn that would be "in a group's interests." Yet this is less true in a sociological sense: group preferences and behaviors follow patterns that can to some degree be related to group positions, even if they lead to miscalculation in relation to group "interest" (Gaventa 1980).

Despite its problems, the interest approach deserves pursuit. It seems odd to imagine one could examine the politics of economic policy without asking *qui bono* and without considering that benefit might shape behavior. Politics and interest interact strongly. Politicians seeking to get and keep power have to fashion coalitions, not just electoral majorities but governing coalitions, combinations of social forces that have producer-group power and whose compliance or even enthusiasm is essential to attaining goals. At a minimum, interest groups and social forces are the raw materials, the essential components from which such coalitions are constructed. In this context, crises are interesting—a curse for the Chinese, a subject for the social scientist, an opportunity or a constraint for politicians. Crises pry open the political scene, throwing traditional relationships into flux. Groups, institutions, and individuals are torn loose from their moorings, their assumptions, their loyalties, their "cognitive road maps." Circumstances become less certain and solutions less obvious. Crises thus render politics more plastic. Political actors have choices to make; they can forge new coalitions, or they can revive old ones. In this process of construction, the structure of the group situation provided political entrepreneurs with both constraints and opportunities. Thus, even to evaluate the limits of interest in explaining an outcome and to identify whether variables mediate it, we need some portrait of the structure of interests. Here, an account of how the production profile of each country fits into the international division of labor proves instructive.

Those who seek policy goals (interest groups) have a need for a politics that will help fulfill their policy. Conversely, those who seek power, whose goals are political, need a policy approach that will suit their policies. This article is about that interaction worked out through the great crisis of the 1930s. The first section briefly defines the major policy alternatives available for coping with the Depression, and the categories of social forces whose preferences are relevant. The second section explores the policy debate in Germany, the United States, Sweden, Britain, and France. The final section interprets these findings.

The Options and Their Political Ramifications

The striking innovation in economic policy during the 1930s was demand-stimulus policy, known in the postwar period as Keynesianism. It is familiar as a countercyclical policy that seeks to correct the deficiency of inadequate demand through deficit spending by governments. Demand-stimulus policy, it has been claimed, saved constitutional government in the capitalist economies by changing the political struggles over economic policy from a zero-sum game to a mixed game. The zero-sum alternatives were posed by the policy programs of the orthodoxies that prevailed in the 1930s, those which were debated at the time and which preceded the innovation of demand stimulus.

The first was *orthodox deflation,* which involved cutting down on costs through lower wages, lower taxes, and less government spending in order to cheapen costs and thereby to attract buyers at home and abroad. It required a defense of the value of the currency and, in that period, its fixed relation to gold.

The second was *the socialization of investment.* The major critique of orthodox deflation at the outset of this period was socialist orthodoxy, which argued that private investment could not sustain a full-employment economy. The only way to avoid the frightful costs of the business cycle was to socialize investment and planning, thereby freeing employment-generating decisions from the interests of a specialized group within the economy, the private investors of capital.

These two alternatives were seen as "zero-sum" in that each requires sacrifices from a major segment of the population. The deflation school insists that high wages and high taxes for transfer payments (unemployment compensation and other benefits) threaten profitability. The owners of capital are discouraged from investing, or even producing, with existing capacity because wages and taxes eat up profits. Wages and wage-sustaining taxes must therefore be cut. Conversely, the socialization of investment school leads to the elimination of the owners of capital. If the private owners of capital are unwilling to lower unemployment, they must be replaced by mechanisms that will.

Each position has a dramatic political implication as well: to attain the economic end, it may be necessary to destroy the constitutional system. The deflationists may be tempted to try authoritarian government as a way of destroying labor's ability to resist wage cuts and welfare reductions through strikes and the ballot box. Conversely, the socializers may seek authoritarian government as a way to break private capital's hold on the economy (in particular, its ability to engage in a "capital strike") and to forestall possible political moves by capital against labor organizations.

The alternatives to these two poles of policy were "mixed games" in the sense that they blurred the effects of policy across different segments of the population and the nature of the sacrifices demanded of each.

Neo-orthodoxy was the "orthodox" break with orthodoxy in that it was derived intellectually from remedies for disorder suggested by classic economic theory, and it preserved private property. Nonetheless, it remained both intellectually and politically controversial. It involved devaluation for the currency, which allows the relaxation of deflation policies since it is not longer necessary to curb imports in defense of the currency via restraint of spending and purchasing; tariffs, which protect industry from imports; and cartelization, which helps share out markets and maintain prices, either officially through government-sponsored agreements or unofficially through private arrangements.

Demand stimulus, or the "unorthodox" break with orthodoxy of either kind, departed intellectually as well as politically from existing traditions. In substance it meant boosting demand through deficit-fianced public works or transfer payments, or both. This would prove to be the new scheme of the 1930s. It may have occurred earlier, through unintended deficits or through specialized spending, but it was not deliberately tried until the 1930s, and even then only sparingly.

Reality, of course, is more confusing than the simplification that generalization requires. Real countries did a mixture of things; some said they were doing one thing and actually did another. The boundaries among actual behaviors blur easily: recent interpretations of the Swedish case, for example, argue that the actual effect of its supposed demand-stimulus policy was far less striking than the common image allows. The United States did not really try demand stimulus until late in the decade, in 1938. Nazi Germany was the most extensive experimenter in the 1930s, and the most successful. Demand stimulus would only come of age after World War II. Nonetheless, reflation through public spending was proposed in many countries even before Keynes published his famous book; attempts were made, experiments were tried, doctrines developed, alliances forged. The postwar pattern took form in the 1930s.

These alternative policies changed the political struggle because they made it possible to attract people across the boundaries defined by the two orthodoxies. With neo-orthodoxy, tariffs helped draw together producers of different sorts—business and agriculture, plus labor in the protected sphere for the end of deflation policy reduced the pressure to cut wages. Demand stimulus altered the game because wages and profits could rise together rather than inversely (see Skidelsky and Crouch in Crouch 1979).

What accounts for the choice of one policy option over others in this period? And what connection was there between the struggle over policy choice and the struggles over political system and political coalitions that occurred at the same time? I seek to explicate the political preconditions of breaking with orthodoxy, and the character of political support that mobilized on behalf of policies in different countries. Why did some countries stop the policy sequence with neo-orthodoxy while others went on to demand stimulus? Descriptively, this means examining what the support coalitions of Nazi Germany, social-democratic Sweden, and New Deal America have in common that enabled more extensive breaks with orthodoxy than occurred in France (save for a few months of the Blum government) and the United Kingdom.

It may at first blush appear that their policy coalitions have nothing in common and that there is no connection between politics and economic policy. What, after all, could be further apart than social-democratic Sweden and Nazi Germany, or Nazi Germany and the United States of the New Deal? Though demand-stimulus policies may in the long run have contributed to the strengthening of democracy at that historical juncture, by helping constitutional regimes deal more effectively with the economic crisis, they were by no means the monopoly of constitutional regimes. Indeed, Germany used such policies more extensively than anyone else in the period and brought the unemployment rate of workers and underutilized capacity down faster than anyone else. With this in mind, we might conclude that since different political systems pursued the same polices, and similar political systems pursued different ones, there is no connection between the two and economic policies are polymorphous—anyone can take up any policy through any political system, so no linkages can be established.

Economic policies are, however, *not* completely polymorphous. Not just anyone supported one or another policy; this was not a randomly distributed set of preferences. Farmers were critical of the market everywhere, while business interests uniformly denounced socialism. In work on the international economic crisis of 1873, I found that the preferences of various groups played a considerable role in explaining the choice of policies in different countries. In exploring the behavior of similar groups during the next great crisis, I see the glimmers of some regularities in these preferences, at the level of interest groups. In the various countries, it may be possible to specify the support base for the alternative polices, the alliances that occurred, and the trade-offs. Furthermore, by specifying what alliances with what terms of trade were possible but were not tried, or were tried and failed, we may explore the similarities among interest groups that, however, express themselves politically in different ways.

Actors and Situations

Let us use a rather crude model of the interest groups that constitute society, adapted from Alexander Gerschenkron's excellent *Bread and Democracy in Germany* (1943).[1] The outstanding feature of Gerschenkron's classification is a disaggregation into three major groupings (agriculture, industry, and labor), each divided into two main camps according to situation in the international economy. Agriculture thus involves large-scale grain-growing estates (Junkers), and small proprietors who used cheap foreign grain as inputs. Industry is split into heavy industry (iron, steel, coal) with very high capital requirements, very strong international competitive pressures, and a need for stable markets; and finished goods manufacturers for whom heavy industry was an input, with high technology, a strong position in international markets, and considerable reliance on consumers as markets. As for labor, Gerschenkron focuses on the German Social-democratic party (SPD) as a bloc. But labor could also be disaggregated, into unionized and nonunionized labor, each caught among frequently conflicting pressures as producers and consumers. Gerschenkron gives some consideration to other groups such as banking, merchants, and shippers, professionals, shopkeepers, and other middle-class strata. In the case he examines, these groups appear not to have separated out with distinctly different positions. Banks, for example, had close relations with different industries and tended to express the needs of their clients (heavy or finished, accordingly); shippers favored policy that would promote trade, lawyers the policies of their clients, and so on.

The situational features of different sectors most likely to account for their varying propensities to ally with labor are international competitiveness (position of the domestic industry in the international division of labor of the product cycle), labor component (labor costs as a percentage of value added), type of market for product (consumer vs. capital goods, including the military dimension and the government as possible buyer), technology (degree of stability), and investment features (minimum capital requirements). The possible combinations of these dimensions are many, but they can be simplified as constituting components of a single variable—international competitiveness.

There are many qualifications and adjustments necessary for this model of social groups, but the country cases will permit us to explore how different groups behaved in relation to the economic policy alternatives for responding to the Depression that were available to the political systems of the day.

The demand-stimulus coalitions of Sweden, the United States, and Germany were, in sum, *cross-sector, cross-class* alliances of groups whose patience with market solutions had run out. In each case farmers made de facto or explicit alliances with certain sectors of business who were themselves seeking help to break from economic orthodoxy, and with certain elements of labor willing to alter old habits to bring about changes. In Sweden and the United States, the labor component of this alliance was provided by the labor organizations themselves. In Germany, of course, it was not, as the union movement was crushed.

Germany

The interwar debate over German economic policy, as well as quarrels over the constitution, social structure, foreign policy, and many other issues, can be seen as the continuation of a complex set of quarrels within German society reaching back to the origins of the German Empire forged by Bismark in 1871. The marriage of iron and rye in the tariff of 1879 is one of the best-known examples of domestic horsetrading among sectors for the national economy (Craig 1964, 1978; Wehler 1970; Bohme 1967; for a critical view, see Rogowski 1982). Heavy industry, the Junkers and smaller farmers, elements of the civil service, banking, and other social groups formed the social base of the coalition that dominated German politics through the end of World War I. It pursued a policy package of protectionism in commercial relations, authoritarianism in politics, naval building, and militarism in foreign policy. Germany did have its counterpart to the British business-labor alliance in support of the cheap loaf and free trade: it contained finished goods manufacturers and high-technology industries strongly oriented toward export, and labor concerned about cheaper food and lower costs. But before 1914, the conservative bloc prevailed.

Military defeat fractured these alignments. Fitfully, and with many obstacles (among them the Kapp putsch, the Ruhr occupation, and hyperinflation), the Social Democrats and the progressive elements of business managed to wriggle away from the iron-rye bloc to form a de facto accommodation, the "Weimar coalition," built around an internationalist economic orientation, democratized labor relations and politics at home, high social insurance benefits, and acquiescence in the post-Versailles international system. The economic collapse of 1929 destroyed the Weimar coalition, opening the way for the resurgence of the old bloc in new, more virulent form (see Abraham 1981 for a very useful account of the policy goals of different interest groups; also Feldman 1977).

The international economy throughout played a great role in shaping the fate of political alignments. As in the prewar period, a major issue of postwar domestic politics was Germany's relationship to the world. Germany again faced two broad alternatives for foreign economic policy, each linked to a particular posture in international relations, domestic constitutional arrangements, and domestic social policy. On the one side was the integration of Germany into an intensified international division of labor, accepting an open economy and the various post-Versailles arrangements. On the other side was resistance to internationalism, shielding Germany from world market forces and possibly using government to prepare the ground for revision of Versailles.

Between these two end points were a variety of combinations. The struggle over economic policy, and the whole shape of German politics and society, turned on the pattern of alignments and coalitions among social actors. Much depended on the relations of different fractions of business to one another, to labor, and to agriculture. While labor and capital were in conflict everywhere over a number of issues, some accommodation was possible and did occur (on the political economy of Weimar, see the important book of Abraham 1981; on the New Deal, see Ferguson 1984).

In Germany, as elsewhere, certain elements of capital were more likely than others to work with labor. Foreign economic policy issues drove elements of German industry into conflict with one another. No element was strong enough by itself to prevail, and so each sought allies. Export industry and labor supported elements of what can be called an "understanding"—there was no formal agreement, such as the Saltsjobaden accord reached in Sweden in 1938, but there was a willingness to accept each other's policies. While all Germans dislike the Versailles Treaty, the export industries and labor were willing to accommodate themselves to it as the price for Germany's integration into a stable international order. After the hyperinflation, industry desperately needed capital to finance the revival of production, and these elements supported the Dawes plan. Integration into an open world economy, access to foreign capital, mass civilian purchasing power, restraint on the drain of inefficient sectors, modernization and rationalization at home—these were the goals of the electrotechnical and chemical industries, symbolized by Siemens and I. G. Farben and individuals such as Carl Duisberg and Walter Rathenau. Fritz Ebert symbolizes the social-democratic side of the Weimar coalition's exchanges: control of the radical elements on the Left, a constitutionalist polity, trade union rights in collective bargaining, full employment, and social insurance programs. Export industry needed labor for political support in resisting autarchy and, economically, as customers for mass consumption's products. And, compared to less efficient business, export industry could (relatively speaking) afford the accommodation, for wages were a smaller proportion of its costs.

In opposition to these internationalists were the members of the prewar iron-rye coalition. Given considerable worldwide expansion of industrial capacity during the war, iron and steel were now in worse shape than before; while German heavy industry remained comparatively efficient, it could not cope with worldwide overproduction. In agriculture, there had been a similarly considerable expansion of production, and the fall of prices marked an agricultural crisis several years before the crash of 1929. While revision of Versailles appealed to nationalists occupying all sorts of "objective" situations, there continued to be some "sociological" basis to it among these economic interests. Heavy industry and agriculture remain more protectionist, more autarchic in policy preferences, and more resistant to accommodating with the trading community abroad and with labor at home.

So long as the world economy was healthy, the pressures for autarchy could be resisted. Exports generated the profits to make an alliance of high technology and labor possible. Foreign loans provided the capital to make the goods that could be sold abroad to earn the foreign exchange that would pay reparations, loans, and wages. But when the world economy collapsed, the alliance came unstuck. The costs and benefits of domestic coalitional behavior changed considerably. Electoral research has documented these shifts at the level of the mass electorate, which abandoned the system's parties for more extreme formations (Lipset 1963; Haberle 1970; on the Nazi electorate, Hamilton 1982). These shifts occurred within a context that has been less clearly explored, the conflict over economic and other policies, strongly shaped by interest groups and the structural situation in which they operate. The flight from the system's parties was a response to the deadlock among them and among the interest groups struggling over different conceptions of policy.

Within the Weimar coalition, the deterioration of the international economy eroded the coalition between labor and the dynamic manufacturers. As exports plummeted, industry's ability to pay the costs of the labor alliance dropped. Without strong markets, high wage bills and transfer payments were too costly. The assertions of heavy industry groups now sounded more plausible to the exporters: a revival of sales required lower prices, which required lower costs, which required lower wages and taxes. In the language of current Euro-American argument, this was a "supply-side" argument. The export sector had been advocating a demand-side view; higher wages helped higher consumption. In the business associations, the export group was weakened, and heavy industry leaders replaced them as spokesmen.

Export and heavy industry both initially supported deflation as a way of cutting costs. Elements of both sectors were soon to turn toward other policies, such as reflation, armaments and exchange controls, corporatism and structured markets. But in both branches the Depression immediately led to sharp conflict with labor.

Labor found itself caught in an increasingly tight pincer, between its preferences for economic policy and its preferences for the maintenance of a constitutional coalition. The trade unions and SPD opposed the deflationary content of Bruning's policy but sustained the government in office in order to preserve the republic and bar the way to the far Right. As defenders of labor in the market, the party and unions opposed the reduction of unemployment benefits, the pressure against wages, and the rollback of state expenditures (in the last they were particularly constrained as the representatives of large numbers of civil servants). To defend labor rights won in the political arena, the SPD felt compelled to support a prosystem government even when that government pursued economic policies contrary to social-democratic goals in the labor market.

SPD leaders, particularly Rudolf Hilferding, the finance minister and leading party intellectual in matters of economic theory, were sharply constrained politically by their economic ideas. They saw no alternative other than full socialization of the economy, for which they have no electoral majority, or operation of the capitalist economy by its own logic, which Hilferding understood according to the same orthodoxy as the pro-deflation economists. Hilferding completely rejected the demand-stimulus ideas that were circulating in Europe. The trade union movement had been persuaded to adopt such a program, the WTB plan, named after Woytinski, a Russian emigré social-democratic economist, Tarnow, a trade union official, and Baade, an agriculture expert. The plan called for deficit-financed public works. In a show-down between union and party leaders, Woytinski and his colleagues were unable to overcome Hilferding's commitment to an orthodox capitalist interpretation of capitalism (Woytinski 1961).

The SPD thus lost an opportunity that was as much political as economic. By 1932, when the debate took place inside the SPD, there was considerable dissatisfaction with economic orthodoxy in all circles of German society, including the varying wings of industry. Among the heavy industrialists there had always been misgiving about the deflationist line. Market mechanisms had not worked well for steel and iron producers in the 1920s. In crisis, they turned readily and rapidly back to familiar policy instruments: tariffs and other forms of autarchy, and government spending, particularly on capital goods such as military items. While demand stimulus per se had not particular theoretical basis among the heavy industrial circles, government assistance in economic development did.

In the context of severe contraction in the world economy, domestic business had a greater affinity for demand-stimulus thinking than did export businesses. For companies seeking to tap the world market, reflating the domestic market is too limited a response; they are likely to seek a revival of international trade. Companies concentrating on the domestic market because of international competitive conditions have already foregone that alternative.

Thus, an acute international depression creates the conditions for a reversal of the previous relations between labor and business. Internationally oriented business shift away from support of high labor purchasing power toward cheaper labor costs, and thus toward the concerns of heavy industry. Labor turns away from consumer concerns of supporting free trade toward producer concerns of preserving jobs, and hence toward heavy industry. The different wings of agriculture draw together to seek market intervention, and hence toward heavy industry. While the issues of conflict (wages and benefits, union rights, social insurance, foreign economic policy) between heavy industry and other groups remain, new possibilities arise for a different combination of groups around other policies.

International crisis may also move an industry or accompany from one bloc to another. While autarchy was generally an unsatisfactory solution for sectors seeking world markets, one very large company in the export block found itself in such deep trouble in 1932 that autarchy seemed attractive. The huge chemical trust I. G. Farben, as James Kurth has notes, had heavily invested in coal gasification. When oil prices dropped sharply in 1931 after the East Texas oil fields came on line, the company desperately sought aid. In the maneuverings of late 1932, Farben preferred the Schleicher variant of intervention (demand-stimulus corporatism with labor participation) over the Hitler version (which excluded labor). Farben leaders did not play an active role in bringing Hitler to power, but they would rally to his policies and, in the end, play a greater role than any other company or industry in the Nazi regime, down to a synthetic rubber plant at Auschwitz (Kurth 1979; Borkin 1978).

In the conflict over economic policy, the behavior of agricultural interests (voters, interest groups, and parties) was vital. German agriculture rebelled against bourgeois economic orthodoxy thoroughly and rapidly. None of the system's parties showed much responsiveness to the countryside's plight. The bourgeois parties defended the market against rural holders' pleas, and the Left saw no reason to help private property, in particular a property owning segment that never gave evidence of willingess to cooperate with labor. There were individuals within the SPD, the bourgeois parties, and the farmers' parties who sought to promote alliances, but they made no headway.

It is not hard to find ample reason for conflict between farmers and workers; indeed, nineteenth and twentieth century history is full of examples. But farmer-labor alliances did occur in the 1930s, in Sweden and in the United States. There is no end of possible explanations for the absence of such alliances in Germany—political culture, interest-group organization, political party structures, market organization, market situation. The approach taken here points toward the weakness of economic modernization in the German countryside, which increased agriculture's dependence on state intervention and inhibited a convergence of interests with efficient industry and labor, as happened in other countries. What is certainly clear is the importance of the relations between labor and agriculture in affecting outcomes.

By 1932, three economic packages were under debate in Germany. The first was a continuation of Bruning's economic orthodoxy. This might have worked to some degree, since the world economy did improve in 1933 and the Bruning government might well have received some credit for improvements. By late 1932, however, the political support for waiting it out had crumbled. A second possibility was to abandon deflation in favor of neo-orthodoxy: devaluation, tariffs, and agricultural price supports, what the United Kingdom did after 1931 and the United States did in separate steps in 1931 and 1933. In Germany, however, devaluation still seemed abhorrent in 1932, and mild neo-orthodoxy seemed too passive to many segments of German society.

The third package involved demand stimulus through deficit-financed spending. It came in two versions, parliamentary and authoritarian. Schleicher tried to organize a quasi-parlimentary version of demand stimulus, and failed. Unlike the American and Swedish experimenters, he excluded agriculture and threatened the special advantages of the Junkers, thereby angering the camarilla around Hindenburg. Labor and buiness could not agree on a package, because labor was unwilling to shoulder the costs as business demanded. In the United States and Sweden, where business came to accept demand stimulus, it did so only when the labor-farmer alliance showed sufficient political strength to force some sectors of business to become more accommodating. In Germany, the attempt was quite different: agriculture was excluded from the Schleicher discussion, which tried to effect a direct bargain between the two actors with the historically deepest antagonism, labor and heavy industry (on business see Feldman 1969; and Turner 1963, 1968a, 1968b, 1969, 1970).

Instead of explicit social bargaining among major social groups within a modified constitutionalism—Schleicher's attempt—Hitler mixed explicit bargaining with certain actors (business and agriculture) with direct mobilization of individuals and the exclusion of their institutionalized representatives (particularly unions and the SPD but some elements of agriculture, white-collar workers, and business as well). Direct accommodation among agriculture and business elites (Von Papen's attempt with the Cabinet of Barons) could not work because it lacked mass support. Hitler could provide just that, tapping unemployed workers who were not unionized, farmers, salaried personnel, and property owners small, medium, and large. Indeed, the social diversity of the Nazi vote is more complex than the traditional stress on the "middlestand" allows. Hitler combined rejection of the orthodox economic alternatives (socialization and the market) with nationalism, a combination that appealed to many different elements of society and did worst with those strongly integrated into alternative interpretations of the world—unions, the Marxist parties, and the Catholic center. But settling the controversy over the Nazi vote will not by itself completely explain either the *Machtergriefung* or the content of policy. After all, in the last normal election, November 1932, Hitler did not exceed 34 percent of the vote. To take power required help from other sources. He got it from the conservatives within agriculture and business who sought a deal—the chancellery for control of labor.

This political bargaining for economic policy is significant. By themselves the economic elites would not have undertaken what Hitler did in economic policy after January 1933, however much they liked the economic results and, at least until the late 1930s, the political ones as well. Neither the economic results nor the political outcomes were the result of the desires of any single group. They emerged from an interaction. Everyone had reasons to prefer some other, "purer" policy and political choice. In this point lies the weakness of many social explanations of fascism, the notion that fascism derives from big business, or the Junkers, or the petty bourgeoisie. Big business in fact preferred the Cabinet of Barons, as did the Junkers; the petty bourgeoisie did not like the bargains fascism struck with big business and the Junkers. Nonetheless, the process that produced the fascist triumph did have a social basis, which cannot be rejected in favor of heavily institutional, individualist, culturalist, or psychological explanations. Thus the heavy industrialists may have preferred the Cabinet of Barons, but they accepted Hitler as preferable to still other alternatives. And while they may have preferred the Cabinet of Barons politically, in economic terms the cabinet had become too conservative and too orthodox for them.

The break from economic orthodoxy required political help. Property owners everywhere were finding it difficult to reconcile a variety of contradictions in their attitudes, preferences, and political behaviors. They wanted defense of property, restraint of labor pressures, and limits on state interference in appropriate ways. Many wanted state aid for an emergency but were reluctant to pay the price of social insurance and state aid for employment. Ordinary "bourgeois" politicians had trouble integrating these various goals in politically effective ways. They appeared to defend capital at the expense of the masses. Hitler had mass support, and a coalition between Nazis and certain social forces gave the government autonomy to try a blend of policies.

The Nazis proved better able than policy makers in other countries to bring down unemployment (and this was true even *before* the upswing in military spending). With extensive public works and government purchasing, Germany ran deficits and infused purchasing power into the economy. Exchange controls and trade restrictions curtailed imports and effectively devalued the mark while maintaining its nominal value. By the end of 1934, unemployment had dropped, and more sharply than anywhere else. In Sweden and the United States, the other countries where some job creation was attempted in this period, actual demand stimulus was far less ample than in Germany and had less effect. Revival in these countries had far more to do with the boost to exports from devaluation, the boost to investment from cheap interest rates, and an upturn in worldwide demand. Thus the first country to try demand stimulus and make it work was, sad to say, Germany under the Nazis (Heyl 1973; Arndt 1944; Milward 1976). (Japan experimented with this policy as well, also at the time the regime was becoming increasingly fascist, but that case is outside the framework of this article: Kindleberger 1973.)

The German case exhibits the impact of international economic crisis on domestic alignments of social forces around economic policies and politics. An important predictor of alliance behavior is the relationship of social groups to the international economy, which is in turn a function of its location within the product cycle: efficient, competitive industries, at the cutting edge of the international distribution of labor, tended to have policy preferences and alliance propensities different from those of industries that found themselves less well positioned, if not in efficiency then in the structure of demand and costs. The crash of 1929 undermined the agreements among social groups that sustained Weimar. As the Depression worsened, demands for policy shifts grew. Situation in the international economy helps predict the direction of these policy shifts, and the structure of policy preferences helps in turn to define the situation within which other variables—political leadership, circumstance, ideology—play a role. The pattern of group support for breaking with orthodoxy in Germany had some remarkable similarities with those of other countries. The sharp difference was the political formula.

The United States

As Ferguson (1984) shows, situation in the international economy affected policy preference and alliance propensities in the United States as well as in Europe. Conflict over foreign economic policy is one of the oldest and most durable issues in American politics. As elsewhere, the conflict can be simplified into a debate between "internationalists" (advocating low tariffs and America's more intense involvement in the international division of labor) and "nationalists." (In U.S. discourse the latter were known for many years as "isolationists," seeking some degree of insulation from the vagaries of the international economy, principally through tariffs.) Core support for the nationalist position came from the large-scale heavy industry of the mid-West—steel was protectionist here as everywhere else in the world. Core support for the internationalist position came from shippers, trade-oriented bankers, and high-technology industries at the export phase of the product cycle.

One conspicuous difference from Europe lies in the situation of agriculture and the related situation of labor. This is, however, a difference not in the explanatory importance of international situation but in its actual content in differing countries. American agriculture was quite efficient; indeed, it was a major source of Europe's problems. The supply of cheap food was therefore not a policy problem either for labor or for industries worried about keeping down costs. In Europe, grain growers were protectionist, while the producers of higher-quality foodstuffs (meat, dairy, etc.) were more likely to favor free trade. In the United States, this policy proclivity of products was reversed. The quality food producers had plenty of cheap domestic grain to use as input in their production and for their own consumption. Since the consumers of these quality foodstuffs were urban residents and industrial workers, whose consumption rose as their incomes rose, this part of the countryside had some interest in promoting the health of domestic industry. Conversely, commodity producers (grain, cotton) sold on world markets; they could not increase their sales by protecting and promoting American industrial growth, but had to export.

The situation of the quality food producers in relation to the other groups facilitated their entry into a protectionist coalition. With cheap food assured, members of the labor movement could follow their interests as industrial producers. The Republican bloc fused in the 1890s thus linked elements of labor, agriculture, and industry around industrial protectionism, in conflict with the internationalist groups drawn from export industry and export agriculture, focused on the Democratic party (Burnham 1970).

The Depression of 1929 ruptured these relationships. Franklin Roosevelt's victory in 1932 put back together what the election of 1896 had ripped asunder—agriculture and labor, both driven away from the GOP by the desire for government action in response to economic distress. In the face of sharply falling prices, the different elements of agriculture converged in clamoring for some sort of corporatistic organization of markets. The large chunks of ethnic working-class electors that had voted Republican now joined up with those workers who had always voted for the Democrats. To that core of electoral and interest-group support came elements of business. The label "business" itself is, however, insufficient: the content, the *types* of business involved, changed over time, as did economic policy.

The first New Deal marked a heavy defeat for internationalists. The United States went off gold, broke up the London Conference, set up the Agricultural Adjustment Administration (AAA) to help agriculture via production controls, marketing arrangements, and price supports, and passed the National Recovery Administration (NRA) to do the same for industry. In place of world markets, the domestic economy would be parceled out among existing producers. Demand-stimulus suggestions existed, but they were marginal to policy discussions. While labor and agriculture provided much of the energy for this approach, it was hardly done in opposition to business. On the contrary, it represented just what a very large portion of American industry increasingly thought had to be done (especially useful on the New Deal are Ferguson 1984, 1985; Skocpol 1980; Skocpol and Finegold 1982; Skocpol and Weir forthcoming).

Yet the coalition behind the first New Deal was itself riddled with fault lines. As policy failed to produce effective results, internal stresses cracked the coalition open. There were acute conflicts within sectors, among sectors, and between business and other groups. Within sectors, fighting increased over the content of the NRA codes. The characteristically conservative notion that self-administration by businessmen freed of politics would overcome conflict proved illusory. Differently situated firms proposed different codes. Compliance without coercion was impossible, and coercion itself was opposed. By the time the Supreme Court found the NRA unconstitutional, business had abandoned it, thereby bringing into the open conflict over what economic policy to following instead. Within business, the partial revival of the world economy exacerbated disagreement about foreign economic policy: internationalists wanted to escape from the Smoot-Hawley tariff and to restore a stable international payments and trading system. At the same time, business and labor fought ever more sharply over the labor relations provisions of the NRA.

These tensions, bursting open the coalition of the first New Deal, reopened various possibilities for policies and politics: a return to deflation, cautious forms of neocorporatism such as the British Conservatives were trying, or more experimentation toward what became the social-democratic model. As in any complex crisis, leadership played a role: Roosevelt took the third route, with significant consequences. The options, and the ingredients of the support coalitions for each option, were profoundly shaped by the economic situation of various actors.

The Second New Deal produced an interrelated set of policies: the Wagner Act, Social Security, continuation and extension of the AAA, pursuit of reciprocal trade negotiations, the Tripartite Monetary Agreement, and conscious demand stimulus in response to the tremendous slump of 1938 (which came from balancing the budget in 1937). This combination of policies entailed exchanges: labor accepted higher food costs in exchange for agriculture's support of a new industrial relations system and social insurance. As Ferguson's modeling predicts, the economic elites from the business side most willing to accept the costs of this exchange were those particularly interested in foreign trade and able to bear higher labor costs.

In policy terms, there was a shift in the political location of demand-stimulus experimentation. It began life as part of an inward-looking, nationalist impulse, an attempt to rescue domestic economies from the ruin of the international one. It was so proposed in Europe and America in the early 1930s and was used that way by the Nazis. Where constitutionalist politics continued, however, demand stimulus was free to seek other sponsors. It took a certain amount of learning—economic, intellectual, and political—to produce acceptance of the faltering steps of prewar Keynesianism. The learning involved sequences of trial and error, policy attempts and policy failures. The full use of demand stimulus did not occur until after 1945, but in the Second New Deal we see the postwar social-democratic model: an open foreign economic policy, full employment fiscal policy, social insurance transfer payments, trade union rights in collective bargaining, high wages, and stable monetary policy.

Sweden

Three Scandinavian countries formed farmer-labor alliances in the 1930s: Denmark in 1932, Sweden later that year, and Norway in 1935. In each country, these "cow trades" represented dramatic breaks with earlier political patterns and also involved dramatic breaks in economic policy. Since the Swedish experience figures so prominently in social science discussions of twentieth century political economy, I concentrate on that case.

The alliance pattern of Swedish economic actors bears strong parallels with that of other countries. The quarrel between protection and free trade split Sweden through World War I. As in Germany, grain growers and locally oriented industries were protectionist while the producers of high-quality foodstuffs, workers, and the high-technology export industries for which Sweden became famous preferred free trade. The first coalition was politically conservative, the second politically liberal. In foreign policy, the former pursued a pro-German policy during World War I, provoking a British blockade. The second alliance overthrew the conservative government under Hammarskjöld, switching Swedish policy dramatically: the pro-British policy allowed the revival of foreign trade and lowering of food costs, suffrage was broadened, and constitutional dominance of the parliament over the crown was established. This "progressive" alliance linked the Social Democrats of labor with export-oriented business (Liberals) and grain-consuming farming (Koblik 1975).

In the 1920s, labor went back to relative isolation, though they did participate in some governing coalitions. High valuation of the currency induced strong pressure to drive down industrial wages. The Agrarian party, among others, showed very strong animosity toward the Social Democrats, while the Liberals and the business groups saw no need to seek labor assistance for policy goals. When the Depression began, the Social Democrats and one major advantage compared to their English and German counterparts—they had been out of power for a number of years.

Sweden's first response to the Depression was orthodox, deflation and no devaluation. When Britain devalued sterling in 1931, the run against the Swedish *krona* forced a policy switch. As the world economy continued to deteriorate, the competitive advantage of devaluation proved limited. Domestic dissatisfaction with market solutions heightened. Farmers sought aid through marketing boards and price supports. The Social Democrats demanded better unemployment compensation and began explicitly to propound deficit-financed public works. While the farmers mobilized bourgeois support for their schemes, at least in piecemeal fashion, that support seemed unstable. Business interests were reluctant to support higher food costs and government intervention in markets, and the bourgeois parties were all reluctant to accept labor's demands. The cow trade between the Swedish SDP and the agrarian party overcame the political obstacles. The surprise at the time was that workers would accept higher food costs and farmers higher work wages, since that particular trade had never occurred before. After the fact, it seems clear and not surprising that these two groups would be the least committed to economic orthodoxy and the most willing to experiment in times of stress.

The business history of the period is not sufficiently detailed to permit careful exploration of differential capacity to accept the costs of participating in such a coalition. Some evidence, however, fits the pattern outlined earlier. Before the Depression, the high-technology export industries and their banking allies, the Wallenbergs, had been the most likely to ally with labor. At the bottom of the Depression, the tension between the two was great: the internationalists wanted to lower wage costs, not to raise them as the cow trade would. Yet size makes a difference: the fortress within which economic nationalism protected domestic demand in the United States and Germany was large; in Sweden, it would have been hopelessly small for Electrolux, Swedish ball bearings, Erickson, and the other firms reliant on international markets. The smaller firms of relatively low technology (building, cement, etc.) were, conversely, sympathetic to the stimulating of domestic purchasing power (Dahmen 1970).

Prior to 1936, the "rejectionist" elements of Swedish industry hoped to break up the cow coalition. When the election of 1936 strengthened it, they sought an alliance instead. The understanding embodied in the Saltsjobaden agreement of 1938 traded business acceptance of social-democratic government, high labor costs (wages and the welfare state), full-employment fiscal policy, and government activism for social services in exchange for labor peace in labor markets (no strikes), continuation of private control over property and capital markets, and openness in relation to the world economy. This pattern has prevailed in Sweden to the present time. The bourgeois coalition that has held office since 1976 has been unable to alter the power relationships that compel the overall policy pattern.

While the new fiscal policy of demand-stimulated employment aroused much attention in Sweden, it would not have much effect on Swedish economic life until after World War II. Sweden's recovery in the 1930s was due much more to the revival of the international economy for reasons completely beyond local control (policies pursued in the major markets of Germany, the United States, and the United Kingdom) and to Swedish policy decisions that took advantage of that revival—the devaluation of 1931 (which was in fact beyond Swedish control as well), low interest rates that stimulated building and investment, and considerable private restructuring of industry (Gustafson 1973; Tilton 1979; Winch 1966; Uhr 1973; and Jonung 1979, 1981). Even in Sweden the improvement remained limited until the war stimulus wiped out unemployment. Demand stimulus and government economic intervention became politically and intellectually respectable in the 1930s, even if their real effects were then limited to agriculture, insurance schemes, and some leadership of direct investment (rural electrification). The gradual economic improvement worked to the benefit of the social Democrats; in this case incumbency was a benefit, allowing the Social Democrats to lock in the coalition's members and the ideas used to launch it (Martin 1979; Koblik 1975; Dahmen 1970; Heckscher 1954; Korpi 1978; Lewin et al. 1972; Lindbeck 1975; Montgomery 1938; Soderpalm 1976; Tingsten 1973; and Nyman 1947).

The United Kingdom

Sweden saw constitutionalist demand stimulus, Germany nonconstitutionalist demand stimulus, and the United States export business adaptation to demand stimulus. The rejection of both socialist orthodoxy and demand stimulus did not (as the "gaming" model referred to above supposed) inexorably lead either to further economic degeneration or to the destruction of constitutional government. Britain shows it was possible to stop with the neo-orthodox moves away from the old ways, without driving labor to rebellion or crushing it with police terror. Nor, indeed, could the mixed-market solution of cheap money in the context of a devalued pound, higher tariffs, and cartelization be called a complete failure.

The common image is that, by sticking to market-oriented orthodoxies, Britain continued to sink and stagnate. It proves to be at least exaggerated, if not quite false. Some recovery occurred, and Britain did better in the 1930s than before (partly a comment on how badly it did in the 1920s). Some historians attribute the improvement to the impact of new inventions— rayons, electrical goods, autos—as the product cycle moved across the Atlantic. The interesting argument, however, concerns not whether some improvement occurred in Britain but whether the strategy pursued was suboptimal and whether labor lost a major opportunity to establish political hegemony like their Swedish counterparts. Unemployment never sank below 10 percent across the decade. Could Britain have done better with demand stimulus? H.W. Arndt (1944) and many other economic historians think so; the neoclassicists think not (Richardson 1967; Youngson 1960; Winch 1969; Hancock 1960, 1962; Kahn 1946; Strange 1971).

There was less policy experimentation in the United Kingdom in the 1930s than in other countries, and a Liberal-Labour (Lib-Lab) coalition pursuing Keynesian policies failed to develop. Examining the relationship of British economic interest groups to the international economy may help account for the specificity of the British case. Two features of the British economy are particularly striking: the finance-trading complex identified with the City, and the relatively small and modernized agricultural sector. The strength of the former reinforced British attachments to orthodoxy and resistance to the inward-looking status of Keynes's ideas in the early 1930s. The weakness of the latter deprived labor and dissident business elements of small-holding property owners as political allies with whom to challenge that orthodoxy.

Despite images of British consensus to the contrary, there had been disagreement about British economic policy for many years. Joseph Chamberlain led Birmingham-centered steel and other industries menaced by the new trading conditions of the post 1873 era to clamor for tariffs. Despite some agricultural and labor support, he failed. The conflict continued in the 1920s. The international banks and their allies (shipping, insurance) pressed for a rapid return to convertibility, and at a high rate; industry feared that a high rate would price its goods out of foreign markets and force deflationary policies, cutting into domestic markets. The bank view prevailed, forcing sharp deflationary pressure that led to the General Strike of 1926 and a major defeat for labor. It is in this context that Ramsay MacDonald came to power in 1929. The defeat of 1926 undermined Labour's willingness to challenge the internationalist orthodoxy, and contributed to that immense concern for the approval of the City which seems characteristic of Labour party politicians (though not union leaders) from MacDonald to Wilson and Callaghan.

The trade unions did press for public works and deficit spending. While serving on the Macmillan Committee, whose mandate was to explore the country's economic plight, Ernest Bevin had been deeply impressed by the failure of the banking-Treasury world to consider the implications of exchange and interest-rate policy for industry and employment. Fighting unemployment by getting factories to produce again appealed to his pragmatic mind, and he led the Trades Union Congress (TUC) to accept the new idea. Some figures in the Labour party supported the notion as well, most notably Oswald Mosley. The two top party officials, MacDonald and Philip Snowden, remained resolutely orthodox (Bullock 1960; Skidelsky 1967).

As the Depression deepened, criticism rose not only in labor ranks but also in the opposition. The Conservatives accepted deflation but wanted tariffs as well, though not devaluation. It was the Liberals who pressed hardest on behalf of public works and deficit budgets, to accompany tariffs or devaluation or both. Almost a decade before the publication of *The General Theory*, Keynes and other economists helped work out for the Liberals a "Programme of Expansion" (its slogan was "We Can Beat Unemployment"). These programmatic statements criticized the stress placed on the pound, arguing that the currency should serve productivity and employment, not the reverse. Keynes and the Liberals accepted devaluation of the pound. Though historically the Liberals were free traders, and continued to criticize the Conservative push for tariffs, Keynes and the Liberals were willing to contemplate devaluation, which has a protectionist effect.

It is by no means easy to explain why it should have been the Liberals who in the late 1920s took up this Chamberlainian theme in the new intellectual guise developed by Keynes. The Liberal social base seems still to have been free-trade oriented elements of industry and agriculture. The sorts of industries that had sustained critiques of banking and free-trade orthodoxy, and complained constantly during the 1920s to various committees, had Conservative party ties, not Liberal ones, and could be pulled over toward the more cautious tariff-cartel version the Tories preferred.

The answer may lie in the dynamics of party rivalry and leadership. the Liberals were, after all, in deep political trouble, and they needed political "product differentiation," arguments with mass appeal. Unemployment was certainly of immense political significance; attacking both Labour and the Conservatives as wrong-headed made political sense, and the solution proposed had th political virtue of being neither clearly protectionist (so as not to offend the powerful "cheap loaf" stance of laboring-class voters) nor orthodox socialist (so as not to offend the middle-class electorate). Leadership also mattered: Lloyd George was a risk taker, looking for arguments for a comeback, and smart enough to be convinced by the reasoning of smart men like Keynes. His behavior contrasts sharply with the intellectual rigidity of Snowden, MacDonald, and Stanley Baldwin (Kavanagh 1973).

Hitching Keynes to the Liberal party base aggravated an already strained situation. As Labour resisted the proffered Lib-Lab alliance, the Liberals crumbled under the pull of competing policy programs. By 1931, so many had defected that it was no longer clear that there remained a large enough "Lib" to construct a working majority even if MacDonald were finally to try for one.

Since the Liberals were the third party, the interpretation of policy debates in the period cannot end with speculation about why they took up Keynes. Breaking with deflationist orthodoxy required help from other social forces and party formations. Elements of the Conservative party were sensitive to the needs of manufacturing industry as distinct from the banking-shipping wing. Such people provided support for some break from the old orthodoxy, but not enough to go the next step. As in America, the major debate in business circles was between classical "free trade-deflation-defense of the pound" orthodoxy and "protectionism-cartelization" deviations. The elements interested in more activist, government-led schemes could not persuade their business compatriots to go along. This is not surprising; elsewhere, firms interested in demand stimulus did not get it by convincing their business brethren of its merits but by allying with other groups intensely dissatisfied with the market mechanisms (labor and agriculture).

In the United Kingdom, the "steel-syndrome" block of business had some "positional" disadvantages compared to their counterparts in other countries. First, in no other country did industry face such a large block of interests tied to international trade and payments (Longstreth 1979; Gilpin 1975; Blank 1977; Beer 1965). As I have suggested, demand stimulus in the first phase appealed primarily to domestically oriented elements of the economy. But no other country at the time had so many interests living off remittances, loans, shipping, and the like; the United States, Germany, and Sweden had fewer foreign investments and did not manage a reserve currency. To some degree, this internationalism inhibited militarism: autarchy could not be appealing to those who lived off international trade and hence militarism lacked an important legitimizing force. Furthermore, agriculture as a sector was smaller in Britain than anywhere else, also the consequence of having been the first industrializer. This meant fewer potential allies for the attack on money, banks, and internationalism. Finally, British labor was very deeply wedded to the cheap loaf, making the construction of a protectionist alliance including labor that much harder. (Though, as the experience of Joseph Chamberlain shows, workers as electors could be won over to protectionism more easily than their representative organizations.)

The most puzzling question of all is why the Labour party did not take up demand stimulus. There is every likelihood that had Labour done so, it could have concluded an alliance with the Liberals. Credit for the post 1932 recovery (a probability whatever the government actually did) would have gone to them, not to the Conservatives. British politics might have looked more like the Swedish variety, dominated by labor for a couple of generations. The interpretative problems are quite similar to those raised when the same question is applied to the German Social Democrats. Snowden, like Hilferding, did not believe in the demand-stimulus arguments; he was operating a market economy, with orthodox rules. MacDonald seems to have been heavily influenced by "good elite opinion," which excluded Keynes and Lloyd George. Thus the top party leadership was socialized into the British "orthodoxy." As in Germany, the trade union leadership may have been more open to new arguments because of a greater pragmatism born of closeness to labor-market conditions. But Bevin could not persuade MacDonald; MacDonald talked endlessly with the Liberals, but failed to make the agreement. In 1931 the Labour party was unified in opposing Snowden and MacDonald, though the issue was cutting unemployment benefits, not a program of public works. It seems highly likely that had the party leadership formed the Lib-Lab alliance around a demand-stimulus scheme, both the TUC and the parliamentary Labour party would have supported it. The subsequent evolution of British policy and politics would then have been quite different.

The actual story is well known and needs no lengthy discussion: MacDonald tried to save the pound through the further deflationary move of cutting unemployment insurance, was expelled from the Labour party, and formed a new government excluding most of the party. The pound quickly proved undefendable. When the financial circles most deeply wedded to a strong currency realized this, MacDonald devalued. Soon afterwards Britain adopted its first significant peacetime tariffs since the Corn Laws. The Conservatives quickly came to dominate the National Government and were swept into power at the next election. Under the impact of tariffs, very low interest rates, innovations, and the revival of demand in other countries, the British economy did improve. Low interest rates plus automobiles and electrification helped spur shifts in residential patterns, and a housing boom ensued. The government helped with electrification, and eventually via military purchases, but demanded stimulus per se did not occur until after World War II.

The British case shows well the interaction between political choice and sectoral constraints. The contours of alternative coalitions supporting different policy options can be detected and appear plausible, but they faced obstacles that, while not insurmountable, appear large. The unique role of the city, the smallness of the agricultural sector, the orientation of labor toward the cheap loaf, and the cultural hegemony of economic orthodoxy in the first nation to have industrialized—these constraints, in the absence of political imagination in the right place (with the Liberals instead of Labour) and with the historical accident of a Labour government in office at the onset of the Depression, proved insurmountable.

France

An extremely cursory glance across the the Channel shows promising similarities between France and the other cases. An undervalued *franc* helped keep the Depression at bay for several years. Products flowed out, gold flowed in, and prosperity prevailed. After 1931, currency devaluations all over the world reversed the relationship, and finally brought the Depression to France. Conservative governments tried the classic deflationary remedy by cutting budgets and pressing on wages. The conservative cabinets drew for support on agriculture, business, and conservative (Catholic) workers, to the exclusion of the labor unions and labor-connected parties. After the march on the Palais Bourbon in 1934, an alternative coalition gradually took shape. The elections of 1936 changed both economic policy and governing coalition; the Popular Front linked together the labor formations, elements of agriculture, and the "republican" bourgeoisie. Léon Blum attempted elements of the social-democratic package being worked out in Sweden and the United States: social insurance, higher wages, and deficit spending. Economic policy, however, was but one of a number of extremely controversial issues weighing down the French party, and but one of the issues that brought down the Popular Front a year late. For my purposes, the important element of the case is the politics of the break with deflation: what groups supported that attempt, and through what political formula? To win the election of 1936, to govern, and to shift economic policy, the Socialists had to construct and to manage a very diverse alliance, from Communists *téléguidé* by Stalin to the highly bourgeois constituency of the Radical party (Goguel 1946). What sorts of farmers, what sorts of bourgeois were willing to link up with elements of labor in such a coalition?

Labor's criticism of orthodoxy was made easier than in Germany and Britain by the exclusion of labor-related organizations from governing coalitions as France entered the Depression. Like any opposition, the Socialists, Communists, and trade unions could mobilize discontent without being judged on actual performance and without being very clear about what compromises each would accept if actually in power. In theoretical terms, the Socialists and Communists interpreted the Depression as a crisis of capitalism to be solved only by socialization of the economy. In the political reality of the mid 1930s, however, socialization was not possible within a constitutionalist framework. The Socialists had long since become defenders of the Republic; the Communists switched to that stance after the Nazi seizure of power in Germany. In formulating a program for labor, both parties sought to accommodate the demands of other groups (agriculture and elements of business) and parties (the Radicals).

As in other countries, agriculture was a major source of discontent with orthodox deflation. As in other countries, bourgeois governments did relatively little to help the countryside deal with plunging prices. Whatever their partisan attachments, farmers agitated for some sort of assistance, be it price supports, government purchases, or marketing agreements. In their discontent with deflation, farmers moved in different directions: some to the Right (Dorgéres, for example), others to the Left (particularly to the Communists, who gained the most votes among the three parties of the Popular Front coalition). Electoral sociology on what sort of farmer moved which way focuses on certain demographic characteristics of farmers (size of holding, location, religion). But it has omitted various situational features: the product raised, the nature of the farm's relationship to markets, recent experience with government policies. In short, rural discontent with orthodox deflation appears clearer than the mechanisms by which that discontent was translated into political action. Large blocs of farmers appear to have been available to support programs of state intervention in the rural economy—no socialization, but corporatism (neo-orthodoxy) (Auge-Laribe 1950; Warner 1960).

In France, as elsewhere, a farmer-labor alliance was not enough. Support from at least some elements of the bourgeoisie was vital, but it materialized only to a limited degree. Bourgeois support for the Popular Front was strong enough to win the election of 1936, sustain defense of the Republic for a few years, and to work out and ratify the Matignon accords as a solution to the sit-down strikes. It was not strong enough to sustain the Blum government in office, to continue the economic program begun in 1936, and in the long run generate a cross-class program of national self-defense. As one of the leading historians of the Popular Front, Georges Dupeux, has written, the moderate social-democratic policy stance of Léon Blum failed because it lacked a necessary partner—a moderate business bourgeoisie (Dupeux 1959).

A situational interpretation of this absent partner would stress the relative weakness in the French economy of strong, internationally competitive, high-technology, low labor-component industries and firms. "Progressive" ideas about business-labor relations received a hearing in France during the interwar years, and Ernest Mercier and Auguste Detoeuf are perhaps the best-known French equivalents to Carl Duisberg. Their industry was electrical equipment. But these figures and industries are strikingly atypical of French economic history from 1870 to 1940, which is full of the destruction of economic pioneers rather than of their success. The men who represented business in the Matignon agreements came from the largest companies, particularly in metallurgy. They were bitterly attacked by the smaller, more backward companies and forced out of offices in the employers' association (Ehrmann 1957; Kuisel 1967). Most French industry was small, labor-intensive, and overwhelmingly protectionist. Few businessmen were in the market for allies to create an open, internationalist strategy.

Small property owners, however, were by no means unanimous defenders of orthodox deflation. In France as elsewhere smallholders were cross-pressured: fearful of labor radicalism, fearful of big business and untrammeled competition. Attacks against *les gros*, the *deux cent familles*, the *mur d'argent* resonated loudly, and were by no means the monopoly of the Left. The Radical party electorate had little sympathy for nationalizing and deep hostility to devaluation, but it did have some sympathy for an effort to break free of deflation.

These conflicting pressures from diverse constituencies put the Blum government into a bind from which, interestingly, "demand-stimulus" experimentation was an easier next move than "neo-orthodoxy." Despite the prior experience of other countries that had vainly sought to defend the currency, virtually all segments of the French public remained attached to the defense of the *franc* Poincaré. Only one politician of any significance, Paul Reynaud, pleaded for devaluation, and he was scorned for his efforts. The Left parties proposed exchange controls instead of devaluation, but this was unacceptable to the Radicals.

Thus orthodoxy had been tried and found wanting, and socialization of the economy and currency devaluation were both unacceptable (Bouvier 1966; Guérin 1970; Kalecki 1938; Lefranc 1974; Marjolin 1938; Sauvy 1967). Reflating the economy through some sort of demand stimulus was the only possibility left. Quite uninfluenced by Keynes, the Socialists drew upon an old tradition in Left thinking about the economy: underconsumption theory. The central predicament of capitalism in this view was the tension between production and consumption: the capitalists' squeezing of the surplus prevented workers from having enough money to buy the output. Higher wages for workers and higher prices for farmers would reflate the economy through higher demand. Through the Matignon agreements and subsequent legislation the Socialists increased wages, constructed a national retirement system, a limited work week, paid vacations, and trade union rights. For agriculture, the Popular Front extended corporatistic marketing arrangements through the Office du Blé.

The effort to resist devaluation failed. Blum refused to do it upon taking office, but by September runs on the *franc* proved unstoppable, and, as in the United Kingdom, a Labour-type government finally gave up monetary orthodoxy when the guardians of that orthodoxy (the bankers, elite economic opinion) said it had to be done (Brower 1968; Bodin and Touchard 1961; Greene 1969; Broué and Dorey 1966; Colton 1966; Ehrmann 1947; Lacouture 1977).

In France neither break with orthodoxy (the full break of demand stimulus, tried first, and the partial break of devaluation, tried second) helped the economy very much. Capital fled the country, inflation was sharp, and production did not increase. Within a year the government fell. New coalitions swung rightward, and unraveled much of the Popular Front's reforms: the work week was lengthened, real wages sank, and unions were ignored or brushed aside. While the coalition of interests that supported the Popular Front looked a lot like those who supported the crisis coalition in Sweden (agriculture, labor, and some elements of business), the solidity of the latter proved far greater than the former's. France thus saw the weakest and least successful demand-stimulus coalition in a parliamentary system.

In exploring these questions, I do not mean to brush aside the other forces that shaped voting and alliances: the existence of a strong Republican, revolutionary, and anticlerical tradition in France among farmers, businessmen, teachers, professionals, and civil servants certainly affected Popular Front politics; so did the example of the collapse of Weimar, which galvanized Republican defense and helped get the Communists to switch over. The coalition may have come into being to save the Republic, but the coalition formed for that purpose also had capabilities in economic policy different from those of the previous (or succeeding) coalitions.

Conclusions

What generalizations does this all-too-rapid *tour d'horizon* sustain? There appears to be some consistency across countries in the "marginal propensity" of various groups to support, or fail to support, demand-stimulus policies in the 1930s. The patience of various actors with orthodoxy and neo-orthodoxy was not uniform. At the level of interest groups (or, in a different usage, social forces) trade unions, agricultural associations, and domestically oriented heavy industry were the first to find appeal in policies that went beyond the market mechanism in general terms, and, more specifically, policies involving government pump priming, and job and demand creation.

At the height of the depression, in 1932–33, these were the groups most likely either to press for or to support state-led solutions to the crisis. The opponents of such moves were likely to be the international wings of the various economic sectors: international (though not domestic) banking, export industries, export-oriented agriculture, and perhaps export-related labor. Later, as economies revived and other issues changed, the politics of demand stimulus changed as well. Conflicts within the reflation coalition over wages, welfare, industrial relations, and foreign economic policy reopened the political struggle (where the survival of constitutional government allowed it), leading to the formation of a new coalition linking internationalism in economic policy to the promotion of demand at home, through fiscal policy, social insurance, and wages.

By and large, this is consistent with the hypothesis that policy preferences toward the Depression can best be explained as a function of a group's "situation" in the economy, where situation is defined as a composite of international competitiveness, labor component, technology, and so on. Situations change—the international distribution of labor, business cycles (long and short), technological innovation, and events are of course constantly in motion. Big changes in situation induce reexamination of policy preferences and of political needs. Actors try one alternative, then if need be another, and we observe *policy sequences*—economic actors move to different policies in response to changing economic circumstances and changing political circumstances.

Deflation was an internationalist strategy. It aimed at beating down domestic costs of production to lower prices, in order to revive foreign and domestic sales. Neo-orthodoxy marked a step toward a nationalist strategy. It funneled domestic demand toward domestic products, given the inadequacy of international demand, and shared out production among existing domestic producers (Hirschman 1945; Kaiser 1980). Demand stimulus entered this policy sequence as an accentuation of economic nationalism, then shifted quite rapidly to association with internationalism. In the 1980s this historical link of demand stimulus to internationalism is under strain, and the strategy is increasingly associated with nationalistic tendencies. Demand stimulus may then have one political meaning in a worsening economic environment, another when things are improving—when the high-technology, lower labor-component, export-oriented industries have an internationalism to sell.

Shifts in policy correspond to shifts in politics, which correspond to shifts in group demands, which in turn correspond to changes in the international economy. A given policy preference is not necessarily in the "interest" of the actor. On the contrary, it is possible to posit a calculus or frame of reference that could make a range of conflicting policies reasonable from the standpoint of different strategies. Thus by one strategy international business should support demand stimulus in 1933, by another it should oppose it. The way out of this interpretative trap is to be sociological, to ask what sorts of strategy various groups actually did prefer. Some groups may tend to evolve certain visions, or shift group preferences, more readily or rapidly than others. When we find such patterns, we can reason backwards to ask what logic underlies these different responses. As I have noted, I am exploring the extent to which that logic may be "situational." This will inevitably sound as if I argue "they had to do it because it was in their interests, and they could do nothing else." But what I wish to convey is "they did it because people occupying that situation were likely to think that way." An adequate critique of the argument, therefore, is not that the reader can think of an alternative strategy which a particular group could in principle have followed. Rather, it would be that a particular group did not follow the expected course; or that some other logic underlies the pattern observed; or that there is no pattern at the level of groups.

Is "situation" the only explanation, or the best one? Alternative interpretations are possible, and I have suggested some of their strengths and limitations. I find it significant, and surprising, that while there are plenty of alternative explanations of the *politics* of the period (fascism, constitutionalism, etc.) there are no alternative explanations of the *policies* of the period. the political culture, political leadership, party system, bureaucratic politics, economic ideology, and international-system explanations of the adoption and rejection of economic policies on a *comparative* basis in the 1930s remain to be constructed. Such explanations—as types—are familiar, but they are familiar because of their use regarding outcomes other than economic policy (Berger 1981).

Discussion of the "best" explanation often stresses too heavily the choice among alternatives rather than the piece of the whole, or the function, that each handled. For example, it is not a question of whether leadership mattered but of what materials leadership could use—what constraints or opportunities were provided by group situation. Thus the classic criticism of Bentleyism—a statement of the groups does not state everything—is correct but incomplete. Such a statement specifies the constraints and opportunities of leadership and other forces. It clarifies the material with which politicians have to work, the structural conditions on which ideologies, earlier experiences, institutional attachments, defense issues, and so on have to work. It suggests the forces that contribute to group strategies. And in world of complex situations, we need more ideas about how groups operate, not fewer (for contrasing approaches see Olson 1982; Piore and Sabel, 1985).

The same point can be made in relation to other causal variables favored in other discourse. I am not *a priori* opposed to institutional or political culture arguments. Institutions obviously affect the struggle for power: for a specified production profile, different institutional arrangements promote different outcomes. Weimar remains the *locus classicus*. Similarly, culture matters: actors rarely understand a situation solely of itself. Prior experiences and analytic approaches shape current analysis. German steel's preference for military over civilian modes of government aid is but one example. But these variables cannot be lifted out of social context and fired off as explanatory cannon. How the institutions matter depends on who is trying to use them. How a particular ideology about political economy affects an actor depends on the actor's situation. The same ideology or institution may produce different outcomes according to the actors on whom they operate.

The contribution of this article (and of the approach it uses) is to structure more carefully the relationship between society and mediating variables by insisting on the importance of the former in making sense out of the latter. To note that at this or that point leadership, or institution, or culture is being used as part of the explanation is no criticism of the argument, since my goal has been from the beginning to see just what these variables might matter. Thus, in the British case, I stress not that leadership was unimportant, but that whatever leader sought to break with orthodoxy would have drawn support (and resistance) from identifiable sources. Looking at why these sources were weaker or stronger in the United Kingdom than in other places tells us something about the likelihood of a particular outcome.

Much of this article has considered whether other policies were possible in each country. But were other *politics* possible, either connected with the actual policy followed or with another policy? My line of inquiry has brought out the importance of a variable neglected in current discourse on political outcomes; the significance of economic policy in shaping preferences for leaders, parties, cabinets, and regimes. The capacity of different political formulae to accommodate various policies can be explored by testing out alternative combinations of support. In some cases the obstacles seem only moderate, for example a Lib-Lab coalition in Britain. In others, the obstacles seem formidable, though not totally impossible, for example in Germany a neo-orthodox policy shift under a moderate constitutionalist (Muller of the

Center party) or a military dictator (Schleicher); or in the same country, a demand-stimulus break under a moderate constitutionalist (Stressman) or a military dictator (Schleicher). There was nothing inevitable about the cow coalition in Sweden, or a Republican incumbency in 1929 helping a Democratic counterattack. Alternative outcomes were thus possible, though only within specific limits whose patterns this article has sought to establish.

The patterns that emerged in the 1930s, and were consolidated in the postwar years, are now under considerable stress. Argument over how to interpret the 1930s is an argument over how to interpret the 1980s, how to predict what is likely to happen, and how to prescribe it. The stretchmarks of previous booms and busts remain, not only in the reality of political conflicts but in the minds of those who fight over interpretation and explanation. Intellectual and political tasks intertwine; the ability to imagine alternatives in both policy options and political formulas may well have a bearing on which solutions succeed. The 1930s were too costly for us not to think about what we can learn from them for the present.

Notes

So many have helped, it is impossible to cite everyone. I wish to thank particularly the reviewers of *International Organization*, many colleagues at the University of California at San Diego, Cornell University, Harvard University's Center for European Studies, and several Swedish Universities; James Kurth and the participants at a special meeting held at Swarthmore College, Albert Hirschman, and Roger Haydon; the National Endowment for the Humanities, and the UCSD Committee on Research.

1. In addition I have been greatly influenced by Moore Jr. (1966), Kurth (1979), Landes (1969), and Vernon (1971); for examples of my approach, see Gourevitch (1977) and (1978).

References

Abraham, D. 1981. *Collapse of the Weimar Republic*, Princeton: Princeton University Press.

Arndt, H. W. 1944. *The Economic Lessons of the Nineteen-Thirties*, Oxford: Oxford University Press.

Aldcroft, D. H., and H. W. Richardson. 1968. *Building in the British Economy between the Wars*, London: Allen and Unwin.

————. 1969. *The British Economy, 1870–1939*, London: Macmillan.

Auge-Laribe, M. 1950. *La politique agricole de la France*, Paris: Presses Universitaires de France.

Bauer, R., Ithiel de Sola Pool, and L. A. Dexter. 1967. *American Business and Public Policy*, Chicago: Aldine-Atherton.

Beer, S. H. 1965. *British Politics in the Collectivist Age*, New York: Alfred A. Knopf.

Berger, S., ed. 1981. *Organizing Interests in Western Europe*, New York: Cambridge University Press.

Blank, S. 1977. "Britain: The Politics of Foreign Economic Policy," in P. Katzenstein, ed., *Between Power and Plenty*, Madison: University of Wisconsin Press.

Bodin, L., and J. Touchard. 1961. *Le Front populaire de 1936*, Paris: Armand Colin.

Bohme, H. 1967. "Big Business Pressure Groups and Bismarck's Turn to Protectionism, 1873–79," *Historical Journal*, 10:218–36.

Borkin, J. 1978. *The Crime and Punishment of I. G. Farben*, New York: Free Press.

Bouvier, J. 1966. "Un débat toujours ouvert: la politique Économique du Front populaire," *Le mouvement social*, No. 54:175–81.

Broué, P., and N. Dorey. 1966. "Critiques de gauche et opposition révolutionnaire au Front populaire (1936–38)," *Le mouvement social*, No. 54: 91–133.

Brower, D. 1968. *The New Jacobins: The French Communist Party and the Popular Front*, Ithaca: Cornell University Press.

Brown, B. 1943. *The Tariff Reform Movement in Britain, 1884–1895*, New York: Columbia University Press.

Burnham, W. D. 1970. *Critical Elections and the Mainsprings of the American Party System*, New York: Norton.

Bullock, A. 1960. *The Life and Times of Ernest Bevin*, vol. 1, London: Heinemann.

Colton, J. 1966. *Léon Blum*, New York: Alfred A. Knopf.

Craig, G. 1964. *The Politics of the Prussian Army, 1640–1945*, New York: Oxford University Press.

———. 1978. *Germany 1866–1945*, Oxford: Clarendon Press.

Crouch, C. 1979. "The State, Capital and Liberal Democracy," in Crouch, ed., *State and Economy in Contemporary Capitalism*, London: Croom Helm.

Dahmen, E. 1970. *Entrepreneurial Activity and the Development of Swedish Industry, 1919–1939*, trans. by A. Leijonhvud, Homewood, IL: Richard D. Irwin.

Dupeux, G. 1959. *Le Front populaire et les elections de 1939*, Paris: Armand Colin.

Ehrmann, H. 1947. *French Labor from Popular Front to Liberation*, New York: Oxford University Press.

———. 1957. *Organized Business in France*, Princeton: Princeton University Press.

Feldman, G. 1969. "The Social and Economic Policies of German Big Business, 1918–29," *American Historical Review*, 75:47–55.

———. 1977. *Iron and Steel in the German Inflation, 1916–23*, Princeton: Princeton University Press.

Ferguson, T. 1984. "From Normalcy to New Deal," *International Organization*, 38.

———. 1985. *Critical Realignment: The Fall of the House of Morgan and the Origins of the New Deal*, New York: Oxford University Press.

Gaventa, J. 1980. *Power and Powerlessness in Appalachia*, Oxford: Clarendon Press.

Gerschenkron, A. 1943. rpt., 1966. *Bread and Democracy in Germany*, New York: Howard Fetig.

Gilpin, R. 1975. *United States Power and the Multinational Corporation*, New York: Basic Books.

Goguel, F. 1946. *La politique des partis sous la IIIe République*, Paris: Seuil.

Gourevitch, P. A. 1977. "International Trade, Domestic Coalitions and Liberty: Comparative Responses to the Crisis of 1873–96," *Journal of Interdisciplinary History*, 8:281–313.

———. 1978. "The Second Image Reversed: The International Sources of Domestic Politics," *International Organization*, 32:881–912.

Greene, N. 1969. *Crisis and Decline: The French Socialist Party in the Popular Front Era*, Ithaca: Cornell University Press.

Gúrin, D. 1970. *Front populaire, révolution manquée*, rev. ed., Paris: Maspéro.

Gustafson, B. 1973. "A Perennial of Doctrinal History: Keynes and the 'Stockholm' School," *Economy and History*, 16:114–28.

Haberle, R. 1970. *From Democracy to Nazism*, Baton Rouge: Louisiana State University Press.

Hamilton, R. 1982. *Who Voted for Hitler*, Princeton: Princeton University Press.

Hancock, K. J. 1960. "Unemployment and the Economists in the 1920s," *Economica*, n.s., 27:305–21.

———. 1962. "Reduction of Unemployment as a Problem of Public Policy, 1920–29," *Economic History Review*, 2d ser., 15:328–43.

Heckscher, E. F. 1954. *An Economic History of Sweden*, trans. by G. Ohlin Cambridge: Harvard University Press.

Heyl, J. D. 1973. "Hitler's Economic Thought: A Reappraisal," *Central European History*, 6:83–96.

Hirschman, A. 1945. *National Power and the Structure of Foreign Trade*, Berkeley: University of California Press.

Jonung, L. 1979. "Knut Wicksell's Norm of Price Stabilization and Swedish Monetary Policy in the 1930s," *Journal of Monetary Economics*, 5.

———. 1981. "The Depression in Sweden and the United States: A Comparison of Causes and Policies," in K. Brunner, ed., *The Great Depression Revisited*, Boston: Marinus Nijhoff.

Kahn, A. 1946. *Great Britain in the World Economy*, New York: Columbia University Press.

Kaiser, D. 1980. *Economic Diplomacy and the Causes of the Second World War*, Princeton: Princeton University Press.

Kalecki, M. 1938. "Lessons of the Blum Experiment," *Economic Journal*, 48:26–41.

Katzenstein, P. 1985. *Corporatism and Change*, Ithaca: Cornell University Press.

Kavanagh, D. A. 1973. "Crisis and Management and Incremental Adaptation in British Politics: The 1931 Crisis of the British Party System," in G. Almond *et al.*, ed., *Crisis, Choice, and Change: Historical Studies of Political Development*, Boston: Little, Brown.

Kindleberger, C. 1973. *The World in Depression, 1929–1939*, Berkeley: University of California Press.

Koblik, S., ed. 1975. *Sweden's Development from Poverty to Affluence*, trans. by J. Johnson, Minneapolis: University of Minnesota Press.

Korpi, W. 1978. *The Working Class in Welfare Capitalism: Work, Unions, and Politics in Sweden*, London: Routledge and Kegan Paul.

Kuisel, R. 1967. *Ernest Mercier: French Technocrat*, Berkeley: University of California Press.

Kurth, J. 1979. "The Political Consequences of the Product Cycle: Industrial History and Political Outcomes," *International Organization*, 33: 1–34.

Lacouture, J. 1977. *Léon Blum*, Paris: Seuil.

Lambi, I. 1963. *Tariffs and Protection in Germany*, Weisbaden: Steiner.

Landes, D. S. 1969. *The Unbound Prometheus: Technological Change and Industrial Development in Western Europe from 1750 to the Present*, Cambridge: Cambridge University Press.

Lange, P. *et al.* 1983. *Unions, Change and Crisis: French and Italian Union Strategy and the Political Economy*, Winchester, MS: Allen and Unwin.

Lefranc, G. 1974. *Histoire du Front populaire*, 2d ed. Paris: Payot.

Lewin, L., B. Jansson, and D. Sorbom. 1972. *The Swedish Electorate, 1887–1968*, Stockholm: Almquist and Wiksell.

Lewis, W. A. 1960. *Economic Survey 1919–1939*, London: Allen and Unwin.

Lindbeck, A. 1975. *Swedish Economic Policy*, London: Macmillan.

Lipset, S. M. 1963. *Political Man*, Garden City, NY: Doubleday.

Longstreth, F. 1979. "The City, Industry and the State," in C. Crouch, ed., *State and Economy in Contemporary Capitalism*, London: Croom Helm.

Marjolin, R. 1938. "Reflections on the Blum Experiment," *Economica*, n. s., 5:177–91.

Martin, A. 1979. "The Dynamics of Change in a Keynesian Political Economy: The Swedish Case and Its Implications," in C. Crouch, ed., *State and Economy in Contemporary Capitalism*, London: Croom Helm.

Milward, A. S. 1976. "Fascism and the Economy," in W. Laqueur, ed., *Fascism, A Reader's Guide: Analyses, Interpretations, Bibliography*, Berkeley: University of California Press.

Montgomery, A. 1938; rpt. 1972. *How Sweden Overcame the Depression, 1930–1933*, New York: Johnson.

Moore, B., Jr. 1966. *The Social Origins of Dictatorship and Democracy*, Boston: Beacon Press.

Nyman, O. 1947. *Svensk parlamentarism 1932–1936; Fran minoritets parlamentarism till majoritetskoalition*, Uppsala: Almquist and Wiksell.

Olson, M. 1982. *The Rise and Decline of Nations*, New Haven: Yale University Press.

Piore, M., C. and Sabel. 1985. *The Industrial Divide: Technology and the Institutions of Coordination and Stabilization in Advanced Industrial Capitalism*, New York: Basic Books.

Richardson, H. W. 1967. *Economic Recovery in Britain, 1932–39*, London: Weidenfeld and Nicolson.

Rogowski, R. 1982. "Iron, Rye, and the Authoritarian Coalition in Germany after 1879." Paper delivered at the American Political Science Association annual meetings, Denver.

Sauvy, A. 1967. *Histoire économique de la France entre les deux guerres*, vol. 2: 1931–39, Paris: Fayard.

Schattschneider, E. E. 1963. *Politics, Pressure and the Tariff*, Hamden, CN: Archon.

Shonfield, A. 1969. *Modern Capitalism*, London: Oxford University Press.

Skidelsky, R. 1967. *Politicians and the Slump*, London: Macmillan.

———. 1979. "The Decline of Keynesian Politics," in C. Crouch, ed., *State and Economy in Contemporary Capitalism*, London: Croom Helm.

Skocpol, T. 1980. "Political Responses to Capitalist Crisis: Neo-Marxist Theories of the State and the Case of the New Deal," *Politics and Society*, 10, 2.

Skocpol, T. and K. Finegold. 1982. "State Capacity and Economic Intervention in the Early New Deal," *Political Science Quarterly*, 97:255–78.

Skocpol, T. and M. Weir. forthcoming. "State Structures, Political Coalitions, and the Possibilities for Social Keynesianism: Responses to the Great Depression in Sweden and the United States".

Soderpalm, S. A. 1976. *Direktorsklubben-Storindustrin i svensk politik under 1930 - och 40 - talen*, Zenit: Raben and Sjorgen.

Strange, S. 1971. *Sterling and British Policy*, London: Oxford University Press.

Taussig, F. 1967. *A Tariff History of the United States*, New York: A. M. Kelley.

Tilton, T. A. 1979. "A Swedish Road to Socialism: Ernst Wifforss and the Ideological Foundations of Swedish Social Democracy," *American Political Science Review*, 51:505–20.

Tingsten, H. 1973. *The Swedish Social Democrats: Their Ideological Development*, trans. by G. Frankel and P. Howard-Rosen, Totowa, NJ: Bedminster Press.

Turner, H. A., Jr. 1963. *Stresemann and the Politics of the Weimar Republic*, Princeton: Princeton University Press.

———. 1968a. "Hitler's Secret Pamphlet for Industrialists, 1927," *Journal of Modern History*, 11:348–74.

———. 1968b. "Emil Kirdorf and the Nazi Party," *Central European History*, 1:324–44.

———. 1969. "Big Business and the Rise of Hitler," *American Historical Review*, 75:56–70.

———. 1970. "The Ruhrlade, Secret Cabinet of Heavy Industry in the Weimar Republic," *Central European History*, 3:195–228.

Uhr, C. G. 1973. "The Emergence of the 'New Economics' in Seden: A Review of a Study by Otto Steiger," *History of Political Economy*, 5:243–60.

Vernon, R. 1971. *Sovereignty at Bay*, New York: Basic Books.

Warner, C. K. 1960. *The Winegrowers of France and the Government since 1875*, New York: Columbia University Press.

Wehler, H. -U. 1970. "Bismarck's Imperialism," *Past and Present*, 48:19–55.

Williams, W. A. 1969. *Roots of the Modern American Empire*, New York: Random House.

Winch, D. 1966. "The Keynesian Revolution in Sweden," *Journal of Political Economy*, 74:168–76.

———. 1969. *Economics and Policy: A Historical Study*, New York: Walker.

Woytinski, V. 1961. *Stormy Passage*, New York: Vanguard.

Youngson, A. 1960. *The British Economy, 1920–57*, Cambridge: Harvard University Press.

10

Silk and Steel: Italy and Japan Between the Two World Wars

WALTER GOLDFRANK

In any attempt to analyze seriously the structural and world-historical forces which contributed to twentieth-century development, certain key features of semi-peripheral states must be incorporated into the analysis, then compared and assessed for their relative weight in that development. Throughout this paper I want to stress the essential comparability of Italy and Japan in terms of the semiperiphery as a whole, their place in the world-system, and their state structures. I shall examine in detail the changes in the Italian and Japanese class structures which were produced by—and became the conditions for—their respective ruling groups' attempts to move from semi-periphery to core. Simultaneously, I shall assess the features which distinguished them such that Japan would overtake Italy in crucial respects before the Second World War and be in a position to surpass Italy, in almost every respect, during the post-war period.

To begin, I offer a set of curiosities concerning these two competitors, illustrative of the range of concerns addressed here. Since the progress made by both Italy and Japan was significantly more substantial and considerably more sophisticated than commonly acknowledged, the following items reflect not only those advances but also the stereotypes held by core observers concerning semi-peripheral states.

Item: In the early 1930s, a Japanese executive, Yoithi Mayeda, made a prophecy which G. E. Hubbard (1938) of the Royal Institute for International Affairs made the epigraph to his marvelous study *Eastern Industrialization and its Effect on the West*. He said, "It is yet to be seen how much we can do with this our 'Greatness in small things.' Human fingers are still the very best machines that mankind do possess, and if the 400,000,000 dextrous

This chapter originally appeared in *Comparative Social Research* 4, pp. 297–315, and is reprinted with permission.

fingers of the Japanese are to be fully employed, we know now what prodigious revolutions they will make in industrial circles. The time may come when we beat the world with the tips of our fingers."

Item: In his often-inapposite comparison of Japanese and German industrialization, David Landes (1965:16) added a further footnote on the manual skill of Japanese workers. "Some have suggested that Japanese children owe their manual dexterity to their training in calligraphy. I myself am inclined to attribute it to eating with chopsticks."

Item: For those who like paradoxes which confound linear accounts of industrial evolution, Japanese conversion to electricity is a case in point. When their textile industry grew in earnest during and after the First World War, electrical energy was also beginning to supersede coal-fueled steam as source of motive power. In coal-poor but hydro-rich Japan this new energy source not only made Japan the world's third largest hydro-electric producer and fifth largest electrical user but also enabled the perpetuation of very small-scale industrial establishments the likes of which had been rendered obsolete at earlier times in Western Europe (Minami 1976).

Item: In the 1930s, the two foreign powers with the greatest interest in the Peruvian banking system were none other than Italy and Japan.

Item: Italian imperialism in Africa is well known, at least in its Ethiopian phase. Less known, if not entirely forgotten, is that during the 1920s the Italians used Eritrean troops to consolidate their hold on Libya, killing over 100,000 Bedouins in an attempt to provide secure land for their agricultural settlements. Less known, too, is that from their base in southern Somaliland, the Italians waged ferocious campaigns agains the North, setting up banana plantations with conscript labor and forcing the overpriced bananas on the Italian market. Again, little known is the fact that in the early 1930s the Ethiopian market had been largely captured by France and (who else?) Japan. A commercial delegation headed by Mitsui representatives had gone to Addis Ababa in 1932 and established political and economic ties by 1933–34 (Mack Smith 1977; Santarelli 1974:269; Schneider 1936:140). Swiss, British, and Americans were also becoming involved in Ethiopia, and, according to Mack Smith, "There was some astonishment [in Italy] that such an 'uncivilized' people could undersell Italians so easily" (1977:64). He further characterizes Italian war propaganda as calling upon patriots to "defend Christianity against barbarian Ethiopians and coloured Japanese." Mussolini's son, Vittorio, described the bombing of Ethiopians as "exceptionally good fun" and characterized war as the "most beautiful and complete of all sports" (Schmidt 1939:202).

Item: It was Mussolini himself who said in 1930, "Fortunately the Italian people are not yet accustomed to eating several times a day, and, having a modest level of living, feel scarcity and suffering less" (Schmidt 1939:121).

In regard to more formal introduction, there are two aspects to be considered: the question of semi-peripheral countries in general and the justification of the present comparative analysis in particular.

Italy and Japan as Semi-Peripheral Countries

Many interesting things have been and can be said about semi-peripheral states as politico-economic units within the changing capitalist world-economy. In important ways, semi-peripheral countries are emblematic of the system as a whole, uniting under their territorial control core and periphery in more of a balance than either core-states or peripheral areas. (The term "pockets of poverty" captures the relatively minor way in which peripheral zones persist within core-states; the notion of "modern enclave" captures the way in which peripheral areas are not without some highly capitalized activities.) This picture of relative semi-peripheral balance must be complicated by the idea of intermediate levels of capitalization and wages: a *balance*, between core-like and peripheral production on the one hand, and *intermediate levels* of production on the other, are two ways, often found together, of arriving for a time at a semi-peripheral position. In the early part of this century, textile production was the quintessential intermediate good—with low-waged, agro-mineral exports quintessentially peripheral and steel and machinery the province of the core: hence, the title, "Silk and Steel." In the course of *this century*, both Japan and Italy pass from silk to steel and beyond. It is a furious passage, through textile production and imperialist war, and in the case of Japan, at least, a passage, finally, from semi-periphery to core. If one cannot think about the semi-periphery without thinking about upward and downward mobility in the world system as a whole, one must simultaneously stress that in any particular period only a few such countries can make the great leap. That is, they are able to garner a large enough share of the most productive technologies and skills and political power to compete more or less effectively with the existing core states. Which brings us back to the question of core and peripheral zones under the control of a particular semi-peripheral state, and to the idea that in a dynamic capitalist world-economy, merely to stand still, relatively speaking, requires effort, and to advance requires both out-competing older core-states and further exploiting peripheries.

In the concrete cases one thinks of the famous Italian Milan-Turin-Genoa northern industrial triangle, of the increasingly productive northern agriculture (in which productivity increased 22 percent between the wars), as compared to the backward and impoverished *mezzogiorno* in which productivity increased only three percent during the same period. Other areas of direct Italian exploitation include the islands, Albania, Libya, and the aforementioned Eritrea, Somaliland, and Ethiopia. Or, for Japan, one thinks of the industry and phenomenally productive rice culture of the main island, along with Hokkaido, and Korea, Taiwan, Manchuria, ultimately much of coastal China and for a brief spell during the second war, most of Southeast Asia. To quote the Japanese President of the South Manchurian Railway Company in 1927: "millet is to be largely cultivated in Manchuria and Mongolia to be exported to Korea for the sustenance of the Koreans, so that as much Korean rice as possible may be imported to Japan (Bix

1972:425). If capitalism, in this new understanding, is expanded reproduction plus primitive accumulation, then the semi-peripheral states best condense the system as a whole. To modify an idea propounded by Wallerstein (1974), *especially* in periods of worldwide stagnation and contraction, do they find the opportunity to move forward, using their relative production cost advantage against the older core states, and their relatively great politico-military power against peripheries and external arenas.

This territorial overview perhaps establishes the plausibility of comparing Italy and Japan. But a more elaborate justification is useful. Most comparative analyses of latecomer industrialization and "fascism" either compare Japan and Germany or Italy and Germany. Comparisons of the first pair aim retrospectively to discover why it was that those two states emerged as the major antagonists of the United States and the other "allies" in the Second World War, finding the key in some combination of the survival of feudal or aristocratic groups, militarism and authoritarian culture (Hayashi 1971). Comparisons of the second pair aim to dissect the causes and consequences of the two principal European fascisms, stressing late national unification, the dislocations of the First World War, the rise of radical petty-bourgeois mass movements, anti-Bolshevism, and weakly institutionalized parliamentary systems (Woolf 1965; Moore 1966; Poulantzas 1976). In some comparative analyses, the Soviet Union is paired with Germany under the totalitarian rubric; in others, it is paired with Japan under the rubric of twentieth-century industrialization, the latter capitalist, the former socialist. From a world-system perspective, only this last pair makes good sense, along with the comparison proposed here between Japan and Italy. For they are both semi-peripheral states moving toward the core, similar in many essential features in the years around the First World War. Germany, on the other hand, was already a core-state by the end of the nineteenth century: the bid of its ruling groups for *hegemony* in the world system has important differences from the Italian and Japanese attempts to achieve rough parity with the pre-existing core powers. In terms of productive structures, Germany was well advanced in the chemical, electrical machinery, and automotive sectors, while Japan and Italy were becoming major producers of textiles. In terms of world politics, Germany instigated the First World War and was demoted and humiliated by the outcome but not greatly damaged physically; stung, but not subdued, to summarize Keynes. Japan and Italy were both secondary partners in the victorious alliance, and disappointed with their share of the spoils (Villari 1929:350).

Some further considerations on comparability as semi-peripheral states are perhaps in order. In the interwar period, Italy and Japan are grouped together as exporters of products which were *declining* as a proportion of all world trade (Tyszynski 1951). Neither was a *major* exporter or importer of agricultural commodities (Tracy 1972:105–114). A recent scholarly summary of the data and literature on Italian foreign trade and industrial structure cannot decide whether Italy is one of, or complementary to, the major imperialist powers (Paradisi 1975:279). In fact, through much of this century's historical and social science literature on Italy runs a stream of ambivalence: Is Italy serious? Was Mussolini a dynamic developer, or a buffoon? Was fascism a "parenthesis" and national nightmare, or did fascism preside over important industrial advance? Welk (1938:153) summarizes thus: "Yet if few fundamental changes have been made in Italian economic life, it must nevertheless be recognized that a surprisingly complete and effective system for the centralized control of the Italian economy has been evolved." And Schneider (1936:128–129) describes Italy's semi-peripheral status this way:

> She is too big to be content with the status of any of her lesser neighbors and too weak to be a "big power." She is, therefore, reduced to what is commonly called a psychological state. . . . It is the moral torment of the big school-boy who cannot "punish" the little school-boy because his father will "punish" him . . . In short, Italy has no equals.

But why not Japan, "within the imperialist camp . . . a pigmy among giants?" (Dower 1974:xxv). After summarizing a large number of materials pertaining to material levels of living and social welfare in contemporary 1970s-Japan, Bennet and Levine remark "The similarities to Italy are striking" (1976:454). But to raise Asian living standards to West European levels is a later development. This paper concentrates on the prior time and has a double theme: Japan and Italy were, in the period in question, more similar to each other than either was to Germany, and their respective politico-economic trajectories offer a set of contrasts that illuminate and specify the utility of the concept of semi-periphery. Why did Japan's economy and political power grow faster than Italy's, making Japan capable of inflicting severe damage on Western interests and bidding for regional hegemony, while Italy could do no better than become Germany's somewhat reluctant junior partner? Does Japan's greater success during the period 1913–1945 help account for its nearly miraculous post-Second World War spurt, once questions of world political power were settled?

To answer these questions and, hence, hopefully to shed some new light on the general question of fascism [which I recently addressed in a worldwide survey (Goldfrank 1978)], leads me to a trinity of orienting ideas derived from my work on the Mexican Revolution (1975, 1979): world system, state structure and class struggle. By world system, I refer to a linked array of regional patterns of accumulation and to the relations among states. By state structure I mean the organizational modes through which repressive and ideological power are exercised and national economic policy pursued. By class struggle I mean the more-or-less organized competition within classes and the conflict between them inside national boundaries. In each of these three areas I would suggest that while Italy and Japan were essentially similar as advanced semi-peripheral formations, from the stand-point of capital Japan had mutually reinforcing and cumulating advantages that overdetermined its relative competitive success.

World System

As an ensemble of relations, the world-system of the period from 1913 to 1945 was convulsed by wars and revolutions, and mired in uneven, but often deep, stagnation. Although I shall not pursue the point in depth here, it is nevertheless necessary to treat war and war-related changes as *integral* to transformation, not as occasional and unusual curses visited on an otherwise peacefully-developing world. As in the time of the Thirty Years' War (1618–1648) and the Napoleonic Wars at the turn of the nineteenth century, the first half of our century was an era of heightened opportunity combined with awful misery. The struggle for world hegemony, ultimately won by the United States, had its own unstable dynamic which helped worsen the cyclical economic troubles; those troubles in turn made the world politics of the era more desperate than any before or since. Both Italy and Japan had been on the rise during the preceding boom, exporting silk and importing capital goods to build up textile production and rudimentary heavy industry. Both suffered from a lack of critical raw materials. Politically, both gained at the expense of declining empires and with the blessing and sponsorship of older core powers. Both entered the First World War on the side of the allies and were disappointed with their share of the fruits. Only Japan joined with the effort to roll back Bolshevism in Russia.

So much for the similarities. The differences, all in Japan's favor, have to do with population and imperialist geography. Japan had a population larger than any East or Southeast Asian country save China, which was then in the throes of warlord fragmentation in the interior and foreign domination on the coast. Nearly all other Asian countries were European colonies whose ruling powers would be defeated or severely threatened by Germany in the Second World War. Japan's colonies in Manchuria, Korea, and Taiwan were rich in resources and population. In addition, Japan could play the racial and cultural "Asian" card against the others.

By contrast, Italy was virtually surrounded by stronger powers. Germany pressed south and eastward, such that Italy had eventually to acquiesce in the Austrian *anschluss* (cf. Santarelli 1974:167). France sat to the northwest; England and France dominated the Mediterranean from Gibralter to Suez. Late into the race for colonies, Italy had been left with the crumbs. The overall contrast could not be clearer: Japan faced a relatively open field while Italy was stuck in a packed territory. And, if Italy was as brutal as Japan in conquest and in colonization, it was not so cost-efficient. Colonization and agricultural projects in Libya brought minimal returns (Segre 1974:164–165). The Ethiopian War cost vast sums and left that territory and its people in no condition to return economic benefits. Italian participation in the Spanish Civil War cost twelve to fourteen billion lire—Mussolini confessed "it bled his country white" (Smith 1968:105)—without paying off in hoped-for coal and steel concessions from Franco. In addition, Spanish involvement marked the transition to Italian subservience to Germany. Japanese capital meanwhile profited from relatively efficient administration of the colonial territories; the Taiwan census is said by demographers to be the most accurate and thorough ever carried out. Finally, there is the startling matter of Japan's export competitiveness in the depression (see Tables 1 and 2), when its share of the world cotton textile market jumped, in large part at he expense of the British, although in Central and South America at Italy's and the United States' expense as well (Halliday 1975:128). This remarkable advance was secured by aggressive marketing in the teeth of high tariffs and/or import quotas in most of the territories controlled by Britain, France, and the United States.

State Structure

Differences in state structure and class struggle help explain this differential success, even as they in turn are partially explained by it. On the former score, one must point above all to the greater degree of centralization of the Japanese state, the greater power of the military within it, and the greater control of state over society. This centralization can be seen in ideology as well as administrative and repressive organization. It is in part based in the distinctive regional economic geography and extends even to the degree of coordination between the state and the most powerful industrial interests. Consider the following:

1. Although its countryside was unquestionably overpopulated, Japan had no real equivalent of the *mezzogiorno*, backward in technique and dominated by corrupt *latifundistas* who had extensive political representation in the capital.
2. While neither Japan nor Italy had a successful parliamentary system, Japan's experience with "bourgeois democracy" was shorter-lived and entailed less mass participation.
3. While corporatism was the official ideology in both states, Japan's seems to have been more effective; according to one authority, Italian corporatism was administrative rather than political or economic, typically putting words before deeds (Vivarelli 1974:651).
4. Nothing so widespread as the Italian fascist movement occurred in Japan; the radical agrarianist politics of assassination and attempted coups that erupted briefly in the 1930s were stopped cold. Halliday (1975:133–140) goes so far as to reject even the term "fascist" as descriptive of the Japanese regime, so continuous was it with the mode of organization which had come before.
5. State economic policy in Japan was more coherent than in Italy, although both made serious mistakes between 1926 and 1932, Italy overvalued the lira in 1926, making its exports less competitive; Japan undervalued the yen in 1932, increasing the quantity of exports unnecessarily much faster than the value. But the Italian drive toward autarky was poorly conceived: the famous battle for wheat, for example,

while succeeding in making Italy virtually self-sufficient in food grains, reinforced the political and social power of the most backward elements, contributed to soil depletion, and took croplands out of valuable fruit and vegetable export production such that first Spain and then, during the civil war and the Palestinian uprising in the late 1930s, the Zionists captured what might have been Italian markets (Schmidt 1939:174).

6. Both governments promoted an increasing concentration of capital and rationalization of production. In Italy, new state enterprises were begun; in Japan state-*zaibatsu* coordination increased and new military *zaibatsu* were started.

7. Both governments expanded the size of their bureaucracies, the Japanese probably more efficiently because they did not have a movement demanding payoffs in government jobs (Salvemini 1936:340–341).

8. Military spending was quite comparable; Japan's went from five percent of GNP (or 16.2 percent of the government budget) in 1931 to 30.2 percent of GNP (or 55.3 percent of government budget) in 1939. Italy's military expenditure went from 5.2 percent of GNP (27.4 percent of the government budget) in 1931 to 11.1 percent of GNP (28 percent of government expenditure) in 1939 and then to 32.9 percent of GNP and 64.4 percent of spending in 1941 (Yamamura 1972: 203; Covino et. al., 1976:189).

9. Mention should also be made of the ideological problems of Italy, given the weight of the church in social life, with Mussolini's uneasy concordat symbolizing the split between fascism as a self-styled renovationist movement and fascism as an accommodationist regime. Although organized competition from below was eliminated, the Church and Confindustria (the industrialists' primary interest association) represented two powerful socialist elements. But if the latter had its Japanese counterpart, the former did not.

Proletarianization Compared

Let me turn now to a comparison of class forces in the two cases, especially the structure and transformation of the working class during this period. Considered in turn will be the structure of production in the city and countryside, differences in the historical and moral element in wages, inter-sectoral wage differences, and the exploitation of female workers. To preview the argument: both Italy and Japan shifted toward heavy industrial production, increasing the proportion of highly-skilled male workers. Because of its greater export competitiveness, Japan was better shielded from the effects of the great depression than Italy, using the flexibility of the historic village and family organization to absorb economic shock. Where Italian fascism compressed wages and attempted to substitute ideology and recreation (*Dopolavoro*, a state-sponsored workers' organization) for autonomous working-class politics, Japanese capital inherited, perpetuated, and/or strengthened a system of greater urban-rural differences, inter-industry differences, exploitation of women, and of lower living standards. These maternal structures are the basis for the relatively *lower* degree of internal repression in the Second World War as the acid test, both in production and in organization—one thinks here particularly of the remarkable penetration of village Japan by the army, a preparation, really, for the postwar land reform—the cumulative results of the prior twenty years become clear.

In terms of productive structure both Italy and Japan remained heavily rural, although this similarity conceals a rather greater amount of village industrial production in the Japanese countryside. Roughly speaking, the absolute size of the rural population of Japan stayed constant throughout the period, with natural increase absorbed in the cities. The prior phenomenal growth in productivity of Japanese agriculture slowed in the 1920s and 1930s, as the limits of intensive rice cultivation were met; fertilizer use became extraordinary. The growth of productivity in Italian agriculture was consistently less; especially in the South, it was negligible. Japanese landlordism was a small-scale affair, and in the wake of the grave rural distress caused by plummeting rice and silk cocoon prices, the army ultimately intervened to alter the payments for rice in favor of the direct producers. In Italy meanwhile, landed property was further concentrated during the thirties, as the battle-for-wheat policies advantaged larger holders, turning many former independent peasants into tenants; the vaunted campaign to rid Italy of rural proletarians resulted in a further increase in tenantry, and, as a whole, the tenants were worse off than either peasants or wage workers had been.

In industrial production, Italy and Japan shared a similar profile (Paradisi 1976:278), with the predominance of intermediate goods and the protected growth of government-subsidized and politically-favored monopolistic heavy industry. Japan ran away with the competition in silk, rayon, and cotton textile exports—even Italian wage cuts were not sufficient to repair the damage of the *cuota novanta* (90 lira = $1). Both were insufficiently competitive in heavy industrial products to export anywhere but to their own colonies. Japan's trade with the so-called "yen bloc" increased from 24 percent to 55 percent of its total trade between 1929 and 1938 (Kindleberger 1973); of its exports, Italy sold all its tires, half its machinery, and two-thirds of its vehicles to its colonies (Tattara and Toniolo 1976:140). In 1935, industry for the first time contributed the largest sectoral share of the Italian GNP—25.3 percent—and that proportion grew to 34.1 percent in 1940 (Vaudagna 1978:194). In terms of the impact of the depression, production fell considerably less in Japan than in Italy after 1929, and it grew much faster in Japan after 1932. In both countries there was a pronounced concentration of capital, although the literature gives a somewhat differential picture. In Italy the most greatly concentrated heavy industries were rescued and protected by the state from competition; the real results of establishing State-Capitalist combines (IRI, ENI, and IMI) would not be felt until the post-war era (Aquarone 1969). In Japan state intervention was more serious, as managerial technocratic elements gained ground within the *zaibatsu* at the expense of the older family owners (Valota 1977:89). In sum, on the strength of its greater export competitiveness, the Japanese textile industry did better than the Italian; the picture in heavy industry is more similar, but the edge in dynamism must be given to the Japanese. Though not without factions, the Japanese bourgeoisie was more compact than the Italian, having neither a powerful landed sector to contend with nor declining textile producers. Nor, to be sure, did it have so politically advanced a proletariat to contain, and so to the structure of the two proletariats I now turn.

A first issue is that of the relative historical and moral elements in the wage level of the two countries. The only direct comparison readily available is reproduced in Table 3. In the 1913 production of raw silk, clearly the wage level in Japan was half that of Italy, which had an industrial wage level in the 1920s half that of France, which in turn was about half that of the United States. But the data on caloric intake provide an indirect measure as well, and there, in Table 4, it can be seen that Japanese levels were considerably below the Italian. Zamagni (1976:351–352) argues that low wages were an integral part of Italian capitalism until 1963, but these were low by West European, not *world* semi-peripheral standards. In fact, it seems that one could summarize much of the literature on the Italian economy in the inter-war period with a negative "Goldilocks" formulation: Italian wages were too high for export competitiveness and too low for the creation of a sizable internal market in consumer durables and other heavy industrial products. Japan, by contrast had the advantage of Asian wage levels in a world where transport costs were falling. (Japan itself would become the second or third largest shipbuilder in the world.) For the first time Asian manufacturers were competing in worldwide markets. The threat from these low-cost products led to drastic retaliation and in turn to Japanese expansion into new markets, including some that had never existed before.

But that is not all; there is a cultural dimension to this contrast. Italian workers were Europeans in aspirations and life-style; many had been involved directly or indirectly in labor migration to France or the United States. Their tastes and wants were those of Europeans. By comparison, Japanese workers pursued traditional Japanese consumer styles, and in the name of "Japaneseness" were more readily denied core-like consumer goods. In addition, to supply consumer demand for traditional wage goods—textiles, soy products, sandals—there existed a large array of small industries keeping employment up and reproduction costs down (see Table 5). In this way, prewar Japan was a preview of Mao's China, as a culturally nationalist, labor-intensive agro-industrial sector reproduced itself while contributing labor and wage goods to the developing heavy industrial sector.

Sectoral differences in wages are another area in which Italian capital faced disadvantages relative to Japan. Table 6 shows the extremely high inter-industry wage difference for 1933 Japan, with the first five industries paying roughly two-and-one-half the wages of the last five and almost twice the wages of the intermediate group. In Italy, the difference between the most and least capital intensive industries was not quite two to one (Zamagni 1976:368–371) throught the 1920s, with the exception of silk reeling; as Table 7 shows, silk-reelers in Japan seem hardly to have been paid at all.

Urban-rural differences are another source of Japanese advantage. The countryside in Japan came to absorb what little excess industrial labor there was during the depression. Meanwhile, as Chart 1 and Table 8 dramatically indicate, the countryside absorbed a most severe relative fall in living standards, hitting a low of around 40 percent of the urban standard in 1930 and recovering to a little better than 50 percent by the end of that decade. While manufacturing real income doubled from 1925 to 1940, agricultural income rose by only about 30 percent, and had more dependents to support. I have not found exactly comparable data for Italy, but Table 9 shows that agricultural incomes remained remarkably stable from 1922 to 1934, declining only a little, and Table 10 shows that while industrial wages moved in the opposite direction from 1929 until 1934, they then fell in a roughly comparable way. That table also shows Japanese industrial wages rising, then falling, during the 1930s, but not below their 1929 level; and Table 5 shows the Japanese to have been much more successful in avoiding unemployment.

Then there is the issue of female exploitation, an area in which Japan perhaps holds the historical record. Tables 11 and 12 show the remarkable extent to which Japanese textile industrialization and factory work in general depended on women workers. Many of them were young; some lived in dormitories or barracks in miserable conditions. Others lived at home and walked or bicycled to work in small village workshops (Saxonhouse 1976; Minami 1976). They had a high ratio of employment turnover regardless of where they lived. The exploitation of women increased during the thirties. As Table 13 shows, from 1930 to 1938 women's wages fell from roughly half to scarcely a third those of men. Again, precisely comparable data for Italy have not appeared, but those summarized in Table 9 suggest that the hardships imposed on Italian workers were about equal in their effect on both sexes.

To summarize briefly: Italian capital was disadvantaged vis-a-vis Japan by its lesser exploitation of women, by the lesser degree of inter-sectoral wage differentials, and by the higher, European historical and moral elements in the wage. This material disadvantage was mirrored in the organizational and political weaknesses of Italian capital as it confronted a working class whose autonomous organs were destroyed, but whose productivity lagged in spite of efforts at political coddling and nationalistic ideological inspiration. The events of the Second World War showed this difference dramatically, as thousands of Italian workers joined or supported a resistance movement that had no counterpart whatever in Japan. In combination with Japan's stronger state structure and more favorable world-system location, the Japanese ruling groups were able to parly these class structural advantages into upward movement matched in this century only by the Soviet Union.

Japan is no longer a pygmy among giants. But Italy, meanwhile, has yet to solve the dilemmas of the *mezzogiorno*, is again exporting labor to the more advanced countries, and is still, in short, a big school-boy.

Notes

The author extends his thanks to David Hammerstein for research assistance, to Elizabeth Sholes for research and editorial help, to the UCSC Comparative History Seminar and Faculty Research Committee for small grants, and to Jim O'Connor and Fred Weaver for comments on an earlier draft.

References

Aquarone, A. 1969. "Italy: The Crisis and Corporative Economy," *Journal of Contemporary History*, 4:37–58.

Bennett, J. W., and S. B. Levine. 1976. "Industrialization and Social Deprivation: Welfare, Environment, and the Post-Industrial Society in Japan," in H. Patrick, ed., *Japanese Industrialization and its Social Consequences*, Berkeley: University of California Press.

Bix, H. 1972. "Japanese Imperialism and the Manchurian Economy, 1900–1931," *China Quarterly*, 51:425–443.

Covino, R. *et al.* 1976. "L'industria dall'economia di guerra alla ricostruzione," in P. Ciocca and G. Toniolo, eds., *L'economia italiana nel periodo fascista*, Bologna: il Mulino.

Dower, J. W. 1975. "Introduction," in J. Halliday, *A Political History of Japanese Capitalism*, New York: Pantheon.

Goldfrank, W. L. 1975. "World System, State Structure, and the Onset of the Mexican Revolution," *Politics and Society*, 5:417–439.

_____. 1978. "Fascism and World Economy," in B. H. Kaplan, ed., *Social Change in the Capitalist World Economy*, Beverly Hills: Sage.

_____. 1979. "Theories of Revolution and Revolution without Theory: The Case of Mexico," *Theory and Society*, 7:135–175.

Halliday, J. 1975. *A Political History of Japanese Capitalism*, New York: Pantheon.

Hayashi, K. 1971. "Japan and Germany in the Interwar Period," in J. W. Morley, ed., *Dilemmas of Growth in Prewar Japan*, Princeton: Princeton University Press.

Hazama, J. 1976. "Historical Changes in the Life Style of Industrial Workers," in H. Patrick, ed., *Japanese Industrialization and its Social Consequences*, Berkeley: University of California Press.

Hubbard, G. E. 1938. *Eastern Industrialization and its Effect on the West*, 2nd ed., London: Oxford University Press.

Kindleberger, C. 1973. *The World in Depression, 1929–1939*, Berkeley: University of California Press.

Landes, D. 1965. "Japan and Europe: Contrasts in Industrialization," in W. W. Lockwood, ed., *The State and Economic Enterprise in Japan*, Princeton: Princeton University Press.

Mack Smith, D. 1977. *Mussolini's Roman Empire*, London: Penguin.

Minami, R. 1976. "The Introduction of Electric Power and its Impact on the Manufacturing Industries: With Special Reference to Smaller Scale Plants," in H. Patrick, ed., *Japanese Industrialization and its Social Consequences*, Berkeley: University of California Press.

Moore, B., Jr. 1966. *Social Origins of Democracy and Dictatorship*, Boston: Beacon Press.

Nakamura, J. I. 1965. "Growth of Japanese Agriculture, 1875–1920," in W. W. Lockwood, ed., *The State and Economic Enterprise in Japan*, Princeton: Princeton University Press.

Ohkawa, Kazushi, and Rosovsky, H. 1960. "The Role of Agriculture in Modern Japanese Economic Development," *Economic Development and Cultural Change*, 9:43–67.

Ono, Akira, and Watanabe, T. 1976. "Changes in Income Inequality in the Japanese Economy," in H. Patrick, ed., *Japanese Industrialization and its Social Consequences*, Berkeley: University of California Press.

Paradisi, M. 1976. "Il comercio estero e la struttura industriale," in P. Ciocca and G. Toniolo, eds., *L'economia italiana nel periodo fascista*, Bologna: il Mulino.

Poulantzas, N. 1976. *Fascism and Dictatorship*, London: New Left Books.

Salvemini, G. 1936. *Under the Axe of Fascism*, New York: Viking.

Santarelli, E. 1974. "The Economic and Political Background of Fascist Imperialism," in R. Sarti, ed., *The Ax Within*, New York: New Viewpoints.

Saxonhouse, G. R. 1976. "Country Girls and Communication among Competitors in the Japanese Cotton-Spinning Industry," in H. Patrick, ed., *Japanese Industrialization and its Social Consequences*, Berkeley: University of California Press.

Schmidt, C. T. 1939. *The Corporate State in Action*, London: Victor Gollancz.

Schneider, H. W. 1936. *The Fascist Government of Italy*, New York: D. Van Nostrand.

Segre, C. G. 1974. *The Fourth Shore*, Chicago: University of Chicago Press.

Shinohara, M. 1964. "Economic Development and Foreign Trade in Pre-War Japan," in C. D. Cowan, ed., *The Economic Development of China and Japan*, New York: Praeger.

Tattara, Giuseppe, and Toniolo, G. 1976. "L'industria manifatturiera: cicli, politiche, e mutamenti di struttura, 1921–1937," in P. Ciocca and G. Toniolo, eds., *L'economia italiana nel periodo fascista*, Bologna: il Mulino.

Tracy, M. 1972. "Agriculture in the Great Depression. World Market Developments and Agricultural Protectionism," in H. van der Wee, ed., *The Great Depression Revisited*, The Hague: Martinus Nijhoff.

Tzszynski, H. 1951. "World Trade in Manufactured Commodities, 1899–1950," *The Manchester School of Economic and Social Studies*, 19:272–304.

Valota, A. 1977. "Continuity of the Prewar Regimes and Development of Democracy in Japan and Italy—An Essay at a Comparison," pp. 87–92 in *Changing Contemporary Japanese Society*, The Research Institute, Momoyama Gakuin University.

Vannutelli, C. 1974. "The Living Standard of Workers," in R. Sarti, ed., *The Ax Within*, New York: New Viewpoints.

Vaudagna, M. 1978. "Structural Change in Fascist Italy," *Journal of Economic History*, 38:181–201.

Villari, L. 1929. *Italy*, New York: Scribner.

Vivarelli, R. 1974. "Italian Fascism," *The Historical Journal*, 17:644–651.

Wallerstein, I. 1974. "Dependence in an Interdependent World: The Limited Possibilities of Transformation within the Capitalist World Economy," *African Studies Review*, 17:1–26.

Welk, W. G. 1938. *Fascist Economic Policy*, New York: Russell and Russell.

Woolf, S. J. 1968. *European Fascism*, London: Penguin.

Yamamura, K. 1972. "Then Came the Gerat Depression: Japan's Interwar Years," in H. van der Wee, ed., *The Great Depression Revisited*, The Hague: Martinus Nijhoff.

————. 1976. "General Trading Companies in Japan—Their Origins and Growth," in H. Patrick, ed., *Japanese Industrialization and its Social Consequences*, Berkeley: University of California Press.

Zamagni, V. 1976. "La dinamica dei salari nel settore industriale." in P. Ciocca and G. Toniolo, eds., *L'economia italiana nel periodo fascista*, Bologna: il Mulino.

TABLE 1

Selected Export Data, 1929-1935

	1929	1930	1931	1932	1933	1934	1935
Quantum of world exports	100	93.0	85.5	74.5	75.5	78.5	82.0
Quantum of Japanese exports	100	88.3	91.0	107.6	119.0	140.6	159.6
Price index (gold) of world exports	100	87.0	67.5	52.5	46.5	43.0	42.0
Price index (gold) of Japanese exports	100	82.8	62.2	35.3	31.6	27.5	26.9
Japanese percentage of world cotton textile exports	22	25	27	34	37	43	44
United Kingdom percentage of world cotton textile imports	37	33	28	32	31	29	28

Source: G. E. Hubbard, Eastern Industrialization and Its Effect on the West (Oxford: Oxford University Press, 1935), pp. 5, 7.

TABLE 2

Costs of Production of No. 40 Cotton Yarn in Various Countries in the 1930's (in Yen)

	(a) Weekly wages per man	(b) Persons required per 1,000 spindles	(c) a x b=c Weekly wages per man per 1,000 spindles	(d) (bales) Weekly output per 1,000 spindles	c/d Costs of production per bale	Index of c/d with Japan eq 100
India	5.5	15.0	82.5	2.4	34.4	260
United Kingdom	18.0	4.0	72.0	2.3	31.4	238
Italy	11.0	5.5	60.5	2.4	25.2	191
Japan	5.8	6.1	35.5	2.7	13.2	100

Source: Miyohei Shinohara in The Economic Development of China and Japan, C. D. Cowan, ed. (London: Allen & Unwin, 1964), page 245.

TABLE 3

Comparison of Wages and Costs of Production in Sericulture in Japan,
Italy, and France in 1913-1914

(Unit: Yen)	Japan	France	Italy
Daily wages in sericulture:			
Male	0.50	1.14	0.95
Female	0.28	0.56	0.43
Cost of production of cocoon per kwans	4.20*	5.17	4.65
Sale prices of cocoon per kwans	4.50	4.98	4.98

Note: *refers to 1916. In 1913, it was far less than 5.36 in 1916.
         1 kan = 3.759 kg.

Source: Miyohei Shinohara in The Economic Development of China
         and Japan, C. D. Cowan, ed. (London: Allen & Unwin,
         1964), page 235.

TABLE 4

Calories Available for Consumption Per Day Per Capita
from Selected Foods

Japan

Period	Grains, Pulses, Potatoes	Meat, Milk, Eggs	Total
1913-1917	2084	10.3	2094
1918-1922	2189	12.1	2201
1923-1927	2031	14.9	2046
1928-1932	1866	38.8	1905
1933-1937	1815	47.2	1862

Italy

| 1926-1930 | | | 2800 |
| 1936-1940 | | | 2650 |

Sources: Nakamura (1965), p. 296; Vannutelli (1974, pp. 156-157).

TABLE 5

Changes in Industrial Employment in Italy,
Japan, and Germany (1929 = 100)

Year	Italy	Japan	Germany
1924	92	90	90
1925	100	92	97
1926	102	93	89
1927	94	99	98
1928	98	99	101
1929	100	100	100
1930	98	101	92
1931	89	100	80
1932	78	98	70
1933	79	101	73
1934	83	106	84
1935	94	111	89
1936	95	116	95
1937	104	119	103
1938	111	123	109
1939	114	128	113

Source: Vera Zamagni in L'economia italiana nel periodo
fascista, Pierluigi Ciocca and Gianni Toniolo,
eds. (Bologna: Il Mulino, 1976), page 346.

TABLE 6

A Comparison of Inter-Industry Wage Structures
of Japan and the United States

	Hourly Wages in Japan (1933)[a] Sen	Hourly Wages in United States (1945)[b] US Cents
Shipbuilding	24.9 (private)	137.0
	25.8 (government)	
Rolling stock	25.6 (private	122.4
	29.9 (government)	
	33.8 (municipal)	
Aeroplanes	27.2 (private)	121.8
	23.0 (government)	
Printing	20.1 (private)	114.0
	19.6 (government)	
Electrical machinery	20.4	105.3
Petroleum refining	16.9	127.6
Rubber	12.8	112.5
Chemicals	14.0 (total)[c]	98.9
Paper	12.3 (private)	88.3
Food processing	15.7 (total)[c]	88.1
Hosiery	9.5	80.0
Canned Food	8.4	80.8
Silk, etc.	4.4	74.4
Textile Goods	7.2 (total)[c]	75.7
Cotton yarn and cloth	7.8	68.4

Notes: [a] From Rodotokei Jitchi Chosahokoku (Report of a Survey on Labour Statistics), 1933.
[b] From Lebergott, "Wage Structures," Review of Economic Statistics (November 1947).
[c] Japanese figures represent broader categories than those for the United States.

Source: Miyohei Shinohara in The Economic Development of China and Japan, C. D. Cowan, ed. (London: Allen & Unwin, 1964), page 246.

TABLE 7

1925 Wages in Lire

Industry	Employed	Hourly Wage	Daily Wage
Wool	65,708	2.03	16.85
Cotton	228,668	1.73	14.38
Silk	160,623	1.31	10.96
Rayon	22,940	1.85	17.44
Steel	48,348	3.23	28.06
Shipbuilding	48,348	3.23	28.06
Machinery	150,313	2.78	24.37

Source: Vera Zamagni in L'economia italiana nel periodo fascista, Pierluigi Ciocca and Gianni Toniolo, eds. (Bologna: Il Mulino, 1976), page 373.

TABLE 8

Real Income Per Gainfully Occupied Person (Relative), Japan (1913-17 = 100)

Year	Primary Industry	Secondary Industry	Tertiary Industry
1913-17	100.0	100.0	100.0
1918-22	125.4	116.0	117.4
1923-27	134.0	136.7	154.1
1928-32	134.0	202.8	202.8
1933-37	151.0	231.8	220.4
1938-42	170.4	274.0	251.7

Source: Kazushi Ohkawa and Henry Rosovsky in Economic Development and Cultural Change 9, page 55.

CHART 1

**Differentials in Per Capita Household Income Between
Urban-Employee Households and Farm Households**

Source: Ono and Watanabe (1976), p. 365.

TABLE 9

Indexes of "Real" Agricultural Wages in Italy, for Men
and Women, by Years, 1922-1934 (1929 = 100)

Daily Wages

Year	Men	Women
1922	106.5	105.4
1923	108.7	108.1
1924	106.5	106.8
1925	100.7	99.3
1926	96.4	96.6
1927	102.9	102
1928	103.6	104.1
1929	100	100
1930	97.8	95.9
1931	97.8	92.2
1932	96.4	92.6
1933	97.8	95.9
1934	98	98.9

Note: *Bertani, in Economia, May 1936, p. 382.

Source: Welk (1936), p. 236.

TABLE 10

Changes in Real Industrial Wages in Italy, Japan,
and Germany, 1924-1939 (1929 = 100)

Year	Italy	Japan	Germany
1924	120	89	64
1925	115	- -	79
1926	112	88	82
1927	114	- -	88
1928	102	- -	98
1929	100	100	100
1930	99	111	95
1931	100	120	91
1932	100	112	85
1933	107	107	89
1934	108	106	93
1935	97	105	94
1936	93	101	96
1937	99	- -	99
1938	97	- -	104
1939	106	- -	107

Source: Vera Zamagni in L'economia italiana nel periodo
fascista, Pierluigi Ciocca and Gianni Toniolo,
eds. (Bologna: Il Mulino, 1976), page 345.

TABLE 11

Proportion of Women Among Factory Workers

(Percentages)

Japan		France	
1909	62.0	1866	42.7
1920	53.0	1881	38.3
1930	52.6	1901	31.5
		1921	31.6
United States		Italy	
1870	24.0	1901	37.4
1880	28.8	1911	46.2
1900	32.6		
1920	24.2		

Source: Saxonhouse (1976), p. 99.

TABLE 12

Females as a Percentage of the Cotton Textile Labor Force

(Percentages)

Japan		United Kingdom		India	
1909	83.0	1835	55.1	1884	22.5
1914	83.3	1847	58.7	1894	25.9
1920	80.0	1867	61.3	1909	22.1
1925	80.6	1878	62.7	1924	21.6
1930	80.6	1895	62.3	1934	18.9

Source: Saxonhouse (1976), p. 100.

TABLE 13

Long-term Trends in Daily Wages (in Sen)

Year	Wages			Real Wage Index 1934-1936 Average=100
	Male	Female	Average	
1882	27	16	19	36.5
1900	41	20	26	40.0
1910	60	30	41	53.1
1920	193	96	140	72.0
1930	194	92	142	101.5
1938	215	73	151	93.2

Source: Hazama (1976), p. 35.

11

The Northeast Asian
Political Economy
Under Two Hegemonies

BRUCE CUMINGS

Introduction

East Asia today is the center of world economic dynamism. Japan in 1980 achieved the number two spot in the world in Gross National Product. It is complemented by the "gang of four," South Korea, Taiwan, Singapore and Hong Kong. These four East Asian developing countries now account for almost twice the export totals of the entire remainder of the Third World and their growth rates are usually the highest in the entire world. Singapore and Hong Kong are difficult to categorize: are they nations? industrial platforms? city-states? Our concern in this paper will be with the Northeastern portion of the East Asian basin: Japan, Korea, and Taiwan.

These four nations (including the two Koreas) in 1978, before the second oil wave, accounted for a combined Gross National Product of about $1.06 trillion, a population of 190 million, an annual growth rate of ten percent, and perhaps $232 billion of world trade. This would compare to a U.S. GNP in 1978 of about $2 trillion, a population of 218 million, a growth rate of four percent, and world trade of $326 billion. After the U.S., no other nation has a higher GNP—the combined GNP of the European Economic Community in 1978 was $1.95 trillion, or less than double the Northeast Asian figure; the average growth rate in the EEC was 2.9 percent. the Soviet Union had a larger population but a lower GNP, and a growth rate estimated at 3.1 percent (Central Intelligence Agency, 1980).

A glance back before World War II suggests that we may need a longer perspective to capture the true dimensions of this growth. Japan's interwar annual growth rate of 4.5 percent doubled the rates of interwar Europe;

Reprinted from *International Organization* 38/1 (winter 1984), Bruce Cumings, "The Origins and Development of the Northeast Asian Political Economy: Industrial Sectors, Product Cycles, and Political Consequences," by permission of The MIT Press, Cambridge, MA. Copyright 1984 by the President and Fellows of Harvard College and of the Massachusetts Institute of Technology.

colonial manufacturing growth in Korea, 1910–1940, averaged ten percent per annum, and overall GNP growth was also in the four percent range, as was Taiwan's. No nation's heavy industrial growth rate was steeper than Japan's in the period 1931–1940; in the textile sector, Japan's automation was ahead of Europe's in 1930. Yet the most recent and careful research on the prewar period now suggests that both Korea and Taiwan experienced higher GDE growth rates than Japan in the period 1911–1938 (Japan, 3.36%; Korea, 3.57%; Taiwan, 3.80%) (Allen 1980:1; also Ohkawa and Rosovsky 1973:74, 82–83; for comparison with Korea and Taiwan, Umemura and Mizoguchi 1981:64).

In the past century Japan, Korea, and Taiwan have also moved fluidly through a classic product-cycle industrialization pattern, Korea and Taiwan of course following in Japan's wake. Japan's industrialization has proceeded through three phases, the last of which is just beginning. The first phase began in the 1880s with textiles being the leading sector; this phase lasted through Japan's rise to world power. In the mid-1930s Japan began the second, heavy phase, based on steel, chemicals, armaments, and ultimately automobiles; this phase did not begin to end until the mid-1960s. The third phase now entered upon emphasized high technology "knowledge" industries such as electronics, communications, computers, and silicon-chip microprocessors.

Within Japan each phase, in good product cycle fashion, has been marked by strong state protection for nascent industries, adoption of foreign technologies, and comparative advantages deriving from cheap labor costs, technological innovation, and "lateness" in world time. In each phase there was a bursting forth into the world market that always struck foreign observers as abrupt and unexpected, thus inspiring both fear and loathing and awe and admiration (Kojima 1977:150–151). The cycle in given industries—textiles, steel, automobiles, light electronics—of origin, rise, apogee and decline has not simply been marked, but often mastered, in Japan; in each industrial life-cycle there is also an appropriate jumping off place, that is, a point at which it pays to let others make the product or at least provide the labor. Taiwan and Korea have historically been receptacles for declining Japanese industries. If we add agriculture to this, we get a pattern in which in the first quarter of this century Korea and Taiwan substituted for the diminishing Japanese agricultural sector, exporting rice and sugar in great amounts to the mother country. (Taiwan was annexed in 1895, Korea in 1910). By mid-1930s Japan had begun to export iron and steel, chemical, and electric-generation industries, although much more to Korea than to Taiwan. In the 1960s and 1970s, both smaller countries have received declining textile and consumer electronic industries from Japan (as well as from the U.S.), and now in the 1980s, some Japanese speak of fobbing off steel and autos in the same direction. All in all the sequence is rather breathtaking.

Thus if there has been a miracle in East Asia, it has not occurred just since 1960; it is profoundly ahistorical to think that it did. Furthermore, it is misleading to take any of these countries one at a time in assessing their industrialization pattern: such an approach through a fallacy of disaggregation misses the fundamental unity and integrity of the *regional* effort in this century. Yet an ahistorical, disaggregated approach is the most common one; it is reinforced by the many differences between the three countries, and by the dominant modernization school in U.S. academic circles, which has produced by far the greatest quantity of literature on East Asian development.

A country-by-country approach (or the modernization approach) is incapable of accounting for a startling phenomenon: the remarkably similar trajectories of Korea and Taiwan in this century. Thus, we find specialists on Korea arguing that its development success "is unique in world history," (Wade and Kim 1978:vi) and Taiwan specialists making similar claims; or we find Taiwan specialists citing the apparent "paradox" of Taiwanese development—i.e., that it developed in a fashion that contradicts the assumptions of the dependency theorists—while not breathing a word about Korea (Greenhalgh 1980 and Simon 1980). And then, of course, both avoid the essential Japanese context of Korean and Taiwan development.

This essay asserts that a proper understanding of the Northeast Asian political economy can only emerge from an approach that posits the systemic interaction of each country with the others, and of the region with the world at large. Remarkable development, yes, but in the *context* of two hegemonic systems: the Japanese imperium to 1945, and intense, if diffuse, American hegemony since the late 1940s. Rapid upward mobility in the world economy has occurred, through the product cycle and other means within a particular and specificable context. Furthermore, only consideration of context can account for the similarities in the Taiwanese and South Korean political economies. Simultaneously, external hegemonic forces have interacted with different domestic societies in Korea and Taiwan, giving rather different political outcomes: this too has been characteristic throughout our century. Korea was more rebellious in 1910 and it is more rebellious today. Our approach, therefore, seeks to explain both the similarities in economic development in the three countries, and the differences in political consequences.

The Origin of the Northeast Asian Political Economy, 1900–1945

However much it may pain the majority of Korean nationalists and the minority of Taiwanese nationalists, the place to begin in comprehending the economic dynamism of this region is with the advent of Japanese imperialism. Japan's imperial experience was different than that of the West in several fundamental respects (Cumings 1981:ch. 1; for a similar emphasis on the colonial state in Taiwan, see Ho 1978:26, 32): it involved the colonization of *contiguous* territory; it involved the location of industry and an infrastructure of communications and transportation *in* the colonies, bringing industry to the labor and raw materials rather than vice-versa; and it was accomplished by a country that always saw itself as *dis*advantaged and *threatened* by more advanced countries—Japan was "weak and puny," Professor Eto Shinkichi has written, and this perception affected the colonial enterprise throughout. All of these characteristics made themselves felt most strongly in Korea, the closest and always the most important of Japan's possessions.

Japan entered upon colonization *late* in world time, in the context of a globe with hundreds of years of colonial experience and where, as King Leopold said three years before the Meiji Restoration, "the world has been pretty well pillaged already." With most of the good colonial territories already spoken for, and with Western powers knocking at the door, Japan had little space for maneuver. Furthermore, for several decades Japan faced the possibility of becoming a dependency, perhaps even a colony, of one of the Western powers. With imperial attention mostly focused on China and its putative vast market, however, Japan got what E. H. Norman called a "breathing space" within which to mobilized its resources and resist the West.

The relative lateness of this endeavor imparted several additional characteristics: first, a posthaste, anticipatory quality in colonial planning; second an extraordinary interest in and mimicking of previous colonial experience; third, a rather quick anachronism to the whole enterprise; last, Japan had little choice but to colonize its contiguous neighbors.

Many have spoken of Japan's defensive reform and industrialization after 1868, and so it was with Japan's colonial expansion: offensive to Taiwanese and Koreans, it looked defensive to Japanese planners in a predatory world. And much like reform at home, the colonial effort had an anticipatory, preconceived, planned aspect to it. The characteristic figure in this architectonic endeavor was therefore not an adventurous Cecil Rhodes type, but an administrator and planner like Goto Shimpei, who played the architect in the Taiwan colony. Much like MITI's role in the Japanese economy today, the colonizers exercised sharp "administrative guidance" in shaping colonial society.

In order to acquire colonies in the first place, Japan had to maximize its comparative advantages by seeking territory close to home. The West, always stretched a bit in East Asia, could in judo-like fashion be dispatched in the near reaches of Japan. Thus, unlike most colonial powers, Japan colonized countries that nearly touched its borders. This then made a close, tight, integral linking of the colony to the metropole feasible. Contiguity could also facilitate the settling of colonial migrants, especially an insular, homogeneous people who abhor distance from the native source, and could raise the potential of extraordinarily rapid exchange-time in market relations. Japan wasted no time in enhancing this through laying railroads, opening ports, and making heavy investments in communications sectors.

The result of Japan's administrative and coercive colonialism was to take two quite different societies and political economies, and mold them into look-alikes (Cumings 1981:chs. 1 and 2; Ho 1978:28–57; Lin 1973:13–28). The first act was a major cadastral survey and land reform: 1898–1906 in Taiwan, 1910–1918 in Korea. North-South trunk railroad lines were laid. Ports were opened. In Taiwan, cane sugar and to a lesser extent rice were promoted in the first phase, making Taiwan second only to Cuba in sugar exports by 1938. In Korea rice exports expanded by leaps and bounds in the 1920s. Agricultural growth was stronger in Taiwan than in Korea; colonial administrators remarked that what could be done with economic incentives in Taiwan required coercion in Korea. Why should this have been so?

Whereas Taiwan had only an aboriginal population for the most part until the eighteenth century, and a small class of Chinese absentee landlords by the end of the nineteenth century (the *ta-tsu-hu*), Korea had a powerful landed class of centuries' duration, melding property-holding and aristocratic privilege in a potent mix (Palais 1975:1–19). Extensive landlordism and tenancy had long development before Japan arrived. Therefore the Japanese found it expedient to root landlords more firmly to the ground, as a means of disciplining peasants and extracting rice for the export market. The landlord class therefore persisted through to 1945, although by then it was tainted by association with imperial rule. In Taiwan, by contrast, and reform at the turn of the century eliminated absentee lords and fostered a class of entrepreneurial landowners, emerging "from below" as they had in Japan. By 1945 most Taiwan landowners were smaller than Korean counterparts and far more productive. Whereas tenancy increased markedly in Korea, it actually decreased in Taiwan during the period 1910–1941. Samuel Ho (1978:43, 57) has concluded that by 1945 agriculture in Taiwan was quite scientific, and change had occurred "without disrupting the traditional system of peasant production." Korea, on the other hand, had frequent peasant protests and rebellions, guerrilla movements in the border region, and above all a huge population movement off the land that severely disrupted the agrarian political economy (Cumings 1981:chs. 8–10). In other words, Korea betrayed most of the features associated with colonial underdevelopment, whereas Taiwan did not. It may be that the very existence of Korea, and subsequently Manchukuo, gave Taiwan its own "breathing space" within the regional imperium. In any case its experience did not conform to the predictions of dependency theorists. And, of course, in Taiwan you get a weak nationalist impulse, and in Korea an extraordinarily strong one.

Although Taiwan seemed to have emerged from the last phase of colonialism relatively unscathed, with few disruptions, Korea was profoundly transformed. The period from 1935 to 1945 was when Korea's industrial revolution began, with most of the usual characteristics: uprooting of peasants from the land, the emergence of a working class, widespread population mobility, and urbanization. Because the Japanese accomplished industrialization from above, however, social change accompanying this revolution was greatest in the lower reaches of society. The social and regional conflicts that racked Korea in the 1945–53 period have their origins in the immense population shifts, agrarian disruptions, and industrial dynamism of the final phase of the Japanese imperium. This was truly a decade-long pressure cooker which deeply effected Korea when the lid was lifted in 1945.

Japan's tightly-held regional political economy in Northeast Asia, and its industrialization of the region (especially Korea and Manchuria), were primarily the results of the crisis of the 1930s depression. As Japan built steel mills, petrochemical complexes, railroads, ports, and even automobile plants in the colonies, Koreans became the mobile human capital moved hither and yon to work at low wages, often combined with militarized mobilization and discipline, in the factories. By 1945 fully 20 percent of the Korean population was residing outside Korea (mostly in Japan and Manchuria) or in a province other than the one in which they were born (usually meaning southern peasants dispatched to north Korean industry). Since most of this population diaspora came from the surplus population of southern farmlands, after the collapse of the Japanese imperium they returned to the south. There, under the hostile gaze of an American occupation from 1945 to 1948, they became rapid converts for radical organizers setting up people's committees, labor unions, left wing parties and, in 1948–50, guerrilla war. Thus there is a relationship between Japan's response to the crisis of the 1930s and America's response to the crisis of the late 1940s in Korea, which led directly to the outbreak of the Korean War and American intervention.

The Postwar Settlement and the Emergence of a New Hegemony

In September 1945, as U.S occupation forces filtered into Japan, an American officer walked into a Mitsui office and introduced himself. The man in the office pointed to a map of the Greater East Asian Co-prosperity Sphere and said, "There it is. We tried. See what you can do with it!" (Emmerson 1978) It was not until 1948 that the U.S. sought to do much with it, however. In the period 1945–47 in Korea, Japan, and Taiwan, society reacted strongly against the effects of imperial militarism and industrial midwifery; an American occupation in Japan led by a nineteenth-century liberal also reacted strongly in the early years against the political economy of prewar Japan, seeking to destroy the Japanese Imperial Army, break up the *zaibatsu*, eliminate rural landlords, and bequeath to the world a reformed and chastened Japan that would never again mix aggression with economic prowess. Unions and leftist parties were unleashed and, with Occupation "New Dealers," mustered a strong enough challenge to the prewar system to, at minimum, establish the countervailing power that enables us to call postwar Japan a democracy. Although the main emphasis was on democratization and an end to militarism, more narrow interests also asserted themselves. The first head of the Economic and Scientific Section of the Occupation, for example, was Robert C. Kramer, a textile industrialist; he and representatives of American textile, rayon, ceramics, and other industries threatened by Japanese competition opposed receiving Japan's economy, particularly in the potent prewar form (Halliday 1975:183–184). American allies, especially the British, also urged that commitments to reform and reparations be carried through, thereby to weaken the competitiveness of Japan in world markets.

There was, however, a sector of American official opinion from the early 1940s on that opposed a punitive occupation, for fear that this would play into the hands of the Soviets and make a reintegration of Japan with the world economy impossible; in essence such people, who included a Japan-ophile faction in the State Department (Iriye 1977:378–407), wanted a Japan revived to *second-rank* economic status and enrolled in an American-managed free trade regime. Such recommendations remained in the background, however, while Japan's American emperor, Gen. Douglas MacArthur, mas-terfully imposed a benevolent tutelage upon the Japanese people.

All this began sharply to change in late 1947, leading to what we might call the Kennan Restoration. George Kennan's policy of containment was always limited and parsimonious, based on the idea that four or five industrial structures existed in the world: the Soviets had one and we have four and things should be kept that way. Only Japan held his interest in Asia; the rest were incontinent regimes and how could one have containment with incontinence? Kennan and his Policy Planning Staff played the key role in pushing through the "reverse course" in Japan.

American policy in the mid-twentieth century resonated with Viner's description of British policy in the eighteenth century: it was governed "by joint and harmonized considerations of power and economics." Security and economic considerations were inextricably mixed. A revived Japan was both a bulwark against the Soviets and a critical element in a reformed and revived world economy. What is surprising, in the multitude of formerly classified documents now available on early postwar Asian policy, is how powerful were the economic voices. In particular, a cluster of bankers and free traders, now dubbed the "Japan Crowd" (Roberts 1979:384–415) were instrumental to the ending of the postwar reforms in Japan, and the revival of the regional political economy that persists today. Economics bulked so large because, as Charles Maier has pointed out, the defeated Axis powers (Japan and West Germany in this case) were to be posted as world centers of capital accumulation and growth, not as centers of political or military power (Maier 1978:45). Thus Japan's economy was reinforced, while its political and military power (beyond its borders) was denuded and shorn. The result is that postwar Japan resembles a *sector* in the world economy as much as a nation-state. Until the 1970s it was a distinctly secondary sector when compared to the U.S., that is, it was returned to semi-peripherality as a (hopefully) permanent second-rank economic power.

As thinking about a revived Japan evolved in 1948–1950 two problems emerged: first, how could Japan's vital but second-rate status be assured; second, how could a prewar political economy that got its raw materials and labor from the Northeast Asian periphery survive in the postwar world without a hinterland? These problems were raised in stunning fashion by George Kennan in a Policy Planning Staff meeting in 1949:

> You have the terrific problem of how the Japanese are going to get along unless they again reopen some sort of empire toward the south. If we really in the Western world could work out controls . . . fool-proof enough and cleverly enough exercised really to have power over what Japan imports in the way of oil and other things . . . we could have veto power over what she does. (Quoted in Maier 1978:185)

Thus, once the decision to revive Japan was made, two questions predominated: the hegemonic problem and the hinterland problem.

In July 1949, the CIA asserted that the U.S. has "an important interest" in "retaining access to Southeast Asia, for its own convenience and because of the great economic importance of that area to western Europe and Japan." It argued that "the basic problem with respect to Japan is to recreate a viable economy. This in turn requires a stabilization of the situation in Southeast Asia and a *modus vivendi* with Communist China." The latter contingency might occur if China could be drawn away from "vassalage toward the USSR" (Central Intelligence Agency 1949). Southeast Asia was the preferred candidate for Japan's hinterland. It would provide markets for Japan's textile and light industrial exports, in exchange for raw materials badly needed in Japan. The problem was that France and England sought to hold the countries in the region exclusively, and that nationalist movements resisted both the Europeans and a reintroduction of the Japanese. Thus, "Anglo-American consensus over Japan dissolved" as the U.S. played the hinterland option. Japan was a threat to sterling bloc trade and currency systems, and was "perforce in the dollar bloc;" the U.S. wanted Japan to earn dollars in the sterling bloc, which had the dual virtue of supporting Japan's revival while encouraging Britain's retreat from empire (Calleo and Rowland 1973:198–202).

For our purposes it is important to note the *triangular* structure of this arrangement: U.S. (core), Japan (semi-periphery), Southeast Asia (periphery). This was clearly articulated in the deliberations leading up to the adoption of NSC 48/1 in late December 1949, a document so important that it might be called the NSC 68 for Asia. This is when the U.S. made the decision to send aid to the Bao Dai regime in Vietnam, not after the Korean War began. The first draft of the paper argued the virtues of a "triangular" trade between the U.S., Japan, and Southeast Asia, giving "certain advantages in production costs of various commodities"—ie., comparative advantage in the product cycle. The paper also called for a positive policy toward Communist-held territory in East Asia: the goal was "to commence the roll-back of Soviet control and influence in the area." The final document changed this phrase to read, "to contain and where feasible to reduce the power and influence of the USSR in Asia" (Truman Library, NSC materials 1949). The roll-back contingency expressed both the fear of continuing communist encroachment, what with the fall of China in 1949, and the search for a Japanese hinterland.

The Korean War had the effect of drawing the effective lines of the "grand area" in East Asia. When the war broke out, the Seventh Fleet was interposed between Taiwan and the mainland, thus suggesting once again an integration of Taiwan with Japan and the world economy. South Korea was almost lost in the summer of 1950. Then, after the Inch'on landing, the course of the fighting opened the realm of feasibility suggested in NSC 48/1; the "contain and reduce" phraseology was used in the State Department to justify the march north, and in passing to wrench North Korea's industrial base away from the communists. A war that had internal, civil origins in Korea—the result of crisis and mass response in the previous fifteen years— became the vehicle for an American redrawing of the lines of the postwar settlement. Roll-back met several hundred thousand Chinese "volunteers," however, and that debacle froze the situation. The geopolitical lines or hegemonic outer limits were thus fixed and they have not been departed from since. Taiwan and South Korea were in, North Korea and Manchuria were out. It remained only to reintroduce Japanese economic influence which was done by the Kennedy administration in the early 1960s in both Taiwan and South Korea.

Dean Acheson remarked in 1954 that "Korea came along and saved us," and the *us* included Japan. The Korean War not only gave a great boost to the Japanese economy, but provided MacArthur with justification for reviving police and military apparatuses and for excluding labor and the left within Japan. With the drawing of the strategic lines of the new Northeast Asian political economy, however, the peculiar nature of American hegemony came to the fore. There is a paradox at the heart of it: nonterritorial in contrast to old world imperialism, organizing great spaces and knocking down barriers to trade, its outer limits are sufficient for keeping countries *in* the system but not sufficient for protecting the home economy against destructive competition, and not sufficient to maintain effective dependency relationships or a frozen hierarchy. The system permits upward mobility. The U.S. retrieved South Korea and Taiwan from oblivion in 1950, but invoking a similar threat to keep them in line in later years was unthinkable. The U.S. keeps Japan on a food, oil, and security dependency, maintaining a light hold on the Japanese jugular; yet invoking that leverage would be disastrous. Outer limits are not enough to bring recalcitrant allies to heel. Furthermore, within those outer limits a dependent but strong state obtains leverage over the American "weak state," weak in the sense of competing centers of power and economic interest, which can be played off against each other (Hirschman 1945). Thus, as Jon Halliday (1975) has argued, Japan in particular got from the postwar settlement a simultaneous dependency and autonomous capability (also Caldwell 1980:ch. 2).

Japan is ultra-dependent on the U.S. or American firms for oil and security, and significantly dependent on the U.S. for food. During the Occupation, the Petroleum Board that set policy was made up of members mostly drawn from American oil majors, and even in the mid-1970s Japan continued to get about 70 percent of its oil deliveries from the majors (Halliday 1975 and Caldwell 1980:ch. 2). In the 1960s and 1970s the U.S. also supplied about 60-70% of Japan's food imports, and in the 1950s used the PL 480 program to sell grain in Japan, Taiwan, and South Korea. All three have been protected markets dependent upon American grain. And, of course, Japan since 1945 has had no military capability remotely commensurate with its economic power. The result is that even today analysts cannot decide if Japan is a superstate or a puny dependency. When Ezra Vogel (1979 confidential) led off a recent Harvard seminar on Japan by saying that "I am really very troubled when I think through the consequences of the rise of Japanese power," Samuel Huntington responded that Japan has "these really fundamental weaknesses—energy, food, and military security." (It is, he thought "an extraordinarily weak country.") The paradox of the postwar Northeast Asian settlement is that they are both right.

Within Japan, after the reverse course took hold, was a formidable political economy for competition in world markets. The *zaibatsu* were less smashed than reformed, prospering again by the mid-1950s in less concentrated form. More important, they were now under *state* influence and control, something that prewar bureaucrats had longed for: the role of the big banks was also enhanced (Johnson 1979; also Allen 1980:108–109). With the *zaibatsu* weakened, the military smashed, and the landlords dispossessed, but with the bureaucracy untouched (the Occupation governed through the existing bureaucracy with few reforms or purges), the postwar Japanese state had more relative autonomy than in the prewar period. It was the great victor of the Occupation. Such autonomy enabled Japan to pursue neo-mercantile policies of restricting entry to Japanese markets, resisting the intrusion of foreign capital, and of course providing various incentives and subsidies to restructure the industrial base in the 1950s and conquer foreign markets in the 1960s and 1970s.

Postwar Korea and Taiwan

The immediate postwar settlement in Taiwan and Korea fundamentally expressed the differences in the two *societies*. Taiwan "drifted aimlessly" in the late 1940s, having to reorient its trade away from Japan and toward China (until 1949); it sold sugar, cement, aluminum, and no food to this now-enlarged periphery (Ho 1978:103 and Lin 1973:27–28). But it remained "an extremely well-ordered society," with "fewer signs of social disintegration" than any place on the Asian mainland (Ho 1978:104). Like Japan, the state emerged stronger once the dust had settled from the inflow of the Kuomintang (KMT) and the China mainlanders in 1945–49. The potent colonial bureaucracy was preserved nearly intact, with its Japanese personnel in many cases staying on well into 1946, while training Taiwanese replacements and continuing in office native bureaucrats who had served in the colonial administration. When the mainlanders took over they added a powerful military component to this state and gave it even more autonomy from society: the Kuomintang had finally found a part of China where its bureaucracy was not hamstrung by provincial warlords and landlords. Thus, for the first time, the Nationalists were able to accomplish a land-reform; they could do so because none of them owned any land in Taiwan. Furthermore, a disproportionate number of experts, technicians, and well-education professionals fled the mainland, adding to Taiwan's already significant fund of human capital. The result, once the seventh fleet drew the outer limit in 1950, was a state with significant relative autonomy, but now far more dependent on the United States than in any previous period of Nationalist rule.

Korea, of course, was divided in 1945. In the North a quick and efficient social and anti-colonial revolution occurred under Soviet auspices, the ultimate (but also in many ways the predictable) societal response to nearly a half century of Japanese imperialism. The South, however, festered for five years through dissent, disorder, and major rebellions in 1946 and 1948, and a significant guerrilla movement in 1948 and 1949. Southern landlords succeeded in recapturing the state in 1945 and 1946, under American auspices, and utilized it in traditional fashion to protect social privilege rather than to foster growth. They prevented major land reform until the Korean War began, and showed no interest in developing the economy. Instead they ruled through draconian police and military organizations. As in Taiwan there was considerable continuity in the bureaucracy from the colonial period, but the Japanese officials had mostly fled when the war ended, and those Korean functionaries who remained were largely unable to function, since they were often hated more than the Japanese excesses but unable to carry forward colonial successes, the regime seemed doomed.

When civil war erupted in June 1950 the North had an easy time of it, sweeping the southern regime away until met with massive American intervention. But paradoxically, the three-month northern occupation of the south, which included a revolutionary land reform in several provinces, cleared the way for an end to landlord dominance in the countryside and land reform on the Taiwan model once the war ended in 1953. By 1953 South Korea further resembled Taiwan in that colonial heavy industry had been amputated by Korea's division, most of it now in the north and beyond reach; like Taiwan southern Korea was the home of light industry and the best rice-producing provinces; during the war many northerners had fled south, also disproportionately including the educated and professional classes; by the war's end the South had a standing army of about 600,000, compared with 75,000 in 1950, so it now approximated the distended Nationalist Army; finally, Syngman Rhee like Chiang Kai-shek had won an ironclad commitment of American defense from communism. So, to put it concisely we can say that by 1953 Taiwan and South Korea once more resembled each other, but what was accomplished with ease in Taiwan required a war in Korea.

Import-Substituting Industrialization
in Taiwan and South Korea

With the underbrush of the early postwar period cleared away, Taiwan and Korea (South-ROK) once again began marching in tandem. Because of the Korean War, Taiwan got a head start on post-colonial industrialization on the typical import-substituting pattern, but by 1953 the ROK was doing the same. Both were enmeshed in a system of American hegemony that brought them economic and military aid on an unheard of scale, but Taiwan's low societal response and the KMT's high relative autonomy gave it more bargaining power with the U.S. The Rhee regime, on the other hand, was penetrated from below by superannuated landlords and from above by a huge American political, economic, and military presence. In the years immediately succeeding the devastation of the war, society was quiet and Rhee ruled through a diffuse authoritarian system that was cruel in its domestic political consequences but incapable of mustering the autonomy to direct growth and unable to withstand the social onslaught that came in 1960. The now-senile Rhee was toppled, the colonial-linked police and military came undone, and the way was clear for a dynamic authoritarian system.

Since 1945 South Korea has received some $13 billion in American military and economic aid, and Taiwan some $5.6 billion. This works out to $600 per capita in Korea and $425 per capita in Taiwan (*C.I.A. Handbook*; also Ho 1978:108–111 and Mason et al. 1980:165). To gauge the true dimensions of this munificence comparative figures are helpful. A statistical compilation by the CIA in 1979 demonstrates that the ROK's total of nearly $6 billion in U.S. economic grants and loans, 1946–78, compares with a *total* for all of Africa of $6.89 billion and for all of Latin American of $14.8 billion; only India, with a population 17 times the size of South Korea, received more ($9.6 billion).

The U.S., of course, did not just give military and economic aid to Taiwan and the ROK but deeply influenced economic programs and the societies themselves. Often it was difficult to know if natives or Americans were writing the plans and policies; the aid missions pushed through land reform on Taiwan and forced it through in Korea; here, in short, was by far the best example in the world of what Wallerstein has called "development by invitation;" if the principle of upward mobility in this system is "many called, few chosen," Taiwan and the ROK were clearly part of the chosen few (Wallerstein 1979). Japan, too, was chosen during this period, if at a higher level in the system; not only were aid totals high, but the U.S. allowed a "simultaneous technological infusion" in the 1950s that brought backward Japanese industries up to speed and started new ones (Ohkawa and Rosovsky 1973:92). American hegemony also had an element of indulgence in these years, no doubt the result of the halcyon American and world boom in the 1950s; U.S. officials tolerated import substitution in Taiwan and the ROK, while chiding both of them for having the state too involved in the economy (i.e., the typical policy of Republican administrations). Thus, the three Northeast Asian political economies had in the 1950s a rare breathing space and incubation allowed to few other peoples in the world; the period set the stage for the breakthroughs of the 1960s, and may be a capitalist analogue of the radical tonic of withdrawal and reorientation by socialist state machineries and societies.

Taiwan and Korea pushed remarkably similar import substitution programs, although the Taiwan program was less fitfull. The key industries were textiles, cement, flat glass, and so on, protected and incubated by a wall of tariffs, overvalued exchanged rates, and other obstacles to foreign entry (on Korea, see Mason et al. 1980:7–8 and Kuznets 1977:48, 71; on Taiwan, see Lin 1973:3–4 and Ho 1978:106). In both countries capitalist parvenus, usually mainlanders in Taiwan and northerners in the ROK, interpenetrated the state, official monopolies, and banks, making windfall profits in import-substituting industries through such connections. Both the KMT and the Rhee regime, after all, grew out of agrarian-bureaucratic traditional systems and had pursued so-called "bureaucratic capitalism," with its "total interpenetration of public and private interests" (Amsden 1970:362). Favored capitalists got to take over formerly Japanese-held industries in Taiwan and the ROK, laying the basis for many of the conglomerates to appear in the 1960s and 1970s (especially in Korea). The phase of "easy" import substitution got going two or three years earlier in Taiwan, and came acropper in 1958–59; it did the same in the ROK in 1960–62, and in both countries a new export-led industrialization began in the early 1960s.

The Export-Led Phase and the Emergence of BAIRs

Readers who know Latin America and especially the work of Guillermo O'Donnell will have noticed that Taiwan and Korea went through industrialization phases that resemble the sequencing of Brazil, Argentina, and other states, even though the import-substituting phase was a good bit shorter in East Asia. It would have continued longer had it not been for opposition by American aid officials, which demonstrates their superior influence in this region of overwhelming American hegemony, when compared to Latin America. But this phase did not have the *political* characteristics of the same phase in Brazil and elsewhere. Politics did not stretch to include workers, peasants, or plural competition for power. There was not the political sequence of inclusion followed by exclusion as the "easy" phase ended and export-led development began (O'Donnell 1973 and the articles by O'Donnell, Cardos, Kaufman, Kurth, Hirschman and Serra in Collier 1979). Labor was excluded in the 1950s and remained excluded in the 1960s; nor did the squeezed middle class of bureaucrats and small businessmen have representation in either Taiwan or South Korea. It is possible to argue, however, that the Korean state was more penetrated by society in the 1950s, both because new capitalists got some influence as the landlord interests receded, and because the U.S. and a small stratum of Korean liberals insisted on a formal democratic structure that occasionally got substantive implementation, if only through students massing in the the streets. The democratic facade could occasionally be invoked. Taiwan, of course, has been ruled under martial law since 1947 in a single-party system, with the KMT having internal organizational principles on Leninist lines. Its politics could easily translate into the new state requisites for export-led development and deepening import-substitution. In Korea, however, such a state had to be reinforced through a major bolstering of bureaucratic, secret police, and party power.

In both countries the export-led program was dictated by the United States. A recent Harvard study explicitly says that in Korea the reform programs were "basically dictated" by the U.S., whereas in Taiwan, Ian Little says A.I.D. pressure was one of the "clearest cases in economic history of cause and effect" (Mason *et al.* 1980:47; Little 1979:474 and Ho 1978:195). Therefore, early–1960s policies tended to have about the same mix in Taiwan and the ROK. Taiwan promulgated a 19-point reform package in 1960 containing extensive reforms of monetary, fiscal, taxation, and trade practices. Korea pursued the same package after the dust had settled in the wake of Park Chung Hee's coup in 1961. Both involved downward reevaluation of currencies to cheapen exports, drastic lowering of tariff barriers that had protected native industries, tax holidays, exemptions, and reductions across the board for firms willing to export, and state guarantees for foreign investment and foreign loans. This package was implemented by 1963 or 1964, and was followed by accelerated depreciation schemes, discounts and subsidies for transportation costs, and monopoly rights for certain firms, usually linked explicitly to export performance. Taiwan established its big Free Export Zone (FEZ) at Kaohsiung in 1965, and Korea followed suit with its Masan FEZ. Both regimes developed long-range planning agencies and multi-year plans; American experts continued riding herd on the planning function (a sort of transnational planning).

Both regimes pursued their comparative advantage in relatively well-educated and skilled, but low-paid labor. This is, of course, the point, and the result of the early 1960s reforms was that Taiwan and the ROK became suppliers of labor to an increasingly far-flung division of production; in the mid-1960s multinational corporations, the World Bank, and the IMF replaced U.S. aid missions as the conduits to the world economy. This pattern is most marked in the East Asian "gang-of-four" LDCs, but it is well known and need not detain us further. More important were the political consequences.

We find in both Taiwan and South Korea by the mid-1960s strong states that bear much comparison to the prewar Japanese model, and to the bureaucratic-authoritarian states in Latin America. Termed NICs (Newly Industrialized Countries) in much of the literature, the Taiwan and Korean variants deserve a more accurate acronym, which I would call BAIRs or Bureaucratic-Authoritarian Industrializing Regimes. These states are ubiq-

uitous in economy and society: penetrating, comprehensive, highly articulated, and relatively autonomous from particular groups and classes.
Furthermore, especially in Korea, we will find that the accumulation of state
power rose considerably at the precise time when the ROK began a deepening
industrialization program in steel, chemicals, ships and automobiles. Taiwan
has developed planning agencies and bureaucracies to go with its existing
strong state, but with society weak we do not find either the occasion or
the necessity for this state to deepen or change its features: once strong
for retaking the mainland and guaranteeing KMT power, it is today strong
for economic development. The best Latin American analogy for Taiwan's
case would be Mexico, where deepening industrialization occurred within
the context of an established authoritarian system, whereas Korea would
be closer to the Argentina case, in which deepening industrialization required
much state strengthening.

Shortly after the 1961 coup, Park and his allies organized the Democratic
Republican Party (DRP), and the Korean Central Intelligence Agency (KCIA).
During much of the 1960s the DRP was the designated vehicle for a stable
politics; its internal structure mimicked the KMT with its democratic-
centralism. But when Park's power was shaken in the period 1969–1971
(he nearly lost the 1971 election to Kim Dae Jung in spite of regime
manipulation), the KCIA emerged as the preferred organization of order.
An arm of the executive, it penetrated nearly every arena of Korean life
with agents in factories, central and local government offices, and university
classrooms. Organized with the help of the U.S. CIA, and working always
in close liaison with the Seoul CIA station, it was an example of transnational
politics to go with the transnational economics. Unfortunately for Park
Chung Hee, the KCIA became so strong that every director came to challenge
his power (Lee Hu-rak, Kim Jae-gyu, Kim Hyong-uk) until finally its chief
shot Park to death over dinner one evening in October, 1979.

The results of a major Harvard project on the Korean economy show
that "Korea, Inc." is "undoubtedly a more apt description of the situation
in Korea than is 'Japan, Inc'." The state is the senior party, with the
corporation lesser partners: "it is the government that is Chairman of the
Board (of Korea, Inc.), with business holding a few directorships" (Chirot
1977:218–220). The Korean *zaibatsu* (the Koreans pronounce it *chaebol*, but
the term is the same) have grown up with the new BAIR. Ten of them are
now in Fortune's 500; like prewar Japanese *zaibatsu* there is great family
interpenetration: the Harvard project found that of current *chaebol* chief
executives, 61.4 percent are firm founders; 7.9 percent are direct descendants
of founders; 12 percent are relatives of founders; only 18.8 percent are
unrelated to the founding family (Cole and Lyman 1971:135; Kuznets 1977:71).
As Gerschenkronian analysis would suggest, "feudal holdovers" have been
an important aspect of late development in East Asia: in the case of prewar
Japanese *zaibatsu*, Korean *chaebol*, and the Taiwanese state (the President
being the son of Chiang Kai-shek), it is the traditional family structure that
provides a basis for organizing industry. The great power of this particular

argument is also revealed in the Northeast Asian socialist case, where the North Korean state is highly interpenetrated by Kim Il Sung's family, and where his son has been chosen as successor.

As in Japan, Korean and Taiwanese big firms exercise paternalistic sway over workers with company dormitories, recreation and hospital facilities, uniforms and company songs. The different labor market in Korea and Taiwan means, however, that there is no permanent employment, working hours are much longer (52 hours/week in the big firms, longer in small firms) and wages much lower in relation to living cost.

Another similarity with the Japanese model is the exclusion of labor, the exploitation of women, and the low state expenditures on social welfare— all three, of course, bound to be more extreme in the periphery than in the core. Social spending is minimal in both countries. In 1973, expenditures on social insurance, public health, public assistance, welfare, and veterans' relief represented 0.97 percent of GNP in the ROK, 1.2 percent in Taiwan; this compares with three percent in Malaysia and 5.3 percent in Japan (Greenhalgh 1980). One can see perfectly the tradeoff between Japan, Korea, and Taiwan here: the latter two spend four to ten percent of GNP on defense, respectively, meaning that Japan can hold defense under one percent; but Japan, by virtue of its "New Deal" during the Occupation and its democratic system, must spend five percent on social programs (still low by world standards). In any case both the ROK and Japan until recently got off with spending about five percent of GNP on defense and welfare combined. Korean and Taiwanese workers must pay the cost in the periphery.

All in all the BAIR model provides a potent mix, fusing state and economic power in pursuit of comparative advantage in world markets. To the extent that hegemonic outer limits are not invoked, we can say that relative autonomy is at any given time greater in Taiwan and Korea than it is in Japan or the United States. Thus it is that both states sought in the early 1970s to use this power to upset transnational and free trade interests by once again import-substituting, this time in heavy industry. Both sought not simply to deepen their industrial structures, but to deepen their self-reliance and independence vs. their hegemonic partners. A key enabling factor here was the massive reentry of Japanese capital (loans and investments) into the ROK and Taiwan in the mid 1960s. Accomplished relatively easily in Taiwan, in Korea as we would predict society reacted strongly and the "normalization" had to be rammed down the throats of protesting students and legislators in 1964–66. But Japan's reentry now gave both regimes a strong proxy to play off against American power and capital: a single hegemony began to turn into a dual hegemony.

Park Chung Hee declared in 1972 that "steel = national power," giving a pithy slogan that symbolizes the deepening industrialization of both countries. The Third Five-year Plan, 1971–6, inaugurated this phase; a similar and coterminous deepening occurred in Taiwan. The ROK got a new integrated steel mill (developed and installed by Japanese technicians), super-tanker shipbuilding capacity, heavy chemical factories and refineries, and an auto industry (with GM, Ford, and Japanese technology) that produced 36,000 cars by 1978. American planners and economists resisted these developments, arguing that heavy industry is unsuited to the factor endowments and small domestic markets of both countries; surplus, idle capacity would be the inevitable result (Lin 1973:131–132). In other words, Korea and Taiwan were violating a rational international division of labor.

The ROK and Taiwan were able to get needed financing and technology for these enterprises from the Japanese in part because the new programs provided the structure necessary to receive declining Japanese heavy industry. This simultaneously increased Taiwanese and Korean autonomy in the world at large, while deepening dependency on Japan. The U.S. was more opposed, and indeed during the same period the Nixon administration dealt the sharpest blows since 1949 to both countries by limiting shoe and textile imports, floating the dollar, recognizing China, and pulling a division of U.S. troops out of the ROK. This set the agenda of conflict for the present: would the northeast Asian political economy continue as joint hegemony, or as an increasingly Japanese preserve?

By the early 1970s, Korea and Taiwan were both transitional between peripheral and semi-peripheral status; in a sense they had recovered the structural position that they held in the last years of the Japanese empire. Vietnam was a periphery for both regimes, as each sent construction teams and other industrial personnel, and Korea sent some 300,000 soldiers over a seven year period (1966–73). The Vietnam War played for the ROK the role that the Korean War played for Japan; labeled "Korea's El Dorado," it accounted for as much as 20 percent of foreign exchange earnings in the late 1960s. Procurements for the war were also important for Taiwan in the same period. By the 1970s, Taiwan exported capital goods, technicians, and foreign aid to several Southeast Asian nations; both countries sent construction teams to the Middle East to recycle petrodollars after the 1973 oil shock. By the late 1970s both nations competed for an intermediate position in the world economy, continuing to export labor-intensive goods to advanced countries and capital-intensive goods to LDCs. Firms in both countries sought to go multinational, looking for cheaper labor costs in Bangladesh, Mexico, and elsewhere, while continuing to supply construction to the Middle East.

Many Are Called but Few Are Chosen: Korea's Export-Led Trap

Export-led development on the Korean and Taiwan model places a number of critical obstacles in the way of upward mobility in the world system. These may be summarized as follows: (1) LDCs need to break into the system of economic exchange at a point other than comparative advantage in labor, that is, in marketing, better technology, or better organization. Yet multinationals provide most of the markets, and utilize "steady-state" or obsolescent technologies. (2) Limited factor endowments and the small domestic markets that characterize such off-shore production inhibit second-stage industrialization and cause early problems of surplus capacity. (3) Rising competition from poorer states means that there is both a critical but short, slim lead over competing LDCs. Multinationals, especially the smaller textile firms, may simply pick up production facilities and move them to countries offering better labor costs. (4) Core-country protectionism will arise to the extent that declining sectors have representation in the polity. Taiwan and Korea met all these problems in the late 1970s, with the added difficulty of inflated oil prices.

In the event, Taiwan was chosen but the ROK was not. Taiwan is beginning to manufacture computers for export (Atari moved a big factory there in 1983) while Korea suffered a loss of six percent of GNP in 1980, the first loss since before the export-led program began. In 1978, the Korean threat to advanced country industries seemed so palpable that Japanese newspapers were filled with wary editorials about "the Korean challenge" and a middle-level State Department official stated that a prime goal of U.S. policy toward Korea was to "manage its articulation with the world economy so that we don't get another Japan there." According to some sources, the Carter administration put off its troop withdrawal plan both to maintain influence in Korea and to stave off ever-increasing Japanese dominance. In June 1979, Jimmy Carter visited Park Chung Hee and toasted him for his stable rule. Six months later Park was assassinated amidst a general political and economic crisis. The timing of the economic crisis is explained by the second oil wave of early 1979, but the cause of the crisis lay deep in the structure of Korea's economic activity. The late 1970s had involved increasing protectionism, declining technology transfer, and increasing necessity to borrow to meet oil expenses and services on previous debt. Furthermore, in dialectical fashion, the remedy that Korea had used to ride out the first oil wave—dispatching construction teams to the Middle East—caused a skilled labor shortage that bid up wages within Korea across the board, thus jeopardizing the ROK's comparative advantage. At the same time, an outward-turning China began eating into Korean textile markets. The big steel, shipbuilding and automobile factories met precisely the obstacle free traders had predicted: when ships and cars could not be sold abroad, the small domestic market could not help out. Korean automobile production in late 1979 and 1980 came to a virtual standstill. Thus, as the economist Yung Chul Park stated, all these problems threatened to "bring the export-led industrialization to a rather abrupt end" (see Park 1981 for a good summary of the ROK's recent economic problems). Korean EPB planners stated that the economy was "uncontrollable" and in a "quandary."

The economic difficulties detonated a political crisis, beginning with vastly enhanced opposition power deployed around Kim Dae Jung, who in turn drew support from textile workers, small businesses and firms with national rather than international interests, and his native southwestern Cholla region which had historically been rebellious and leftist, and which had been left out of much of the growth of the previous fifteen years. Major urban insurrections occurred in Pusan and Masan, southeastern cities, in the fall of 1979. Some 700 labor strikes were recorded in 1979–80, and in April 1980 miners took over a small town east of Seoul and held it for several days. In May, hundreds of thousands of students and common people flooded the streets of Seoul, leading to martial law, which in turn touched off a province-wide rebellion in S. Cholla and the capture of the provincial capital by rebels who held it for a week. Korea seemed to be on the verge of disintegrating on the Iran model, but unlike Iran the military did not fracture and a new general, Chun Doo Hwan, executed a multi-stage coup: within the military in December 1979, within the KCIA in April 1980, and throughout the state apparatus in summer 1980. Through withering repression the strong societal reaction was quieted, but at the cost of a deep radicalization of remaining protesters.

In the aftermath of this rebellious period, the Korean state intervened continuously to revive the economy's comparative advantage in the world system. The state sponsored the sectoral reorganization of several large conglomerates, on the principle of one *chaebol* for each industrial sector. For the first time the ROK publicly referred to the "organic" nature of its perimeter defense relationship with Japan, as justification for demanding at least $6 billion in Japanese loans and aid.

Finally, the state accomplished a thorough repression of labor in outlawing strikes and unions, closely surveilling any and all organizing activity, and driving down wages. Thus in 1981 labor productivity increased 16 percent while wages went down five percent in real terms. GNP growth of 6.4 percent recovered the loss of 1980. Yet the period 1978–83 has seriously weakened the ROK in its competition with Taiwan for advantageous position in the world economy.

In a major study of the Korean economy published in 1979, the World Bank stated that "the burden of external debt is being steadily reduced," and agreed with Korean planners that a growth rate for exports of 16 percent and for GNP of 9 to 10 percent per year could be sustained through the 1980s. It noted that "confidence in Korea's ability to meet its external debt service obligations is based on the continuation of rapid export growth." Since the 1980 downturn the economy has grown only in the 5 to 6 percent range, debts have more than doubled since 1979, to a total external debt of $42 billion, third largest in the world, and export growth has tumbled badly. Growing by double digit rates throughout the 1970s, and by 17 percent in the bad year of 1980 (to $17.2 billion), exports reached $21 billion at the end of 1981 and by mid-1983 were no higher than $22 billion on an annual basis. In other works exports growth has been dead in the water since 1981. Taiwan's exports have not been booming, either, but its external debt is no more than $7 billion and the slowing of export growth has had no apparent ripple effect on internal politics.

Thus, in 1983 as in the rest of this century, Taiwan continues its smooth development, in spite of losing major security guarantees and in spite of structural obstacles to its model of development. South Korea, on the contrary, plays out its history of economic dynamism mixed with spasmodic social reaction. Today its development programs hangs in the balance.

Conclusions

This article has sought to demonstrate the shaping and conditioning effects of economic forces on three distinct societies, peoples, and cultures, and the effects of industrial product cycles on a regional political economy. Japan, Taiwan, and South Korea have come to have similar economic structures (although in different temporal sequences), and all three, with markedly different traditional polities, have adopted quite similar political models and roles for the state. The BAIR model of relative state autonomy, central coordination, bureaucratic short- and long-range planning, high mobility in moving in and out of industrial sectors, private concentration in big conglomerates, exclusion of labor, exploitation of women, low expenditures on social welfare and, in prewar Japan and contemporary South Korea and Taiwan, militarization and authoritarian repression, is found in all three nations. When one is compared to another the differences are also salient, but when all three are compared to the rest of the world the similarities are remarkable.

We have also argued that industrial development in Japan, Korea and Taiwan cannot be considered as an individual country phenomenon, but instead as a regional phenomenon in which a tripartite hierarchy of core, semi-periphery and periphery was created in the first part of the twentieth century and then slowly recreated after World War II. The smooth development of Taiwan has its counterpart in the spasmodic and troubled development of Korea, and neither can be understood apart from Japan. Not only was Taiwan's society less restive, and its state less penetrated by societal constraint, but it also had breathing space occasioned by Japan's greater attention to Korea and Manchuria before 1945, and American "development by invitation" after 1950. In short, the developmental "successes" of Taiwan and Korea are historically and regionally specific, and therefore provide no readily adaptably models for other developing countries interested in emulation.

The evidence also strongly suggests that a hegemonic system is necessary for the functioning of this regional political economy: unilateral colonialism until 1945, U.S. hegemony since 1945. Today there is increasing competition between American and Japanese hegemony over semi-peripheral Taiwan and South Korea, but as years pass there may well be sharper competition over a new hinterland, People's China. Will the U.S. or Japan, or both, organize Chinese labor in the world system? And as Chinese labor-intensive exports increase, whither Taiwan and South Korea?

Notes

A version of this article was first presented at the Conference on Industrial Sectors and World Markets, Swarthmore College, September 1981, and at the Santa Cruz conference which is the basis of this volume. Readers wishing fuller elaboration and documentation should consult the above article, and my *Origins of the Korean War: Liberation and the Emergence of Separate Regimes, 1945–1947* (1981).

References

Amsden, A. H. 1970. "Taiwan's Economic History: A Case of Etatisme and a Challenge to Dependency Theory," *Modern China*, 5:3.

Allen, G. C. 1980. *Japan's Economic Policy*, London: MacMillan Press.

Caldwell, M. 1980. "Petroleum Politics in Japan: State and Industry in a Changing Policy Context," Ph.D. dissertation, University of Wisconsin.

Calleo, D. P., and B. M. Rowland. 1973. *America and the World Political Economy: Atlantic Dreams and National Realities*, Bloomington: University of Indiana Press.

Chirot, D. 1977. *Social Change in the Twentieth Century*, New York: Harcourt, Brace, Jovanovich.

Cole, D. C., and P. N. Lyman. 1971. *Korean Development: The Interplay of Politics and Economics*, Cambridge: Harvard University Press.

Collier, D., ed. 1979. *The New Authoritarianism in Latin America*, Princeton: Princeton University Press.

Cumings, B. 1981. *The Origins of the Korean War: Liberation and the Emergence of Separate Regimes*, Princeton: Princeton University Press.

Emmerson, J. K. 1978. *The Japanese Thread: A Life in the U.S. Foreign Service*, New York: Holt Rinehart and Winston.

Greenhalgh, S. 1980. "Dependency, Distribution and the Taiwan 'Paradox'," paper presented at the Taiwan Political Economy Workshop, Columbia University, December 18–20.

Halliday, J. 1975. *A Political History of Japanese Capitalism*, New York: Pantheon Books.

Hirschman, A. O. 1945. *National Power and the Structure of Foreign Trade*, Berkeley: University of Calfiornia Press.

Ho, S. 1978. *The Economic Development of Taiwan 1860–1970*, New Haven: Yale University Press.

Iriye, A. 1977. "Continuities in U.S.-Japanese Relations, 1941–1949," in Y. Nagai and A. Iriye, eds., *The Origins of the Cold War in Asia*, Tokyo: University of Tokyo Press and New York: Columbia University Press.

Johnson, C. 1979. "A Japan Model?" unpublished paper presented at American Discussion Group on U.S. Policy toward Japan, Harvard University, December 13.

Kojima, K. 1977. *Japan and a New World Economic Order*, Boulder: Westview Press.

Kuznets, P. W. 1977. *Economic Growth and Structure in the Republic of Korea*, New Haven: Yale University Press.

Lin, C. 1973. *Industrialization in Taiwan, 1946–1972: Trade and Import-Substitution Policies for Developing Countries*, New York: Praeger.

Little, I. M. D. 1979. "An Economic Renaissance," in W. Galenson, ed., *Economic Growth and Structural Change in Taiwan*, Ithaca: Cornell University Press.

Maier, C. S. 1978. "The Politics of Productivity: Foundations of American International Economic Policy after World War II," in P. J. Katzenstein, ed., *Between Power and Plenty: Foreign Economic Policies of Advanced Industrial States*, Madison: University of Wisconsin Press.

Mason, E. S. *et al.* 1980. *The Economic and Social Modernization of the Republic of Korea*, Cambridge: Harvard University Press.

O'Donnell, G. A. 1973. *Modernization and Bureaucratic-Authoritarianism in South American Politics*, Berkeley: University of California Institute for International Studies.

Ohkawa, K., and H. Rosovsky. 1973. *Japanese Economic Growth: Trend Acceleration in the Twentieth Century*, Stanford: Stanford University.

Palais, J. P. 1975. *Politics and Policy in Traditional Korea*, Cambridge: Harvard University Press.

Park, Y. C. 1981. "Recent Economic Developments in Korea," paper presented to the Seminar on Korea, Columbia University, April 24.

Roberts, J. G. 1977. "The 'Japan Crowd' and the Zaibatsu Restoration," *The Japan Interpretor*, 12: 384–415.

Simon, D. 1980. "U.S. Assistance, Land Reform, and Taiwan's Political Economy," paper presented at the Taiwan Political Economy Workshop, Columbia University, December 18–20.

Umemura, M., and T. Mizoguchi, eds. 1981. *Quantitative Studies on the Economic History of the Japanese Empire, 1890–1940*, Tokyo: Hitotsubashi University.

U.S. Central Intelligence Agency. 1980. *Handbook of Economic Statistics, 1979*, Washington, DC: National Foreign Assessment Center.

———. ORE 69–49. July 14, 1949. "Relative U.S. Security Interest in the European-Mediterranean Area and the Far East," HST/PSF file, Memos, 1945–49, box #249.

U.S. National Security Council. October 26, 1949. Draft paper, NSC 48, in NSC materials, Harry S. Truman Library, box #207.

Vogel, E.F. 1979. "Growing Japanese Economic Capabilities and the U.S.-Japan Relationship," summary of the first meeting of the American Discussion Group on U.S. Policy Toward Japan, Harvard University, December 13, "confidential."

Wade, L. L., and B. S. Kim. 1978. *Economic Development of South Korea: The Political Economy of Success*, New York: Preager.

Wallerstein, I. 1979. "Dependence in an Interdependent World," in I. Wallerstein, *Capitalist World Economy*, Cambridge: Cambridge University Press.

About the Contributors

Michael Adas is professor of history at Rutgers University and is the author of books and articles on South and Southeast Asia, most recently *Prophets of Rebellion* (1979).

Robert Bezucha is professor of history at Amherst College. He is the author of *The Lyon Uprising of 1834* (1974).

Edmund Burke, III, is professor of history at the University of California, Santa Cruz, and is the author of *Prelude to Protectorate in Morocco* (1976) and the editor (with I. M. Lapidus) of *Islam, Politics and Social Movements* (forthcoming).

Craig Calhoun has written *The Question of Class Struggle: Social Foundations of Popular Radicalism During the Industrial Revolution* (1982). He is associate professor of sociology at the University of North Carolina, Chapel Hill.

Bruce Cumings is professor at the School of International Relations at the University of Washington, Seattle. He has written *The Origins of the Korean War: Liberation and the Emergence of Separate Regimes, 1945–1947* (1981).

Walter Goldfrank is professor of sociology at the University of California, Santa Cruz. He is the editor of *The World System of Capitalism: Past and Present* (1979) and articles on the sociology of Mexican revolution and the world system.

Peter Gourevitch is professor of political science at the University of California, San Diego, and has written *Paris and the Provinces: The Politics of Local Government Reform in France* (1980) and is the editor of *Unions and Economic Crisis: Britain, West Germany and Sweden* (1984).

Jeffery Paige is professor of sociology at the University of Michigan and the author of *Agrarian Revolution* (1975).

Gareth Stedman Jones teaches English and European history at Christ Church College, Cambridge University. He is the author of *Languages of Class* (1983).

Mark Traugott is associate professor of sociology at the University of California, Santa Cruz. He is the author of *Armies of the Poor: Determinants of Working Class Participation in the Parisian Insurrection of June 1848* (1985).

Michael Watts is associate professor of geography at the University of California, Berkeley. He has written *Silent Violence: Food, Famine and Peasantry in Northern Nigeria* (1983).

Index